W9-DJF-125

The Prayers of Man

The Catholic
Theological Union
LIBRARY
Chicago, Ill.

Translations by Rex Benedict

THE

PRAYERS

OF MAN

*From Primitive Peoples to
Present Times*

Compiled by
Alfonso M. di Nola

Edited by
Patrick O'Connor

New York

Ivan Obolensky, Inc.

The Catholic
Theological Union
LIBRARY
Chicago, Ill.
WITHDRAWN

English translation © 1961 by Ivan Obolensky, Inc.

Library of Congress Catalog Card Number: 60-13420

All rights reserved under Pan-American and International Copyright Conventions. Published simultaneously in the Dominion of Canada by George J. McLeod Limited, Toronto.

First Printing

Manufactured in the United States of America by The Haddon Craftsmen, Scranton, Pennsylvania.

Designed by Alfred Manso

Introduction

The selections making up this compilation represent an exhaustive study of one of the central phenomena of religious life—prayer. Prayer characterizes the spirit of a religion, a religious epoch, or a religious man, with far more efficacy than mythology, legend, dogma, morals or theology. The history of prayer is the history of the religious development of mankind. Aside from its documentary value, this compilation, though in the main limited to the confines of liturgical prayer, with the intentional exclusion of the lofty voices of personal, aliturgical prayer, seeks to catch the suggestive rhythms of an eternal dialogue between man and God, between the space-time imprisoned creature and the cosmic energies around him, from the most elementary form in which this dialogue is expressed to the most complex religious experience.

Prayer is the heart, the center-most point of religion. It is not in dogmas, institutions, rites or in moral ideas that we are permitted to perceive the substance of religious life, but in prayer. Prayer is the individual and collective reaction of the religious soul when confronted with the cosmos. The individualization and the analysis of these reactions are the means by which we shall succeed not only in reaching—

in its intimacy and germination—the essence of the religious fact, but also by which we may interpret, in their exact functions, the single elements that go into the making of every positive religion: the rites, the liturgies, the myths, the theologies.

On the basis of this premise, what is the place of prayer in the complex acts and functions that constitute an historic religion?

Prayer is a ritual form by means of which individuals or collective groups put themselves in communication with divine forces in order to enjoin, ask, promise, glorify, and confidently abandon themselves to a sense of knowledge of their own limitations.

Such an attempt at definition places prayer among the religious manifestations that stabilize the opening of an emotional circuit between the two fundamental terms of the religious experience—God and man.

Prayer may take any number of different forms: it may be persuasive, insinuating, imploring, harsh, demanding, broken, weeping, exuberant, contrite, joyous. As a consequence it is possible to include exorcism in the various forms of prayer. There is also the simple prayer of request, of bowing down, of thanksgiving, the hymn of praise and glorification and any other prayer that opens up a relationship between God and man.

Personal, individual prayer precedes liturgical prayer, and is a preliminary condition of it. Evidently the initial God-man relationship is wholly sealed off in the innermost places of the individual soul: a predisposition, an inclination of the soul to ask, to glorify, to abandon itself. Prayer, in its initial intimate stage, may be considered an unexpressed spiritual condition. Erasmus of Rotterdam individualizes prayer as the elevation of the mind to God, which in itself is a prayer.

The transition from personal prayer to liturgy is almost always the work of a great mystic or the prophetic souls who shape and form religious movements.

A study of liturgical prayer reveals the psychological mechanisms out of which are born the impulse—a purely interior impulse—to pray and the concrete manifestations of prayer: words and gestures.

The singularity of liturgical prayer lies in the fact that it has undergone changes wrought by the passing from the limits of a religious personality to the collective personality. As a consequence it has adapted itself to the laws that govern the collective life.

Personal prayer, whether exorcism, invocation, hymn or sworn vow becomes formula, not in the sense that it becomes emptied of its primitive emotional energy, but in the sense that it becomes solidified and crystallized in form.

When official liturgies decay, it is necessary to examine the only true cause behind and decadence of religious spirituality: the religious predisposition of the spirit. Liturgical prayer, even when it bears the marks of fatigue and fails to excite any response in the life of the collective group always conserves its full emotional impact for the souls religiously oriented and disposed: St. Paul "To give life to the spirit by use of the word."

It is this spiritual orientation that each reader should keep in mind if, behind the words we have gathered for him, he wishes to glimpse the flames of those religions that shook the world.

THE EDITOR

Acknowledgments

The editor wishes to thank Mr. Norman Petteway and Mr. Joseph Mask of The New York Public Library, Mr. Abraham Berger of that library's Jewish Division, and especially Mr. Francis W. Paar of the Oriental Division whose deep knowledge of Oriental literature and whose patience were of inestimable value.

The editor also wishes to thank the staff of The Union Theological Seminary Library, Mrs. Ethel Keech Logan, Assistant to the Educational Director of The Salvation Army, The Jehovah's Witnesses East Manhattan Congregation and the Seventh-Day Adventist Church, New York Center.

Grateful acknowledgment should also be made to Mr. Edward Fenton, Miss Katherine Richardson, Mr. Fred Burns, Mr. and Mrs. Kenneth Cameron and finally to Norma Lee Clark for her devotion, generosity and encouragement.

Contents

BARUNDI

MADAGASCAR

ALGERIA

RWALA BEDOUINS

DINKA

YAO

SHILLUK

The Religions of Pre-Columbian America

PERU

China

THE NATIONAL RELIGION OF ANTIQUITY

BUDDHISM

TAOISM

CHINESE MOHAMMEDANISM

Tibet

Japan

India

Siam

Egypt

Mesopotamia

Iran

The Hebrews

The Greeks and Romans

Christianity

MOZARABIC LITURGY

LUTHERANISM

WALDENSIAN EVANGELIC CHURCH

ANGLICAN COMMUNION

Islam

The Primitives

MANJAS—ETHIOPIAN HIGHLANDS

To Nature

This is a prayer used in ritual feasts of the new year, during the January-February moon. It is recited by *ba-wan-tua,* the patriarch, following the benediction of newborn babies and after a series of ritual ceremonies.

Mountains, marshes, near land, far land, be good to us.
Bisorube, Gbozon, their haunting souls, be clement to us.
Let the beasts, your children, come, and let them get caught in the big
     fire that we shall light tomorrow.
We shall give the finest cuts and we will offer their hearts and livers
     as a sacrifice.
Protect the hunters, keep them from all injuries and from death.

PYGMIES

Chant for the Consecration of Arms

        Khmvoum, O Khmvoum, Thou are the Lord,
        O Creator, the Lord of all,

3

Master of the forest, Master of things,
Master of the men, O Khmvoum;
And we, the smallest, we are but servants.
Master of the men, O Khmvoum,
Command, O Master of Life and Death,
We shall obey.

Presentation of an Infant

Lifting the newborn child toward the sun, the father prays:
To thee, the Creator, to thee, the Powerful,
I offer this fresh bud,
New fruit of the ancient tree.
Thou art the master, we thy children.
To thee, the Creator, to thee, the Powerful,
Khmvoum, Khmvoum,
I offer this new plant.

Funeral Hymn

The creature is born, it fades away, it dies,
And comes then the great cold.

Chorus: It is the great cold of the night, it is the dark.

The bird comes, it flies, it dies,
And comes then the great cold.

Chorus: It is the great cold of the night, it is the dark.

The fish swim away, it goes, it dies,
And comes then the great cold.

Chorus: It is the great cold of the night, it is the dark.

Man is born, he eats and sleeps. He fades away,
And comes then the great cold.

Chorus: It is the great cold of the night, it is the dark.

And the sky lights up, the eyes are closed,
The star shines.

Chorus: The cold down here, the light up there.

Man is gone, the prisoner is freed,
The shadow has disappeared.

Chorus: The shadow has disappeared.

Khmvoum, Khmvoum, hear our call.

Chorus: Khmvoum, Khmvoum, hear our call.

Song of the Rainbow

The Pygmy chants this psalm when the rainbow appears during certain ritualistic conditions; he ceases work, rises, and arranges his arrow in the same direction and position as the rainbow.

Khwa, ye, O Khwa. Rainbow, O Rainbow,
You shine high up there, so high
Above the forest so vast,
In the center of the black clouds,
Splitting the dark sky,
You bend under yourself,
Victorious of the fight,
The roaring thunder,
Roaring so terribly, angry.
Was it angry with us?
In the middle of the black clouds,
Splitting the dark sky,
As a knife splits the too ripe fruit.
Rainbow, Rainbow.
And it ran away,
The man-killer thunder,
As run the antelope before the panther;
And it ran away,
Rainbow, Rainbow,
Powerful bow of the Great Hunter,
Of the Great Hunter who tracks the herd of clouds
Like a herd of frightened elephants,
Rainbow, extend our thanks to Him.
Tell Him[1]: Do not be angry.
Tell Him: Do not be irritated.
Tell Him: Do not kill us,
For we are very frightened.
Rainbow, tell Him

To the Moon

> O Mother Moon, O Mother Moon, deh!
> Mother of living things,
> Hear us, O Mother Moon,
> Listen to our voice, O Mother Moon,
> O Mother Moon, O Mother Moon, deh!

Against the Elephant of the Evil Spirit

> Now he is driven by evil spirits of the forest,
> The old elephant, he who sired the herd;
> Now he wanders alone, unwanted by young females.
> O Father Elephant, where now is thy potency,
> That masculine potency thou once trumpeted so proudly?
> Driven by evil spirits of the forest
> The old elephant comes crashing toward our huts.
> May thine eyes be blinded, O Father Elephant,
> And thine ears not hear the young child's wail;
> May thy great feet not crush our huts,
> O Father Elephant, O Father Elephant.

Formula Against Spectral Hands of the Forest

Both this and the preceding prayers are uttered as protection against "malign hands," or *ogiri,* the wandering souls of witch doctors, cannibals, and criminals.

> Ogiri, Thou who ate men on earth.
> Ogiri, do not come near our huts.
> We have seen thy eyes glitter in the black night.
> O Ogiri
> We have heard thy teeth gnashing, *kra, kra.*
> O Ogiri
> Thou who ate men on earth.
> O Ogiri that we knew so well,
> Do not come near our huts.

To Celeste the Serpent, Against Snakebites

The serpent Totemico, or Celeste, is the tribe's guardian, and this prayer is addressed to him to gain protection against reptiles.

When the foot, in the night
Stumbles against the obstacle that shrinks and rears and bites,
Let, O Snake, Thou our Father, Father of our Tribe,
We are Thy sons,
Let it be a branch that rears and strikes,
But not one of Thy sharp-toothed children,
O Father of the tribe, we are Thy sons.

Litany

This prayer is chanted by a group of women, walking.

> Morning has risen;
> Asobe, take away from us every pain,
> Every ill,
> Every mishap;
> Asobe, let us come safely home.

Against the Storm

> Epilipili, Epilipili,
> Do not let the rains come.
> The rains fall,
> The rains come
> To burden us with misery.
> Thy sons are in the forest;
> Let the rain be slow,
> Let the rain be slow.

FANG

To the Spirit of the Race

The Spirit is believed to dwell in a coffer holding the skulls of tribal ancestors. During initiation ceremonies for the young the coffer is held up by the head of the family to which the initiate belongs, and he offers the following prayer.

> Thou who art deathless,
> Who knowest not death,

Who livest always,
Never feeling the cold sleep,
Thy children have come
To gather around thee.
O Father, gird up thy strength,
Penetrate them with thy shadow,
O Father who never dies,
O Father of our race.

A Chant

Nzame is on high, Man is below.
Nzame is Nzame, Man is Man.
Each to himself, each in his dwelling.

Dance and Incantation for the Ngil

Ngil: By the consecrated ashes of the chosen victim
of the wandering spirits of the nights,
erring through the dark forest . . .
Forever . . .
Never . . .
Chorus: Yo, yo, never.
Ngil: Spirits of the dead who have seen no funeral sacrifices . . .
Chorus: Yo, yo, never.
Ngil: Dead who have not crossed yet
crossed the river of tears . . .
Chorus: Yo, yo, never.
Ngil: The river of tears and sighs . . .
Chorus: The river of tears and sighs.
Ngil: The river of infinite repose . . .
Chorus: The river of infinite repose.
Ngil: Spirits of the night, dark spirits,
Our protectors . . .
Chorus: Our protectors.
Ngil: You, my son, be protected, you, my son,
be protected forever.
Chorus: Yo, yo, forever.

Invocation of a Sorcerer

O Thou who rule strength, Thou spirit of virile energy,
Thou can do all, and without Thee, I am powerless, I am powerless;
I who am consecrated to Thee, I who am pledged to Thee, O Spirit,
      from Thee I get my strength, my power. Thou brought me the gift.
Spirit of Force, I call Thee. Acknowledge my call.
Come, Come.
Thou must come, I gave Thee what Thou asked me
The sacrifice has been given, sacrifice has been given in the forest;
Spirit, I am Thine, Thou are mine, come to me.

Elegy for the Baobab Tree

This prayer is directed to the sacred baobab tree, in the belief that, like important personages, sacred trees cannot die until a three-day funeral ceremony has been concluded. The death of this divinity is preceded and revealed by the death of certain individuals considered to be its sons.

> For a long time he hath begot him sons,
> Whose births built houses.
> His son died without a funeral.
> But here is the missing sacrifice,
> A freshet poured into his mouth,
> The mouth of burial.

Formula for the Divinatory Sacrifice of a Chicken

When the rains do not arrive on time, a chicken is sacrificed to Nyule, the Goddess-Earth or Goddess-Forest, to determine whether the community is in a state of sin or a state of grace. The group's moral worthiness or unworthiness to receive rainfall is divined by the position of the dead chicken, according to the formula below.

If it is the hand of God that holds back the rain, the sacrificial victim dies with its breast up. But if boys or young men have had sexual relations with women in the forest, the chicken's breast remains in sight.

Sacrificial Prayer to the Masked Divine One

This sacrificial prayer is offered on behalf of a man who has killed a poisoner. Do is a powerful divinity who gives strength to certain age groups, to masked persons, and to the initiated.

We have come to thee, O Do, to ask for life. Help us to cling to it. Thou well knowest that the person who has slain a poisoner must make haste. We know thou art a strong God, and have faith in thee. Hasten to help us cling to life, and those whom thou hast protected will gather sea shells for thee and buy a goat to offer up to thee. Here is the water we pour out to thee with one hand, and thou acceptest it with two hands.

WAPOKOMO—LAKE TANA

Three Invocations

O God, give us peace, give us tranquillity, and let good fortune come to us.

Let the one who put a jinx on the village die. Let him die, he who thought evil thoughts against us. Also give us fish.

O God, give us rain, we are in misery, we suffer with our sons, send us the clouds that bring the rain. We pray Thee, O Lord our Father, to send us the rain.

Let her who is sick, O God, receive from Thee health and peace, and her village and her children and her husband. Let her get up and go to work, let her work in the kitchen, let her find peace again.

BANTU

Formula for the Kou Biyeketa Ceremony

Abousaye! Akhwari![2] Here is the child. Let him grow tall, let him grow into manhood with your medicines. Let his sweat be pure, let the stains go, let them go to Chibouri, let them go to Nkhabelane![3] Let the child play happily, let him be like his friends. This is not my first try. You gave me these drugs; let them protect the child against sickness so that no one can say they are powerless.

Formula for the Burial Rite

This formula is uttered by the dead man's younger brother, who holds a small branch that was in the hand of the dead one until the earth covered him over.

You, my forefathers, you have congregated here today. Do you not see this? You have taken him with you. I am alone now. I am dead, I implore you, who are so far, since he has gone back to you, let us remain in peace. He has not left us with hate. Let us weep softly over him, in peace. Let us help each other in our pain, even his wife's parents.

Two Formulas of the Dlaya Chilongo Rites

Dlaya Chilongo are the rites which give legitimacy to marriages consummated between members forbidden to enter into matrimony. The first formula belongs to the rites of northern clans; the married couple is freed from the matrimonial taboo by eating the liver of a sacrificed animal. The second formula belongs to the Ronga clan; it is spoken by the bride's father while two goats are sacrificed in front of her mother's hut.

You have acted with strong determination! Now eat the liver! Eat it in the full light of day, not in the dark! It will be a mhamba, an offering to the gods.

You, gods, look! We have done it in the daylight. It has not been done by stealth. Bless them, give them children.

So be it! They have decided to marry each other; you, gods of the boy and girl, unite them together so that they do not hate each other; let them not remind each other that they are brother and sister; let their union not be spoilt by such remembrances, nor by other people saying to them: You have been guilty of witchcraft! You have married your relative!

In Praise of Sneezing

Bupsaye! Boukhwari! I pray you. I am not angry with you. Remain with me and let me sneeze. Give me sleep and let me live so that I can go my way, so that I can find a dead antelope in the forest and hoist it on my shoulders, so that I can go and kill Ndlopfou bou kene, an elephant.[4] Now it is enough, oh, my nose.

An Offering of Tobacco to Gods of the Family

Here is some tobacco! Come all of you and take a pinch, and do not be angry with me when I snuff, nor say that I deprive you of your share.

For One Who Departs

This prayer is recited by a witch doctor in the doorway of a person preparing to depart. During the recitation the witch doctor must spit a decoction he has prepared on the traveler, then wash the traveler's body with it.

Gently! Smoothly! I say so. Death does not come to him for whom prayer is made; death only comes to him who trusts in his own strength! Let misfortune depart, let it go to Shiburi, and Nkhabelane. Let him travel safely; let him trample on his enemies; let thorns sleep, let lions sleep; let him drink water wherever he goes, and let that water make him happy, by the strength of this herb.

For One Who Is Sick

When someone is sick, an appeal of a divinatory nature is made to the group of family gods, to whom an expiatory sacrifice must be made. The prayer below accompanies the sacrifice of a chicken. Before reciting it, the officiant plucks a few feathers from the fowl's neck and spits on the bloody tips.

You, our gods, here is our mhamba. Bless this child and make him live and grow; make him rich, so that when we visit him, he may be able to kill an ox for us. . . . You are useless, you gods; you only give us trouble! For, although we give you offerings, you do not listen to us! We are deprived of everything! You ——— *(naming the god who was angry, and who induced the other gods to come and do harm to the village by making the child ill),* you are full of hatred! You do not enrich us! All those who succeed do so by the help of their gods! Now we have made you this gift! Call your ancestors; call also the gods of this sick boy's father, because his father's people did not steal his mother: these people, of this clan, came in the daylight.[5] So come here to the altar! Eat and distribute amongst yourselves our ox according to your wisdom.

Sacred Chant

Let the meat not stick in your throats!
Eat, you chiefs, you ancestor gods. . . .
They are coming [the oxen]; they see me, whilst I mourn you,

my father and my mother, whilst I remain outside, where I receive
life from you, who are below; I remain, I am a miserable wretch.
The oxen are slain! Slay the oxen! Here they are. I mourn you.
Let us eat them together, you father and mother. Give me life and
give it also to my children. Let us eat these oxen which I possess,
but I possess them for you. Let us not suffer from complaints of
the chest here in our home.
This is the song by which we accompany you, as you return below.
Let us remain in good health.

Offering

> Mulungu, here is your food.
> We wish for rain, for wives, for cattle and for goats to raise;
> And we pray God that our people do not die from sickness.

Incantation for the Sword

The Bantu weapon-maker casts this incantation over a new sword he has
forged; the enchantment is instilled in the weapon by rubbing it with a piece
of magic wood called *kianduri*.

If the owner of this meets with an enemy, may you go straight and
kill your adversary; but if you are launched at one who has no evil in
his heart, may you miss him and pass on either side without entering
into his body.

Song for the Offering Ceremony

This chant accompanies the purification ceremonies which always precede
a sacrificial offering.

Heart return to the place.
The seeker of the thing has found it.
Drawer, bring the little bud of the water of the rain, that the little
boys may eat for themselves the herbs and salad plants of the deserted
homesteads.

For the Purification of Widows and Widowers

The purification of a widow or a widower is achieved by rubbing his or her
house, and the individual as well, with the contents from the stomach of a
sacrificed animal. The people requesting purification must seat themselves on
a black pelt, where the ceremony is carried out. At its conclusion the stomach

contents are mixed with incense and burned as an offering to the gods while this chant is intoned.

Tlhatlhadinwanen, take the smoke, there it is, take it right up to the place of the Molelale, Molelale, chief of the clouds.

Exorcism

Help me, you spirits of the Ngoni.[6]
I have received from your hands this medicine; therefore they must come forth at once from my sick one.

If by chance he has swallowed a snake or a toad that hinders the spirits from coming forth, compel these animals to flee so that there can be a way for the ghosts to depart.

UBANGI

Dancing Song for the Excision of the Clitoris

The clitoridotomy, or excision of the clitoris, is a puberty rite practiced in Sudan; in the central basin of the Nile and in Ethiopia the mutilation is more complex and crude.

The *ganzas* sing to the surgeon:

Before this we walked painlessly.
Why did you mock us?
When Korlo created us to make love,
He gave us a Wi-zu-gore.[7]
You took it away today, as it was taken away from you.
You gave us a great hurt, as it was given to you.
Maybe you think that we shall die,
But why?
You did not die, you, so we shall not die, either,
And we know that you did a good job, so that we can
    make love well.

They sing again at the end of the operation:

When we were circumcised, it hurt a great deal;
All of us, we thought that we would die.
Now we are strong and the pain is gone.

Tell our mothers, our brothers, our relatives, our neigh-
    bors, to come and admire our dancing.
They will see how pretty and well dressed for the dance
    we are
And also how happy and strong we are.

BAMBARA

Placating the Sacred Animal

This is used in the killing of *n'tana* (the sacred animal), and in all other
ritual violations perpetrated against him. The guilty person confesses his sin
to one of the older members of the group. The latter takes a fistful of straw
and bends it in two. Where the straws split, he puts a cluster of flowers, and
then, while the other crouches at his feet, waves the straw and flowers over
the head of the sinner. He makes three circles in this manner, while chanting
the ritual formula *A*. The formula indicated by *B* is the confession of the
believer; *dege* is millet flour sprinkled in water.

a)   Someone has come to me, he has said that he killed or ate our
n'tana. Any wound that he gets is because of the n'tana that he killed
or ate. Any sickness he gets will be because of the n'tana that he killed
or ate. Let now the sickness from which he suffers be cured.

b)   My Father, forgive me, I have killed —— [here the name of the
sacred animal], I give you some dege; I spread the dege in your honor.
Grant me peace. Forgive me. Grant me a happy fate. Deliver me from
bad sickness, deliver me from suffering.

For a Family Sacrifice

I offer thee this dege, this d'lo [nuts] and this chicken, in the
sacrifice that I carry out in my name and in the name of my children. Keep us safe from the suba [evil witches], from all evil and
ugly spirits. Be good to us, keep us from sickness, give us women,
healthy children, and take care to send us rain; give us physical vigor,
and in all ways preserve us that we might gather a bountiful crop.

An Offering of the Brotherhood of N'Tomo

N'tomo is a secret association for young men. The initiate offers up a chicken
to the boy leader (*n'tomotis.*), and then prostrates himself before the tree of

genius, swearing never to reveal the rites and teachings to the uninitiated or to young girls. Once yearly the members make a sacrificial offering in honor of *n'tomo*. This is a great feast day that terminates with collective flagellation. The following prayer accompanies the sacrifice.

N'tomo yea, see this chicken, a beautiful chicken, no? N'tomo, in all our names, I offer thee this chicken as a sacrifice.

Shower us with blessings, defend us from the furious genii of the thorn-brakes and from evil spirts. Make us strong and vigorous. Send us an abundance of food and drink, keep us safe from sickness. Give us rains and good crops, O N'tomo, and bless us with happy families.

Burial Prayer

In the complicated ceremonial practices of Bambara burial rites, the body is wrapped in a hide and then deposited under the *goua*—a rude awning that casts a little shadow over the dwelling—after which, aided by a witch doctor, those present pay their respects to the deceased. Formula *A* is shouted at the beginning of the ceremony by the herald. Formula *B* closes the first part of the ceremony. Formula *C* is recited while the witch doctor leans over the grave and pours water from a gourd on the body. The last formula is chanted by women, accompanied by a rhythmic beating of hands, while the earth is being shoveled into the grave.

a)   Pray do not get angry, we love you, we respect you, be happy while you stay in the Lahara.

b)   Give us rain when the hibernating time comes, give us a plentiful crop, a spry old age, some children, some wives, give us well-being.

c)   See this water, do not get angry, forgive us, give us rain when the hibernating time comes and a plentiful crop. Should wind come from the west or east, from the south or north, let it be favorable. Give us a long life, many children, some wives, and well-being.

d)   Our Father is dead, we have been told, he is dead. But he will come back. Young men, close the grave and do not let a suba [evil witch] or a hyena or a wild beast carry the corpse away.

BARUNDI

To Kiranga

Kiranga is a demigod. Public and private cults are dedicated to him, the former being of an initiative type. The god takes possession of a person in a mediumistic manner. The one obsessed, who has already been marked with special maladies by the god, then becomes a *kiranga* himself, thus determining the identification between god and creature. Once this identification has been established, the obsessed takes the name *Nyakere,* which means "wedded to god," and is admitted into the Bishegu caste. Upon this occasion the inhabitants of the kraal file before him and chant the following prayer.

> Reign! O Lord of the cattle of the Burundi,
> Living Biheko,
> Ryangombe of the Burundi,
> Reign, our refuge.
> Send me children, O Lord of the cattle of the Burundi.
> Help me to build.
> Grant me strength.
> Be beneficient.
> If I receive so much
> To thee I will make a sacrifice of brew
> And offer up to thee in sacrifice one barren cow.

MADAGASCAR

To Zanar and Niang

Zanar and Niang are the creators of the world.

> O Zanar, not to thee do we lift our voices.
> One need not pray to a God who is good.
> But we must placate the wrath of Niang.
> O Niang! wicked and powerful God, let not the
> thunder rumble over our poor heads; let not the
> furious sea break over its banks; spare our tender
> fruits; do not burn the rice before it has flowered;
> don't bring catastrophe and suffering down on our
> women; force no woman to see the hope of her old
>   age borne away and buried at sea.
> O Niang! Don't destroy the good works of Zanar.
> Thou rulest over the wicked and their number is
>   sufficiently great.
> Do not torment the good among us.

To the Earth

Have mercy upon me, O Earth! It is upon thee that I dwell, it is thou that givest to me my food and the water that I drink, it is thou that givest me clothes. Be merciful toward me, O Earth! Thou takest from me the wife without whom I cannot live, thou takest from me the children that are my joy, takest my friends that are dear to me, and takest even my father and mother.

ALGERIA

A Song

> Man is but small in the presence of Allah!
> He is small when he stands up,
> small when he walks,
> small when he works,
> for then the world is greater than he.
> But man is great when he lies down,
> for then his spirit rises
> into unknown worlds,
> rises toward heaven.
> Our life is a book of mystery
> written by Allah, mysterious and all-powerful;
> and only in sleep is it given
> to search through the pages of this book!
> Sleep, sleep, sleep!
> Sleep is close to death,
> and death is close to God.

RWALA BEDOUINS

Prayers for Rain

The chants selected are part of a complicated ritual designed to call forth rain. Women carry in procession the "Umm al-rejt," or Rain Mother, who is represented by a long stick, at the top of which are tied women's garments. The bearer of the simulacre passes from tent to tent, chanting formula *A*. Following her are groups of girls who chant formula *B* while gathering up offerings of grain and other edibles. Formula *C* is then chanted by the bearer, who weeps for the weakening of the camel which she loves, for the camel is dying of thirst. Formula *D* is a chant of liberation and probably serves to indicate the arrival of rain. The last strophe is an invocation to the wolf, who is not shackled by the winds and, wandering in the desert, has seen ancient customs and habits abandoned. He knows the story of Abu Zejd and of his beloved 'Alja, popular heroes of Bedouin folk tales.

a)

O Mother of Rain, rain upon us!
Moisten the cloak of our shepherd.
O Mother of Rain, rain upon us!
Slake our thirst with torrential rain.
O Mother of Rain, rain upon us!
Mete out our share from the gauge of Allah.
O Mother of Rain, rain upon us!
Cause a torrent to fall upon us.

b)

O Mother of Rain, rain upon us!
Thy ill will torments us still.
O Mother of Rain, rain upon us!
Clouds of dust still blind us.
O Mother of Rain, rain upon us!
The specter of death speeds toward us.
O Mother of Rain, O famished one!
The great cold hath destroyed us.

c)

Place me upon a tender young camel
and hold back whoever would restrain me.
The tears of my eyes are used up,
spent for those from whom I have been parted.

d)

Place me upon a bay horse,
feed me with the fruit of the date.
O, may Allah prolong their lives,
For they have liberated me.

e)

O wolf, O thou that strugglest with the burning wind of the south!
Drive away the freezing gust of the wind of the north.
Surely thou has seen 'Alja and Abu Zejd,
who will live forever in high ways.

Caravan Leaders' Prayer

This invocation to Allah is sung by the Bedouins when their caravans stop at watering places in the desert where the flow of water is poor. Watering the thirsty camels is a serious and dangerous task, for the animals are not always manageable and in their rush to drink they may trample one another to death. If twenty camels must sate their thirst at one of these poor water holes, it is necessary for ten men to work furiously for over four hours.

> O Lord, thou who art our guide,
> help us to accomplish speedily our wishes;
> fill with water our ships that have brought us to desperation.

DINKA

Religious Song

> In the time when God created all things, He created the sun.
> And the sun is born and dies and comes again.
>   He created the Moon,
> And the moon is born and dies and comes again.
>   He created the stars,
> And the stars are born and die and come again.
>   He created man.
> And man is born and dies and comes not again.

Hymns to Dengdit

a)
Father Rain falls into a solitary place.
Father Rain falls into a solitary place.
The Lord was in untrodden ground.
Hold the Father well, He holds our few souls.
Hold the Rain well, He holds our few souls.

b)
My ant[8] hoes the marsh grass and rests, hand on hip.
My ant hoes the marsh grass and rests, hand on hip.
Have I not given of my substance to man?
Have I not given of my substance to the spikes of the marsh grass, alas.

c)
Who will laugh?
The cattle-ant and the ant of the boat
Who will possess a homestead?
Unite the ants to a head.
Who will laugh?
The cattle-ant and the ant of the boat.
The ants have gone to Rain [as their] head
And the Fish-lord has not appeared.
Let us worship.

A Chant

Truly, God the Creator is there,
And we say: Far off is Der, the Father, up there.
God, the Creator, is near,
And we say: He is not here.

A Chant

On us shall descend some awful curse,
Like the curse that descended in far-off times.
Thus speaketh the Creator of men,
But the men refuse to listen.
On us shall descend some awful curse,
Like the curse that descended in far-off times:
We have but one word to say:
Idle about! Sink in sloth!
Men of such kind will gain nothing from the Father,
For they know not his voice.
He is the one who loves Man.

Prayers to Nhialic

Nhialic is another name for the Supreme Being, and means "He who is above."

a)

O Father, Creator, God, I ask thy help!
I invoke Thee, O my Father!
To Thee, Father, I turn,
To Thee, my God, I turn,

O Father, I turn to Thee.
God, my Father, I pray to Thee.
To Thee, in the time of the new moon,
I address my plea.
God recognizes my forebears who are reconciled with him.

b)

Come all and implore God to give life to Man,
Come all and receive life from God.
Rain mixed with sunbeams will gain us life.

c)

Ask life for the flocks, the herds, and men.
Sacrifice the white ox, that God may draw nigh,
That the Father may give us life.
Deng and Abuk are invoking life.
Sacrifice the white ox, that God may draw nigh.

d)

Now let us reunite!
The Father has life to give,
The Great Man has life.

e)

O Father, Creator, come! We are reunited.
Give life to herds and flocks and men.
O Father, come!
How can I reconcile myself with thee?
Go invoke the Lord!

A Prayer for Rain

Cry out for rain.
The Man on High sends no rain.
Cry out for rain.
He sends no rain.

Abandoned

God has forsaken us,
The creator of the sun refuses us life.
O cold-white moon,
The creator of the sun refuses us life.

Prayers of Faith

a)

> God has turned his back on us,
> The words of men have made him wrathful.
> And yet he will turn about again.
> God has turned his back on us.

b)

> We are the children of our Maker
> And do not fear that he will kill us.
> We are the children of God
> And do not fear that he will kill.

c)

> How, in the time of privation,
> Will the people live?
> In the time of privation
> I will not fear.

d)

> Because I have prayed and prayed,
> The word of the Lord will not be mocked,
> His good word will ever keep thee.

Evening Prayer

> Now that evening has fallen,
> To God, the Creator, I will turn in prayer,
> Knowing that he will help me.
> I know the Father will help me.

Prayer of a Dying Man

> And though I behold a man hate me,
> I will love him.
> O God, Father, help me, Father!
> O God, Creator, help me, Father!
> And even though I behold a man hate me,
> I will love him.

Chants

a)

> O Deng, O Father, O most high Deng,
> O Father Deng, the great ancient one.

b)

> Dengdit refuses to hear us, Dengdit turns away.
> When he is not honored, he takes offense.
> O Father Deng, don't abandon me,
> O Father Deng, don't thrust me into the arms
>   of the Malign Spirit.

c)

> I ask of Deng: Where art thou gone?
> Come, Father, with a gift from the Man on High.
> The gift is from God.
> I turn to Deng, and he will listen,
> I turn to Him, and he will hearken.

A Prayer for Recovery

> O great Deng, let her live,
> Let her recover and escape from death,
> O great Deng, let her live!

To Morning

> Abuk, Deng, rise up in glory,
> Day is breaking.
> Deng Maiwal, give me thy blessing, give me life.

Sacrificial Offering to Nhialic

> O Nhialic, thou alone generated them,
> Thou alone made them.
> No one finds them odious.
> O merciful Nhialic, turn thine eyes upon life.
> No one is powerful.
> Accept this ox.
> I have paid the price.
> Now let them live.

A Bloodless Offering to Nhialic

Let us lift our voices in prayer,
Offering up an ox to the Creator.
May this ox be permitted to grow old,
That we might gain good health.
Let us lift our voices in prayer,
Offering up an ox to the Creator.
The Creator of the sky gives us peace,
Gives us food.

For Rain

Spring rain comes driving down like clubs on the heads of the people.
And the people say: Up there the Father knows.
But we do not know if He is showering us with blessings or if it is His
wish instead to chastise the clan.

YAO

Instructions for the Initiation

You, my pupil, now you are initiated.
Respect your mother and your father.
See that you do not enter the house unannounced, lest you should find
them embracing.
Do not be afraid of women, but sleep with them, bathe with them; when
you have finished, let her rub you; when you have finished, she should
salute you, saying 'Masakam,' and you must answer, 'Marhaba.'
You must take care when you see the new moon, you might get hurt.
Beware of women during their courses; this is dangerous, it causes many
diseases.

SHILLUK

To Juok and Nyakang

In this prayer Juok is the name of the Supreme Being who, with only minor differences of phonetics, is claimed by almost all the Nilotic ethnic groups. His spirit is invisible and omnipresent. Nyakang (Nikawng) is a mediating goddess between men and Juok, and Dok (Dag) is Nyakang's son.

We praise you, you who are God. Protect us, we are in your hands, protect us, save me. You and Nyakang, you are the ones who created; people are in your hands, and it is you who gave the rain. The sun is yours, and the river is yours, you are Nyakang. You came from under the sun, you and your father, you two saved the earth, and your son, Dok, you subdued all the people. The cow is here for you and the blood will go to God and you.

Dancing Song for Juok

I pray to Juok, God the giver. God the protector; I have taken God to me and have become fearful to my enemies, so that they scarcely dare attack me.

Sacrifice to the Dead Father

We praise you, you, who are God, it was you who gave me my father, who begot me. I pray to you also, my father. Why did you go to earth and keep silence? Was not this your house before? When evil comes to your house, why do you not pray to God? Your house is given as a plaything to the people. You went to the presence of God, and we thought that nothing evil would befall us again after you left. Now help, God. Why do you leave this responsibility of saving on God alone? God's spirit becomes tired from work and he leaves people and they die. Why do you not see and save us? You went to the ground, and you have forgotten that a person from another house does not guard yours.

In Ruins

O Shilluk, cause of the ruination of our lands;
Why not turn again to God, up there?
Why not turn again to the real God?

To God the protector who looks after the country?
To God the giver who looks after the country?

A Chant to Nyikango

> Nyikango, call upon God,
> for He has created men,
> for he sends forth the rain.

Another Chant to Nyikango

> I call upon Grandfather Nyikango,
> I spread the palms of my hands in prayer:
> O Nyikango, implore God,
> who hath created the earth.

A Third Chant to Nyikango

> O sharpener of spears, little Yelo,
> call upon God,
> who has generated men,
> until he grants rain to Nyikango, sharpener of spears.

To Dywok and to the Ancestors

To Thou, who art God, we raise praises. Protect us. We are in Thy hands. Protect us and spare us. Thou and Nyikang art the ones who generate life, all men are in Thy hands. And Thou, Nyikang, art the only help of God in saving us, Thou art the granter of rain. The sun is Thine, the sea is Thine, for Thou art Nyikang. Thou comest here from the subsolar regions. Through Thy efforts and the father's the world was saved. And to Thy son Dok all men give obedience. Behold here the cow, and its blood shall be scattered for God and for Thee. Hear now, all of you, you men of earth, and be saved. Whoever transgresses your word shall die.

To Dywok

> King Nyikango refuses to help us.
> Nyidung, the son of Yor, presented himself
> to God's face, and was helped.
> He stood up on his feet and found help.

Offering for a Cure

I implore thee, thou God,
I pray to thee during the night.
How are all people kept by thee all days!
And thou walkest in the midst of the high grass.
I walk with thee: when I sleep in the house, I sleep with thee.
To thee I pray for food, and thou givest it to the people;
    and water to drink; and the souls are kept alive by thee.
There is no one above thee, thou God.
Thou becamest the grandfather of Nyikango; it is thou, Nyikango, who
    walkest with God; thou becamest the grandfather of man and thy
    son Dak.
If a famine comes, is it not given by thee?
So as this cow stands here, is it not thee; if she dies, does her blood not
    go to thee?
Thou God, to whom shall we pray, is it not to thee?
Thou God, and thou who becamest Nyikango, and thy son Dak!
But the soul of man, is not thine own?
It is thou who liftest up the sick.

GIUR

To the Magic Spear

The magic spear has mysterious origins, and the Giur always have it at the
forefront of their ranks when attacking enemies. On such occasions the following prayer is recited by the bearer of the magic spear.

Thou has brought us here to help us.
Tomorrow we must fight: none of us shall fall, but only the enemy.
If one of us is wounded, let it not be to the death, but so that he can
    be borne home.
With thee let it be granted to us to recover our wives and children that
    are taken prisoner by the enemy.

Morning Prayer

      Thou, O Jouk, who hast created all men,
      Let my family be forever happy,

I have not offended against my father and my mother,
I have not sinned with my neighbor's wife,
there is no sin in me, I am innocent:
I have stolen nothing, I have killed no one
without cause; grant contentment
to everyone of my house.

Taking Possession of a New Camp

When the Giur clear out a new place in the forest to build a camp or a new
house, they sacrifice a rooster and a goat to Jouk and recite the following
prayer of propitiation.

I pray to Thee, Jouk.
I have come to shave your head.[9]
Let me dwell in peace,
let the grain ripen;
let no harm come to me
when I cut the trees.
Now I have bought[10] thee, killing
a goat. Let me remain happy.

To Bring the Rain

In a public ceremony the recitation of this formula is entrusted to *ngade
acek*, the "person of the creative spirit," a member of the community possessed
by the spirit.

We make this sacrifice in order to have rain.
If thou hearest our prayer, grant us rain.
Thou art our father, everyone is here to ask rain of thee.
We are sinners.
If one of us engages in strife today,
if one of us sheds blood, we will not have rain.
Thou art our father. Grant us rain.
The earth is dry, our families, ruined.
Thou art our father. Grant us rain.

Before Fighting with the Enemy

O spear of my old grandfather,
I go now into the fight.

May my youths not stumble.
May the arrows fly into empty air,
not touching the youths.
We are not entering into war without cause.
Once you slew my brother,
You slew my cousin.
You slew my grandfather, too.
May my spear today strike you in the back.
We've got to avenge our own blood.

For a Sick Child

This formula is sung by *ngade acek* over the person who is sick. During the song he shakes his weapon over the patient and then casts water upon all present, as well as blood from a sacrificed sheep.

Jouk, my father, help us heal this—
since I have never taken anything from others,
I stole nothing in order to marry his mother—
I have no sin upon my soul.
Now I redeem the child from you with a ram.
Leave us the child, grant that he recover.

For the Fertility of a Woman

Thou, Jouk, who art our father and hast created all of us,
thou knowest this woman is ours,
and we wish her to bear children—
grant children to her.
Should we die tomorrow, no children of ours will remain—
grant children to her.
If she bears a son, his name will be the name of his grandfather.
If she bears a daughter, her name will be the name of her grandmother.
Grant children to her.
Would it be displeasing to thee if many children surrounded us?
Spirit of the father, spirit of the grandfather, you who dwell now
    in the skies,
Are displeased that we ask for children?
Grant children to her.
Should we die without them, who will guard the family?
Your name and ours shall be forgotten upon the earth.

Grant us this night good dreams,
that we will die leaving many children behind us.

ZULU

A Prayer

Yes! Yes! I implore you, O grandfathers who completed so many
noble undertakings! After having sacrificed this bull which belongs to
you, I pray to you, asking you every kind of prosperity. I cannot deny
you nourishment, since you have given me all the herds that are here,
and if you ask of me the nourishment that you have given me, is it not
just that I return it to you? Grant us many beasts to fill these tables!
Grant us much grain, so that many people may come to inhabit this
village which is yours and so may make much tumult to your glory!
Grant us numerous offspring, so that this village may be much populated
and your names may never be extinguished!

Prayer of Offering

Here is our food. All you spirits of our tribe, invite each other. I do
not say that you are jealous, but you who have raised this sick man,
summon all the spirits. Come, all of you, to eat this food.

Prayer

When have we ever forgotten to make sacrifices to you and to
enumerate your honorable names? Why are you so miserly? If you do
not improve, we will let all your honorable names fall into oblivion.
What will your fate be then! You will have to go and feed on locusts.
Improve: else we will forget you. For whose good is it that we make
sacrifices and celebrate the praises? You bring us neither harvests nor
abundant herds. You show no gratitude whatever for all the trouble
we take. However, we do not wish to estrange ourselves completely from
you and we will say to other men that we do not completely possess
the spirits of our forebears. You will suffer from it. We are angry with
you.

LOBI

Invocation to the River

This invocation belongs to a group of ceremonies that accompany the sowing and the harvesting. It is also used in connection with a certain legume, the leaves of which contain a drug—Theprosia Vogelii—widely used along the Gulf of Guinea, in the Cameroons and in the Congo, for fishing. If used properly, this herb makes the fish very excited and then leaves them paralyzed, so that they are easy to catch. Before using the drug, the Lobi fisherman goes to a place in the river that is frequented by hippopotamuses and crocodiles, recites this prayer, and offers a baby chick as a sacrifice.

O river, I beg leave to take fish from thee, as my ancestors did before me.
The antelope leaps and its young learns not to climb.
In such a manner the sons of men do as their fathers did.
O river, rise up, engulf your sharp-toothed monsters, and permit our
young men to enter the water and enjoy themselves with the fish without
     being harmed.
If there is acceptance from you, then show it by accepting this baby
chick. If not, if you cannot control the monsters, if one of them should
     harm our sons, then show it by refusing to accept this baby chick.

For the Migration

When famine forces the tribe to move, a priest chants the following prayer over the new territory.

Sie, Dyohourete, Dyorfoute, Dyolinnte, and all the priests of the Earth
     who lived before me have observed this custom, and now it is my
     turn.
The famine is upon us. We have no millet, maize, or beans.
Our cattle, sheep, and goats are dead, as are our chickens.
The women and children are hungry.
Therefore we have decided to set up our homes in this unoccupied place.
O nurturing Earth, we offer thee this chicken; accept it, we beseech
thee, and in exchange give us bountiful harvests, numerous herds and
flocks, and many children. Keep us free from sickness, epidemics and
     all evils.

To the River

This is part of the initiation ritual of the Dyoro Sect and is recited by the priest while the *silisinsi,* members or candidates of the sect, remain motionless on the banks of the river. In the text the name Batiè refers to a certain locality and Kana, to an ancient priest of the sect.

The whole of Batiè belongs to the river. O Kana, it is out of thanks to the great things thou hast done that so many people are gathered here today. May they be blessed, may they see no evil, and may they dwell safely in their homes. And if that happens, I recognize that the Land of Batiè truly protects its men, and with these shells given to me I shall buy an ox to offer up to the river. If it is true that thou art here, O River, and hear me, let the hippopotamuses come out, that our children may see them.

LANGO

A Ceremony of the Gayo Tango

During the *gayo tango,* or purification ceremony at the birth of twins, all the men are daubed with flour. Then an old woman, brandishing a millet stalk on which she has spit, rubs soup from the pot on the breasts of the men and women and chants the following prayer.

Pu! Thou, God, hast come upon us. We accept thee. Stay, stay thou with us favorably. May the children be well; may their mother be well. Any animal that comes before us, let our spears fall on its body. Any man who seeks us, let us kill him and rejoice.

To the Spirit of the Air

O men-children,
come along, pray to God!
O children,
come along, pray to God!
Pray to our God!
Our ancestor has descended here below.
It would be madness to deride the spirits.
The Spirit of the Air is something great,
pursuing us over his wide plains.

HOTTENTOTS

Prayer for Rain

> O Tsuni-Goam, father of fathers, thou our father,
> Tell Nanub to let the rain come down in torrents.

Prayer

O Haitsi-Eibib, O thou our forebear, grant me good fortune to find
honey and roots in order to please thee.

To Tsuigoa, the Ancestor

> O Tsuigoa,
> father of fathers,
> thou art our father.
> Let the rain fall from storm clouds,
> Let our herds live.
> Let us live.
> Alas, I am so weak,
> I am thirsty, I am hungry.
> Oh, could I but eat the fruit of the fields!
> Art thou not our father,
> father of fathers,
> O Tsuigoa?
> O, could we but praise thee,
> could we but show our gratefulness!
> Thou, father of fathers,
> thou, our Master,
> O Tsuigoa!

KONDE

Morning Prayer

We rise up in the morning, before the day, to betake ourselves to our
labor, to prepare our harvest. Protect us from the tiger and from the
serpent and from every stumbling block.

In Time of Famine

Mbamba, Kiara, you have denied us rain, grant us rain so that we may not die. Deliver us from death by starvation. For thou art our father and we are your children. Thou hast created us. Why, then, dost thou wish us to die? Give us maize, bananas, and beans. Thou hast given us feet to walk with, arms to work with, and even sons: grant us also rain so that we may harvest!

When Enemies Draw Near

Our enemies approach. O God, fortify our arms, grant us strength.

Harvest Prayer

May our grain bear so much fruit that it be forgotten on the ground and that it lets fall along the path so much that next year when we go forth to seed, the fields and the pathways will be covered with green grain.

To Boora Pennu

O Boora Pennu, thou alone hast created us and hast given us the capacity to feel hunger. So we need grain and we must have fertile fields.

BAKANGO

Against the Rain

Father, thy children are in great anguish.
Calm the tempest, for here live many of thy children.
Seest thou not that we are dying?

MASAI

For the Return of the Warriors

Engai is the name of the Supreme Being.

                Engai, Engai, tear out . . .
Chorus: The brand marks of the people.[11]

                Tear out, tear out . . .
Chorus: The brand marks of the people.

                Girls, be not silent . . .
Chorus: It is being prayed to Engai.

                Tear out, tear out . . .
Chorus: The brand marks of the people.

                Venus who is rising . . .
Chorus: And the evening star,

                Tear out . . .
Chorus: The brand marks of the people.

                The clouds of snow capped mountains, tear out . . .
Chorus: The brand marks of the people.

                He who waits till the heavens are red, tear out . . .
Chorus: The brand marks of the people.

Prayer Before a Raid

                Let us say to Engai—grant us many cattle!
Chorus: He will grant it.

                Grant us life!
Chorus: He will grant it.

                Grant us health and happiness!
Chorus: He will grant it.

Grant us victory!

Chorus: He will grant it.

Grant us much booty!

Chorus: He will grant it.

Morning Prayer

God of my needfulness, grant me something to eat, give me milk, give me sons, give me great herds, give me meat, O my father.

KIKUYU

Propitiation for the Harvest

Ngai is the name of the Supreme Being.

Mwene-Nyaga, you who have brought us rain and have given us a good harvest, let people eat grain of this harvest calmly and peacefully.

Chorus: Peace, praise ye, Ngai, peace be with us.

Do not bring us any surprise or depression.

Chorus: Peace, praise ye, Ngai, peace be with us.

Guard us against illness of people and our herds and flocks, so that we may enjoy this season's harvest in tranquillity.

Chorus: Peace, praise ye, Ngai, peace be with us.

For Opening the Assembly of the Ancients

Say ye, the elders may have wisdom and speak with one voice.

Chorus: Praise ye Ngai. Peace be with us.
Say ye that the country may have tranquillity and the people may continue to increase.

Chorus: Praise ye Ngai. Peace be with us.

Say ye that the people and the flocks and herds may prosper and be free from illness.

Chorus: Praise ye Ngai. Peace be with us.

Say ye the fields may bear much fruit and the land may continue to be fertile.

Chorus: Praise ye Ngai. Peace be with us.

A Chief's Prayer Favoring Routledge, the Ethnologist

O God, accept this sacrifice, because the white man has come to my fireside. When the white man falls ill, see that neither he nor his wife become very sick. The white man has come to us from his country, from the other side of the water: he is a good man and is considerate to those who work for him. If the white man and his wife fall ill, see that they do not become very sick, because I and the white man have come together to make a sacrifice to thee. Do not let them die because we are sacrificing a very fat ram to thee. From very far has the white man come to us, and now we have agreed to offer up to thee a sacrifice. Wherever he goes, see that he does not fall ill; because he is a good man and also extremely rich, and I too am good, and rich; and I and the white man live in such good accord as though we were sons of the same mother. God, we have set aside for thee a big ram. The white man and his wife and I and my people are going to sacrifice for thee on the trunk of a tree a ram, a very valuable ram. See that I do not fall very ill, for I have taught him to pray to thee as though he were a true Mkikuyu.

LOZI

Benediction of the Sowing

O Nyamba, you are the creator of all. Today we, your creatures, prostrate ourselves before you in supplication. We have no strength. You who have created us have all power. We bring you our seed and all our implements, that you may bless them and bless us also so that we may make good use of them by the power which comes from you, our creator.

BARONGA

Against a Thief

O Heaven, thou hast two eyes that see well both by day and by night. They have stolen my goods and deny it. Come and reveal them. May they be destroyed!

CAMEROON

For a Wife

Thou alone, O God, hath ordained that we marry women. Therefore grant that my wife, now sick, recover speedily.

DJAGGA

Entreaty

This formula is recited each morning after the person has made the ritual spit in the direction of the sun.

O Ruwa, protect me and mine!

Vows

These two vows are uttered by the same person, the second being used if it seems that the first has not been heard.

a)

O spirit, thou that hast taken possession of this man, give back his health, and I will reward what you do and I will sacrifice a goat to you.

b)

This is the goat, O my father, continue to turn your eyes toward the sick one until he is cured. Grant my prayer, grant my prayer, O king, O earth, O heaven, let yourself be moved. If you have taken possession of him, give him back his health, O Lord, and you will receive another sacrifice.

Leaving for War

Ruwa, my chief, take me by the hand and lead me in safety. Grant me also an ox, O chief, so that I may offer you a sacrifice.

To the Spirits

Keep me in life and grant me health. O what else must I do, in your opinion? Have patience: I wish to cut grain until I have earned a goat, to offer up to you. If you hinder me in any way, will you then perhaps receive anything? Never. And your colleagues will make fun of you. Therefore, watch over me and you will receive your due.

CONGO

Funeral Chant

O great Nzambi, what thou hast made is good, but thou hast brought a great sorrow to us with death. Thou shouldst have planned in some way that we would not be subject to death. O Nzambi, we are afflicted with great sadness.

TANGANYIKA

Fisherman's Prayer

O Spirit, grant us a calm lake, little wind, little rain, so that the canoes may proceed well, so that they may proceed speedily.

GALLA

Daily Prayer

If enemies should come, let not your small worm die, but stretch your hand over him.

MENSA

To the New Moon

May you be for us a moon of joy and happiness. Let the young become strong and the grown man maintain his strength, the pregnant woman be delivered and the woman who has given birth, suckle her child. Let the stranger come to the end of his journey and those who remain at home dwell safely in their houses. Let the flocks that go to feed in the pastures return happily. May you be a moon of harvest and of calves. May you be a moon of restoration and of good health.

RUWANDA

Chief's Prayer at the Engagement of His Daughter

O father, forebear of my daughter, this is the ox that we are sacrificing for you. Go up to the mountains, call your servants, assemble all your people for this banquet, all your warriors. This is your ox, chosen for you by your people. Sit and eat it, you and your people.

EWE

To Ask Protection During an Act of Magic

I have no saliva in my mouth. Thou art the possessor of saliva. Come then and spit upon this medicine.

For Peace and Harmony

May peace reign over the earth, may the gourd cup agree with the vessel. May their heads agree and every ill word be driven out into the wilderness, into the virgin forest.

In War

We were at home and suddenly we heard the report that there was war. You are our chief. That is why we have come to you to pray that you march at our head, in the war, to guide us. In our homeland, at Anlo, there is no forest where we may hide. But you, O Nyigibla of our ancestors, you are the forest wherein we may be safe. Call together, therefore, all your warriors, so that they may wage this war for us, for we have no strength whatever.

To Mawu Sodza

O Mawu Sodza, mother of men, mother of beasts. If thou givest to man, thou givest truly. If thou deniest to man, thou deniest truly. In thy greatness, I am great and agree to thy will.

Vow

I pray to you, grant me a son.
If you grant my prayer, I will show you my gratitude and offer a goat
    up to you.

MALAYA

Incantation Against the Langsuirs

The Langsuirs are "birth demons" that issue forth from the ghost of a woman who died in childbirth. They prey on newborn babies, somewhat the way the ancient European vampire was supposed to do.

Langhui, Langhua,
Your beak is stumpy,
Your feathers are cloth of silk,
Your eyes are "crab's-eye" beans,[12]
Your heart, a young areca-nut,
Your blood, thread in water,
Your veins, the thread for binding on cock's-spurs,
Your bone, twigs of the giant bamboo
Your tail, a fan from China.[13]

Descend, O Venom, ascend,
Neutralize the Venom in the bones, neutralize it in the veins,
Neutralize it in the joints,
Neutralize it within the house, neutralize it within the jungle.
Descend, O Venom, ascend Neutralizer,
And lock up this Langsuir.
Descend, O Venom, ascend Neutralizer.

Incantation Against the Savage Hunter

A symbolic offering of water is often substituted for the blood offering
referred to in the prayer.

Oho, thou Demon Hunter,
Accept this bowl of blood we offer,
And use it up to cook your mushrooms;
But go ahunting here no longer,
Hunt only in the slough of Ali
And in the Swamp of the Mahang trees,
With your good hound whose name is Tampoi,
Your hound whose name is Tampoi,
Your hound whose name is Koing,
Your hound whose name is Sukum,
Your hound whose name is Langsat.
Lo, here I draw my jungle chopper
To cut the Neutralizing Creeper,
To cut in twain the Giant Creeper,
And snuff out thus the Demon Hunter.
Come thou ahunting here no longer,
But hasten back to where thou cam'st from,
Return unto the slough of Ali.

Charm for Driving out Devils

One, Two, Three, Four, Five, Six, Seven,
Be cool, O Fever, cool and frigid.
In flesh and bones and joints and sinews
Pluck forth, expel, all fiends and devils;
Be opened, loosed, ye fiends and devils;
Drive forth, I beg, all fiends and devils.
Busu, bring thou the sucking flour-ball,

Busu, bring thou the flour-paste antidote,
To allay these pangs in the flesh and sinews.
And thou, O Fever, be thou cooled,
And all the fiends and devils driven forth
From out the heart, from out the spirit.
Busu, bring thou the Tenglang blossom,
And chant in the leaf cell, the leaf chamber.
Bring, Busu, all these fiends together,
And drive them forth before your knife blade
Unto the rock that's called Perimbum;
Foul be Perimbum with them ever.

Inwalling Spell

A spell used by the Mantras to acquire invulnerability.

Hong![14] O Horn, Shoot of Iron.
Offering of the wise to the forest in solitude.
I am walled round with rock, I recline walled round by the earth, with my face downward. Cover me, O Air; may my enemies be ever at the Selaguri plant. Tear off the husk within. Hang a thick mist before the eyes of him who looks at me. Come, thick mist, the concealer, and render me invisible to all enemies, opponents, and assailants. Thou that art the true and holy instructor, descend, and pray that I may touch, by the invocation of invisibility, all the eyes of my enemies, opponents, and assailants.

Charm for Invoking the Rice-Soul

Belonging to the Jacun-Blandas, this is one of the numerous prayers in the rituals and cults of rice.

Rice-boat male[15] and Rice-boat female,
Cluck, cluck, cluck! your souls I summon,
Both the girl-child and the boy-child.
Soul of Rice-plants,[16] S'lotan, Borak,
Jambi, Pulut,[17] Maize, Bananas.
Thus into the house we bear you,
In the soil no longer slumber,
Slumber now within the curtains.[18]

To the Spirit of Incense

This invocation is used in connection with the burning of incense, which is one of the most common forms of sacrifice in this part of Asia. The Moslem influence on indigenous religions is also apparent.

Zabur[19] Hijau is your name, O Incense,
Zabur Bajang, the name of your Mother,
Zabur Puteh, the name of your Fumes,
Scales from the person of God's Apostle[20] were your origin.
May you fumigate the Seven Tiers of the Earth,
May you fumigate the Seven Tiers of the Sky,
And serve as a summons to all Spirits, to those which have become
 Saints of God.
The Spirits of God's elect, who dwell in the Halo of the Sun,
And whose resort is the Ka'bah of Allah,
Who dwell at the Gate of the Spaces of Heaven,
And whose resort is the White Diamond
In the interior of Egypt, at morn and eve;
Who know how to make the dead branch live,
And the withered blossom unfold its petals,
And to perform the word of Allah;
By the grace of the creed "There is no god but Allah."

Against the Hantu Songkei

Hantu is the generic Malayan term for "demon and captive spirit"; *Songkei* means "that which unties a knot." In Malaya demons frequently enter into and tinker with animal traps and bird cages, setting the captives free and molesting the hunters. The demon is represented as a spirit invisible from the chest down, with a big nose and eyes so large that he can see everything around him. The following incantation is recited to neutralize his malign influence.

Peace be with you, grandson of the Specter Huntsman,
Whose dwelling place is a solitary patch of primeval forest,
Whose chair is the nook between the buttresses of trees,
Whose leaning post, the wild Areca palm,
Whose roof, the leaves of the Resam,
Whose mattress, leaves of the Lerek,
Whose swing, the tree Medang Jelawei,
And whose swing-ropes are Malacca-cane-plants,

The Gift of His Highness Sultan Berumbangan,
Who dwelt at Pagar Ruyong,
In the House whose posts were heart of the Tree-nettle,
Whose threshold a Stem of Spinach,
Strewn over with stems of the Purut-purut,
Whose Body-hairs were inverted
And whose Breasts were four in number,
To whom belonged the Casting-net for Flies,
And whose drum was "headed" with the skins of lice.
Break not faith with me
Or you shall be killed by the Impact of the Sanctity of the Four Corners
    of the World,
Killed by the Impact of the Forty-four Angels,
Killed by the Impact of the Pillar of the Ka'bah,
Killed by the Thrust of the sacred Lump of Iron,
Killed by the Shaft of the Thunderbolt,
Killed by the Pounce of Twilight Lightning,
Killed by the Impact of the Thirty Sections of the Koran,
Killed by the Impact of the Saying,
"There is no god but Allah."

Charm for the Ceremony of Erecting the Center Post

Ho, Raja Guru, Majaraja Guru,[21]
You are the sons of Batara Guru.
I know the origin from which you spring,
From the Flashing of Lightning's spurs;
I know the origin from which you spring,
From the Brightening of Daybreak.
Ho, Specter of the Earth, Brains of the Earth, Demon of the Earth,
Retire ye hence to the depths of the Ocean,
To the peace of the primeval forest;
Betwixt you and me
Division was made by Adam.

LOLO

Benediction at a Wedding

a)

May the God, Apu Uosa, fill you with grace!
Protect you by day, defend you at night!
May he send you many children: sons to the father, sons to the mother!
May the sons live to be ninety-nine, the daughters, to be seventy-seven:
    and this for eleven hundred years!
Divine assistance! Nocturnal vigilance!

b)

Libations! Libations!
to the protective spirits on high,
to Apu Uosa the God,
to the wandering spirits below,
to the spirits of the mountains,
to the spirits of the valleys,
to the spirits of the east,
to the spirits of the west,
to the spirits of the north,
to the spirits of the south,
To the bride and groom, together, libation!
May the spirits on high, as well as the spirits below, fill you with grace!

c)

Divine assistance! Nocturnal vigilance! Rather than see you so much as damage a toenail, the good spirits scatter out before you. The good spirits precede you, keep your way cleared of obstacles, that you might not so much as damage a fingernail! The good spirits are cushions, and not a hair of your head shall be harmed. O you, the thirty good persons in the shadows, come out into the light, and may light follow you! Libation!

d)

When you go together in the daytime to the mountain and the evil spirit
    follows,
May the evil spirit be kept at a distance!
If the evil spirit comes, keep it at a distance!
If it is the evil spirit X, keep it at a distance!

If it is the evil spirit Z, keep it at a distance!

When the young bride goes out of the village, and if the demon of the
forest should molest her, let her go away, and keep him at his
distance

And from this moment forth let the evil spirits vanish!

Vanish also the ominous signs!

Away with the evil way!

Away with sickness!

A Divining Prayer

Formula A is used in "divining the scale." A weight is suspended from a
cord and the spirits are named. When the spirit responsible for the sickness
is mentioned, the weight begins to move. Formula B: The shoulder blade of a
sheep is put on the fire and a priest waits for the openings to appear. When
they do, he interprets them and makes his divination.

a) Divining the scale:

We know that you, O powerful spirit ———, are the cause of the sickness.

We present you with this gift, asking you to grant relief to the sufferer
and commute his suffering into joy.

b) Divining the shoulder blade:

Come running, come running, all of you, spirits of the mountains, spirits
of the forests, spirits of the torrents!

Spirit of Mountain X, spirit of Forest Y, spirit of Fountain Z, come
running, come running!

It behooves you to tell us why the chief, Matu of the Black Bone, is
stricken by a malady that threatens his days. You, sharp-eyed goat,
will certainly know the secret. Reveal it! Will the chief live, or die?

For the Dead

Among the Lolos of Tonchino the priest recites this prayer to enclose sensitive souls or vital spirits (pho) in the coffin, to insure that they, the sensitive
souls, will be buried with the body.

I have readied a pleasant dwelling place for you,
I pray you, enter.
To a delicious place will I conduct you.
There you will dwell in peace,
You will not be annoyed by visits from your children.

Your descendants will pay tribute to you.
Compensate them by according them your protection!

ARMENIAN

Hymn to the Birth of Vagahu

Vagahu is the national hero of the Armenians, the god of war and courage.

The heavens and the earth travailed,
There travailed also the purple sea,
The travail held
The red reed in the sea.
Through the hollow of the reed a smoke rose,
Through the hollow of the reed a flame rose,
And out of the flame ran forth a youth.
He had hair of fire,
He had a beard of flame,
And his eyes were suns.

TELEUTS

A Prayer to Ulgan

Dweller on high,
O Tangara Kan, Kan of Abyyas,
Thou who makest the grass grow,
Bringest leaves to the trees,
Shapest flesh on the thigh,
Givest hair to the head,
Creator of every living thing,
Ruler of the heavens,
Lighter of the stars!
O the sixty powerful princes that surround thee,
Who took my father from me!
Creator of all living things,
Ruler of the heavens,

Lighter of the stars!
Give me, O God, herds and flocks,
Give me bread!
Give to every house a master,
O Creator of every living thing,
Ruler of the heavens,
Lighter of the stars!
In the name of the Father I beseech thee.
Give me, O Father, prosperity,
Dwell here with the master of my house,
Dwell with the flocks in the field.
May the gods grant us happiness,
O Creator of every living thing,
Ruler of the heavens,
Lighter of the stars!

For Rain

Prayer recited by a rainmaker (*yadasti*) while pouring a magic potion into the sacred fire.

Kaira Kan, Kaira Kan!
Alas! Alas! Alas!
For the width of a hand
Cause the sky to open,
Open it for the width of a needle point!
I belong to the race of rainmakers,
I, the root of the evergreen tree.
And I call Tobu,
I call Kuldurak.
Tie the earth's umbilical to the sky,
Tie the sky's umbilical to the earth!
I call Pastygan, my forebear.
Open the rivulet from the sky.
For the width of a hand
Cause the sky to open,
Open it for the width of a needle point!
I cross over the high mountains
From the fountains of Abakan.
Kaira Kan, Kaira Kan!
Alas! Alas! Alas!

Keep them safe from the evil eye,
Keep them from harm!
When an evil spirit approaches them,
Hand them your golden bow.
With the bow and blowpipe thrust back
The evil spirit.
And keep away spirits of the storm,
That they bring no howling winds!
Keep every evil far away!
Lead them to the good things!
Cause the spirit to reawaken,
Strengthen the roots of the heather.

To the Power of Bai Ulgan

He who moves the sun and moon,
Who on high rolls the white clouds around,
Who strikes with lightning in the dark forest,
Who measured out everything with shovel and spoon,
He, the bearer of lightning, the hurler of thunder,
When he stamps his feet upon the earth,
How the universe trembles!
And how the outcast's heart burns inside his breast!

A Prayer to Mai-ana, Protector of Children

O Mother-Fire, with the thirty flashing heads,
O virgin of the many heads,
Who cooks the food,
Who thaws the bitter freeze,
Come wrap around us
And be a father!
Come wrap around us
And be a mother!
You, who scatter all impurities in the sea,
Who with the white splinter severs the umbilical cord,
Who dips your cup in the sea of milk,
And whose playground lies on Mount Surum!
O Mai-ana of the silken tresses!
Surrounded by forty virgins, O pure Mai-ana!
Surrounded by thirty virgins, O pure Mai-ana!

O Mai-ana of the immaculate mouth!
You who descended from white Ulgan,
You who descended from the colored moon,
You who descended from the colored sun,
You who descended supported by a forked stick,
Who came here, leaning on a golden bow,
You, O Mai-ana of the fair hair!
Do not terrify the children!
Guide them by their little shoulders,
Clasp them to you,
Take them under your right arm,
Nurture them at your breast.
Thou wearest three bows of various colors,
And three steps lead to thy throne.
Thou, O Ulgan, created horses to ride,
Created flocks and herds,
Created women with long tresses,
Filled the earth with peace.
Thou didst lead them out of the abyss,
Out of the pit so deep that
Not even an echo could make its way.
Thou didst fix the earth on its cardinal points,
Thou didst create the wondrous soul of man,
O great Father,
Wearing the mysterious many-colored headpiece.
We have faith in thee,
To thee we sacrifice all earthly passions.
And by means of reason elevate ourselves toward thee.

Two Prayers to the Spirit of Earth

a)

My mountain of iron, that the sun cannot encircle,
My mountain of gold, that the moon cannot encircle,
You who grant mercy to my flocks in their pens,
Will not some impurity remain to defile us?
On our eyelash will there not be a tear?

b)

O Sumar-Ulan, my mountain,
O Sut my sea, Sumar my mountain,
May his pronounced decisions be worth gold,

May he bring peace to this hoary head!
And the mountains, rivers, seas reply:
Do not forget us, do not abandon us!
May the people dwell on the earth!

To the Wandering Spirit of a Dead Man

Return to your Yar-Su,
To your seventy mountains,
To your seven beams,
To your four walls,
To your house,
To your fireside!
Do not show yourself to the evil eye,
Nor meet the evil one.
Return to the father who nourishes you
And the mother who gives you food.

To Fire

Fire is the central feature of shamanistic rituals.

The blinding Fire is united with Kan Ayas,
Smoke spreads over all the universe.
You strip the morning sun of its power
And the evening moon has lost its vital force.
You have gathered in the wayfarers,
United those who were separated,
O dominator of flaming Fire,
Stone fireplace, blackened with smoke,
Hot, terrible flame!

To Ot Ana, the Fire

O Mother-Fire, wearing thirty flashing crowns,
Whose ears are curved reeds,
Virgin of the forty heads,
Who leaps and descends with sureness,
Who dances on billows,
Plunge your head into your dwelling!
While you dance on the billows,

Incline your head, O adored one!
Lord of three hearths,
Orum tuldyn mugi.
Resplendent in azure, O Kan here descended,
Descended here to prevent destruction.
Dressed in green silk,
O red-lipped laughing flame!
It is the father who strikes the flint
And the mother who lights you.
O Mother-Fire with the thirty flashing crowns,
Whose ears are curved reeds,
You cause white flowers to bud
And the white Nasar to open,
You cause blue flowers to bud
And the blue Nasar to open.
O Mother-Fire, wearing thirty flashing crowns,
Who leaps and descends with sureness,
O virgin of the forty heads,
Resplendent in the light of seven clarities!
You are the fire that flashes in the hearth,
That thaws the bitter cold
And cooks the food.

Prayers and Formulas in a Ceremony Honoring Ulgan

The shaman begins the ceremony by calling forth the spirits with a roll
on the drum:

Come, young cloud,
Press down on my back!
People, press down on my shoulders,
Come to me!
Tang Sary, son of heaven,
O Kergidai, son of Ulgan!
Thou, who art my eye to see,
My hand to grasp,
My foot to walk,
My fingers to hold on,
Sounding forth, come to my right.

The spirits, through the mouth of the same shaman, reply:
Ah, I come, ahi! O Shaman, here I am!

Then the shaman leans the drum forward and slowly sweeps his arm
above it to indicate that the spirit is now imprisoned in the drum. He
continues:

> With the yellow cane club,
> With the dun-colored horses!
> With the bridles of yellow silk
> And with the blankets of yellow silk!
> O Kan Karkys, son of Ulgan,
> Come to my right,
> Thou who, beating the Orbu, demands.

The spirit:
> Here I am. I come!

And again the shaman:

> Astride red camels
> With reins of red silk,
> With the rainbow,
> Come here to my right
> O Father Kysugen Tengra,
> Sounding forth like Yalama!

And the spirit replies:
> Here I am. I come!

The shaman again calls forth the spirits:
> He who rides on thunder,
> He who comes laughing with lightning bolts,
> That is he!
> Autumn clouds charged with thunder,
> Clouds of spring, flashing lightning,
> Thy footsteps explode and rumble
> O my father, Mergan Kan,
> Come to my right side,
> Sounding forth like Yalama!

The spirit replies:
> Here I am. I come!

Prayers for the Sacrificial Banquet to Honor Ulgan

This prayer to Ulgan is recited by the shaman when he makes the sacrifice
in honor of the ancestors and the protective spirits of the earth.

a)

For the new waxing of the moon,
For the bright splendor of the sun,
When the old year goes out,
And the new year comes in,
When autumn is a riot of color,
When the tall reeds bend
To the rippling wind:
I offer thee up the bowl
With the fine aroma of food,
O Kaira Kan, here is thy gift!

b)

Now that the old year has gone out,
Now that the new year has come in,
May he support it with both his shoulders,
May he lift it with his head!
And if he should not support it with both shoulders,
If he should not lift it with his head,
May his lot be chastisement,
Chastisement for all time!
And so accept it, O Kaira Kan!

To the Powerful Ones of Abakan and Altai

Heroes of Altai,
You in bright furs, like silk,
You on powerful red horses,
Come to my side!
Thou, Mordo Kan, powerful lord
Of the founts of Abakan
And the thousand-crested mountain,
Where thou dwellest, O Mordo Kan,
Hearken! Come to my side!
Hearken, O prince, to my words,
Thou art ornate in gilded bells,
Who conquered the sixty champions,
Thou who were chosen for the battle,
O Altai Kan, powerful prince!
Ornate in silver bells,
Who smote the forty champions,

Chosen for the struggle,
O Altai Kan, powerful prince!
Thou who did thrust the sword to the hilt,
O father, Altai Kan,
Whom no horse was strong enough to carry,
Come, singing, to my side!

To the Celestial Markut Birds

Celestial birds, O five Markut,
With powerful claws of copper
And beak of steel.
Vast sweeping wings
That cover the moon on the left
And the sun on the right.
Mother of the nine eagles,
Who flies supremely around Edil,
O Mother, come singing to my side,
Come joyously to my right eye,
Alight on my right shoulder.

To the Protective Spirit of the Race

Thou who flyest like scattered seed,
Rattling like the falling hail,
Thou descendant of Musygan Kan,
O my father, Kem Totoi.
From the side of the moon
There comes a golden sign,
From the side of the sun
There comes a silver sign.
Thou who veilest the moon,
Who shadoweth the sun,
Thou who hast twelve high steps,
Who hast twelve levels of games,
And thirteen seats of joy.

Prayer to the Spirit of the Door

Thou art the wise lord
And I am thy stupid servant.

Thou art a mighty lord,
I am the slave seeking the door of prayer.
Which prince must I beseech,
To whom of all these lords should I pray?
Thou, the servant of these princes,
Guide to all the lords,
Send me a new ambassador
To show me the way!

Here the shaman alters the tone of his voice and replies as if he were
the spirit being evoked:

Beseech Pyrkam Tengre,
Pray to Father Pyrkam
In humility,
Receive the orders of this prince.
Seek Pyrkam Tengre.

Prayer to Ulgan

This prayer is part of the Ustugu ceremony.

Thou art he who thunders from on high,
Who shatters all the doors,
Who strikes the rocks together
To touch off flames.
Thou art he who destroys the dark forest,
Swallowing it up in one mouthful in thy spoon,
He who sets the wood to crackling with fire,
Crushes the solid boulder
And hurls the pieces in the tinderbox.
When thou rumblest,
The universe doth tremble,
And if thou stompest thy feet
Dark forests plunge into the abyss.
In outcast people
Trembles the outcast heart,
And in thine own people
Wavers the fleshly heart.
The bouncing hailstones, like white boulders,
Hammer on Altai Kan.
Do not be harsh with us!

We ask thy mercy.
With these hailstones like white boulders
Do not hammer thy people,
Thou who art the sky adorned with sun and moon,
Who turnest the sun and the moon,
Thou who settest the clouds to rolling,
Who frightest the outcast heart
And tear the fleshy heart.

Prayer to Altai

I address myself to Altai,
"O my Altai!"—and I pray.
Ever stronger will he make my people,
Granting prosperity from generation to generation.
When sickness comes,
He will drive it away;
When terror comes,
He will scatter it to the winds.
May he be an impenetrable shield against misfortune
And an invincible armor against the enemy.
O young green forests hiding by the river!
O wild-leaping foliage dancing in verdant growth!
I invoke thee with the voice of a singing bird:
Will thou grant us health and abundance this new year?
Will I live a happy and peaceful life
In the sky's clear light, here atop my Altai?
Lead me not into shadows,
Lead me not into evil.
As long as my hair is not gray,
Will thou grant me life among my people?
Will I live in the midst of my people
Without being done an offense?
Will thou give me strength?
Lead me not into evil!
Let me not die young!
May I dwell untroubled
Under this clear light,
May I live with my people
And know not evil!
And may the God that I profess

Be merciful unto me!
May my people, who sing thy praises,
Be not brought to harm,
But dwell joyously;
May my name, for one month,
Know no evil!
I bless my people
And let this be my blessing:
O my venerated God,
In the name of my love,
Grant me mercy!

TARTARS OF ABAKAN

Death Lament

This lamentation is attributed to the old prince of the Sagai and his wife Agylangko, and was said at the death of their children.

Why did you give me flocks and herds to cover the steppes?
Instead of covering the steppes with herds
You could have given me children.
Though my house is filled, why did you give it, O my God?
Instead of heaping my house with goods,
Why did you not give me a child?

Sacrificial Prayers

In order that life not cease,
That destruction fall not on the house,
According to the ritual of our forebears,
Let us pray.
Let us bow our heads and bend our shoulders:
And may the prayer be heard in the sky,
May it reach the pure creator, God!
          The Celebrant: O mysterious sky!
          The People: O mysterious sky!
According to the ritual of our forebears, I turn to thee,
O beautiful birch of silver bark and golden leaf,
With nine branches

Not one of thy tender roots will we sever
As we dig thee from the black earth
To carry thee to the white mountaintop
And plant thee there.
Before thee we kneel and bend our heads.
May the prayer be heard in the sky,
May each word reach the pure creator.

> The Celebrant: O mysterious sky!
> The People: O mysterious sky!

After having bound the snowy black-cheeked lamb,
After having turned thrice about the silver birch,
We bring thee the victim—
First we gut it in thy name.
May our offering reach the gods
And gain us protection!

> The Celebrant: O mysterious sky!
> The People: O mysterious sky!

For the dwellings of my people,
For the grass in the pasture of the flocks,
For the young mares' feed,
May this offering reach the sky!
According to the ritual of our forebears, let us pray
Let us kneel and bow our heads.
May the prayer be heard in the sky,
May every word reach the pure creator!

> The Celebrant: O mysterious sky!
> The People: O mysterious sky!

Let not storms crash upon the earth,
Let not misery descend upon us!
Cause grass to grow on the black soil,
Cause black rain to fall from the sky!
We beseech thee:
May our words be heard in the nine skies!
May our words be heard by the nine creators
Who dwell in the realm of the nine skies!

> The Celebrant: O mysterious sky!
> The People: O mysterious sky!

Grant us strength
Which does not weaken,
Grant us fortune
Which does not wane!

According to the ritual of our forebears, let us pray!
May the prayer be heard by the gods!

              The Celebrant: O mysterious sky!
              The People: O mysterious sky!

That we may be granted long lives
And teeth as strong as a horse!
According to the ritual of our forebears,
We have offered a victim to the pure gods,
And having gutted it
Under the silver birch.
Beneath this azure sky,
On the black and turning earth,
From the reaches of the black lands
To the limits of the God-Sky,
We offer this victim to the gods,
That the life force
Created by the gods for men
Not cease.
May our offering reach the gods!

              The Celebrant: O mysterious sky!
              The People: O mysterious sky!

A Prayer to Fire

You, O Fire, our mother with thirty teeth,
Our mother-in-law with forty teeth,
Who provides for us by day
And protects us at night,
You light the way for those who depart,
Lead others homeward.
Now the moon is waning
And the old year flees.
The new year is consecrated to your service
And I come bearing coolness for your hot mouth.
You dance at twilight,
Flinging your tresses about.
You ride a red mare of three springs,
Your red camel cloak flying in the wind;
In the evening light you seem a tender youth.
You lash yourself with luminous whips of silk,
You are the defender of the black-haired men

And defender of the grazing herds.
You rest in the shadow of the silver birch;
We offer you a castrated snowy-white lamb,
Quench your burning thirst
With the shank of mutton
Roasted over nine fiery spits.
Nine strips of red and white adorn you,
We offer you cold breast of mutton
You wear a princely cuirass,
Dressed in red and many folds of sable.
We sprinkle you with the milk of the white cow
While invocations rise to the precious name of the splendid moon.
Fifty are the tresses that fall on your neck and shoulders,
Sixty the tresses that fall down your back.
In front of your garment flows the Abakan,
Behind your garment, the winding Jenissei,
Through your garment run chains of mountains,
In your veins the rivers flow.

MONGOLS

A Prayer to Fire

O sovereign mother Fire, born of the elm,
Reared on the mountaintops of Khangai-khan and Burchatukhan!
Born of the separation of earth and sky,
Issuing forth in the footprints of Etugu
And generated by the sovereign of Tengri!
O mother, whose father is hard steel,
Whose mother is the burning stone,
Whose forebears are the elms,
Your splendor rises to the sky
And passes over the earth.
You are the Fire rained down by those who dwell on high
And ignited by Czaress Uluken.
To you, O goddess mother, we offer yellow butter,
A white calf with a tawny head.
We bring you a strong son,
A beautiful bride,

And a pretty daughter.
To you, O mother, whose eyes turn ever upward,
We offer a glass of wine,
A handful of fat.
Grant prosperity to the bride and groom
And to all the people.
All honor to you!

BURYATS

A Hymn to Buxa Noyon

Buxa Noyon is one of the three celestial khans sent down to earth. His name means "bull prince," and he is supposed to determine the birth and destiny of all Buryats. *Se-ex* is an invocation of no particular significance, though it is often repeated in Buryat prayers.

Se-ex!
Bearer of gifts,
O Esege Malan Tengeri,
You who determine the birth of Buryats,
Buxa Noyon, O father,
Buxtan Xatun, O mother!
From the heights of the great sky,
Clearing away the fiery sunset,
Come sit upon the earth
With your vast figure.
In your slithering bark
Slide down the ocean's shore
On a joyous route, swimming and skimming
The bright milk sea.
Crashing with your powerful horn
Against Mount Humer,
You come to rest on a royal throne
Stretching out over all the earth.
In great black shoes
A limitless path unfolds
Over the vast land,
Letting you come to rest on earth.

Prayer Chant of the Shaman Banquet

A shaman chant for the sacrificial banquet dedicated to divine powers.

O nine Bozintais,
Resplendent blacksmiths,
With dancing sparks,
With licking flames,
With powerful, tinkling tools,
With anvils of solid iron,
With strident files and rasps,
With a bellows of ninety-nine mouths
Attached to the jingling bells.
On the banks of the Black Sea
Forge your great black caldrons,
Bring flying coals of black squirrels,
Ride your black-spotted steeds.
On the banks of the Yellow Sea
Forge your great yellow caldrons,
Bring your flying coals of yellow squirrels,
Ride your yellow-spotted steeds.
O! You possess flying coals of squirrel and ermine,
You possess silk of many colors!
You descend to the darker regions
As if you were on a mountaintop,
As if you were on Mount Sojan,
And you slip along the rivers
As if they were the shimmering ocean.
You descend to the lower regions,
Carrying a hammer in your right hand,
A gigantic anvil on your back,
Balancing a great silver slug on your chest,
Forging irons in your left hand.
In your forges
There are powerful incantations.
In your bellows
There is wondrous magic.

To Powerful Gods

You, O lords of the echo in mountain passes,
You, O lords of the wind blowing over the sea,
My princes, you who dwell in the mountains,
My gods, who dwell in the forest.
Support us in our sorrow,
During the lean years be generous,
In the months of hardship, grant us abundance.
When we are seated inside our huts,
Do not bring danger down upon us,
And when we are outside,
Do not put our strength to a trial.
In the dark night, give us light,
In the heat of day, give us shade.
Keep evil far from us,
Bring good things near.
Play the part of creator,
Save us from every peril.
Do not cause the sweat to stream from our brows,
Do not let our hearts tremble.
You guardians of our lives,
Who bring food to our mouths,
Cause the sun to shine
Through the door of our huts,
Cause us to see the sun
Through the holes in our huts.

For the Sacrificial Banquet

Against my mouth press another mouth,
Against my tongue press another tongue,
Against my stomach press another stomach,
Against my hands press other hands,
Against my feet press other feet.
And now, O dominating gods, do you understand
The nature of my prayer? Why I invoke you?

Evocation for the Soul of a Dead Man

Abosi is your father,
Ersin, your mother;

You are named Irdeni. . . .
Where are you,
Where have you gone?
Your family has come from far-away lands,
They, who were so close to you for all your life,
Sit weeping in the hut.
Eyes filled with tears, they stare at the walls
And recall the sweet life they had with you
And weep and wail, torn by so much pain.
The little children, begotten of thy body,
Cry out for you and sob:
"Father, where are you? Come back to us!"
Hear their cries and come back soon!
                    A-xurui!

All your brothers,
Your aged parents, the old ones of the village,
All your friends and companions
Are gathered here.
Midst tears and prayers they are calling you.
You could return to them.
If you hear their entreaties and their calls,
Speedily return to your parents!
                    A-xurui!

Your little horse is saddled
And awaits you.
Come, return to your little horse.
If you treat him like this,
Any fool may ride him.
Have pity on your horses
And hurry back to them.
                    A-xurui!

Waiting also,
Neat and clean,
Untouched by dust,
Are all your splendid garments.
Return
And take them!
For many years
May you enjoy them
                    A-xurui!

Come, the house
Is all in order,

Shining splendidly.
Return
And claim it.
For many years
May you enjoy it.

                A-xurui!

Your loving wife,
Your dear children,
So suddenly orphaned,
Are wailing and sobbing.
They call you, hearts filled with pain:
"O father, where are you?"
Listen to them, have pity on them
And return.

                A-xurui!

Your many horses
Are neighing and calling you
And asking:
"Master, where are you?
Come back to us!"

                A-xurui!

Bleating sadly,
Your flocks of sheep
Are calling to their master.
Return to them.

                A-xurui!

The dog that you raised
Is baying mournfully
In the courtyard.
Return to him.

                A-xurui!

The fire you lit in the hearth
Will yet burn ten thousand years.
Your good body
Will be safe and sound for another ninety years.

                A-xurui!

Do not abandon your immense wealth,
Your regal dwelling.
Come back,
Reclaim it,
Make it prosper!

                A-xurui!

Look! The table is laid
With your favorite delicacies:
With sweet-sour tarak,
With the nourishing amxan,
With the cooked salamat,
With golden yellow butter in great bowls
And whipped cream on the tarak.
Look! The cooked meat, the fat meat,
Ready in a plate.
And there is tea with sugar,
And there are sweetmeats.
Return and eat,
Enjoy these delicacies!
And listen to them call you:
The family, the old people of the village,
The neighbors and your relatives near and far.
Midst tears and sad songs
They express their grief.
In their aprons
They bring you the choicest morsels
And the most varied drinks.
Together they sing and pray
That you will return.
                    A-xurui!
Know this well:
The land of the dead
Is cold and dark and desolate.
While this shining world
Is warm and gay.
Therefore return.
You will be honored master.
You in your land will be honored.
            A-xurui—A-xurui—A-xurui

YUGURS

A Curse

To the raging wastes of the black sea, there may you go!
Three times may you open the black door of Erluk!

To the raging wastes of the yellow sea, there may you go!
To the whirling yellow storm, there may you go!
To ride the yellow running camel, there may you go!
To where the yellow arrow is drawn, there may you go!
To the raging wastes of the red sea, there may you go!
To the whirling red storm, there may you go!
To the advancing bearers of red gems, there may you go!
To the advancing bearers of red hides, there may you go!

TUNGUS

Prayer of the Dunankan Clan

An orphan stammers nonsense,
But you lend an ear to all she says.
O Anduris, guardian of our door, warmer of our house,
Father of the south, of southern lands, our defender,
O Anduris, our father, listen!
Sickness has struck the family.
O defend your people from the evil lower world.
Each who prostrates himself before you,
Each who prays before you,
Has offered up the clean burnt hides.
Purify us with water from the boiling fountain,
Protect us against calamity.
Cure each person of every family
Who is prostrate before you.
Drive, O father, the sickness of the children
Far from him who beseeches you:
Keep, O mother, from sickness
Anyone who now invokes thee:
Wash him with cool waters from the spring,
Lift up his head from the pillow.
Make him grow stronger from day to day,
Give air to his lungs and make him rise from his bed.
Cure his sickness wholly
And purify his bowels!
Keep the eight generations unbroken.

Thus I, since midnight, with a good heart
And good words, have implored.

A Sacrificial Prayer of the Malakul Clan

O virile Enduri, you who come from the south,
    who are seated in front of the great door,
Father, who has taken your place at the door,
Mother, who are seated in the corner,
Hear me!
We are certain
There is a reason for this reunion,
That to you in sacrifice may be offered a pig and a boar.
The sacrificial board weighs heavily,
The ritual victim lies upon it, eyes straight ahead.
Our tongues utter senseless things, lovingly.
Fail not to give an ear
To him who prays before thee,
To all who kneel before your face.
Hear each plea!

To the Polar Sun

O sun!
Permit us to pass our days prosperously;
Do not abandon us in the future,
Until the warm spring breezes come!

Prayer for the Dead of the Dunankan Clan

Dweller in the shade!
You who clamber on the jagged mountain peaks,
Who rush along the sharp stone path,
Voicelessly whispering along the shadowed ancestral path,
You who thrust your eyes ahead, toward the dark path,
And wander aimlessly by the nine sepulchers,
Where there can be no hiding,
O seat yourselves here, cross-legged,
By the side of the hut
And listen to the old man speak of the world of the dead.
Listen carefully to the old man from the nether world.

To him who speaks, who built the thick straw hut.
Will you understand him when he speaks to you?
Will you accept anything from your slow-witted son,
From him whose roof is worm-eaten and rotten,
Blackened with soot,
From one who is as dazed and stupid as the wood?
May the disemboweled victim be acceptable to you,
Partake of it cheerfully in the thick straw hut!
Eat the blood, eat the soup, eat the liver!
Here, I lift the meat on the offering plate,
Where I have piled it high as a mountain,
Where I have cast it like a weight.
Grant us good hunting!
When you accept,
Your slow-witted son is grateful.
Turn your glances toward the black hound,
Go forth along the harsh rock pathway.
Covered with nets,
Go forth.

YAKUT

Consecration of Sour Milk

This formula is used in the consecration of sour milk to be conserved for winter use. It is recited by the oldest member of the group, who lifts his cup to the gods.

Toyon! We thank you!
You have given us summer,
You have given us many lambs and colts,
And an abundance of milk.
You cast spring over the forest
And covered the fields with green.
Soon will come harvest time
And the gathering of the grain,
A time much desired by us.
To thee, Ay Toyon, we lift this crock and whey,
To thee go our fervent prayers:
Bless us and our flocks!

Send nourishing green-grass to our plains,
Send health to our flocks.
Ay Toyon, accept our offer!
Drink of the offering and bless it.
Thus, when we sip it,
We shall be strong and happy.

A Hymn to Superior Spirits

A hymn used by the shamans in curing certain illnesses.

The powerful bull of the plain,
The horse of the steppe,
The powerful bull of the plain bawls,
The horse of the steppe neighs.
I am above all of them,
I am the man,
I am the man of abilities,
I am the man created by the infinite God.
Come! horse of the steppe,
And learn!
Come! O marvelous bull,
And respond!
O mighty God, command:
Wherever I go,
Listen with your ears.
No one accompanies me
When I fail to say: Come!
No one draws nigh to me
If I command it otherwise.
Anyone can lift up his eyes,
Anyone can listen: Attention!
Bear it in mind,
All of you,
All of you who are there!
You on my left side, O woman with the club,
Should I choose a false path, warn me!
Command me!
O my lady, my mother,
Show my errors to me
And show me the road to follow.

Fly ahead of me,
Open the way,
Prepare the path.
O spirit of the sun
That dwells in the jungle-south,
O mother of light
Who are jealous,
I turn to thee, imploring
Keep your shadows high, very high!
And you who dwell in the west on the mountaintop,
O my lordly forebear of the great strength,
The powerful hill,
Come to me!
And you, venerable charmer of the flames,
With the gray beard,
I implore thee!
Give approval to all my thoughts
And to all my desires.
Listen to me,
Listen to all my prayers, all my prayers!

To Albys, for an Ailing Maiden

Albys is a divinity.

> All together let us smoke tobacco,
> Let us all drink wine.
> All together let us ride a horse,
> Let us all wear furs.
> We shall not keep hidden
> What we have learned.
> We shall preserve
> What we have found.

Marriage Ceremony

We are decided here and now to join our son and daughter. Therefore O goddess of Fire, hearken and be witness. Protect this pair from every illness, watch over them so that they may grow old.

CELEBES

For a Journey

We are bound for ——. Smooth away the difficulties of the road for us and give us sunlight!

BATAK

To Find a Bride

Grant me a good dream, a beneficent dream. If I shall truly marry the daughter of ——, if she is to be the companion of my well-being, the companion of my fortune, and if we are to grow old together, make it apparent to me, O Ancestors.

Prayer for Ourselves

Sanctify us and make us great, so that our worth may be like unto that of the illustrious ones, so that our happiness may be that of the blessed, as the worth of princes, on mountains and in the valley.

TROBRIAND ISLANDS

Enchantment of Love

Let his name be forgotten, let his name be cast aside,
Forgotten at sunset, cast aside at sunrise,
Cast aside at sunset, forgotten at sunrise.
A bird is on Baku, a bird glutted with nourishment.
I will deaden it!
His bright mint-magic, I will deaden it.[22]
His kayro'iwa magic, I will deaden it.
His libomatu magic, I will deaden it.
His magic of copulation, I will deaden it.

His magic of the horizontal position, I will deaden it.
His movement of response, I will deaden it.
His tender caress, I will deaden it.
His searing kiss, I will deaden it.
His tight clutch, I will deaden it.
His carnal vigor, I will deaden it.
My kabisilowa incantation now twists inside thee like a worm.
The road which leads through the brush to the mountains is now open,
The road which leads to the tatter-heap of memories is now closed.[23]

NAVIGATORS ISLANDS

Offering

> The old grandmother stands before thee.
> Turn your benevolent gaze upon this family.
> Grant it growth and prosperity.
> Keep it in good health.
> Make our plants productive
> And cause the food to grow.
> Let us live in the midst of abundance.

POLYNESIA

Hymn of Creation

> He alone existed. Taaroa was his name.
> In the immense void was neither earth nor sky,
> Neither man nor sea.
> Taaroa calls, no one replies.
> For he alone existed, he himself became the universe.
> Taaroa is the root, the rock.
> Taaroa is the sand.
> And thus he was called.
> Taaroa is the light.
> Taaroa is the inner thing.
> Taaroa is the germ.

Taaroa is the support.
Taaroa is wise.
He made the land,
The sacred land of Hawaii,
As a body and a sea shell for Taaroa.
The earth began to move.
O foundations, O rocks,
O sands, come hither!
Gather here and knead
The earth together.
But they won't knead together.
The seven skies explain: make ignorance cease.
He creates the skies, and brings light.
Immobility ceases.
He brings order out of time.
Then the foundations are kneaded,
Kneaded the rocks,
Kneaded the sands,
And the skies close,
The skies lift up
To leave the abyss and finish the land of Hawaii.

ROCKY MOUNTAINS

Medicine Chant

A chant used to open the ceremony that takes place before the gathering of medicinal herbs and roots.

Yes, I hear you, my friends of the Metai,
All of you who here surround me.
Who makes this river flow?
The Great Spirit makes this river flow;
Watch me closely, my friends,
Examine me and understand me, my companions.
Who makes good tribes and people march together?
A bird makes good tribes and people march together.
I fly over all space.
Wherever I meet an animal, I destroy it.

I tear out your heart, O animal,
I touch your heart, I touch your heart.
Who looks on me believes he looks on fire.
I can bring water down from above,
But I cannot make it rise from depths to where I stand.
I can make things resemble death;
I have made a man resemble death.
I can make things resemble death.
I have made a woman resemble death.
I can make things resemble death;
I have made a child resemble death;
I am so; so much can I do, my friends;
Every animal, my friends . . . I kill it, my friends.

PATAGONIA

Prayer

O father! Great man!
King of this earth,
Favor me each day with nourishment.
Give me good water and sweet sleep.
I am poor. Art thou hungry?
Here is a morsel from my poor table.
Eat it if you wish.

OSAGE

Prayer

Wakanda, have pity on me—for I am poor.
Give me what I need,
Let me win against my enemies.
Grant me thy aid,
That I might steal many horses.

MANI

To the Great Ancient Ones

Ho, Aged One, ecka,[24]
At a time when there were gathered together seven persons,[25]
You sat in the seventh place, it is said,
And of the Seven, you alone possessed knowledge of all things,
Aged One, ecka.
When in their longing for protection and guidance,
The people sought in their minds for a way,
They beheld you seated with assured permanency and endurance,
In the center where converged the paths,
There, exposed to the violence of the four winds, you sat,
Possessed with power to receive supplications,
Aged One, ecka.

INDIANS OF THE GREAT PLAINS

To the Sun

This hymn to the sun, which in many ways repeats the ancient traditions of pre-Columbian sun cults, is still used by Indians of the Great Plains. It is part of the Sun Dance, an annual celebration, lasting eight days, that is performed to fulfill a collective or individual vow. The pageant consists of an action-drama in which there are processions, symbolic dances and chants of a narra-tive-historic kind. In pre-Columbian times a human being was sacrificed to the sun; later this came to be only an offering of thanks, a cosmic thanksgiving in which the people put themselves in direct communication with the Sun Father. This hymn is delivered by a chief during the proceedings.

Great Sun Power, I am praying for my people that they may be happy in the summer and that they may live through the cold of winter. Many are sick and in want. Pity them and let them survive. Grant that they may live long and have abundance. May we go through these ceremonies correctly, as you taught our forefathers to do in the days that are past. If we make mistakes, pity us. Help us, Mother Earth, for we depend upon your goodness. Let there be rain to water the prairies, that the grass may grow long and the berries be abundant.

O Morning Star! when you look down upon us, give us peace and refreshing sleep. Great Spirit! bless our children, friends, and visitors
through a happy life. May our trails lie straight and level before us.
Let us live to be old. We are all your children and ask these things
with good hearts.

Blackfoot Prayer to the Four Directions

A prayer embracing cosmic values.

To the West:
Over there are the mountains. May you see them as long as you
live, for from them you must receive your sweet pine as incense.

To the North:
Strength will come from the North. May you look for many years
upon the Star that never moves.

To the East:
Old age will come from below, where lies the light of the Sun.

To the South:
May the warm winds of the South bring you success in securing food.

Ritual Hymn of the Omahas

This belongs to the ritual of the Pebble Society and is chanted in commem-
oration of the Great Rock that Wakanda, the Supreme Being, caused to
emerge from the waters at the beginning of the world. The rock was destined
as a dwelling place for the souls of animals that were wandering in chaos.

Toward the coming of the Sun
There the people of every kind gathered,
And great animals of every kind,
Verily all gathered together as well as people.
Insects, also, of every description,
Verily all gathered there together,
By what means or manner we know not.
Verily one alone of all these was the greatest,
Inspiring to all minds,
The great white rock,
Standing and reaching as high as the heavens, wrapped in mist,

Verily as high as the heavens.
Thus my little ones shall speak of me;
As long as they shall travel in life's path, thus shall they speak of me.
Such were the words, it has been said.

Then, next in rank,
Thou, male of the crane, stoodst with thy long beak
And thy neck none like to it in length,
There with thy beak didst thou strike the earth.

This shall be the legend
Of the people of yore, the red people,
Thus my little ones shall speak of me.

Then next in rank stood the male gray wolf, whose cry,
Though uttered without effort, verily made the earth to tremble,
Even the stable earth to tremble.
Each shall be the legend of the people.

Then next in rank stood Hega, the buzzard, with his red neck.
Calmly he stood, his great wings spread, letting the heat of the sun
    straighten his feathers.
Slowly he flapped his wings,
Then floated away, as though without effort,
Thus displaying a power often to be spoken of by the old men in
    their teachings.

NAVAJOS

Hymn to the Thunderbird

This hymn belongs to the nine-day ritual of the Night Chant. The chant invokes Thunder, which, as frequently happens in Indian hymns, is represented by a bird or a nest of birds. At times the thunderbird is depicted as an enormous animal with a lake of water on his back and lightning flashing from his eyes. The term *Tsegihi* in the first verse represents one of the most sacred Navajo localities.

In Tsegihi,
In the house made of dawn,

In the house made of evening twilight,
In the house made of dark cloud,
In the house made of rain and mist, of pollen, of grasshoppers,
Where the dark mist curtains the doorway,
The path to which is on the rainbow,
Where the zigzag lightning stands high on top,
Oh, male divinity!
With your moccasins of dark cloud, come to us,
With your leggings and shirt and headdress of dark cloud, come to us,
With your mind enveloped in dark cloud, come to us,
With the dark thunder above you, come to us, soaring,
With the shapen cloud at your feet, come to us, soaring,
With the far darkness made of the dark cloud over your head, come
    to us, soaring.
With the far darkness made of the rain and the mist over your head,
    come to us, soaring.
With the zigzag lightning flung out on high over your head,
With the rainbow hanging high over your head, come to us, soaring.
With the far darkness made of the dark cloud on the ends of your wings,
With the far darkness made of the rain and the mist on the ends of
    your wings, come to us, soaring.
With the zigzag lightning, with the rainbow hanging high on the
    ends of your wings, come to us, soaring.
With the near darkness made of the dark cloud of the rain and the
    mist, come to us,
With the darkness on the earth, come to us.
With these I wish the foam floating on the flowing water over the roots
    of the great corn.
I have made your sacrifice,
I have prepared a smoke for you,
My feet restore for me.
My limbs restore, my body restore, my mind restore, my voice restore
    for me.
Today, take out your spell for me,
Today, take away your spell for me,
Away from me you have taken it,
Far off from me it is taken,
Far off you have done it.
Happily I recover,
Happily I become cool,

My eyes regain their power, my head cools, my limbs regain their
    strength, I hear again.
Happily for me the spell is taken off,
Happily I walk; impervious to pain, I walk; light within, I walk;
    joyous, I walk.
Abundant dark clouds I desire,
An abundance of vegetation I desire,
An abundance of pollen, abundant dew, I desire.
Happily may fair white corn, to the ends of the earth, come with you,
Happily may fair yellow corn, fair blue corn, fair corn of all kinds,
    plants of all kinds, goods of all kinds, jewels of all kinds, to the
    ends of the earth, come with you.
With these before you, happily may they come with you,
With these behind, below, above, around you, happily may they come
    with you,
Thus you accomplish your tasks.
Happily, the old men will regard you,
Happily, the old women will regard you,
The young men and the young women will regard you,
The children will regard you,
The chiefs will regard you,
Happily, as they scatter in different directions, they will regard you,
Happily, as they approach their homes, they will regard you.
May their roads home be on the trail of peace,
Happily may they all return.
In beauty I walk,
With beauty before me, I walk,
With beauty behind me, I walk,
With beauty above and about me, I walk.
It is finished in beauty.
It is finished in beauty.

PUEBLOS

Announcement of the Rain Dance

    The call of the village crier announcing the beginning of the Rain Dance.

All people awake, open your eyes, arise,
Become children of light, vigorous, active, sprightly.

Hasten clouds from the four world quarters;
Come snow in plenty, that water may be abundant when summer comes;
Come ice, cover the fields, that the planting may yield abundance.
Let all hearts be glad!
The knowing ones will assemble in four days;
They will encircle the village, dancing and singing their lays . . .
That moisture may come in abundance.

KWAKIUTL

Cannibal Chants

Among the Kwakiutls the initiate at a cannibalistic ceremony is called
hamatsa. Following are some the sacred *hamatsa.*

Food will be given to me, food will be given to me, because I obtained
    this magic treasure.
I am swallowing food alive: I eat living men.
I swallow wealth; I swallow the wealth that my father is giving away.

Now I am going to eat,
My face is ghastly pale.
I shall eat what is given to me by Baxbakualanuchsiwae.

You will be known all over the World; you will be known all over
    the world, as far as the edge of the world, you went to Baxbakua-
    lanuchsiwae, and there you first ate dried human flesh.
You were led to his cannibal pole in the place of honor in his house,
    and his house is our world.
You were led to his cannibal pole at the right-hand side of our world.

UITOTO

Cannibalistic Chant to the God Husiniamui

Down below, behind the sons of men, before the blood-covered site
where the sun rises, my begotten are to be found in the middle of the
blood-stained stage, at the foot of my tree of blood. The enraged ones

are performing there, they are grinding down the skull of the captive
and burning bird feathers. Near the sky, in the flooding rivers of blood,
are the rocks of my warlike will. Down below, on the village square, men
move with rage, grinding down the captives.

KEKEKEE

Corn Harvest

Thou, O God, thou my Lord,
thou my mother, thou my father,
Lord of the Mountains and of the Valleys.
Now and similarly in three suns, in three days,
the harvest of the corn will begin,
in the presence of thy mouth, in the presence of thy face,
Lord of the Mountains and of the Valleys!
Then reveal it to me, too, in the presence of my body, in the presence
    of my soul.
I offer thee a morsel of thy food and of thy drink.
It is practically nothing, what I offer thee.
But I have many, and lovely, things
For my food and for my drink:
it is thou who hast shown them to my soul, to my body,
thou, my mother, thou, my father!
I will begin my harvesting therefore,
But not today will I complete my harvest
in the presence of thy mouth, in the presence of thy face.
Who knows for how many suns, who knows for how many days, I
    will reap?
It is not seemly to be hasty, searching through the weeds:
I will only labor slowly.
Who knows when I will be able to speak to thee again,
O my father, O my mother!
Angel, Lord of the Mountains and of the Valleys!
But to begin to pray to thee again,
Why should I not do so, O my God?

JAWARRA

At the Death of a Member of the Clan

O Jawahu, thou hast taken him from us without his ever having left his field and his family. Lead him beside his friends that thou hast cut down before him, so that he may hunt and find food.

CORA INDIANS

Offertory

Tchakan, I here give you this offering so that you will give me permission to bathe.

SIOUX

Warrior's Vow

I promise thee a calico shirt and a dress, O Wakanda. I will also give you a blanket if you grant that I return whole and well to my fireside after having killed a Pawnee.

Voyager's Prayer

Thou, O God, Lord of the mountains and of the valleys! I have given thee a very small portion of thy food and of thy drink. And while I continue on my way, beneath thy feet, beneath thy hands, I, a voyager. It does not hurt thee, it does not even trouble thee, to grant me every kind of creature, great and small, O my father! Thou hast many creatures, the wild peacock, the wild pheasant, the boar: show them to me, open up my eyes and set them upon my road. Then I may see them; then I will watch out for them. I am beneath thy feet, beneath thy hands. I am well, O Lord of the mountains and of the valleys.

In thy power, in thy thought, all things are abundant. I would have everything.

Now perhaps I will have to eat my maize cake dry, and yet I am in a stretch of land which is abundant with game. Let God see that here there is nothing living; perhaps I will not carry away, and I will not bag here more than a wild peacock. Meanwhile I am looking, I am searching, O my God, O my father, O my mother.

But I do not say, I do not think, other than this: There is not much, there is nothing very good to feed you and to give you to drink that I can carry here.

And whatever comes, this is what I say, this is what I think: O God, thou art my mother, thou art my father.

Meanwhile I am going to sleep beneath thy feet, beneath thy hands O Lord of the mountains and of the valleys, Ruler of the trees, ruler of the vines.

Tomorrow the sun will return, tomorrow the light of the sun will return. I no longer know where I am. Who is my father? Who is my mother? Thou alone O God, thou seest me, thou shieldest me on every path, in every darkness, in the face of all obstacles, that thou wouldst hide, thou O God my Lord, O Ruler of the mountains and of the valleys.

I do not say, I do not think, that this must go on, that this must cease. This is what I have said: thou endurest, thou forgettest my faults.

HOPI

To Bring the Rain

> Come here, Thunder, and look!
> Come here, Cold, and see it rain!
> Thunder strikes and makes it hot.
> All seeds grow when it is hot.
> Corn in blossom,
> Beans in blossom,
> Your face on gardens looks.
> Watermelon plant, muskmelon plant,
> Your face on gardens looks.
> Aha-aha-ehe-ihe.

Ceremonial Chant of the Antelope Serpent

Listen, oh my father. I am standing here,
Why come not the clouds from the east, west, the north, or
    the south?

Why bring they not the rain? The corn is weary
And has ceased to grow.
I have prepared my prayer stick, why comes not the rain?
Why hear I not the rumbling of the clouds,
The noise of the falling waters?
The frogs cry, but no rain comes.
Why comes not the clouds and the rain?

Notes

1. Tell the Supreme Being.
2. Religious terms used to invoke the gods, and meaning "gently,"
"sweetly."
3. The top of the world.
4. Bump into a pretty maid.
5. The paternal side of the family did not carry the mother off against
her will, a reprehensible act for a Bantu, but duly paid the fee (lobola) in
accordance with local customs.
6. An order of gods or spirits.
7. Wi-zu-gore—clitoris.
8. In Denka hymns Dengdit, the Supreme Being, habitually speaks of
men as ants.
9. By cutting down the vegetation.
10. I've paid the price by offering up the sacrifice.
11. The enemy of the people.
12. Calcite specks found in crabs.
13. This listing of the qualities and characteristics of the spirit being evoked
is explained by the belief—common in all forms of magic—that the
evocation is effective only if all the attributes of the spirit have been
enumerated.
14. No Malayan can explain the meaning of the word *Hong,* except that
it is used in original Malayan invocations in the same way as the Arabic
Bismallah in these times. It is deemed a very unhallowed word, of great
power, and so *panas* (hot) that if any man uses a *Hong* invocation three
times, nothing that he undertakes will succeed and he will live, powerful yet
miserable, able to afflict or assist others but unable to help himself. It appears
to be considered as a recognition of an Essence or First Principle beyond
God, and an appeal to it for power which God has not granted to man.
Horn is the name given to hard horns or hornlike parts of animals believed
to possess magical or medicinal properties.
The Malayans cannot affix any definite meaning to the first two lines of
this spell. They might be translated as a better "magical" science for protection
when alone in the forest, or as an appeal to give the individual solitude, as
when surrounded by a forest.
15. The rice-boat, or *puan,* as it is called in Malaya, is a boat-shaped
wooden box (with a built-out end), in which rice is deposited by Malayans

on ceremonial occasions, or in processions, such as that of a wedding, etc.

16. *Selotan,* or *S'lotan, Borak,* and *Jambi,* are the names of the best kinds of rice *padi* grown in the district.

17. *Pulut* is a glutinous rice used chiefly with turmeric on ceremonial occasions.

18. Literally a "mosquito-curtain"—a graphic touch.

19. *Zabur* is Arabic for "psalm," especially for the Psalms of David; the connection here is not clear.

20. Another account derives the origin of incense from the "eye gum of the Prophet Mohammed's eyes."

21. The *guru* are the genii of destruction, represented here as the children of Batara Guru or Shiva Batara Guru, one of the very few figures in the Malaya pantheon conserving all the features of the Hindu prototype, Shiva.

22. This form of magic falls into that species of incantation which annuls by recitation. *Magic* known as *kayro'iwa* and *libomatu* is erotic. Horizontal magic refers to a position of coupling which is indicated in the native tongue precisely by the word "horizontal."

23. The jungle is open to the maiden though she may not enter the village.

24. The word *ecka* may be roughly translated as "I desire," "I crave," "I implore," or "I seek," but it has no exact English equivalent.

25. The spirits of the seven directions: north, south, east, west, above, below, and here.

*

The Religions of
Pre-Columbian America

In Time of Pestilence, to Tezcatlipoca

This prayer and those following it have obviously been altered by the Franciscan missionaries. Doubtless they were attempting to demonstrate the ingenuous goodness of Aztec customs and these people's essential predisposition to accept the Christian word.

O our powerful Lord, beneath whose wings we find protection, shelter and defense, thou who art invisible and untouchable, like the night and like the air, behold me here, humble and wretched, daring to appear before thy majesty! I appear, stammering graceless words, like one who has stumbled and has lost his path. I am afraid, therefore, with my great trouble, to provoke your wrath against me and to arouse your indignation, instead of placating you.

Thou, O Lord, do with my body whatever pleases thee: thou hast by now abandoned us, according to the preordained plans of heaven and hell. And upon us, in these days, have fallen thy vexation and indignation, wherefore the great and multiple afflictions arising from thy wrath have submerged us and laid us low, like unto stones and spears and thunderbolts hurled upon us unfortunates who dwell in

93

this world. And now there is a great pestilence that devours and destroys us, O strong and all-powerful Lord!

O our Lord, powerful, merciful, invisible, untouchable, to whose will all things are obedient, at whose disposition depends the running of the universe, to whom all things are subject, what then is the judgment of thy divine heart?

Hast thou perhaps decided to abandon thy people and thy race forever? Hast thou perhaps truly decided that they totally perish and that not even their memory shall remain in the world, and that the place of their dwelling shall become a mountain wilderness and a stony desert? And would you perhaps allow your temples and places of prayer and the altars and the buildings erected for your services to become neglected and no trace of them remain?

Could it be possible that your wrath and your punishment and your angry fury are completely implacable, until they have brought about our utter destruction? Is it by this time confirmed in your divine counsel that thou no longer have mercy, that thou must no longer pity us, until all the thunderbolts of your fury shall have been used up to destroy and abandon us. All remain like stupefied men, without thought and without hope of any assistance. The young children are dying now of hunger, for there is nothing to drink or to eat, there is no one to console and caress them, not a single woman is left who can give the breast to those who are still suckling, for by this time fathers and mothers are dead and they have left their children orphans, unprotected, without any succor. They suffer for the sins of their fathers.

O most human Lord, thou knowest that thy people are like infants who, after having been whipped and punished, weep and sob and repent of what they have done. So, these poor creatures, for the punishment that thou hast inflicted upon them, weep and sigh and accuse themselves, remembering and regretting their sins in thy presence.

Most human, most merciful, most noble, most precious Lord, let the punishment already endured be sufficient and let an end to it be granted them, so that they may reform, and let those still be punished who alone, granted such an end to their affliction, do not reform. Forgive them and suffer their faults, ceasing your wrath and anger. Let the pleasure and satisfaction that thou hast taken in the punishment which thou hast inflicted be sufficient unto thee. Let them be finished at last, O Lord, the smoke and the fog of your anger, let the furious flaring fire of your wrath be placated, let peace and clarity come, let thy people return as small birds to sing and celebrate the sun. Grant them a time of peace so that they may call upon thee and praise thee and be grateful unto thee.

Tezcatlipoca, in Time of War

Most human, most merciful Lord, invisible and untouchable protector and defender, by whose judgment and wisdom we are ruled and governed, under whose empire we live, Lord of battles, it is by now certain that a great war is in preparation. The Earth God is opening his throat, eager to gulp down the blood of those who are to die. The Sun and the god of war called Tlaltecultli rejoice in it. They offer food and drink to the gods of the sky and the underworld, inviting them to partake of the blood and flesh of the men who are destined to die in this war.

The gods of the sky and of the underworld are already reconnoitering to find out which men are to conquer and which are to be conquered, which of them are destined to wipe out and which of them are destined to be wiped out; whose blood they are to drink and whose flesh they are to devour: so that the fathers and mothers of the noble youths are still unknowing as to which of their sons are destined to die.

O most human Lord, Lord of Battles, Ruler of all, thou who art called Tezcatlipoca, invisible and untouchable, we pray to thee so that those whom thou has destined to die in this war shall be welcomed in the House of the Sun, in the sky, with love and honor. May they ascend to thee and be housed among the valiant and the heroes fallen in battle, with Quitzicquaquatzin and Maceuhcatzin and Ilacauepantzin and Ixtlilcuechahuac and Ihuiltemoc and Chauacuetzin and all the bravest and most celebrated champions who fell in the war prior to this one, with those who are rendering the tribute of joyous praise to the Sun. May they share with them in the eternal glory and in the never-ending riches, may they forever continue to savor the sweetness of all the flowers delightful and sweet to the taste.

To Tezcatlipoca, for a New Chief

Today, a truly auspicious day, a sun has risen, illuminating us, bringing us its clarity and splendor, almost as though a precious stone, a precious sapphire, were set in it. A new light has appeared, a new clarity has been brought to us, a new leader has been sent to us, a more splendid ruler who will rule over us and govern our people and take on the burden of trade and the weight of public concerns.

Already, O Lord, this poor man has accepted and received the honor and the nobility which your majesty has granted him. He has already taken on the glory and the treasure. He has already adorned his hands and his feet, his head, ears, and lips with a chin strap, jeweled pendants, bracelets, and moccasins. O Lord, do not let these symbols, shows, and ornaments become a cause for pride and presumption, but grant, O Lord, that he serve thee loyally and humbly. Grant, O most human Lord, that he rule and govern with prudence and wisdom in the place that thou has entrusted to him. Be pleased to ordain that he commit no ill that might offend thee. Deign to go with him and be his guide. And if it fall otherwise, command that men shrink from him, that he be detested from this moment, and that he die in battle at the hand of his enemies, and that he enter the House of the Sun, where he shall be cared for like a precious stone and his heart guarded like a sapphire. And offer up his body and his heart to the Lord Sun, dying in battle as one valiant and courageous: that would be better than to be dishonored and despised, abhorred and detested in this world for his errors and his faults.

Confession

O most human Lord, protector and defender of all, thou hast already heard the confession of this poor sinner, by means of which he has made public, in your presence, his distresses and his faults, or, kept some of his sins secret.

If he has done so, if he has mocked thy majesty, and, with irreverence, has offended it, may he be flung into an abyss, into a deep pit; by himself enchained, by himself ensnared in a net. Of himself he will have deserved blindness and paralysis, the consumption of all his members, poverty and misfortune. Alas, if this poor sinner has had the rashness to commit this offense against thy majesty, against thee who art master and ruler of all, who takest heed of all things, of his own doing he has fashioned his fetter, his degradation and delusion, thy majesty will seest it—for thou, incorporeal and invisible, seest all—and if it has happened, that he of his own free will has placed himself in his present danger and jeopardy, since this is a region of incorruptible justice and severe judgment; it is like the limpid water in which thou, O Lord, wash the faults of all those who righteously confess themselves. Now, if by chance he has incurred his perdition and the shortening of his days, or if, on the other hand, he has spoken the whole truth and is freed and loosed from his sinful faults, he has received the forgiveness of those he had incurred, as one who stumbles and falls in thy presence, offending thee by various faults and of himself stained and flung into a deep pit and into a bottomless well. Like a man wretched and without strength, he has fallen and now is filled with pain and remorse for his whole past; his body and his heart are saddened and uneasy, what he has done weighs heavily upon him and therefore he firmly proposes never to offend thee again.

To Tlaloc, for Rain

O most human Lord and generous giver, sovereign of all things green and of the grain, Lord of the earthly paradise, Lord of incense.

Great is our sorrow, Lord, to see the whole earth parched with thirst, unable to create, unable to produce grain and trees and anything to sustain us. As a father and mother it conceived us and suckled us with the grain and fruit it bore: and now all is burned, all is lost, nothing reappears, inasmuch as the Gods of Tlaloque have borne everything away with them and concealed it in their hiding places, in their dwelling which is the earthly paradise. O most merciful Lord, Ruler of all things green and of the rubber, and of fragrant and medicinal herbs, we implore thee to look with a benign eye upon the people of thy race, of thy reign, of thy possessions, who are now spent, lost, in peril and dying. All things are perishing, and even the beasts and the animals and the birds die and fall without any cure.

Succor the God of the Earth, O Lord, with a little rain, for he conceives and sustains us when there is water. Grant, O Lord, to the people to receive this boon and this favor from thy hand. Grant that the people deserve to see and rejoice in green things and plants which are like precious stones and fruit and the sustenance of the Tlaloques. Let the dry clouds carry the rain and scatter it over us. Deign, O Lord, to grant that animals and plants be merry and rejoice; grant that the birds and the precious feathered flyers, like the quechol and the zacuan, soar and sing and taste green buds again.

With a great sighing and anguish of heart, I call upon and invoke all ye that are Gods of Water, ye that sleep in the four corners of the world, in the east, in the west, to the south, and to the north, ye that dwell in the cavities of the earth or in the deep caverns, so that ye may come and console this poor people, and water the earth, for the eyes of the inhabitants of the earth, men, beasts and birds, may, with renewed hope, praise your persons.

O Lords, deign to come!

From the Ritual Bath of the Newborn

a)

Before the bath. The midwife to the Goddess of the Waters of Chal-chiuhtlicue:

O eagle, O tiger, O valiant one, O my grandchild!

You have come into this world where your father and mother, the Great Lord and the Great Lady, have sent you. You were created and conceived in your house, which is the dwelling of the supreme ones, the Great Lord and the Great Lady who remain above the nine skies. Be united now with your mother, the Goddess of the Waters that are called Chalchiuhtlicue and Chalchiuhtlatonac.

b)

While the midwife gives the newly-born the water to taste, wetting her finger and putting it to its mouth:

Take it, receive it!

This is what you must live with upon the earth, by means of which you will grow and become strong. This is the water by which we are sustained, by means of which we obtain what we need in order to live upon the earth.

Take it!

c)

While the midwife pours water upon the head of the newly-born:

My grandson, my child, receive and take the water of the Lord of the World, the water which is our life, which makes the body grow and invigorates it and which serves to wash and purify. I pray that this water of celestial blue, clear blue, enter into your body and live in it. I pray that it destroy and carry away from you every ill and all the adversities that were joined in you from the beginning of the world, for we men are entrusted into her hands, she being our mother Chal-chiuhtlicue.

d)

While raising the child with both arms from the ground to the sky:

Lord, thou seest here your creature that you have sent into this place of sorrow, of affliction, and of penitents which is the world. Grant it, O Lord, your gifts and your breath, for thou art the great God.

And with you may the great goddess grant them.

e)
While raising the newly-born to the sky the second time:

Lady who art mother of the heavens and who is called Citlaltonac and also Citlalicue, to thee my words are directed. I implore thee to give, impress upon, and inspire this, your creature, with your power, whatever it may be.

f)
While raising the newly-born for the third time.

O Lords, celestial gods and goddesses who dwell on high, this is your creature: Deign to implant in it your power and to blow your breath into it in order that it have life upon earth.

g)
While raising it for the fourth time:

Lords Sun and Tlalteculti, who are our mother and father, behold this creature which is like a bird of rich plumage, like the zacuan or quechol. It is yours, and I have decided to offer it to you, Lords Sun, who are called also Tonametl and Xipilli and Quauhtli and Ocelotl, like a tiger painted brown and black, valiant in war. Remember that this creature is yours, that it belongs to your house and to your patrimony, that it was made to serve thee and to offer thee food and drink. He belongs to the family of soldiers and warriors who fight on the field of battle.

Hymn to Tlaloc

Tlaloc or Tlalocatuecutli, lord of paradise, appears here in his true function as god of the waters and terrestrial fecundity.

In Mexico the god appears; thy banner is unfolded in all directions, and no one weeps.
I, thy god, have returned again, I have turned again to the place of abundance of blood sacrifices; there, when the day grows old, I am beheld as a god.
Thy work is that of a noble magician; truly thou hast made thyself to be of our flesh; thou hast made thyself, and who dare affront thee?
Truly, he who affronts me does not find himself well with me; my fathers took by the head the tigers and the serpents.
In Tlalocan, in the verdant house, they play at ball, they cast the reeds.

Go forth, go forth to where the clouds are spread abundantly, where
the thick mist makes the cloudy house of Tlaloc.
There with strong voice I rise up and cry aloud.
Go ye forth to seek me, seek for the words which I have said, as I
rise, a terrible one, and cry aloud.
After four years they shall go forth, not to be known, not to be num-
bered, they shall descend to the beautiful house, to unite together
and know the doctrine.
Go forth, go forth to where the clouds are spread abundantly, where
the thick mist makes the cloudy house of Tlaloc.

Hymn to the Mother of the Gods, Teteuynan, the Nurturing Earth

Hail to our mother, who caused the yellow flowers to blossom, who
scattered the seeds of the maguey as she came forth from Paradise.
Hail to our mother, who poured forth flowers in abundance, who
scattered the seeds of the maguey as she came forth from Paradise.
Hail to our mother, who caused the yellow flowers to blossom, she
who scattered the seeds of the maguey as she came forth from Paradise.
Hail to the goddess who shines in the thornbush like a bright butterfly.
Ho! she is our mother, goddess of the earth, she supplies food in the
desert to the wild beasts, and causes them to live.
Thus, thus, you see her to be an ever-fresh model of liberality toward
all flesh.
And as you see the goddess of the earth do to the wild beasts, so also
does she toward the green herbs and the fishes.

Hymn to Ixcozauhqui

Ixcozauhqui, or Xintecuhtli, "he who has yellow eyes," the "lord of eyes,"
the "lord of comets," was the year god, fire god, and god of green growth.

In the Hall of Flames let me not put to shame my ancestors; descending
there, let me not put you to shame.
I fasten a rope to the sacred tree, I twist it in eight folds, that by it
I, a magician, may descend to the magical house.
Begin your song in the Hall of Flames; begin your song in the Hall of
Flames; why does the magician not come forth? Why does he not
rise up?

Let his subjects assist in the Hall of Flames; he appears, he appears, let his subjects assist.

Let the servants never cease the song in the Hall of Flames; let them rejoice greatly, let them dance wonderfully.

Call ye for the woman with abundant hair, whose care is the mist and the rain, call ye for her.

Hymn to Ciuacoatl

Ciuacoatl, the serpent-woman, called "the gift of our flesh," was mother of the human species.

Quilazli, plumed with eagle feathers, with the crest of eagles, painted with serpents' blood, comes with her hoe, beating her drum, from Colhuacan.[1]

She alone, who is our flesh, goddess of the fields and shrubs, is strong to support us.

With the hoe, with the hoe, with hands full, with the hoe, with hands full, the goddess of the fields is strong to support us.

With a broom in her hands the goddess of the fields strongly supports us.

Our mother is as twelve eagles, goddess of drum-beating, filling the fields of tzioac and maguey like our lord Mixcoatl.[2]

She is our mother, a goddess of war, our mother, a goddess of war, an example and a companion from the home of our ancestors [Colhuacan].

She comes forth, she appears when war is waged, she protects us in war, that we shall not be destroyed, an example and companion from the home of our ancestors.

She comes adorned in the ancient manner with the eagle crest, in the ancient manner with the eagle crest.

Hymn Sung Every Eight Years During the Fasts on Bread and Water

The flower in my heart blossoms and spreads abroad in the middle of the night,

Tonan has satisfied her passion, the goddess Tlazolteotl has satisfied her passion.

I, Cinteotl,[3] was born in Paradise, I come from the place of flowers. I am the only flower, the new, the glorious one.

Cinteotl was born from the water; he came born as a mortal, as a youth, from the cerulean home of the fishes, a new, a glorious god.

He shone forth as the sun; his mother dwelt in the house of the dawn, varied in hue as the quechol bird, a new, a glorious flower.

I came forth on the earth, even to the market place like a mortal, even I, Quetzalcoatl,[4] great and glorious.

Be ye happy under the flower bush varied in hue as the quetzal bird; listen to the quechol singing to the gods; listen to the singing of the quechol along the river; hear its flute along the river in the house of the reeds.

Alas! would that my flowers would cease from dying; our flesh is as flowers, even as flowers in the place of flowers.

He plays at ball, he plays at ball, the servant of marvelous skill; he plays at ball, the precious servant; look at him; even the ruler of the nobles follows him to his house.

O youths! O youths! follow the example of your ancestors; make yourselves equal to them in the ball court; establish yourselves in your houses.

She goes to the mart, they carry Kochiquetzal to the mart; she speaks at Cholula; she startles my heart; she startles my heart; she has not finished, the priest knows her; where the merchants sell green jade earrings she is to be seen, in the place of wonders she is to be seen.

Sleep, sleep, sleep, I fold my hands to sleep, I, O woman, sleep.

To Xochiquetzal, Goddess of Flowers and of Love

I, Xochiquetzal, come from the Land of Rain and Cloud.
The devoted Piltzintecutli[5] weeps and seeks Xochiquetzal;
I must go to the Land of Putrefaction.[6]

To Chicomecoatl, Goddess of Corn

Goddess of the seven ears of corn, rise, for thou, our mother, must leave us now. You must go toward your country Tlalocan. Rise, awaken, for our mother must leave us now and return to her own country, Tlalocan.

To Xipe-Totec, the One With the Coat of Skin

"Our skin-clad lord" is the most important and terrible Mexican divinity of vegetation. He is pictured wearing a cloak of human skin, taken from a sacrificed prisoner. His greatest feast day was the "feast of the skinning of man," held during the spring at the first sign of new vegetation in the land. During the festivities, prisoners were sacrificed, their skins carved from them, and their bodies eaten. The skins were then used to make a garment for those representing the god. Xipe-Totec wore an emerald-green garment, the color of vegetation in germination, but his predominant color was yellow, symbol of ripeness and grain. The prayer that follows is one of the chants recited during the festival.

Thou nighttime drinker, why dost thou delay?
Put on thy disguise—thy golden garment, put it on!
My Lord, let thine emerald waters come descending!
Now is the old tree changed to green plumage—
The Fire-Snake is transformed into the Quetzal.

It may be that I am to die, I, the young maize plant;
Like an emerald is my heart; gold would I see it be;
I shall be happy when first it is ripe—the war chief born!
My Lord, when there is abundance in the maize fields,
I shall look to thy mountains, verily thy worshippers;
I shall be happy when first it is ripe—the war chief born!

PERU

Grand Hymn to Viracocha

Viracocha was the supreme god of the Incas.

O Vira-cocha! Lord of the universe;
Whether thou art male,
Whether thou art female,
Lord of reproduction,
Whatsoever thou mayest be,
O Lord of divination,
Where art thou?
Thou mayest be above,
Thou mayest be below,
Or perhaps around
Thy splendid throne and scepter.
Oh, hear me!
From the sky above,
In which thou mayest be,
From the sea beneath,

In which thou mayest be,
Creator of the world,
Maker of all men;
Lord of all Lords,
My eyes fail me
For longing to see thee;
For the sole desire to know thee.
Might I behold thee,
Might I know thee,
Might I consider thee.
Might I understand thee.
Oh, look down upon me,
For thou knowest me.
The sun—the moon—
The day—the night—
Spring—winter,
Are not ordained in vain
By thee, O Vira-cocha!
They all travel
To the assigned place;
They all arrive
At their destined ends,
Whithersoever thou pleasest.
Thy royal scepter
Thou holdest.
Oh, hear me,
Oh, choose me,
Let it not be
That I should tire,
That I should die.

Prayer to Viracocha

O Viracocha, thou art the creator, the conqueror, the infinite spirit, wherever thou art, the spirit always equal as far as infinity: thou who giveth life and strength to man by saying, "Be a man," "Be a woman" —and as you say so, giveth life and granteth them health, freeing them from evil: thou that dwellest in the highest of the heavens, in the thunder, in the storm cloud, hear our prayer, grant us eternal life, have us in thy keeping and accept this offering as it pleaseth thee, O Viracocha.

To the Goddess of Rain

> Beautiful goddess, daughter of the sky,
> With an urn full of water
> That your brother then shatters
> When the storm unleashes
> Thunder and lightning!
> Beautiful goddess, king's daughter!
> And then give us showers,
> Mild showers! Nevertheless, you also
> Often scatter snowflakes, and often hail,
> For so hath He, the universal spirit,
> He the God of the World, Viracocha,
> Enjoined and commanded you.

To the Sun

O Creator, thou who sayest, "Let there be night," the dawn, the day, the sunset, Grant to the Sun, your son, that when he rises, he may see peace everywhere. Preserve him so that he may give light to the men whom thou hast created.

O Creator, O Sun, thou who art in peace and well-being, give light to this nation, keep it ever sane and happy.

To Pachacamac

Pachacamac is a god-creator venerated by the coastal Incas. He is a spiritual and invisible essence who gives life to the universe.

> Pity my tears,
> Pity my anguish.
> The most distressed
> Of thy children,
> The most distressed of thy servants,
> Implores thee with tears.
> Grant the miracle
> Of thy waters,
> Grant the gift of rain,
> To this unfortunate
> Person,
> To this creature
> Thou hast created.

Propitiation of the Seed

This is one of the celebrated triumphal chants used by the Incas in the magic-religious ceremonies of propitiating the seed. The word *jailli* is a triumphal shout which probably means "victory." The Nustes were virgins who had taken vows to the sun god and lived together in a community.

Men: Ho! *jailli,* ho! *jailli.*
            Here is digging-stick, here the furrow,
            Here the sweat and here the toil.
Women: Huzzah, men, huzzah!
Men: Ho! *jailli,* ho! *jailli.*
            Where the Nusta, where the fair one?
            Where the seed, where the triumph?
Women: Huzzah, the seed, huzzah!
Men: Ho! *jailli,* ho! *jailli.*
            Great Sun, Mighty Father,
            Watch the sowing, that it prosper.
Women: Huzzah, Sun, Huzzah!
Men: Ho! *jailli,* ho! *jailli.*
            In the belly of Mother Earth
            May it germinate and fructify.
Women: Huzzah, Earth Mother, huzzah!
Men: Ho! *jailli,* ho! *jailli.*
Women: Here the Nusta, here the fair one,
            Here the man, here the toil,
            Huzzah, man, huzzah!

Notes

1. Colhuacan, the Ararat of America, is a peak on which Coxcox came to rest in his cypress raft after the deluge.
2. Mixcoatl, or "nebulous serpent," is a divinity of the hunt to which savage animals are sacrificed.
3. Cinteotl is the Mexican Demeter.
4. Quetzalcoatl, "the plumed serpent," is god of the air and of human arts.
5. The sun god.
6. Because his mistress is dead, the sun goes to seek her beyond the tomb.

✳

China

CHINA

The National Religion of Antiquity

Hymns and prayers from "To Transcendent Beings" to "For the Imperial Sacrifice of the New Year, Ch'ing Dynasty," all belong to rituals of the imperial cult. Hymns from "To Transcendent Beings" to "For the Emperor Wu" are to be found in the annals of the first Hans and were chanted by Emperor Ou while making imperial offerings to the Sovereign On High and to the Sovereigns of the Five Regions. They date from the period 113–110 B.C. In this liturgy the sky cult is conjoined with that of the imperial ancestors and the genii of heaven and earth, while in later liturgies each of these divine entities were worshiped singly.

To Transcendent Beings

We have chosen the time and the day, in the respectful hope of a
    meeting.
We burn some fat mixed with mugwort, to invite in the four regions.
May the nine celestial spaces open, may the transcendent beings appear.
May they cause great benefits to descend, and an abundant blessing.

The chariots of the transcendent beings roll along on the black clouds.
They are drawn by black dragons, and ornamented by feathered
    banners.

Their descent is rapid, like the wind, like a horse let loose.
On the left the green dragon, on the right, the white tiger, escort them.

The coming of the transcendent beings is sudden and mysterious.
The rain has purified the air before them, and they arrive as if flying.
When they have arrived, they are saluted, without being seen; and
hearts are moved, as if one saw them.
When they are seated, the music resounds; one cheers them up, one
satisfies them, until dawn.

The victim offered is young and tender, the meats are plentiful and
smell good.
There is an amphora of cinnamon wine to rejoice the Genii who have
come from the eight regions.
Satisfied, the transcendent beings bless those taking part in their varied
costumes; and admire the rich decorations of the temple.

To Heaven, the Sovereign, the Supreme One

> The Sovereign descends on the central mound,
> the four regions of space serve him for a temple.
> Energetically concentrate your unsteady thoughts,
> cause your mind to keep itself in its place.
> May purity and concord reign everywhere,
> may the whole empire enjoy peace.
> May queen Earth, rich and fertile,
> appear radiant in her yellow robe.

To the Mound of the East: Spring

Under the influence of the vernal yang, the vegetation is reborn.
The time of fertilizing rains, the time of love.

The thunder resounds and awakes the hibernating creatures.
That which seemed dead revives, and pursues its destiny.

May the innumerable new beings live their life to its end.
May the crowd of the living fully enjoy the happiness of the vernal
spring.

To the Mound of the South: Summer

> The red light grows, the heat increases,
> The flowering trees are in their full splendor.

After the flowers will come the fruits, plentiful and savory.
We will offer to the Genii the products of the earth.

They will grant us in exchange consoling benedictions.
If the Genii protect us, we will perpetuate ourselves without limit.

To the Mound of the West: Autumn

The West is the region of the white light,
the autumn wind gently kills the vegetation.

But the seeds of the plants are preserved,
those that contain the germ of the future spring.

May all which is harmful dry up and die,
may every inauspicious influence cease for ever.

Barbarous peoples, obey with fear, practice virtue,
be submissive and not rebellious, rectify and mend your hearts.

To the Mound of the North: Winter

Somber is the region of the North. All the beings which hibernate have
gone into the earth.
The vegetables have lost their leaves, and the frost freezes the land.
May all spirit of rebellion be set aside, may morals and customs remain
good.
May the multitude of the people, remembering their origin, retain love
for simplicity.
May all, acting with equity, increase mutual confidence.
May they make offerings, may they prepare the lands, in order that the
next harvest may be abundant.

To the Heaven and the Earth

The yin and yang cited in the hymn are the passive-feminine and active-
masculine forces of the world, the two fundamental energies.

O! Heaven, noble and sublime author, O! Earth, rich and fertile mother,
firmament and soil, you whose incessant action and reaction produce
the four seasons,
sun, moon and stars, in constant and regular course,
yin and yang, and you five natural agents, who always recommence
revolutions scarcely finished,

clouds, winds, lightnings, rain and dew, which procure abundance for
  the people . . .
The series of successions having caused me to ascend in my turn the
  imperial throne,
it is incumbent upon me to express to you the universal gratitude, to
  thank you for your benefits.
I have therefore prepared this feast for you, I present to you these
  offerings,
in the hope that, they being pleasing to you, you will avert from my
  empire every scourge and make everything prosper.
Roll drums, resound flutes, dancers wave your feathers
in order that, through the transcendent virtue of our flags, the barbarian
  peoples may be drawn to us.

For the Emperor Wu

The emperor Wu hoped one day to ascend alive to heaven, as had the
legendary Huang-ti, on a chariot drawn by six dragons. The hymn given here
was sung in his name, in order to invite that team.

> Majestic, from antiquity, the sun rises and sets;
> time passes, without men having any power over it;
> the four seasons serve them, but do not belong to them;
> the years flow like water; I see that all passes away.
>
> That which I desire is immortality.
> The hymn to the six dragons rejoices my heart.
> Why do they delay? Why do they still not descend?
> I await them, May they come!

Liturgical Hymn of the Chin Dynasty
(FIFTH CENTURY A.D.)

The official history informs us that, in 405 A.D., in China, of ten families,
nine practiced Buddhism. In this Buddhist medium the old Chinese religion,
with its official worship, was preseved as a state institution, just as the first
Han had made it in the second century B.C. The second Han dynasty has not
bequeathed us any liturgical documents, but there remain some fine hymns
from the Chin Dynasty.

> August are the Chin,
> who, in recompense for their good work,
> have received from Heaven the lasting mandate
> to procure the happiness of all the principalities.

All the principalities being happy,
and all the omens being propitious,
with respect we offer, on his mound,
this sacrifice to the August One on high.

May this sacrifice to the August One on high
be for us the pledge of all happinesses!
May our ancestors be glorified,
who have co-operated with Heaven.

We offer victims, chants,
and the perfume of virtues,
in order that Heaven may bless us,
and cause all to turn to good in the four regions.

Offering to the Celestial Genii

Let us prepare the great mound,
to receive the Genii on high.
Let us arouse our ardor,
for the transcendent beings are approaching.

The red fires blaze,
the perfumed woodpiles smoke,
violet flames escape therefrom,
and then form a dark cloud.

The body of the Genii
has neither form nor face.
It transports itself everywhere,
invisible by reason of its tenuity.

The arrival of the Genii
is announced by a gleam,
without any sound being heard,
without any motion being noticed.

When they have arrived,
if they are satisfied,
their joy and their peace
communicate themselves to our hearts.

When they are seated
and rejoicing with us,
the clouds give rain,
the favorable winds blow.

May the accents of the music
unite with the words of the chants.
May the symphony resound,
for the Genii are there listening.

They are assembled there,
enjoying the incense burnt for them,
enjoying the offered meats,
enjoying the contents of the great hanap.

They accept with pleasure,
they delight in the offerings,
they bless the great Chin,
and cause happiness to descend upon them.

From the imperial capital,
this benediction extends within the four seas,
guaranteeing that the dynasty will reign prosperous,
until the exhaustion of the portion which Heaven has allotted it.

To the Patron of the Soil

This hymn is also from the Chin Dynasty, and reflects the persistence of agrarian rites, honoring the spirits of earth and soil.

Today is the auspicious day
of the Genii of the mound, the Patron of the soil.
The whole population is gathered together,
to pray and make offerings under his tree.

We offer to him eggs, meat, leeks, garlic, and pickles.
The weather is fine, our hearts are joyful.
Let the drinking cup pass and re-pass.

To the Sky
(SUI DYNASTY)

The violet palace [the quadrilateral of the Great Bear] shines.
There resides, invisible and mysterious, the Supreme One,
who casts his looks down on the earth.
O noble and high Supreme Heaven,
here are set out the stones [lapis lazuli] that we offer to you,
here are the victims immolated for you.

See all these ministers,
the music and the banners.
Cast your looks on these stones of your color.
May the smoke of the sacrifice ascend to you.
Give us happiness,
for these testimonies of veneration.

To the Celestial and Terrestrial Genii

With affected hearts,
we look at the space,
in sincere hope,
with respectful sentiments.
Coming out of the mysterious,
the Genii descend, invisible.
With veneration, the emperor
and his ministers raise their eyes [toward them].
We have done all that can be done
to open the way to the Genii,
to cause these transcendental intelligences to come,
to entertain them with respect,
after having evoked them in the azure heights,
and in the dark depths.

To the Sky
(T'ANG DYNASTY)

The mound is ready.
Our hearts, also.
The bamboo flutes sound.
The wooden cithers vibrate.
The rites unfold with majesty,
the bells and the gongs sound,
to honor the Sovereign on high,
in the hope that he will bless us.

To the Sky
(T'ANG DYNASTY)

Adoration to the Supreme!
Veneration in the sacrifice!

Abundance and purity.
The music is ready.
The Lord on high comes to enjoy himself.
He will give us happiness,
benediction for our offerings,
and will cause everything to be for our good.

Liturgical Hymn
(SUNG DYNASTY)

August is the Sovereign on high,
whose influence extends to all the regions.
On the occasion of this beginning of the return of the luminous prin-
ciple [winter solstice],
We offer to it this sacrifice, as has been the custom from time im-
memorial.
Our vessels are full of abundant and pure gifts.
A perfume of virtue exhales from our offerings.
May he who guides the good deign to accept them,
and cause to descend on us, in exchange, numerous benedictions.
Noble is the ancestor of our race,
he who received the mandate of Heaven.
He has equaled in virtue the emperors of old,
and filled all the regions with his renown.
Then he ascended to be with the Sovereign on high.
Let us prove our piety by these offerings,
in order that prosperity may descend upon us,
for years without end.

Liturgical Hymn
(SUNG DYNASTY)

The azure and luminous vault
covers the earth.
We humbly request
that on which the people live [a good harvest].
Exhausted by the drought,
we humbly request, by this ceremony,
favorable rain,
which will procure us corn.

To the Sky
(YÜAN MONGOLIAN DYNASTY)

The august Sovereign on high
having seen with pleasure his virtues,
has installed in heaven our glorified Ancestor,
and has established our dynasty in glory and peace.
It is therefore right that, remembering his favors with a filial sense,
we should present to him our offerings and our gratitude.
If the Sovereign on high should stoop to aid us,
all blessings will come to us together.
Pure are our victims,
abundant are our meat offerings;
the knives of the carvers are active,
the blood and fat are presented.
We offer, with reverence, our salutations and our silks,
the smell of the offerings rises.
The Sovereign on high comes down to us,
regales himself on them, and rejoices in our virtues.

To Heaven
(YÜAN MONGOLIAN DYNASTY)

Heaven is so great!
The Sovereign of the empire regales the One on high,
and his Ancestor who is with him,
respectfully asking a transcendental blessing.
Considering his merits and his constancy,
may it continue to rest on him,
until he also shall ascend to the skies.
That is what we ask, by these symbolic rites.

Before the Ancestral Tablet
(YÜAN MONGOLIAN DYNASTY)

The tablet of the Ancestor is in the temple,
his spiritual soul is in the heavens.
[Come for the sacrifice], after the offerings and the music,
it returns to the invisible heights.
But not without having left a mysterious benediction,
which will cause all our enterprises to succeed,
considering the piety of the emperor, throughout innumerable years.

Let us offer incense, let us worship,
the innumerable Genii come to enjoy.
Satiated with our offerings,
the transcendent Genii go back again.
The seasons will be favorable, the year will be fertile.
The wind and the rain will come just in time.
To the emperor, ten thousand years of life, and infinite happiness.

For the Imperial Sacrifice
(MING DYNASTY)

These hymns date from the year 1368.

Before the offering, the invitation:

The azure spreads in an immense vault, covering the world below.
This round mound is the point of the empire where all the Genii gather
    together.
Small ants though we are,
We receive them with veneration.
Their faces shine like gold and jade.
Their dragon-drawn chariots run on the clouds.
They arrive at this mound.
To you, very noble ones, veneration!

During the offering:

As a little child,
I [the emperor] implore the mercy of Heaven my father,
I trust in the benevolence of Heaven.
I have taken all the trouble that I could.
Here are odoriferous libations,
here are choice meats.
I have prepared them in the joy of my heart,
to give pleasure to you, O Genii [Heaven].
After this offering is over,
may your benediction always remain on me!

While the fire is consuming the offerings:

On the mound burn the victims and the silks.
We hope they will ascend to the palace of the Sovereign.
We have offered him the sacrifice of the mound.
We hope that we will be aware of it, in his luminous palace.

Dismissing the Genii:

May the flags wave!
The dragon- and phoenix-drawn chariots strain.
Go, ascend to the heights!
Leave to us, with your blessing, lasting prosperity.

Imperial Prayer
(MING DYNASTY)

In this prayer the emperor addresses himself to the spirits to tell them that the name of God has been changed from Hao T'ien Shang Ti, Supreme Sovereign of the Splendid Sky, to Huang T'ien Shang Ti, Supreme Sovereign of the August Sky.

On the first day of the coming month, we shall reverently lead our officers and people to honor the great name of Shang Ti, dwelling in the sovereign heavens, looking up to the lofty nine-vaulted azure dome. Beforehand we inform you, all ye celestial and all ye terrestrial spirits, and will trouble you, on our behalf, to exert your spiritual power, and display your most earnest endeavors, communicating our poor desire to Shang Ti, and praying Him graciously to grant us acceptance and regard, and to be pleased with the title which we shall reverently present. For this purpose we have made this paper for your information. All ye spirits should be well aware of our purpose. Ye are respectfully informed.

For the Sacrifice
(MING DYNASTY)

Of old, in the beginning, there was the great chaos, without form and dark. The five elements had not begun to revolve, nor the sun and moon to shine. In the midst thereof there presented itself neither form nor sound. Thou, O Spiritual Sovereign, camest forth in Thy presidency, and first did divide the gross from the pure (the ethereal from the material). Thou madest heaven; Thou madest earth; Thou madest man. All things got their being, with their reproducing power.

For Presenting a New Name
(MING DYNASTY)

O Ti, when Thou hadst opened the course for the inactive [yin] and active [yang] forces of matter to operate, Thy making work went on. Thou didst produce, O Spirit, the sun and moon, and five planets; and pure and beautiful was their light. The vault of heaven was spread out like a curtain, and the square earth supported all on it, and all creatures were happy. I, Thy servant, presume reverently to thank Thee, and, while I worship, present the notice to thee, O Ti, calling Thee Sovereign.

Presentation of the Jade Scepter
(MING DYNASTY)

Thou hast vouchsafed, O Ti, to hear us, for Thou regardest us as our Father. I, Thy child, dull and unenlightened, am unable to show forth my feelings. I thank Thee that Thou hast accepted the intimation. Honorable is Thy great name; with reverence we spread out these precious stones and silk, and, as swallows rejoicing in the spring, praise Thy abundant love.

The Offering of Food
(MING DYNASTY)

The great feast has been set forth, and the sound of our joy is like thunder. The Sovereign Spirit vouchsafes to enjoy our offering and his servant's heart is within him like a particle of dust. The meat has been boiled in the large caldrons, and the fragrant provisions have been prepared. Enjoy the offering, O Ti, and then shall all the people have happiness. I, Thy servant, receiving Thy favors, am blessed indeed.

A drink-offering was made with the following:

The great and lofty One sends down His favor and regard, which we, in our insignificance, are hardly sufficient to receive. I, His simple servant, while I worship, present this precious cup to Him, whose years have no end.

A thanksgiving followed in these words:

When Ti, the Lord, had so decreed, He called into existence the three powers [heaven, earth, and man]. Between heaven and earth He separately disposed men and things, all overspread by the heavens. I, His small servant, beg His [favoring] decree, to enlighten me, His vassal; so may I ever appear before Him in the empyrean.

At the second drink-offering it was said:

All the numerous tribes of animated beings are indebted to Thy favor for their beginning. Men and creatures are emparadised, O Ti, in

Thy love. All living things are indebted to Thy goodness, but who knows whence his blessings come to him? It is Thou alone, O Lord, who art the true parent of all things.

Again, at the third and final drink-offering, it was said:

The precious feast is wide displayed; the gem-adorned tables are arranged; the pearly spirits are presented, with music and dancing. The spirit of harmony reigns; men and creatures are happy. The breast of His servant is troubled, that he can make no recompense [for such goodness].

When the offerings were removed, it was further said:

The service of song is completed, but our poor sincerity cannot be fully expressed. Thy sovereign goodness is infinite. As a potter hast Thou made all living things. Great and small are curtained round [by Thee from harm]. As engraven on the heart of Thy poor servant is the sense of Thy goodness, but my feelings cannot be fully displayed. With great kindness Thou dost bear with us, and notwithstanding our demerits, dost grant us life and prosperity.

For the Offering of the Cup and the Plate
(MING DYNASTY)

a)

With reverent ceremonies the record has been presented; and Thou, O Sovereign Spirit, hast deigned to accept our service. The dances have been performed, and nine times the music has resounded. Grant, O Ti, Thy great blessing to increase the happiness of my House. The instruments of metal and precious stones have given out their melody; the jeweled girdles of the officers have emitted their tinklings. Spirits and men rejoice together, praising Ti the Lord. What limit, what measure can there be, while we celebrate his great name? Forever He setteth fast the high heavens, and establisheth the solid earth. His government is everlasting. His poor servant, I bow my head, and lay it in the dust, bathed in His grace and glory.

b)

We have worshiped and written the Great Name on this gemlike sheet. Now we display it before Ti, and place it in the fire. These valuable offerings of silks and fine meats we burn, also, with these sincere prayers, that they may ascend in volumes of flames up to the distant azure. All the ends of the earth look up to Him. All human beings, all things on the earth, rejoice together in the Great Name.

For the Imperial Sacrifice of the New Year
(CH'ING DYNASTY)

I, your subject, by hereditary succession son of heaven, having received from above the gracious decree to nourish and console the inhabitants of all regions, think with sympathy of all men, earnestly desirous of their prosperity. At present looking to the approach of the day Sin and the spring plowing, which is about to take place, I earnestly look up, hoping for merciful protection. I bring my subjects and servants with offerings of food in abundance, a reverential sacrifice to Shang-te. Humbly I pray for thy downward glance, and may rain be granted for the production of all sorts of grain and the success of all agricultural labors.

Ode of Thanksgiving

An ode of thanksgiving for an abundant year. Used in autumn and winter, it was directed to the Father of Agriculture, the first Agrarian, How-tseih.

Abundant is the year, with much millet and much rice;
And we have our high granaries,
With myriads, and hundreds of thousands, and millions of measures
    in them;
For spirits and sweet spirits,
To present to our ancestors, male and female,
And to supply all our ceremonies.
The blessings sent down on us are of every kind.

For the Ancestral Sacrifice

Originally used for a sacrifice celebrated by the Emperor Wu in honor of his father, Wan, this hymn then made its way into common liturgies celebrating the ancestral sacrifice and was chanted at the moment the sacrificial vases were removed.

They come full of harmony;
They are here, in all gravity;
The princes assisting,
While the Son of Heaven looks profound.
While I present this noble bull,

And they assist me in setting forth the sacrifice,
O great and august Father,
Comfort me, your filial son!
With penetrating wisdom thou didst play the man,
A sovereign with the gifts both of peace and war,
Giving rest even to great Heaven,
And ensuring prosperity to thy descendants.
Thou comfortest me with the eyebrows of longevity;
Thou makest me great with manifold blessings.
I offer this sacrifice to my meritorious father,
And to my accomplished mother.

Ode of Propitiation

Principally used in the spring to propitiate a fruitful season.

They clear away the grass and the bushes;
And the ground is laid open by their plows.
In thousands of pairs they remove the roots,
Some in the low wet lands, some along the dikes.
There are the master and his eldest son;
His younger sons, and all their children;
Their strong helpers, and their hired servants.
How the noise of their eating the viands brought to them resounds!
The husbands think lovingly of their wives;
The wives keep close to their husbands.
Then with their sharp plowshares
They set to work on the south-lying acres.
They sow their different kinds of grain,
Each seed containing in it a germ of life.
In unbroken lines rises the blade,
And, well nourished, the stalks grow long.
Luxuriant looks the young grain,
And the weeders go among it in multitudes.
Then come the reapers in crowds,
And the grain is piled up in the fields,
Myriads, and hundreds of thousands, and millions of stacks
For spirits and for sweet spirits,
To offer to our ancestors, male and female,
And to provide for all ceremonies.
Fragrant is their aroma,

Enhancing the glory of the State:
Like pepper is their smell,
To give comfort to the aged.
It is not here only that there is this abundance;
It is not now only that there is such a time:
From of old it has been thus.

To Drive Away Drought

It is said that this ode was uttered by Prince Suen when a drought threatened.

Bright was that milky way,
Shining and revolving in the sky.
The king said: Oh!
What crime is chargeable on us now,
That Heaven thus sends down death and disorder?
Famine comes again and again.
There is no victim I have grudged;
Our maces and other tokens are exhausted:
How is it that I am not heard?
The drought is excessive;
Its fervors become more and more tormenting.
I have not ceased offering pure sacrifices;
From the border altars I have gone to the ancestral temple.
To the Powers above and below I have presented my offerings and then
        buried them:
There is no Spirit whom I have not honored.
How-tseih is not equal to the occasion;
God does not come to us.
This wasting and ruin of our country—
Would that it fell only on me!
The drought is excessive,
And I may not try to excuse myself.
I am full of terror and feel the peril,
Like the clap of thunder or the roll.
Of the remnant of Chow, among the black-haired people,
There will not be half a man left;
Nor will God from His great heaven
Exempt even me.
Shall we not mingle our fears together?

The sacrifices to my ancestors will be extinguished.
The drought is excessive,
And it cannot be stopped.
More fierce and fiery,
It is leaving me no place.
My end is near;
I have none to look up to, none to look round to.
The many dukes and their ministers of the past
Give me no help.
O ye parents and nearer ancestors,
How can ye bear to see us thus?
The drought is excessive;
Parched are the hills, and the streams are dried.
The demon of drought exercises his oppression,
As if scattering flames and fire.
My heart is terrified with the heat;
My sorrowing heart is as if on fire.
The many dukes and their ministers of the past
Do not hear me.
O God, from Thy great heaven,
Grant me the liberty to withdraw into retirement!
The drought is excessive;
I struggle, and fear to go away.
How is it I am afflicted with this drought?
I cannot ascertain the cause of it.
In praying for a good year I was abundantly early;
I was not late in sacrificing to the Spirits of the four quarters and of
     the land.
God in the great heaven
Does not consider me.
Reverent to the intelligent Spirits,
I ought not to be thus the object of their anger.
The drought is excessive;
All is dispersion, and the bonds of government are relaxed.
Reduced to extremities are the heads of departments;
Full of distress are my chief minister,
The master of the horse, the commander of the guards,
The chief cook, and my attendants.
There is no one who has not tried to help the people,
They have not refrained on the ground of being unable;
I look up to the great heaven;

Why am I plunged in this sorrow?
I look up to the great heaven,
But its stars sparkle bright.
My great officers and excellent men,
Ye have drawn near to Heaven with reverence with all your powers.
Death is approaching,
But do not cast away what you have done.
You are seeking not for me only,
But to give rest to all our departments.
I look up to the great heaven;
When shall I be favored with repose?

From the Ceremony of Placing the Beret on a Shi

These pieces were said by the *Tcho*—a prior and public magistrate, one of whose duties was to recite prayers. The ritual was used in connection with the *shi,* sons of functionaries or magistrates.

At the first capping:

In this auspicious month, and on this lucky day, we endow you with the headgear for the first time. Put from you your childish thoughts and see that you keep guard upon the virtues of your manhood. Then shall your years all be fair, and your good fortune grow from more to more.

At the second capping:

In this lucky month, at this auspicious hour, we add to your garments. Guard reverently your demeanor, preserve the integrity of your virtue. Then will your years be without end, and good luck attend you forever and ever.

At the third capping:

In this best of years, and most auspicious of months, we complete the tale of your robes. Your kinsmen are all here to perfect this virtuous act. May your years be agelong, and Heaven's blessing attend you.

The blessing when the must is drunk:

Sweet must and strong, good meats, fine flavors. Take them reverently and offer them, that you may confirm your good fortune, and receive the blessing of Heaven, and life everlasting.

The blessing at the pledging; for the first cup:

Fine wine and clear, good food, right time. As we first put on your headgear, your kinsmen are all here. Filial piety and brother love are at their best. See that you keep them so.

At the second cup:

Fine wine well cleared; good relish and dried flesh. We add to your robes, for the rites have their order. Pour out your libation from this noble cup, and may Heaven's blessing be yours.

At the third cup:

Fine wine, good flavors, holders of splint and wood decked for the feast. We complete the tale of your robes. The meat is divided and laid on the stand. May Heaven's blessing attend you, and happiness beyond all bound.

The blessing at the giving of the "style."

Now that the ceremony is complete, I announce your Style in this auspicious month, and on this lucky day. May that Style become greatly honored, and may you attain to eminence, holding fast to what is right, for right leads to happiness. May you receive and ever hold this gift.

Ritual Sacrifice to the Sky, by Yüan Shih-k'ai

These belong to the ritual sacrifice to the sky; their composition was ordered by President Yüan Shih-k'ai in 1914. The Taoist influence is evident. While the woodpile [lit to notify Heaven] is burning:

With eyes raised toward the azure celestial vault,
we who, for the good of the people, have just remolded our country
with reverence prepare the great sacrifice of the mound,
on the auspicious day when the yang modality is reborn [solstice].
Thoughtfully, we express our sincere respect,
that the flame of this woodpile should announce on high.
From the purple palace descends a train of clouds,
the way of the Genii who have come out of the nine gates.
We raise our eyes toward them with fear and with joy,
hoping that their advent in such great numbers will bring us happiness.

During the libation and the offering of jade and silk:

The pavilion of the Great Origin is adorned with flags.
All is ready for the great sacrifice.
It is about to be offered with joy and respect.
The wine is poured out, the jade and the silk are offered.
We lift our heads, moved by fear,
asking that our people may be heard.

While the benediction is descending:

The sacrifice is offered and the chariots of the celestial guests are about
    to start back.
Everything has gone off well, the benediction has been given,
A perfume spreads like a tenuous vapor.
The green dragon and the white tiger return from it, satisfied.
Gently the banners of the transcendent being wave.
Our people may count on their protection.

An Offering to Confucius
According to the Ritual of President Yüan Shih-k'ai

Invitation of the spirit:

He is great, the greatest of the Sages,
the master and the model of all the ages.
Let us make to him a respectful offering!
The music sounds. Everything is arranged.

Oblation:

Since our people has existed, there has been no master like him.
The vows we offer in this temple are those which have always been
    offered there.
This mound and these buildings [of the Great School] have often
    witnessed this ceremony,
These vessels and these baskets thus arranged.

Attending the spirit back:

August Great School, model to all others,
preserver of the doctrine of the Master,
you have again seen the offering in its usual surroundings.
It is finished. Virtue will spread about new perfume.

BUDDHISM

From Mahayana Ritual: Liberation of the Animals

When a pious layman has brought to the convent some living animals, quadrupeds, birds, or fish which he wishes to set at liberty, and has presented them to a monk, the latter ought first, in conformity with rule XLV,[1] to say to them cordially:

> Oh! How deeply you are plunged in ignorance! . . .
> Oh! How I pity you! . . .
> Oh! How I desire your salvation! . . .

Then he will recite over them the following formula:

I invoke the Buddha, his Law and his Order. Here are some living beings which, having been taken in nets, were on the point of being put to death. Most fortunately they met ——, a pious and compassionate man, who saved their lives. Now I, monk ——, wish, according to the Mahayana ritual, to lead them to commend themselves to Buddha, to his Law and to his Order. But they are, as a penalty for their past sins, deprived of intelligence to the point of not being able to understand me. Therefore I pray the Buddha, his Law and his Order, to enlighten the darkness of their understanding, and to draw them, out of compassion toward them.

Then, after a pause, the illumination supposedly having been obtained, the monk addresses himself to the animals and says:

Living beings who are present here before me, commend yourselves to Buddha, to his Law and to his Order.

As the animals are supposed to have obeyed, the monk will henceforth call them disciples of Buddha. He teaches them the fundamental dogma, that the succession of existences is the great evil; that they should withdraw themselves from that wheel, through faith in Buddha and through the practice of his precepts. He exhorts them to believe and to practice, to persevere and to advance during their future existences, to preserve themselves carefully from heretical teachings, etc. Finally, the monk says to the animals:

Disciples of Buddha, you are now admitted and instructed. I am now going to confess for you your past sins, in order that you may obtain the remission of them. Follow, whilst repenting, the words which I am about to pronounce. . . . For all the evil that I have done in times past, in consequence of my ignorance, of my covetousness, of my insubordination; all the sins which I could have committed by the body, by the mouth, or by thought, I confess and repent of them.

Then the monk sprinkles the animals with water on which he has first pronounced this invocation:

O Buddhas who live in the heights, cause your virtue to descend into this water, in order that a force may be diffused in it for the purification of all beings.

After the sprinkling is done, the monk concludes:

I hope that after this liberation these disciples of Buddha will not fall any more into the hands of the wicked, will not be any more caught in nets or traps, and will not any more swallow fishhooks. I hope they will live free and peacefully, until their natural death. I hope that, after that death, they will be reborn men or devas, will do good, will make progress in the way, and will finally reach the end. I hope also that their benefactor, ———, will be blest in this life, and enlightened more and more.

Rhythmic Address of the Presiding Elder

Bowing the head, we venerate the Buddha, his Law and his Order. We are here gathered together to fulfill the disciplinary rule, the observance of which will cause the true doctrine to last forever. The extent of the precepts is as vast as the sea. They are precious, more so than those treasures which one never is tired of searching for. It is in order to protect the treasure of the precepts of the Sage that we are gathered together here. Therefore listen to me, in order that the cases of degradation and the cases of penitence may be avoided. Listen to me, all you who are assembled here. And you Buddhas of the past, Vipasyin, Sikhin, Visvabhu, Krakucchanda, Kanakamuni, Kasyapa, Sakyamuni, all you, full of all virtue and worthy of universal veneration, help me to speak. I greatly desire to say that which I have to say. Wise hearers, be so good all as to listen to me. —A man deprived of his feet, cannot walk. In the same way he who lives without rule cannot be reborn a deva in the heavens. He who wishes to be reborn in the heavens must, during this terrestrial life, carefully and unceasingly observe the precepts, which are like his [moral] feet, and not injure them. —A coachman who, before crossing a dangerous pass, sees that he has lost a bolt from the wheel, or that his axle-tree is cracked, is he not anxious? Thus he who has violated the precepts will be anxious at the hour of death. A man who beholds his face in a mirror is happy or distressed, according as he is handsome or ugly. The reading of the precepts produces an analogous effect. According as they have observed or violated them, the hearers are pleased or distressed. When two armies join battle, the brave advance, the cowards retire. Thus it is when the precepts are promulgated; those who are innocent have confidence, those who are guilty are afraid. As the king excels other men, as the ocean excels all the waters, as the moon excels all the stars, as the Buddha excels all the Sages, thus, among all the treatises of discipline, it is the formulary which excels all the others. So the Buddha has laid it down as a rule from which one cannot obtain exemption, that it should be read every fortnight.

The Paradise of Amithaba

A dithyramb of Tsan A-mi-touo Fouo kie di Tan-Loan, in which the spiritual essence of Amidista can be clearly seen.

O Amitabha, light without equal . . .
O Amitabha, infinite splendor . . .
so pure and so calm . . .
so sweet and so consoling . . .
How we desire to be reborn with thee!
Thou whose power is without limits . . .
Thou toward whom the beings of all the worlds turn,
How beautiful is thy kingdom,
where the breeze sows flowers under the feet of the blessed. . . .
How we desire to be reborn with thee!
How beautiful is thy kingdom,
where the finest music resounds,
where the most precious perfumes rise,
where all beings are saints . . .
How we desire to be reborn with thee!
Foolishly, during numberless existences,
we have renewed the karma which binds us to the earth.
Oh! guard us henceforth, sweet light,

that we lose no more the wisdom of the heart!
We exalt thy knowledge and thy works,
we desire that all may go to thee;
that no obstacle may prevent any being
from being reborn in peace and happiness with you!

Amidista Formula of Repentance

We here assembled to venerate and pray, confess with repentance, before all the Buddhas and P'usas, before the Genii of heaven of the earth and of the air, before the Judges of the hells, that, during numberless existences, we have perhaps committed many crimes, wounded some Buddha, killed some arhant, ill-treated our parents or our relations, sinned through luxury or theft or slandering. We have perhaps incurred the worst penalties, in the hot hells and in the cold hells. Terrified by this thought, we now proclaim our repentance. We all wish that all our sins may be destroyed in such a way that none of them remains. All, and with all our hearts, we have given ourselves to Amitabha.

A Verse from Masses for the Dead, Amidista

Thou perfect master,
Who shinest upon all things and all men,
As gleaming moonlight plays upon a thousand waters at the same time!
Thy great compassion does not pass by a single creature.
Steadily and quietly sails the great ship of compassion across the sea
    of sorrow.
Thou art the great physician for a sick and impure world,
In pity giving the invitation to the "Paradise of the West."

From the Ritual in Praise of the Sect of Hsien Shou

The Hsien Shou sect, named for its founder, is strong in northern China. Its principal scripture is the Sutra of the Diadem of Buddha: Huan Yen Ching. The Ritual of Praise reflects the depth of feeling in which the sect holds its fundamental scripture, and is also important because it documents the manner in which the Mahayanist makes his vows.

I prostrate myself and give honor to the Hua-yen Sutra, through which
    is revealed, as in a vast ocean-mirror, the true aspect of the nature of
    life.

Lo! all kinds of light are reflected from the lofty brilliant one [Vairocana].

[By him stands] in unceasing activity, the omnipresent P'u-hsien [Samantabhadra],

Revealing the different laws of the true model of life in their harmonious operation.

Lung-shu [Nagarjuna] himself, from his dragon castle, takes part in this choir of recitation.

Shih-ch'a [Siksananda], from Kashgar [Yu-tien], joins in with the most sublime voice.

In one moment was revealed the mysterious and magnificent way of salvation, which is given in the perfect Mahayana.

The true and secret method of transformation into the real nature of a Buddha was shown forth.

The whole thing was firmly established as grasped with the hands, seen with the eyes, uttered from the mouth with a believing heart,

Producing the firm conviction that the great law of cause and effect lies behind all the phenomena.

Out of this conviction the heart is filled with joy by seeing or hearing about virtuous people who make the great decision to attain the highest wisdom and compassion,

And in this way to launch out for the great aim of the perfect life of compassion and enlightenment, the wisdom called sa-p'o-jo [Sarvajua].

Hail to thee, Vairocana, thou great creator and master of religion, thou merciful worthy one from the realms above; all unite in the chanting of the precious verses of the golden text.

Spreading out the text roll, attached to the precious cylinder, all the dust in the empty space [the heavenly planetary matter] flocked in from everywhere, all the world ages were melted together in one harmony —proclaiming the 10,095,048 words, continued in the eighty-one volumes of the Huayen Ching, embracing the most perfect school of Buddhism [the perfect Mahayana]—the broad and catholic Buddhism presented by the Huayen Sutra.

If a man really has the desire to come to a full understanding of all the Buddhas of the three world periods [past, present, and future],

Certainly he will in due time reach the point when he will comprehend [perceive] the true laws of nature. He will experience the whole thing in his own heart. If there are people who wish truly to present offerings, let them remember always to give reverence

To the Buddhas and bodhisattvas from the seven different places gathered in the nine different assemblies;

If there are people who wish to bear witness about and proclaim the ta-ts'ang and enter into and permanently proclaim, let them study the teaching of this sutra regarding the five categories of cause and effect and the four divisions dealing with discipline.

If there are people who wish to perform the uninterrupted sacrifices, let them study the description about the ninety divisions of the bodhisattvas and all living beings.

If there are people who wish to comprehend and enter into the permanent function of proclaiming the law,

Let them emerge into the all-embracing doctrines of the Hua-yen Sutra.

I prostrate myself and make the vow:

I, ——, through my whole life, through generation after generation, everywhere, in every spot,

Will always have my eyes fixed upon this sutra; the sounds of this sutra shall always ring in my ears; the words of this sutra shall always go forth from my mouth; my hands shall always be busy with the copying of this sutra; in my heart I will always ponder upon this sutra.

May I, through my whole life, through generation after generation, everywhere, in every spot, always approach all the saints of the hua-ts'ang.[2]

May I always be under the gracious protection and influence of the saints of the hua-ts'ang. May I be able to give a full account of all that this sutra contains. May I be like

The shan-ts'ai bodhisattva.

> May I be like the Master of Power, Wen-shu bodhisattva
> May I be like the bodhisattva Kuan-yin
> May I be like the Buddha Vairocana.

May I get the full benefit of this sutra.

> May I in this way get the benefit of this great vow.
> May I get the benefit of the four categories of grace and the three states of existence.

May I, together with all living beings in the universe, be helped in the work of blotting out all the sins and impurities which I have carried with me through eternity. May I, together with all other living beings, be helped so that all the boundless sins and impurities which I have accumulated through the past eternities, through all the stages of evolution, through all the boundless stages of emptines, be blotted out.

May I, together with the other living beings who are under the sign of the four graces and the three existences, be helped so that all the boundless cases of accumulated grievances and hostility through the past eternities, through all the stages of evolution, through the boundless stages of emptiness, be settled and wiped out.

May I, together with the whole creation who lives under the sign of the four graces and the three existences, be partakers of the boundless happiness and wisdom which has been stored up from the past eternities throughout all the stages of evolution, through the un- limited stages of emptiness.

May we all together join in the great journey toward the glorious and solemn meeting place of the upper world and unitedly be partakers of the perfect.

Compassion and wisdom in the logos-square.

Hail to thee, thou all-embracing Hua-yen Sutra and thou universal meeting place of Buddhas and bodhisattvas described in the Hua- yen Sutra. [To be sung three times]

To Ti Tsang-P'u Sa (Kshitigarbha Bodhisattva)

O Bodhisattva of the World of Darkness, Thy glory is difficult to describe.

Realize our hopes by showing Thy true face and diffusing this over every place,

That the beings on the three lower paths of the six paths of transmigra- tion may hearken to the glorious Law,

And the ten classes of beings which have been called into existence by the four modes of birth may bathe their heads with Thy merciful favors.

May the light of Thy precious pearl shine as far as the roads which lead to the celestial halls,

And Thy metal crosier knock open the gates of hell!

We sincerely wish the soul of the deceased may enjoy the favor of being introduced [into the region of bliss],

And on the lotus-terrace [the Universe] may worship the merciful Honourable Ones [Buddhas and Bodhisattvas].

Prayer for the Deceased

The preceding is a prayer to the miraculous infernal redeemer. The one following is an invocation frequently written on strips of silk. The monks repeat it in a sobbing voice during Amidist ceremonies for the deceased.

OM. May Thy nimbus call to Thee the real soul of the deceased Wen-ju, the chief of the Yang family, upon whom the Imperial house of Ts'ing has conferred the honorary title of the sixth degree and who was a graduate of this district with the dignity of Archivist of the Imperial Academy of Learning. May his soul speedily repair to the regions of the West to entrust itself to the process of transformation into an independent existence of careless diversion amidst the lotus-tanks; may it receive and enjoy the treasures and food [which surviving relations sacrifice to it], being entirely extricated from the bitter wheel of transmigration. AHUM.

TAOISM

To the Essence of the Supreme One

A prayer of the sixth century A.D. in which the influence of the Christian-Basilidian heresies on Taoism are apparent.

> Essence of the Supreme One,
> Spirit of the obscure mystery,
> You who produce all beings
> and who can purify all,
> before invoking you I sprinkle myself
> and place myself in this pure place.
> By order of the Sovereign Lord
> the seven celestial torches were lit.
> They send their rays on this earth,
> lighting and protecting all living beings.
> Assistants and ministers of the right and left,
> brilliant and redoubtable intellects;
> O chief of the heavenly army
> and you five thunder-bearers.
> Leave for a moment the golden palace,
> come to this dusty world,
> to deliver us from dangers and evils,
> to protect and prolong our lives.
> Extend to us your power,
> extinguish that which is bad and impure,

bless all those who live,
give repose to the dead.
May those who disobey you perish.
May they who obey you prosper.
The seven celestial torches shine,
spreading their light on our persons.
May this protecting light
cause us to live always!
With respect we offer incense.
With reverence we express our devotion.

Liturgical Hymn of the Eleventh Century

This hymn was used in collective services to the Pure August One, and belongs to Taoist rituals of the eleventh and twelfth centuries, or the vulgar era. During this period Taoism, in order to hold back the Amidist movement, absorbed some characteristics of the religion it was struggling against, thus becoming itself a theism.

Venerable celestial, Pure August One,
Sovereign Lord seated above the azure vault,
I and all those present desire that each word that we are about to utter
may be a homage to your sacred name,
may benefit our deceased ancestors and our living relatives,
all those who live in this dusty world,
and the souls who are plunged in the darkness of the long night.
O You who are resplendent, shining with light,
in the city of white jade, in the palace of yellow gold,
You, the saintliest and purest of all beings,
You who wage war against all evils and save from all misfortunes . . .
Enlightening light, penetrating light,
purifying light, consoling light,
invincible Lord of the azure heaven,
Compassionate father of all beings . . .
Oh! that all might understand what is sinful!
Oh! that all may obtain complete pardon!
May their evil passions be extinguished!
May their circumspection preserve them from the hells!
Preserve us from incredulity, from doubt,
from gluttony, impurity, envy;
from vain imaginations and frivolous affections;

from all which deludes or defiles!
May our minds be concentrated, may our thoughts be pure,
may our heart be empty, may our bodies be chaste!
Preserve us from ambition and covetousness,
make us calm, patient, persevering!
Help the sick and all who suffer,
protect the hermits against serpents and tigers,
navigators against the fury of the waves,
peaceable men against robbers and brigands!
Drive from us all contagion,
caterpillars and grasshoppers.
Preserve us from drought, flood, and fire,
from tyranny, from captivity.
Deliver from the hells those who are tormented there.
Put an end to the sufferings of the famished pretas.
Grant to animals that they be reborn higher in the scale.
Give peace to the peoples of the earth.
Preserve us from war and a violent death.
Give prosperity to the countries and the nations.
Enlighten all men with the doctrine which saves.
Cause to be reborn that which is dead, and to become green again that
    which is dried up.

CHINESE MOHAMMEDANISM

Invocation of the Lord

O venerable and great Lord, we pray thee to help us to serve thee,
we pray thee to pardon our sins. We believe in thee. We put all our
trust in thee. We praise thee. We are full of thankfulness toward thee.
We proclaim thy kindnesses. O venerable and great Lord, we prostrate
ourselves before thee only. We wish faithfully to walk in thy ways. We
wish to serve thee with zeal. We confide in thy pity. We fear thy judgments.

Notes

1. Rule XLV of the Mahayana reads: "Every time that [the monk] meets
an animal, he must wish for his entrance along the path of salvation. This
shall be done by reawakening the necessary reason. Everywhere, in the

mountains or on the plains, the disciple of Buddha must keep this vow in his heart toward all living creatures of the region, even toward those invisible to the eye. For whoever lets die in his heart the desire to save all living creatures has sinned."

2. The world above.

*

Tibet

TIBET

For the Transmigration

O ye Knowledge-Holding Deities, pray hearken unto me;
Lead me on the Path, out of your great love.
When [I am] wandering in the Sangsara, because of intensified
    propensities,
On the bright light-path of the Simultaneously-born Wisdom
May the bands of Heroes, the Knowledge-Holders, lead me;
May the bands of the Mothers, the Kakınis, be [my] rear guard;
May they save me from the fearful ambuscades of the Bardo,
And place me in the pure Paradise Realms.

For the Transmigration

Alas! when wandering in the Sangsara because of the power of violent
    anger,
On the radiant light-path of the Mirror-like Wisdom,
May [I] be led by the Bhagavan Vajra-Sattva,
May the Divine Mother Mamaki be [my] rear guard;
May [I] be led safely across the fearful ambush of the Bardo;
And may [I] be placed in the state of the All-perfect Buddhahood.

143

For the Transmigration

Alas! when [I am] wandering in the Sangsara, through force of over-
powering illusions,
On the light-path of the abandonment of fright, fear, and awe,
May the bands of the Bhagavans, the Peaceful and Wrathful Ones,
lead [me];
May the bands of the Wrathful Goddesses Rich in Space be [my]
rear guard,
And save me from the fearful ambuscades of the Bardo,
And place me in the state of the Perfectly-Enlightened Buddhas.
When wandering alone, separated from dear friends,
When the void forms one's own thoughts are shining here,
May the Buddhas, exerting the force of their grace,
Cause not to come the fear, awe, and terror in the Bardo.
When the five bright Wisdom-Lights are shining here,
May recognition come without dread and without awe;
When the divine bodies of the Peaceful and the Wrathful are shining
here,
May the assurance of fearlessness be obtained and the Bardo be
recognized.
When, by the power of evil karma, misery is being tasted,
May the tutelary deities dissipate the misery;
When the natural sound of Reality is reverberating [like] a thousand
thunders,
May they be transmuted into the sounds of the Six Syllables.
When unprotected, karma having to be followed here,
I beseech the Gracious Compassionate [One] to protect me;
When suffering miseries of karmic propensities here,
May the blissfulness of the Clear Light dawn;
May the Five Elements not rise up as enemies;
But may I behold the realms of the Five Orders of the Enlightened Ones.

Instructions for the Dead

O nobly-born on the Fourteenth Day, the Four Female Doorkeepers,
also issuing from within thine own brain, will come to shine upon thee.
Again recognize. From the east [quarter] of thy brain will come to
shine the White Tiger-Headed Goat-Holding Goddess, bearing a scalp
filled with blood in her left [hand]; from the south, the Yellow Sow-
Headed Noose-Holding Goddess; from the west, the Red Lion-Headed

Iron-Chain-Holding Goddess; and from the north, the Green Serpent-Headed Bell-Holding Goddess. Thus issue the Four Female Doorkeepers also from within thine own brain and come to shine upon thee; as tutelary deities, recognize them.

O nobly-born, on the outer Circle of these thirty wrathful deities, Herukas, the twenty-eight various-headed mighty goddesses, bearing various weapons, issuing from within thine own brain, will come to shine upon thee. Fear that not. Recognize whatever shineth to be the thought-forms of thine own intellectual faculties. At this vitally important time, recollect the select teachings of the guru.

O nobly-born, [there will dawn] from the east the Dark-Brown Yak-headed Rakshasa-Goddess, holding a dorje and a skull; and the Reddish-Yellow Serpent-Headed Brahma-Goddess, holding a lotus in her hand; and the Greenish-Black Leopard-Headed Great-Goddess, holding a trident in her hand; and the Blue Monkey-Headed Goddess of Inquisitiveness, holding a wheel; and the Red Snow-Bear-Headed Virgin-Goddess, bearing a short spear in the hand; and the White Bear-Headed Indra-Goddess, holding an intestine-noose in the hand: [these], the Six Yoginis of the East, issuing from within the [eastern quarter of thine own] brain, will come to shine upon thee; fear that not.

O nobly-born, from the south [will dawn] the Yellow Bat-Headed Delight-Goddess, holding a shaving-knife in the hand; and the Red Makara-Headed Peaceful-[Goddess], holding an urn in the hand; and the Red Scorpion-Headed Amrita-Goddess, holding a lotus in the hand; and the White Kite-Headed Moon-Goddess, holding a dorje in the hand; and the Dark-Green Fox-Headed Baton-Goddess, flourishing a club in the hand; and the Yellowish-Black Tiger-Headed Rakshasi, holding a skull [filled with] blood in the hand: [these] the Six Yoginis of the South, issuing from within the [southern quarter of thine own] brain, will come to shine upon thee; fear that not.

O nobly-born, from the west [will dawn] the Greenish-Black Vulture-Headed Eater-Goddess, holding a baton in the hand; and the Red Horse-Headed Delight-Goddess, holding a huge trunk of a corpse; and the White Eagle-Headed Mighty-Goddess, holding a club in the hand; and the Yellow Dog-Headed Rakshasi, holding a dorje in the hand and a shaving-knife and cutting [with this]; and the Red Hoopoo-Headed Desire-Goddess, holding, aimed, a bow and arrow in the hand, and the Green Stag-Headed Wealth-Guardian Goddess, holding an urn in the hand: [these], the Six Yoginis of the West, issuing from within the [western quarter of thine own] brain, will come to shine upon thee; fear that not.

O nobly-born, from the north [will dawn] the Blue Wolf-Headed

Wind-Goddess, waving a pennant in the hand; and the Red Ibex-Headed Woman-Goddess, holding a pointed stake in the hand; and the Black Sow-Headed Sow-Goddess, holding a noose of fangs in the hand; and the Red Crow-Headed Thunderbolt-Goddess, holding an infant corpse in the hand; and the Greenish-Black Elephant-Headed Big-Nosed Goddess, holding in the hand a big corpse and drinking blood from a skull; and the Blue Serpent-Headed Water-Goddess, holding in the hand a serpent noose: [these], the Six Yoginis of the North, issuing from within [the northern quarter of] thine own brain, will come to shine upon thee; fear that not.

O nobly-born, the Four Yoginis of the Door, issuing from within the brain, will come to shine upon thee: from the east, the Black Cuckoo-Headed Mystic Goddess, holding an iron hook in the hand; from the south, the Yellow Goat-Headed Mystic Goddess, holding a noose in the hand; from the west, the Red Lion-Headed Mystic Goddess, holding an iron chain in the hand; and from the north, the Greenish-Black Serpent-Headed Mystic Goddess: [these], the Four Doorkeeping Yoginis, issuing from within the brain, will come to shine upon thee.

Since these Twenty-eight Mighty Goddesses emanate from the bodily powers of Ratna-Sambhava, [He] of the Six Heruka Deities, recognize them.

O nobly-born, the Peaceful Deities emanate from the Voidness of the Dharma-Kaya; recognize them. From the Radiance of the Dharma-Kaya emanate the Wrathful Deities; recognize them.

At this time when the Fifty-eight Blood-Drinking Deities emanating from thine own brain come to shine upon thee, if thou knowest them to be the radiances of thine own intellect, thou wilt merge, in the state of at-one-ment, into the body of the Blood-Drinking Ones there and then, and obtain Buddhahood.

O nobly-born, by not recognizing now, and by fleeing from the deities out of fear, again sufferings will come to overpower thee. If this be not known, fear being begotten of the Blood-Drinking Deities, [one is] awed and terrified and fainteth away: one's own thought-forms turn into illusory appearances, and one wandereth into the Sangsara; if one be not awed and terrified, one will not wander into the Sangsara.

Furthermore, the bodies of the largest of the Peaceful and Wrathful Deities are equal [in vastness] to the limits of the heavens; the intermediate, as big as Mt. Meru; the smallest, equal to eighteen bodies such as thine own body, set one upon another. Be not terrified at that; be not awed. If all existing phenomena shining forth as divine shapes and radiances be recognized to be the emanations of one's own intellect,

Buddhahood will be obtained at that very instant of recognition. The saying, "Buddhahood will be obtained in a moment [of time]" is that which applieth now. Bearing this in mind, one will obtain Buddhahood by merging, in at-one-ment, into the Radiances and the Kayas.

O nobly-born, whatever fearful and terrifying visions thou mayst see, recognize them to be thine own thought-forms.

O nobly-born, if thou recognize not, and be frightened, then all the Peaceful Deities will shine forth in the shape of Maha-Kala; and all the Wrathful Deities will shine [forth] in the form of Dharma-Raja, the Lord of Death; and thine own thought-forms becoming illusions [or Maras], thou wilt wander into the Sangsara.

O nobly-born, if one recognize not one's own thought-forms, however learned one may be in the Scriptures—both Sutras and Tantras—although practicing religion for a kalpa, one obtaineth not Buddhahood. If one recognize one's own thought-forms, by one important art and by one word, Buddhahood is obtained.

✳

Japan

Prayer of the Great Purification

This *norito* may be found in the Yengishiki No. X. Two great purifications are held annually, on the last day of the sixth and seventh lunar phases. These dates, with the adoption of the Gregorian calendar, are fixed as June 30 and December 31. The prayer read on these occasions is entitled: Minazuki Tsugomori non O-harae, or Nakatomi no dotoba, the Words of Nakatomi. In ancient times it was recited by a member of the Nakatomi family, the family to which tradition delegated the religious functions of the Mikado.

He[1] says: Give ear, all ye Imperial Princes, Princes, Ministers of State, and functionaries who are here assembled, and hearken every one to the Great Purification by which at this year's interlune of the sixth month he deigns to purge and absolve all manner of faults and transgressions which may have been committed by those who serve in the Imperial Court, whether they wear the scarf or the shoulder strap, whether they bear on their back the quiver or gird on them the sword, the eighty attendants of the attendants, including, moreover, all those who do duty in the various offices of State.

He says: Hearken, all of you. The sovereign dear ancestors[2] who divinely dwell in the Plain of High Heaven, having summoned to an assembly the eight hundred myriads of deities, held divine counsel with them, and then gave command, saying: "Let our August Grand-child hold serene rule over the fertile reed-plain, the region of fair rice ears [Japan], as a land of peace.

But in the realm thus assigned to him there were savage deities. These were called to a divine account and expelled with a divine expulsion. Moreover, the rocks, trees, and smallest leaves of grass which had power of speech were put to silence. Then they dispatched him down-ward from his celestial everlasting throne, cleaving as he went with an awful way-cleaving the many-piled clouds of Heaven, and delivered to him the Land. At the middle point of the lands of the four quarters thus entrusted to him, Yamato, the High-Sun-Land, was established as a peaceful land, and there was built here for the Sovereign Grandchild a fair Palace wherewithal to shelter him from sun and sky [rain], with massy pillars based deep on the nethermost rocks and upraising to the Plain of High Heaven the crossbeams of its roof.

Now of the various faults and transgressions to be committed by the celestial race destined more and more to people this land of his peaceful rule, some are of Heaven, to wit, the breaking down of divisions be-tween rice fields, filling up of irrigation channels, removing water pipes, sowing seed over again, planting skewers, flaying alive, flaying back-ward. These are distinguished as Heavenly offenses.

Earthly offenses which will be committed are the cutting of living bodies, the cutting of dead bodies, leprosy, kokumi,[3] incest of a man with his mother or daughter, with his mother-in-law or stepdaughter, bestiality, calamities from creeping things, from the high Gods [light-ning], and from high birds,[4] killing animals, bewitchments.

Whensoever they may be committed, let the Great Nakatomi, in ac-cordance with the custom of the Heavenly Palace, cut heavenly saplings at the top and cut them at the bottom and make thereof a complete array of one thousand stands for offerings.

Having trimmed rushes of heaven at the top and trimmed them at the bottom, let him split them into manifold slivers.

Then let him recite the mighty ritual words of the celestial ritual. When he does so, the Gods of Heaven, thrusting open the adamantine door of Heaven and cleaving the many-piled clouds of Heaven with an awful way-cleaving, will lend ear. The Gods of Earth, climbing to the tops of the high mountains and to the tops of the low mountains, sweeping apart the mists of the high mountains and the mists of the low mountains, will lend ear. When they have thus lent ear, all offenses

whatsoever will be annulled, from the Court of the Sovereign Grandchild to the provinces of the four quarters of the Under-Heaven.

As the many-piled clouds of Heaven are scattered by the breath of the
Wind Gods; as the morning breezes and the evening breezes dissipate
the dense morning vapors and the dense evening vapors; as a huge ship,
moored in a great harbor, casting off its stern moorings, casting off its
bow moorings, drives forth into the great sea-plain; as yonder thick
brushwood is smitten and cleared away by the sharp sickle forged in
the fire, so shall all offenses be utterly annulled. Therefore he [the
Mikado] is graciously pleased to purify and cleanse them away. The
Goddess called Se-ori-tsu-hime, who dwells in the rapids of the swift
streams whose cataracts tumble headlong from the tops of the high
mountains and from the tops of the low mountains, will bear them out
into the great sea-plain. Thereupon the Goddess called Haya-aki-tsu-
hime, who dwells in the myriad meetings of the tides of the myriad
brine-paths of the myriad ways of the currents of the boisterous sea,
will swallow them up. And the God Ibuki-do-nushi, who dwells in the
Root Country, the Bottom Country.[5] Then the Goddess Haya-sasura-
hime, who dwells in the Root Country, the Bottom Country will banish
and abolish them. When they have been so destroyed, everyone, from
the servants of the Imperial Court to the four quarters of the Under-
Heaven, will remain void of all offenses whatsoever.

Attend, therefore, all of you to this Great Purification, by which he
is graciously pleased at sunset on this interlunar day of the sixth month
of this year to purify and cleanse you, having led hither a horse as an
animal that pricks up its ears at the Plain of High-Heaven.

He says: Ye diviners [Urabe] of the four provinces, remove them to
the great river-way and abolish them.

Prayer for the Purification of an Altar

Izanagi and Izanami are the two most important deities, for they created
Japan.

In reverence and awe: The great gods of the purification place who
came into existence when the Great God Izanagi deigned to wash and
purify himself on the plain of Ahagi (east) of Tachibana (near) the
River Woto in Himuka in Tsukushi, shall deign to purify and deign
to cleanse whatever there may be of sins and pollutions committed in-
advertently or deliberately by the officials serving here today. Listen
to these my words. Thus I say reverentially.

Two Noritos

Yengishiki, numbers 14 and 27. The feast called Onie, or Oname-matsuri, also Daijoe or Daijosai, gave solemn religious sanction to the sovereignty of each emperor. The occasion was the accession of the Mikado to the throne. During the celebration the emperor made an offering of new rice brought to him from two different provinces, assuring himself of the absolute ritual purity of the offering. An offering of vestments and material was also made, during which *norito A* was pronounced. The main part of the celebration was represented by the emperor's offering and by the act of adoration made by him through special offerings of sixty white jewels mixed with jewels of red and green, of a gold and silver mounted sword, of a mirror and fifty vessels of edibles, all accompanied by a complicated series of symbols. For the latter offerings *norito B* was read by Idzumo no Miyakko, the hereditary chief priest of Kitsuki in Idzumo of the temple affiliated with Hinokuma in Kii. This caste of priests claimed to be descendants of the God Ama no hohi, who appears in the cycle of Ohonamoch.

a)
The offering of cloth and wearing apparel:

He says: Hearken! all ye assembled kannushi and hafuri.[6] I humbly declare in the presence of the sovereign Gods, who, according to the command of the dear divine ancestor and dear divine ancestress who dwell in the Plain of High Heaven, bear sway as Heavenly Shrines and Earthly Shrines.

He says: To the end that on the middle day of the Hare of the eleventh month of this year, the Sovereign Grandchild may partake of the Great Food as Heavenly Food, as Long Food, as Distant Food, I pray that ye sovereign Gods will jointly undertake to bless his reign, to be firm and enduring and give it happiness as a prosperous reign. Therefore, on behalf of the Sovereign Grandchild, who will rule peacefully and serenely for one thousand autumns, and five hundred autumns with festive ruddy countenance, do I set forth these fair offerings, namely, bright cloth and shining cloth, soft cloth and rough cloth.

Hearken! all of you to this fulfilling of praises as the morning sun rises in glory.

He says: More especially would I enjoin on the kannushi and hafuri with all due ceremony to receive, take up, and present the offerings purely provided by the Imbe, hanging stout straps on weak shoulders.

b) The words of blessing of the Miyakko of Idzumo.

Among the many tens of days that be, on this day, this living day,

this perfect day, do I ——, Miyakko of the Land of Idzumo, humbly
declare with deepest reverence, to wit: With the object of pronouncing
a blessing on the great august reign of our Sovereign Lord, who rules
the Great-eight-island country as—with fear be it said—a wise manifest
deity, and blessing it as a long and great reign, did I, hanging stout
straps on weak shoulders[7] fastening the cords of the sacred offerings,
wearing the celestial cap, shearing and spreading the coarse grass as a
sacred mat in the sacred house, blackening the sacred vessels, dwelling in
pure retirement by the celestial sake jars, calming the deities in their
calm shrines by the avoidance of impurity, did service first to the Great
God of Kumano, Kushi mikenu, our divine ancestor, the Great-Grand-
child of Izanagi, and to Ohonamochi, the maker of the land, for whom
within the blue hill-confines of the province of Idzumo the temple pillars
have been stoutly planted on the rock roots below, while the projecting
crossbeams of the roof are exalted to the Plain of High Heaven. Thereafter I did worship to the Sovereign Gods who dwell in the one hundred
and eighty-six shrines.

Then as the morning sun went up in glory, there came these good
words of divine blessing, to wit: When Takami-musubi and Kami mi-
musubi, the High-Heaven divine ancestors, bestowed upon the Sovereign
Grandchild this subcelestial Great-eight-island country, Ama no hohi,
the remote divine ancestor of the Omi of Idzumo was sent by them to
view the condition of the land. Forcing his way through the eightfold
clouds of Heaven, soaring across the sky, soaring over the earth, he
surveyed the Under-Heaven on all sides, and made report that the Fair-
Ear-Land of the Rich-Reed-Plain was a savage land where there were
Gods who in the daytime swarmed like flies in the fifth month and at
night shone like fire pots, and where the rocks, trees, and blue-water
foam had power of speech. However, he promised that it should be subdued so that the Sovereign Grandchild might rule it serenely as a peaceful land. Therefore his son Ame-hina-dori, and with him Futsunushi,
were sent down from Heaven. They drove out and subdued the savage
deities, and persuaded the Great God who made the Land to divide off
the visible outward things of the Great-eight-island country.

Then Ohonamochi said: In the land to be governed by the Sovereign
Grandchild and called Great Yamato I will make my own gentle spirit
to be attached to an eight-hand mirror, and enshrined in Miha, under
the title of Yamato no Oho-mono-nushi kushi-mika-tama no mikoto
[great-thing-master-wondrous-awful-spirit], the spirit of my son Ajisuki-
taka-hikone to be enshrined at Kamo in Katsuraki; that of Kotoshironushi, at Unade; and that of Kaya narumi, at Asuka; dedicating them to

dwell there divinely as near guardian deities of the Sovereign Grand-child. He then went to rest in the shrine of fertile Kitsuki. Thereupon the Sovereign dear divine ancestor and ancestress gave command saying: Do thou Hohi no Mikoto bless the Sovereign's long age so that it may be firm and enduring, and make it happy as a prosperous age.

In accordance with this injunction, I [his successor] perform this service of blessing, and as the morning sun rises in glory, bring tribute of congratulatory divine treasures in token of the God's [Hohi] regard and in token of the Omi's [his own] regard. These white jewels are a prediction of the great august white hairs (to which your majesty will reach). The red jewels are the august, healthful, ruddy countenance, and the green-estuary jewels are the harmonious fitness with which your majesty will establish far and wide, as with a broad sword blade, his lasting great august reign over the Great-eight-island country which he governs. As this white horse plants firmly his forehoofs and his hind-hoofs, so will the pillars of the Great Palace be set firmly on the upper rocks and frozen firmly on the lower rocks. The prick-up of his ears is a sign that Your Majesty will, with ears ever more erect, rule the Under-Heaven. As a token that the visible deity shall peacefully and serenely rule the Great-eight-island country as long as Heaven and Earth, the Sun and Moon endure, I offer these congratulatory divine treasures by way of respect from the God, and by way of these auspicious words of divine congratulation delivered to me from Heaven.

A Prayer for Harvest

This *norito* was read at the feast of Toshigoi no Matsuri, Office of Harvest Prayers, in honor of the 3132 official temples of the entire Shinto pantheon. It was read on the fourth day of the second month, during the sowing of the rice. The offerings prepared by the Imbe consisted of cloth of various kinds, models of swords, shields, lances, arrows, quivers, deer horns, hoes, beer, fish, edible algae, salt, and woven mats. When the ceremony was held in the temples of Ise, a horse was added. In every case a white horse, a rooster, and a boar were sent to Mitosh-no-kami, the divinity of harvest, and a horse was also sent to each of the nineteen other divinities, including the god of gen-eration and the aquatic divinities of Yamato. During the complicated cere-mony, Nakatomi, read this *norito,* which is the first of the Yengishiki col-lection and designed to prevent damage to the rice crop. During the ceremony, the hafuri echoed each strophe with *O,* which corresponds to the Hebrew "amen."

He says: Hearken, all ye assembled Kannushi and Hafuri.

He says: I humbly declare in the presence of the Sovereign Gods, whose praises are fulfilled as Heavenly Deities and as Earthly Deities, by command of the Sovereign, dear, divine ancestor and ancestress who divinely dwell in the Plain of High-Heaven. In the second month of this year the Sovereign Grandchild is graciously pleased to pray for harvest, and I, therefore, as the morning sun rises in glory, offer up this plenteous offering, thus fulfilling your praise.

He says: I humbly declare in the presence of the Sovereign Gods of the harvest.

If the Sovereign Gods will bestow in ears a hand's breadth long and ears abundant the latter harvest which they will bestow, the latter harvest produced by the labor of men from whose arms the foam drips down, on whose opposing thighs the mud is gathered, I will fulfill their praises by humbly offering first fruits, of ears a thousand, of ears many a hundred, raising up the tops of the sake jars; and setting in rows the bellies of the sake jars, in juice and in ear will I present them; of things growing in the great moor-plain, sweet herbs and bitter herbs; of things that dwell in the blue sea-plain, the broad of fin and the narrow of fin; edible seaweed, too, from the offing and seaweed from the shore; of clothing, bright stuffs and shiny stuffs, soft stuffs and coarse stuffs— with these I will fulfill your praises. [In the meantime] having furnished a white horse, a white boar, and a white cock, with things of various kinds before the Sovereign Gods of the Harvest, I fulfill their praises by humbly presenting these plenteous offerings of the Sovereign Grand-child.

He says: I humbly declare in the presence of the Sovereign Gods whose praises the chief priestess fulfills, and I fulfill your praises, namely, Kami-musubi, Taka-mi-musubi, Ikumusubi, Taru-musubi, Tama-tsume-musubi, Oho-miya no me, Oho-mi-ketsu no kami, and Kotoshironushi. Because you bless the Sovereign Grandchild's reign as a long reign, firm and enduring, and render it a happy and prosperous reign, I fulfill your praises as our Sovereign dear, divine ancestor and ancestress by making these plenteous offerings on his behalf.

He says: I humbly declare in the presence of the Sovereign Gods whose praises the priestess of Wigasuri fulfills. I fulfill your praises, repeating your names, to wit, Live Well, Blessing Well, Long-Rope Well Asuha and Hahigi. Whereas, on the nethermost rock-root ruled by the Sovereign Gods the palace pillars have been raised stout and high, and the projecting crossbeams exalted to the Plain of High-Heaven, furnishing a fair abode for the Sovereign Grandchild, wherein, finding shelter from the rain and shelter from the sun, he serenely governs in peace the world on all sides, I fulfill your praises by making these plenteous offerings on his behalf.

He says: I humbly declare in the presence of the Sovereign Gods, whose praises are fulfilled by the priestess of the Gate. Repeating your names, to wit, Kushi-iha-mado [wondrous rock-gate] and Toyo-iha-mado [rich rock-gate,] I fulfill your praises. Whereas you guard the gates of the four quarters by night and day, obstructing the passage like manifold piles of rock, and whether you open them in the morning or close them in the evening, guard below against unfriendly things coming from below, and guard above against unfriendly things coming from above, I fulfill your praises by making these offerings on behalf of the Sovereign Grandchild.

He says: I humbly declare in the presence of the Sovereign Gods, whose praises the priestess of Ikushima [live-island] or region fulfills. Repeating your names, to wit, Iku-kuni [live country] and Taru-kuni [perfect country], I fulfill your praises. Because you, the Sovereign Gods who rule the islands many tens in number, wherever the frog of the valley finds his way, wherever the ocean foam extends, making wide the narrow regions and the steep regions, level, have granted these many islands to him, every one, I fulfill your praises by making these plenteous offerings on behalf of the Sovereign Grandchild.

He says: More especially do I humbly declare in the mighty presence of the Great Heaven-shining Deity who dwells in Ise. Because the Great Deity has bestowed on him the lands of the four quarters over which her glance extends as far as where the wall of Heaven rises, as far as where the bounds of Earth stand up, as far as the blue clouds are diffused, as far as where the white clouds settle down opposite, by the blue sea-plain, as far as the prows of ships can go without letting dry their poles and oars; by land, as far as the hoofs of horses can go, with tightened baggage cords, treading their way among rock roots and tree roots where the long road extends, continuously widening the narrow regions and making the steep regions level, drawing together, as it were, the distant regions by throwing over them [a net of] many ropes—therefore will the first fruits for the Sovereign Great Deity be piled up in her mighty presence like a range of hills, leaving the remainder for him tranquilly to partake of.

Moreover, whereas you bless the Sovereign Grandchild's reign as a long reign, firm and enduring, and render it a happy and prosperous reign, I plunge down my neck, as a cormorant, in reverence to you as our Sovereign's dear, divine ancestress, and fulfill your praises by making these plenteous offerings on his behalf.

He says: I humbly declare in the presence of the Sovereign Gods who dwell in the Crown lands and name your august names, to wit—Takechi,

Katsuraki, Tohochi, Shiki, Yamanobe, and Sofu. Whereas the Sovereign Grandchild partakes of, as his long food, his distant food, the sweet herbs and bitter herbs which grow in and are brought from the six Crown lands aforesaid, I fulfill your praises by making these plenteous offerings on his behalf. I humbly declare in the presence of the Sovereign Gods who dwell in the mountain-mouths and name your august names to wit—Asuka, Ihare, Osaka, Hatsuse, Unebi, and Miminashi. Whereas the great trees and the small trees which grow on the near mountains and on the far mountains are cut at the root and at the top, and brought to furnish a fair abode for the Sovereign Grandchild, wherein, sheltered from the rain and sun, he serenely governs in peace the lands of the four quarters, I fulfill your praises by making these plenteous offerings on his behalf.

He says: I humbly declare in the presence of the Gods who dwell in the water-partings, and name your august names, to wit—Yoshinu, Uda, Tsuge, and Katsuraki, fulfill your praises. If you, the Sovereign Gods, will bestow in ears many a hand's breadth long, and ears abundant the latter harvest which you will bestow, I will fulfill your praises by offering first fruits in ear and in juice, raising up the tops of the sake jars and filling and setting in a row the bellies of the sake jars. The Sovereign Grandchild will then partake with ruddy countenance of that which remains as the corn of his august morning meals and his august evening meals, for his long food and for his distant food. Therefore do I now fulfill your praises by making these plenteous offerings on his behalf.

Lend ear, all of you.

He says: More especially, let the Kannushi and Hafuri, having received the offerings which the Imbe, hanging stout straps on weak shoulders, have prepared with purity, take them away and offer them in all due form.

Two Noritos of the Moon Feast

This festival was held in honor of the gods of the "Greater Shrines." Its name connotes a monthly feast, but it was really celebrated only twice a year, on the eleventh day of the sixth and twelfth months.

He says: By the great command of the Mikado, I humbly declare in the mighty presence of the Great Deity whose praises are fulfilled [in the shrine built] upon the nethermost rock-roots on the bank of the River Isuzu in Watarahi. I, of —— rank, of —— name, humbly repeat his commands, as his envoy to convey hither and make offering of the customary great offerings of Praying-for-Harvest in the second month.

He says: Hearken, all ye kannushi and momo-imi, to this celestial, this great, norito, which I humbly pronounce in the mighty presence of the Heaven-Shining Great Deity, whose praises are fulfilled in Uji of Watarahi, where on the bank of the River Isuzu the pillars of the Great Shrine are stoutly erected, and the projecting crossbeams are exalted to the Plain of High-Heaven. (Here the Negi and Uchi-bito, priests of lower rank, answer "O", that is, "Yes," or "Amen.") Bless the life of our Sovereign as a long life, let his reign be prosperous, firm, and enduring as a pile of multitudinous rocks, and show thy favor to the princes born of him. As to the functionaries of every rank, down to the peasants of the four quarters of the Under-Heaven, make the five grains which they long and peacefully cultivate to flourish abundantly. Favor them with thy protection, and grant them thy blessing.

On this seventeenth day of the sixth month, as the morning sun rises in glory, I fulfill thy praises, setting before thee in ample measure, like seas and mountains, the tribute yarn and the great food offerings of holy rice and sake, provided according to custom by the consecrated peasants of the three districts, and the various localities of the various provinces, while the Great Nakatomi himself is hidden in offering branches. Hearken, all ye kannushi and mono-imi.

He says: This service is likewise addressed to the Aramatsuri shrine and to the Tsukiyomi [Moon-God] shrine.

(The kannushi again answer O.)

Luck-Wishing or Blessing of the Great Palace

This ceremony was performed on the morning after the Kamu image and the Nihi-name. It honored three deities: the two Yabune no Kami, or House deities, and Oho-miya no me, a personified Lady Chamberlain. It was a ceremony of purification and blessing of the imperial palace. Officers of the royal house came carrying four jewel boxes containing precious stones, pieces of bark from the mulberry tree, rice, and rice wine in bottles. The offerings were then carried in procession by specially appointed priests to the door of the palace, where they were deposited. At this point the ritual declarations were formulated in accordance with a fixed liturgy. After this the procession entered the palace. A priestess entered the audience room and scattered rice, while others conducted the same ceremony out in other rooms. Meanwhile the Imbe hung precious stones in every corner of the room. The Nakatomi remained in the southeast part of the palace and continued to read the ritual in a low voice. Finally the entire procession passed into the Mikado's bathroom and draped other precious stones

on the fixtures. The ancient *norito* which follows was read during the course
of the ceremony.

When by command of the dear, divine ancestor and ancestress who
divinely dwell in the Plain of High Heaven the Sovereign Grandchild
was made to take his seat on the high august throne of Heaven, and
when the Heavenly Emblems, namely, the mirror and the sword, were
delivered to him, these words of blessing were pronounced: "Let our
sovereign great offspring, the Sovereign Grandchild, receiving over the
celestial Sun-succession on this high throne of Heaven, rule tranquilly
for myriads of thousands of autumns, for long autumns, over the
Great-Eight-islands, the Rich Reed-plain, Land of fair rice ears, as a
peaceful country." With these words they delivered it unto him. Then,
celestial counsel having been held, they put to silence the rock-roots and
tree-roots, even to the smallest blades of grass, that previously had power
of speech. And for the Sovereign Grandchild who in Heavenly Sun-
succession rules the Under-Heaven, to which he had descended, trees are
now cut down with the sacred axes of the Imbe in the great valleys and
the small valleys of the secluded mountains, and sacrifice having been
made of their tops and bottoms to the God of the mountains, the middle
parts are brought forth and set up as sacred pillars with sacred mattocks
to form a fair palace wherein the Sovereign Grandchild finds shelter
from the sky and shelter from the sun. To thee, therefore, Ya-bune no
Mikoto [the palace treated as a God], I address these heavenly, wondrous, auspicious words of calm and blessing.

He says: I humbly declare the names of the gods who calmly and
peacefully watch that this Great Palace where he holds rule, as far
downward as the lowermost rock-roots, suffer no harm from reptiles
among its bottom-ropes,[8] as far upward as the blue clouds are diffused in
the Plain of High Heaven, may suffer no harm from flying birds in the
celestial smoke-hole, that the joinings of the firmly planted pillars, and
of the crossbeams, rafters, doors, and windows may not move or make
a noise, that there may be no slackening of the tied rope-knots and no
dishevelment of the roof-thatch, no creaking of the floor-joints or alarms
by night. I humbly praise your honored names, to wit, Yabune Kuku-
nochi no Mikoto and Yabune Toyo-uke hime no Mikoto [House-tree
God and House-food Goddess]. And inasmuch as you humbly preserve
the Sovereign's Grandchild's reign to be firm and enduring, and humbly
bless it as a lasting, prosperous, and perfect reign, the Imbe no Sukune,
adding shining cloth and lustrous fine cloth to the countless strings of
fair jewels prepared by the sacred jewelmakers, with observance of purity

and avoidance of pollution, and hanging stout straps on weak shoulders [will offer them to you], with words of blessing and calm. And let the Gods Kamu-nahobi and Oho-nahobi peacefully and tranquilly exercise their office, correcting, whether in things heard or in things seen, any omission which he make make in so doing.

More especially does he humbly fulfill her praises because, within the same Palace as the Sovereign Grandchild, she blocks the way and takes cognizance and makes choice of the persons who go in and out, with words amends and mollifies the hurry and roughness of Gods, keeps from error the hands and feet of the scarf-wearing attendants and the strap-wearing attendants who serve the morning meal and the evening meal of the Sovereign Grandchild, preventing the Imperial Princes, Princes, Ministers of State, and all the functionaries from indulging their several inclinations and causing them, pure of evil intents and base hearts, to attend in the Palace with a Palace-attendance, and to serve in the Palace with a Palace-service, and amending to eye and ear all faults and errors, so that their duties may be performed peacefully and tranquilly.

Invocation of the Kami Who Prevent Disasters

This *norito* was read during the Michi-ahe no Matsuri ceremony and was used to invoke the Sahe no kami, the Kami or divinities who prevent disasters, also called "divinities of the road." These gods, whose emblem is a club, are closely tied to the phallic cult. In Japan, the phallus represents not only the power of procreation but also animal vigor and life. The second representation has prophylactic and magic applications against the forces of evil and also against contagious diseases.

I humbly declare in the presence of the Sovereign Gods, whose functions first began in the Plain of High Heaven when they fulfilled the praises of the Sovereign Grandchild by guarding the great eight-road-forks like a multitudinous assemblage of rocks,[9] naming your honored names, to wit, Yachimata-hiko, Yachimata-hime, and Kunado, I fulfill your praises. Whenever from the Root-country, the Bottom-country, there may come savage and unfriendly beings, consort not and parley not with them; but if they go below, keep watch below; if they go above, keep watch above, protecting us against pollution with a night guarding and with a day guarding. The offerings I furnish in your honor are bright cloth, shining cloth, soft cloth, and rough cloth. Of sake I raise up the tops of the jars and fill and range in order the bellies of the jars. [Grain] in juice and in ear I offer you. Of things that dwell in the mountains and on the moors I offer the soft of hair and the coarse of hair. Of things that dwell in the blue sea-plain, the broad of fin and the narrow of fin, even to the weeds of the offing and the weeds of the shore. Peacefully partaking of these plenteous offerings, which I lay before you in full measure like a cross range of hills, hold guard on the highways like a multitudinous assemblage of rocks, preserving from pollution the Sovereign Grandchild firmly and enduringly, and bless his reign to be a prosperous reign.

Also be pleased peacefully to preserve from pollution the Imperial Princes, the Princes, the Ministers of State, and the functionaries, including, moreover, the people of the Under Heaven. I, as official of the Department of Religion, humbly fulfill your praises by this celestial, this great, pronouncement.

Fire-Calming Service

This ceremony was performed on the last days of the sixth and twelfth months by the Urabe, or diviners, at the four outer corners of the Imperial palace, in order to prevent its destruction by fire. The Urabe kindled a fire by means of the fire-drill, worshiped it, and read the following *norito* (No. 12).

I humbly declare according to the celestial, the great pronouncement delivered to the Sovereign Grandchild by his Sovereign dear, divine ancestor and ancestress when they granted to him the Under-Heaven, commanding him to rule tranquilly as a peaceful realm the fair Rice-ear-land of the Rich-reed-plain, as follows: "The two Gods Izanagi and Izanami, having become united as husband and wife, procreated the eighty countries and the eighty islands and gave birth to the eight hundred myriads of deities. When Izanami's last son, the God Homusubi [fire-growth] was born, her pudenda were burnt and she became rock-concealed.

She said, "For nights seven and for days seven look not on me, oh, my husband."

But before the seven days were fulfilled, Izanagi, wondering at her concealment, viewed her, and behold, her pudenda had been burnt in giving birth to the Fire. "Oh, my honored husband," said Izanami, "thou hast insulted me by looking on me despite my having besought thee to refrain from doing so at such a time. Therefore thou must govern the upper world and I, the lower world."

"So saying, she was rock-concealed. When she had reached the Even Pass of Yomi, she bethought herself: "I gave birth to, and left behind me in the upper world ruled by my honored husband, an evil-hearted child."

So she went back and gave birth to other children, namely, the God of Water, the Gourd, the River-weed, and the Clay-mountain-lady, four kinds in all. Moreover, she taught him, saying, "When the temper of this evil-hearted child becomes violent, do thou assuage it with the Water-God, the Gourd, the River-weed, and the Clay-mountain-lady."

Therefore do I fulfill thy praises as follows: To the end that thou mayest deign to control thy transports against the Palace of the Sovereign Grandchild, I offer thee bright cloth, shining cloth, smooth cloth, and rough cloth of various colors. Of things which dwell in the blue sea-plain, I offer the broad of fin and the narrow of fin, even unto the weeds of the offing and the weeds of the shore. Of sake, I raise up the tops of the jars, and fill and range in order the bellies of the jars. Nor do I omit rice, cleaned and in the husk. Heaping up these things like a cross-range of hills, I fulfill thy praises according to the Celestial, the Great, pronouncement.

Notes

1. "He" is the officiating Nakatomi, speaking on behalf of Mikado.

2. The divine forebears are the gods of the sun and the moon, Takamusubi and Amaterasu.

3. An uncertain term which probably signifies some grotesque malady.

4. Either an allusion to birds whose droppings might render food impure or to rapacious birds that swoop down to attack children and animals.

5. Two names for hell.

6. Classes of priests.

7. A formula equivalent to donning priestly vestments for the offering.

8. This refers to the ancient Japanese custom of tying the foundation beams with cords.

9. These divinities were worshiped at crossroads and invoked as "divinities of the crossroads."

*

India

INDIA

In selecting the hymns and prayers to represent the great religious traditions of India, we have not adhered to the false tripartition of Vedaism-Brahmanism-Hinduism. In order that the reader may make whatever distinctions in this sense he chooses, we set forth a general grouping of the various works to be found in the present section. Those belonging to the Vedaic epoch run from "To Agni" to "Glorification of the Sun, Considered as a Brahma-Karin"; the Hindu selections run from "Invocation to Visnu" to "A Prayer to Sri," and then from "To Visnu" to "After the Dinner"; those of Brahmanism run from "The Preservative Karmas" to "Prayers for the Practice of Yoga." Documents belonging to Indian Buddhism run from "Angulimala Paritta" to "Glorification of the Buddha," while the excerpts from "Evocation of Kwun" to "Judiciary Oath" are from Siamese Buddhism and contain mixtures of indigenous and Hindu elements.

To Agni

I glorify Agni,[1] the high priest of the sacrifice, the divine, the ministrant who presents the oblation to the gods and is the possessor of great wealth;

May that Agni, who is to be celebrated by both ancient and modern sages, conduct the gods hither.

Through Agni the worshiper obtains that affluence which increases day by day, which is the source of fame and the multiplier of mankind.

Agni, the unobstructed sacrifice of which thou art on every side the protector, assuredly reaches the gods.

May Agni, the presenter of oblations, the attainer of knowledge, he who is true, renowned, and divine, come hither with the gods. Whatever good thou mayest, Agni, bestow upon the giver of the oblation, that, verily, Angiras shall revert to thee.

We approach thee, Agni, with reverential homage in our thoughts, daily, both morning and evening;

Thee, the radiant, the protector of sacrifices, the constant illuminator of truth, increasing in thine own dwelling.

Agni, be unto us easy of access; as is a father to his son; be ever present with us for our good.

To Indra and to the Mortar

It is known that most of the Rig-Veda hymns concern the complicated ceremony accompanying the sacrifice of the soma, the inebriating acid drink made from an unidentified plant (perhaps the Sarcostemma acidum, of the family Asclepiadaceae), the stem of which is crushed with stones. In the following hymn there is a reference to the use of the mortar, the only such reference in the whole Rig-Veda.

Indra,[2] as the broad-based stone is raised to express the Soma juice, recognize and partake of the effusions of the mortar.

Indra, in the rite in which the two platters for containing the juice—as broad as a woman's hips—are employed, recognize and partake of the effusions of the mortar.

Indra, in the rite in which the housewife repeats egress from and ingress into the sacrificial chamber, recognize and partake of the effusions of the mortar.

When they bind the churning-staff with a cord, like reins to restrain a horse, Indra, recognize and partake of the effusions of the mortar.

If, indeed, O Mortar, thou art present in every house, give forth in this rite a lusty sound, like the drum of a victorious host.

Lord of the forest, as the wind gently blows before thee, so do thou, O Mortar, prepare the Soma juice, for the beverage of Indra.

Implements of sacrifice, bestowers of food, loud-sounding, sport, like the horses of Indra champing the grain.

Do you two forest lords, of pleasing form, prepare, with agreeable libations, our sweet juices, for Indra.

Bring the remains of the Soma juice upon the platters; sprinkle it upon the blades of Kusa grass; and place the remainder upon the cow-hide.

To Indra

I declare the former valorous deeds of Indra, which the thunderer has achieved: he clove the cloud; he cast the waters down to earth; he broke a way for the torrents of the mountains.

He clove the cloud, seeking refuge on the mountain: TwashTri[3] sharpened his far-whirling bolt: the flowing waters quickly hastened to the ocean, like cows hastening to their calves.

Impetuous as a bull, he quaffed the Soma juice: he drank the libation at the triple sacrifice. Maghavan took his shaft, the thunderbolt, and, with it, struck the first-born of the clouds.

Inasmuch, Indra, as thou hast divided the first-born of the clouds, thou hast destroyed the delusions of the deluders; and, then, engendering the sun, the dawn, the firmament, thou hast not left an enemy to oppose thee.

With his vast destroying thunderbolt, Indra struck the darkling mutilated Vritra. As the trunks of trees are felled by the ax, so lies Ahi, prostrate on the earth.

The arrogant Vritra, as if unequaled, defied Indra, the mighty hero, the destroyer of many, the scatterer of foes; he has not escaped the contact of the fate of Indra's enemies. The foe of Indra has crushed the banks of the rivers.

Having neither hand nor foot, he defied Indra, who struck him with the thunderbolt upon his mountainlike shoulder, like one emasculated who pretends to virility: then Vritra, mutilated of many members, slept.

The waters that delight the mind of men flow over him, recumbent on this earth, as a river bursts through its broken banks. Ahi has been prostrated beneath the feet of the waters, which Vritra, by his might, had obstructed.

The mother Vritra was bending over her son when Indra struck her nether part with his shaft. So the mother was above, and the son underneath; and Danu slept with her son, like a cow with its calf.

The waters carry off the nameless body of Vritra, tossed into the midst of the never-stopping, never-resting currents. The foe of Indra has slept through a long darkness.

The waters, the wives of the destroyer, guarded by Ahi, stood obstructed, like the cows by Pani: but, by slaying Vritra, Indra set open the cave that had confined them.

When the single resplendent Vritra returned the blow, Indra by the thunderbolt, thou becamest furious, like a horse's tail. Thou hast rescued the kine; thou hast won, hero, the Soma juice; thou hast let loose the seven rivers to flow.

Neither the lightning nor the thunder discharged by Vritra, nor the rain which he showered, nor the thunderbolt, harmed Indra when he and Ahi contended, and Maghavan triumphed, also over other attacks.

When fear entered, Indra, into thy heart, when about to slay Ahi, what other destroyer of him didst thou look for, that, alarmed, thou didst traverse ninety and nine streams, like a swift hawk?

Then Indra, the wielder of the thunderbolt, became the sovereign of all that is movable or immovable, of hornless and horned cattle; and as he abides the monarch of men, he comprehended all things within him; as the circumference comprehends the spokes of a wheel.

To Brahmanaspati

Rise up, Brahmanaspati,[4] Devoted to the gods, we solicit thee. Bounteous Maruts,[5] may he who praises you obtain wealth, yielding excellent steeds and eminent vigor.

May Brahmanaspati approach us: may the goddess, speaker of truth, approach us: may the gods drive away every adversary, and, present, conduct us to the sacrifice which is beneficial to aman, and abounds with respectably presented offerings.

He who presents to the ministrant wealth fit to be accepted enjoys inexhaustible abundance: for him we worship Ila, attended by brave warriors, inflicting much injury, receiving none.

Verily, Brahmanaspati proclaims the sacred prayer in which the divinities Indra, Varuna, Mitra, and Aryaman have made their abode.

Let us recite gods, that felicitous and faultless prayer at sacrifices. If you, leaders, desire to hear this prayer, then will all that is to be spoken reach unto you.

Who except Brahmanaspati may approach the man who is devoted to the gods, by whom the clipped sacred grass is spread? The giver of the oblation has proceeded, with the priests, to the hall of sacrifice; for he has a dwelling abounding, internally, with precious things.

Let Brahmanaspati concentrate his strength. Associated with the regal divinities, he slays the foe: in the time of danger, he maintains his station: armed with the thunderbolt, there is no encourager nor discourager of him, a great battle or a small.

To Surya, the Sun

His coursers bear on high the divine all-knowing Sun, that he may be seen by all the worlds.

At the approach of the all-illuminating Sun, the constellations depart, with the night, like thieves.

His illuminating rays behold men in succession, like a blazing fire.

Thou, Surya, outstrippest all in speed; thou art visible to all; thou art the source of light; thou shinest throughout the entire firmament.

Thou risest in the presence of the Maruts, thou risest in the presence of the whole region of heaven.

With that light with which thou, the purifier and defender from evil, lookest upon this creature-bearing world.

Thou traversest the vast ethereal space, measuring days and nights and contemplating all that have birth.

Divine and light-diffusing Surya, thy seven coursers bear thee, bright-haired, in thy ear.

The Sun has yoked the seven mares that safely draw his chariot, and comes with them self-harnessed.

Beholding the up-springing light above the darkness, we approach the divine Sun, among the gods, the excellent light.

Radiant with benevolent light, rising today, and mounting into the highest heaven, do thou, O Sun, remove the sickness of my heart and the yellowness of my body.

Let us transfer the yellowness of my body to the parrots, to the starlings, or to the Haritala tree.

This Aditya has risen with all his might, destroying my adversary; for I am unable to resist my enemy.

To the Maruts

Offer, Nodhas, earnest praise to the company of the Maruts, the senders of rain and ripeners of fruit, deserving of adoration. Composed, and with folded hands, I utter the praises conceived in my mind, which are efficacious in sacred rites and flow readily as the waters.

They were born, handsome and vigorous, from the sky, the sons of Rudra, the conquerors of their foes, pure from sin and purifying all, radiant as suns, powerful as evil spirits, diffusers of raindrops and of fearful forms.

Youthful Rudras, and undecaying, destructive of those who do not worship the gods, of unobstructed progress, and immovable as mountains, they are desirous of granting the wishes of the worshiper, and, by their strength, agitate all substances, whether of heaven or of earth.

They decorate their persons with various ornaments; they have placed, for elegance, brilliant garlands on their breasts; lances are borne upon their shoulders, and, with them and their own strength, have they been born, leaders, from the sky.

Enriching their worshiper, agitating the clouds, devourers of foes, they create the winds and lightnings by their power. The circumambient and agitating Maruts milk heavenly udders and sprinkle the earth with the water.

The munificent Maruts scatter the nutritious waters, as priests, at sacrifices, the clarified butter. As grooms lead forth a horse, they bring forth, for its rain, the fleet-moving cloud, and milk it, thundering and unexhausted.

Vast, possessed of knowledge, bright-shining, like mountains in stability, and quick in motion, you, like elephants, break down the forests when you put vigor into your ruddy mares.

The most wise Maruts roar like lions: the all-knowing are graceful as the spotted deer, destroying their foes, delighting their worshipers: of deadly strength in their anger, they come, with their antelopes and their arms, to defend the sacrificer against interruption.

Maruts, who are distinguished in troops, who are benevolent to men, who are heroes, and whose strength is deadly in your anger, you make heaven and earth resound [at your coming]; your [glory] sits in the seat-furnished chariots, conspicuous as [a beautiful] form, or as the lovely lightning.

The Maruts, who are all-knowing, combined with strength, loud-sounding, repellers of foes, of infinite prowess, whose weapon of offense is Indra, and who are leaders of men, hold in their hands the shaft.

Augmenters of rain, they drive, with golden wheels, the clouds asunder, as elephants in a herd break down the trees in their way. They are honored with sacrifices, visitants of the hall of offering, spontaneous assailers of their foes, subverters of what are stable, immovable themselves, and wearers of shining weapons.

We invoke, with praise, the foe-destroying, all-purifying, water-shedding, all-surveying band of Maruts, the offspring of Rudra. Priests, to obtain prosperity, have recourse to the dust-raising and powerful band of Maruts, receiving libations from sacred vessels and showering down benefits.

The man whom, Maruts, you defend, with your protection quickly surpasses all men in strength: with his horses, he acquires food, and with his men, riches: he performs the required worship; and he prospers.

Maruts, grant to your wealthy [worshipers, a son], eminent for good works, invincible in battle, illustrious, the annihilator of his adversaries, the seizer of wealth, the deserver of praise, and all-discerning. May we cherish such a son, and such a grandson, for a hundred winters.

Grant us, Maruts, durable riches, attended by posterity, and mortifying to our enemies—riches reckoned by hundreds and thousands, and ever increasing. May they who have acquired wealth by pious acts come hither, quickly, in the morning.

To Ushas, the Dawn, and to the Aswins

Ushas, the dawn, is the beautiful young girl who flings open the doors of the sky. Some mythologists also consider her the mother of the sun. The Aswins are possessors of horses, two handsome brothers who precede Aurora, probably personifications of Venus in her twin role of evening star and morning star. They are considered beneficient saviors.

These divinites of the morning have spread light over the world: they make manifest the light in the eastern portion of the firmament, brightening all things, like warriors burnishing their weapons: the radiant and progressing mothers of the earth, they travel daily on their course.

Their purple rays have readily shot upwards; they have yoked the easily yoked and ruddy kine to their ear; the deities of the dawn have restored, as of yore, the consciousness of sentient creatures, and, bright-rayed, have attended upon the glorious sun.

The female leaders of the morning illuminate with their inherent radiance the remotest parts of the heaven, with a simultaneous effort— like warriors with their shining arms, in the van of battle—bringing every kind of food to the performer of good works, to the bountiful, and to the worshiper who presents libations.

Ushas cuts off the accumulated gloom, as a barber cuts off the hair; she bares her bosom, as a cow yields her udder to the milker; and, as cattle hasten to their pastures, she speeds to the east, and, shedding light upon all the world, dissipates the darkness.

Her brilliant light is first seen toward the east: it spreads and disperses the thick darkness. She anoints her beauty, as the priests anoint the sacrificial food in sacrifices. The daughter of the sky awaits the glorious sun.

We have crossed over the boundary of darkness. Ushas restores the consciousness of living beings. Bright-shining, she smiles, like a flatterer, to obtain favor, and, lovely in all her radiance, she has swallowed, for our delight, the darkness.

The brilliant daughter of the sky, the exciter of pleasant voices, is praised by the descendants of Gotama. Ushas, grant us food, associated with progeny and dependants and distinguished by horses and cattle.

May I obtain, Ushas, that ample wealth which confers fame, posterity, troops of slaves, and is characterized by horses—which thou, who aboundest in riches and art the giver of food, displayest when gratified by hymns and holy sacrifices.

The divine Ushas, having lighted up the whole world, spreads, expanding with her radiance, toward the west, arousing all living creatures to their labors. She hears the speech of all endowed with thought.

The divine and ancient Ushas, born again and again, and bright with unchanging hues, wastes away the life of a mortal, like the wife of a hunter cutting up and dividing the birds.

She has been seen illuminating the boundaries of the sky, and driving into disappearance the spontaneously retiring night. Wearing away the ages of the human race, she shines with light, like the bride of the Sun. The affluent and adorable Ushas has sent her rays abroad—as a cowherd drives the cattle to pasture—and spreads, expansive, like flowing water. She is beheld associated with the rays of the sun, unimpeding sacred ceremonies.

Ushas, possessor of food, bring us that various wealth by which we may sustain sons and grandsons.

Luminous Ushas, possessor of cows and horses, true of speech, dawn here, today, upon this ceremony, that is to bring us wealth.

Possessor of food, Ushas, yoke, indeed, today, your purple steeds, and bring to us all good things.

Aswins, destroyers of foes, turn, with favorable intentions, your chariot toward our abode, which contains cattle and gold.

Aswins, who have sent adorable light from heaven to man, bring us strength.

May the steeds, awakened at dawn, bring hither, to drink the Soma juice, the divine Aswins—who are the givers of happiness, the destroyers of foes—seated in a golden chariot.

To Rudra

We offer these praises to the mighty Rudra[6] with the braided hair, the destroyer of heroes, in order that health may be enjoyed by bipeds and quadrupeds, and that all beings in this village may be well nourished and exempt from disease.

Be gracious to us, Rudra. Grant us happiness; for we worship the destroyer of heroes with oblations. And, by thy directions, Rudra, may we obtain that freedom from disease and exemption from dangers, which our progenitor, Manu, bestowed upon us, having obtained them from the gods.

Rudra, showerer of benefits, may we obtain, through our worship of the gods, the favor of thee, who art the destroyer of heroes. Come to our posterity, purposing to promote their happiness, while we, having our sons in safety, offer thee oblations.

We invoke, for our preservation, the illustrious Rudra, the accomplisher of sacrifices, the tortuous, the wise. May he remove far from us his celestial wrath; for we earnestly solicit his favor.

We invoke, from heaven, with reverence, him who has excellent food, who is radiant, and has braided hair, who is brilliant, and is to be ascertained by sacred study, holding in his hands excellent medicaments. May he grant us health, defensive armor, and a secure dwelling.

This praise, the sweetest of the sweet, and cause of increase to the reciter, is addressed to Rudra, the father of the Maruts. Immortal Rudra, grant us food sufficient for mortals, and bestow happiness on me, my son, and my grandson.

Injure not, Rudra, those amongst us who are old, or young, who are capable of begetting, or who are begotten, nor a father, nor a mother; nor afflict our precious persons.

Harm us not, Rudra, in our sons, or grandsons, or other male descendants, nor in our cattle, nor in our horses. Inflamed with anger, kill not our valiant men; for we, presenting clarified butter, perpetually invoke thee.

I restore to thee the praises derived from thee, as a shepherd returns his sheep to their owner. Father of the Maruts, bestow happiness upon me, Thy auspicious benignity is the cause of successive delight: therefore, we especially solicit thy protection.

Destroyer of heroes, may thy cow-killing or man-slaying weapon be far away; and let the felicity granted by thee be ours. Favor us! Speak, brilliant hero, in our behalf; and grant us, thou who art mighty over the two realms of heaven and earth, prosperity.

Desirous of protection, we have said: Reverence be to him. May Rudra, with the Maruts, hear our invocation: and may Mitra, Varuna, Aditi, ocean, earth, and heaven, be favorable to this our prayer.

To Vayu, the Wind

Let thy swift coursers, Vayu, bring thee quickly hither, that thou mayst be the first to drink; the first of the gods to drink of the Soma libation. May our upraised, discriminating, and sincere praise be acceptable to thy mind: come with thy steed-yoked ear for the libation to be presented to thee; come, Vayu, for granting the objects of our worship.

May the exhilarating drops of the libation exhilarate thee, Vayu, being fitly prepared, doing their office, administered opportunely, rendered efficacious by our praises, and flowing in the season: for which purpose thy docile and active steeds, the Niyuts, attending thy presence, bring thee to the sacrificial hall to accept the offering; to the sacrifice in which the pious priests represent their desires.

Vayu yokes to his ear his two red horses; Vayu yokes his purple steeds: Vayu yokes his two unwearied coursers to his ear to bear their burden; for most able are they to bear the burden. Arouse, Vayu, the intelligent sacrificer, as a gallant awakens his sleeping mistress: summon heaven and earth; light up the dawn; light up the dawn to receive thy sacrificial food.

For thee, the brilliant dawns, rising from afar, spread abroad their auspicious raiment in inviting rays, in variegated and glorious rays: for thee, the cow that yields ambrosia milks all kinds of treasure: thou begetest the Maruts, of the firmament, for the purpose of showering rain; for the purpose of replenishing the rivers.

For thee, the bright, pure, quick-flowing Soma juices, potent for exhilaration, are eager for the fire of oblation; are eager for the cloud-showering waters. The timid and anxious worshiper praises thee, who art auspicious, for driving away thieves, for thou defendest from all beings as the reward of our righteousness: thou protectest us from the fear of evil spirits, as the reward of our righteousness.

Thou Vayu, who art preceded by none, art entitled to drink first of these our libations: thou art entitled to drink of the effused juices, moreover, of all oblations and sin-offerings of men: for thee, their cattle yield milk; for thee they yield butter.

Agli Aditya

I present continually, with the ladle [of speech], these oblation-dropping hymns to the royal A'dityas: May Mitra, Aryaman, Bhaga, the multipresent Varuna, the powerful Ansa, hear us.

May those of equal exploits, Mitra, Aryaman, Varuna, be pleased today by this my praise; they who are A'dityas, luminous, purified by showers, who abandon none [that worship them], who are irreproachable, unassailable.

Those A'dityas, mighty, profound, unsubdued, subduing, many-eyed, behold the innermost thoughts of men, whether wicked or virtuous, whether far from or nigh to those royal deities.

The divine A'dityas are the upholders of all things, movable or immovable; the protectors of the universe; the provident in acts; the collection of rain; the possessors of veracity; the acquitters of our debts.

May I be conscious, A'dityas, of this your protection, the cause of happiness and security in danger; Aryaman, Mitra, and Varuna, may I, through your guidance, escape the sins which are like pitfalls in my path.

Aryaman, Mitra, and Varuna, easy is the path [you show us], and free from thorns, and pleasant; therefore, A'dityas, lead us by it: speak to us favorably, and grant us happiness difficult to be disturbed.

May Aditi, the mother of royal sons, place us beyond the malice of our enemies: may Aryaman lead us by easy paths, and may we, blessed with many descendants and safe from harm, attain the great happiness of Mitra and Varuna.

They uphold the three worlds, the three powerful ones, make manifest the desirable dwelling of the water to the water-seizing sun.

Let thy horses yoked to the chariot bring thee, Indra, the yellow-jawed, desiring [the sacrifice], to the vicinity of the worshipers; when thou, desiring the sacrifice prepared by the ten fingers, drinkest of the collected sweet-flavored Soma, let them bring thee to the battle.

Lord of horses, thou didst drink of previous libations, this sacrifice is for thee alone; exhilarate thyself, Indra, with the sweet Soma; showerer of copious rain, shower it into thy belly.

To Mitra

Mitra,[7] when praised, animates men to exertion: Indra sustains both the earth and heaven: Mitra looks upon men with unclosing eyes: offer to Mitra the oblations of clarified butter.

May that mortal enjoy abundance, Mitra, who presents thee, Aditya, [with offerings] at the sacred rite; protected by thee, he is not harmed; he is not overcome by any one; sin reaches him not, either from afar or nigh.

May we, exempt from disease, rejoicing in [abundant] food, roaming free over the wide [expanse of the] earth, diligent in the worship of Aditya, ever be in the good favor of Mitra.

This Mitra has been engendered adorable and to be served, the sovereign [over all], endowed with vigor, the creator [of the universe]; may we ever be in the good favor, in the auspicious approbation, of this adorable [Aditya].

The great Aditya, who animates men to exertion, is to be approached with reverence: he is the giver of happiness to him who praises him: offer with fire the acceptable libation of that most glorifiable Mitra.

Desirable food and most renowned wealth are [the gifts] of the divine Mitra, the supporter of man.

The renowned Mitra, who by his might presides over heaven, is he who presides over the earth by [the gift of] food.

The five classes of men have repaired to the victorious Mitra, for he supports all the gods.

Mitra is he who amongst gods and men bestows food as the reward of pious acts upon the man who has prepared [for him] the lopped sacred grass.

To Heaven and Earth

Vast and most excellent Heaven and Earth, be present with splendor at this [sacrifice, attracted] by sanctifying hymns; since that the showerer sounds everywhere with [his] heralds, the rapid [winds], passing through the two spacious and mighty [regions].

May the divine, adorable, benevolent, fertilizing, truthful, unoppressive Heaven and Earth, the leaders of sacrifice, whose sons are the gods, be present with the adorable gods [attracted] by sanctifying hymns.

Verily he was the doer of a good work in the regions, who generated these two, Heaven and Earth, and, firm of purpose, gave an impulse by his deed to the two vast, immovable, beautiful, unsupported worlds.

May Heaven and Earth, vast, universal, adorable, united in satisfaction, and disposed to give us food, protect us with our spacious dwellings, inhabited by our wives, and may we for our [pious] acts be possessed of chariots and slaves.

We offer earnest praise to you both, resplendent [Heaven and Earth]; we approach you who are pure, to offer adoration.

Mutually sanctifying [each other] of your own substance, you shine by your own power, and ever bear away the offering.

Mighty [Heaven and Earth], you fulfill the desires of your friend:

distributing food and giving sustenance, you have sat down at the sacrifice.

To Prthiví, the Earth[8]

Verily thou sustainest here, Prthiví, the fracture of the mountains: mighty and most excellent, thou art she who delightest the earth by thy greatness.

Wanderer in various ways, thy worshipers hymn thee with [sacred] songs; thee who, bright-hued, tossest the swollen [cloud] like a neighing horse.

Thou who, with solid earth, sustainest by thy strength the forest lords when the showers of thy cloud fall from the shining sky.

To Indra and the Cows[9]

May the Cows come and bring good fortune; let them lie down in [our] stalls and be pleased with us: may the many-colored kine here be prolific, and yield milk for Indra on many dawns.

Indra grants the desires of the man who offers to him sacrifice and praise; he ever bestows upon him wealth, and deprives him not of that which is his own: again and again increasing his riches, he places the devout man in an inaccessible fortress.

Let not the Cows be lost: let no thief carry them away: let no hostile weapon fall upon them: may the master of the cattle be long possessed of those with which he sacrifices, and which he presents to the gods.

Let not the dust-spurning [war]horse reach them; nor let them fall in the way of sacrificial consecration: let the cattle of the man who offers sacrifice wander about at large and without fear.

May the Cows be [for our] affluence: may Indra grant me cattle: may the Cows yield the food of the first libation: these Cows, oh men, are the Indra, the Indra whom I desire with heart and mind.

Do you, Cows, give us nourishment: render the emaciated, the unlovely body the reverse: do you, whose lowing is auspicious, make my dwelling prosperous: great is the abundance that is attributed to you in religious assemblies.

May you, Cows, have many calves grazing upon good pasture and drinking pure water at accessible ponds: may no thief be your master, no beast of prey [assail you], and may the [fatal] weapon of Rudra avoid you.

Let the nourishment of the Cows be solicited, let the vigor of the bull [be requested], Indra, for thy invigoration.

To Vishnu[10]

The mortal desirous of wealth quickly obtains it who presents [offerings] to the widely renowned Vishnu, who worships him with entirely devoted mind, who adores so great a benefactor of mankind.

Vishnu, granter of desires, show us that favorable disposition which is benevolent to all, unmixed [with exception], so that there may be to us the attainment of easily acquired, ample, steed-comprising, all-delighting riches.

This deity, by his great power, traversed with three [steps] the many-lustrous earth; may Vishnu, the most powerful of the powerful, rule over us, for illustrious is the name of the mighty one.

This Vishnu traversed the earth for a dwelling which he was desirous of giving to his eulogist; firm are the people who are his praisers; he who is the engenderer of good has made a spacious dwelling [for his worshipers].

Resplendent Vishnu, I, the master of the offering, knowing the objects that are to be known, glorify today thy name: I, who am feeble, praise thee who art powerful, dwelling in a remote region of this world.

What is to be proclaimed, Vishnu, of thee, when thou sayest, I am Sipivishta? Conceal not from us thy real form, although thou hast engaged under a different form in battle.

I offer, Vishnu, the oblation placed before thee with the exclamation Vashat; be pleased, Sipivishta, with my offering: may my laudatory hymns magnify thee; and do you [gods] ever cherish us with blessings.

Against Demons, Malign Spirits, and Witches

Indra and Soma,[11] afflict, destroy the Rakshasas; showerers [of benefits] cast down those who delight in darkness; put to flight the stupid [spirits]; consume, slay, drive away, utterly exterminate the cannibals.

Indra and Soma, fall upon the destructive [Rakshasa] and the performer of unprofitable acts, so that, consumed [by your wrath], he may perish like the offering cast into the fire; retain implacable hatred to the hater of Brahmans, the cannibal, the hideous, the vile [Rakshasa].

Indra and Soma, chastise the malignant [Rakshasas], having plunged them in surrounding and inextricable darkness, so that not one of them may again issue from it: so may your wrathful might be triumphant over them.

Indra and Soma, display from heaven your fatal [weapon], the extirpator from earth of the malignant [Rakshasas]: put forth from the clouds the consuming [thunderbolt], wherewith you slay the increasing Rakshas race.

Indra and Soma, scatter around [your weapons] from the sky, pierce their sides with fiery scorching adamantine [weapons], so that they may depart without a sound.

May this praise invest you, Indra and Soma, who are mighty, on every side, as a girth [encompasses] a horse—that praise which I offer to you both with pure devotion: do you, like two kings, accept this my homage.

Come with rapid steeds, slay the oppressive mischievous Rakshasas: let there be no happiness, Indra and Soma, to the malignant, who harasses us with his oppression.

May he who with false calumnies maligns me behaving with a pure heart, may such a speaker of falsehood, Indra, cease to be, like water held in the hand.

May Soma give to the serpent, or toss upon the lap of Nirriti, those who with designing [accusations] persecute me, a speaker of sincerity, and those who by spiteful [calumnies] vilify all that is good in me.

May he, Agni, who strives to destroy the essence of our food, of our horses, of our cattle, of our bodies—the adversary, the thief, the robber —go to destruction, and be deprived both of person and of progeny.

May he be deprived of bodily [existence] and of posterity; may he be cast down below all the three worlds; may his reputation, Gods, be blighted who seeks our destruction by day or by night.

To the understanding man there is perfect discrimination, the words of truth and falsehood are mutually at variance; of these two, Soma verily cherishes that which is true and right: he destroys the false.

Soma instigates not the wicked; he instigates not the strong man dealing in falsehood: he destroys the Rakshasa, he destroys the speaker of untruth; and both remain in the bondage of Indra.

If I am one following false gods, if I approach the gods in vain, then Agni [punish me]. If [we be not such, then] why, Játavedas, art thou angry with us? Let the utterers of falsehood incur thy chastisement.

May I this day die if I am a spirit of ill, or if I have ever injured the life of any man: mayest thou be deprived [Rálsjasa] of thy ten sons, who hast falsely called me by such an appellation.

May Indra slay with his mighty weapon him who calls me the Yátudhána, which I am not—the Rakshasa, who says [of himself], I am pure: may he, the vilest of all beings, perish.

May the cruel female fiend who, throwing off the concealment of her person, wanders about at night like an owl, fall headlong down into the unbounded caverns: may the stones that grind the Soma destroy the Rakshasas by their noise.

Stay, Maruts, amongst the people, desirous [of protecting them]; seize the Rakshasas, grind them to pieces: whether they fly about like birds by night or whether they have offered obstruction to the sacred sacrifice.

Hurl, Indra, thy thunderbolt from heaven; sanctify, Maghavan, [the worshiper] sharpened by the Soma beverage: slay with the thunderbolt the Rakshasas, on the east, on the west, on the south, on the north.

They advance, accompanied by dogs: desirous to destroy him, they assail the indomitable Indra: Sakra whets his thunderbolt for the miscreants; quickly let him hurl the bolt upon the fiends.

Indra has ever been the discomfiter of the evil spirits coming to obstruct [the rites of] the offerers of oblations: Sakra advances, crushing the present Rakshasas, as a hatchet cuts down [the trees of] a forest, as [a mallet smashes] the earthen vessels.

Destroy the evil spirit, whether in the form of an owl or of an owlet, of a dog or of a duck, of a hawk or of a vulture; slay the Rakshasas, Indra [with the thunderbolt] as with a stone.

Let not the Rakshasas do us harm: let the dawn drive away the pairs of evil spirits, exclaiming, "What now is this?" May the earth protect us from terrestrial, the firmament protect us from celestial, wickedness.

Slay, Indra, the Yátudhána, whether in the form of a man or of a woman doing mischief by her deceptions; may those who sport in murder perish decapitated; let them not behold the rising sun.

Soma, do thou and Indra severally watch [the Rakshasas], be wary, be vigilant, hurl the thunderbolt at the malignant Rakshasas.

To the Waters[12]

[Honored] by adoration, let the advancing Soma approach the celestial waters like the celerity of the mind: offer abundant [sacrificial] food and perfect praise for the sake of Mitra and Varuna, and for [Indra] the rapid mover.

Priests, since you are charged with the libation, desiring [to present it], proceed to the waters desiring [to receive it], to those [waters] which the red hawk beholds descending [from the clouds]: do you, dextrous-handed [priests], cast today that flood [of Soma] into [the consecrated water].

Go, priests, to the water, to the reservoir; worship the grandson of the waters with oblations: may he today give you the consecrated water, and do you pour forth to him the sweet-flavored Soma.

[He] who shines, without fuel, in the midst of the waters, he whom the pious worship at sacrifices; grandson of the waters, give us those sweet waters by which [mixed with the Soma-juice], Indra is elevated to heroism.

Those waters with which Soma sports and delights as a man [sports] with elegant young damsels: do thou, priest, approach to obtain them: when thou sprinklest them [in libation], purify [them with the filter] along with the plants [the Soma].

Verily, as young damsels welcome a youth, when desiring [them], he comes to them desiring [him], so the priests and their praise and the divine waters agree in mind and contemplate [their mutual assistance].

Present, waters, the sweet-flavored god-exhilarating mixture to that Indra who has made an issue for you when enveloped [by the clouds]; who has liberated you from a great calamity.

Send forth, rivers, the sweet-flavored beverage to him who is your germ, a well of the sweet [Soma-juice], that beverage which is mixed with butter adorable at sacrifices: hear, opulent waters, my invocation.

Send, rivers, [to our sacrifice] that exhilarating wave, the beverage of Indra, which sends us both [kinds of fruit], exciting exhilaration, desirous [of mixing with the Soma], generated in the firmament; spreading through the three [worlds], flowing [amidst the vessels of sacrifice], a well [of satisfaction to the gods].

Praise, Rishi, the waters like [those] of the cloud-warring Indra, falling in many showers, returning, flowing to mix [with the Soma], the mothers of the world and its protectresses, augmenting and combining [with the Soma].

Direct our sacrifice to the worship of the gods; direct our adoration to the acquirement of wealth; open the udder on the occasion of [this] rite; be to us, waters, the givers of felicity.

Opulent waters, you rule over riches; you support good fortune, pious rites, and immortality; you are the protectresses of wealth and of offspring: may Saraswati bestow all this opulence on him who praises you.

I behold you, waters, coming to [the sacrifice], conveying the butter, the water, the sweet [Soma-juices]: conversing mentally with the priests, and bringing the well-effused Soma for Indra.

These opulent and life-sustaining [waters] have come [to my sacrifice]: friendly priests, make them sit down; place them on the sacred grass, ye offerers of the Soma, conversing with the grandson of the waters.

The waters desiring [it] have come to this sacred grass, and wishing to satisfy the gods, have sat down at our sacrifice: express, priests, the Soma for Indra; to you the worship of the gods is easy.

In Praise of Herbs

I think of the hundred and seven applications of the brown-tinted plants, which are ancient, being generated for the gods before the three ages.

Mothers [of mankind] a hundred are your applications, a thousand-fold is your growth; do you who fulfill a hundred functions make this my [people] free from disease.

Rejoice, plants, bearing abundant flowers and fruit, triumphing together [over disease] like [victorious] horses, sprouting forth, bearing [men safe] beyond [disease].

"Plants!" thus I hail you, the divine mothers [of mankind]. I will give to thee, oh physician, a horse, a cow, a garment—yea, even myself.

Your abode is in the Aswattha, your dwelling is established in the Palása, you are assuredly the distributers of cattle, inasmuch as you bestow them on the physician.

Where, plants, you are congregated like princes [assembled] in battle, there the sage is designated a physician, the destroyer of evil spirits, the extirpator of disease.

The Aswavatí, the Somavatí, the Úrjayantí, the Udojasa—all these plants I praise for the purpose of overcoming this disease.

The virtues of the plants which are desirous of bestowing wealth issue from them, man, [toward] thy body like cattle from the pen.

Verily Ishkriti is your mother, therefore are you [also] Nishkritis; you are flying streams; if [a man] is ill, you cure him.

The universal all-pervading plants assail [diseases] as a thief [attacks] a cowshed; they drive out whatever infirmity of body there may be.

As soon as I take these plants in my hand, making [the sick man] strong, the soul of the malady perishes before [their application] as [life is driven away from the presence] of the seizer of life.

From him, oh plants, in whom you creep from limb to limb, from joint to joint, you drive away disease like a mighty [prince] stationed in the midst of his host.

Fly forth, sickness, with the jay, with the blue jay, with the velocity of the wind, perish along with the iguana.

Let each of you, plants, go to the other, approach the one [to the vicinity] of the other; thus being all mutually joined together, attend to this my speech.

Whether bearing fruit or barren, whether flowering or flowerless, may they, the progeny of Brihaspati, liberate us from sin.

May they liberate me from the sin produced by curse, from the sin caused by Varuna, from the fetters of Yama, from all guilt caused by the gods.

The plants, falling from heaven, said, "The man, whom living we pervade, will not perish."

The plants which have the Soma for their king, and are numerous and all-seeing, of them thou [O Soma-plant] are the best; be very bountiful to the affectionate heart.

Plants, which have the Soma for your king, who are scattered over the earth, the offspring of Brihaspati, give vigor to this [infirm body].

Let not the digger hurt you, nor [the sick person] for whom I dig you up; may all my bipeds and quadrupeds be free from disease.

Both the plants that hear this [prayer], and those which are removed far off, all coming together, give vigor to this [infirm body].

All the plants, together with Soma their king, declare, "We save him, O King, to whom the Brahman administers [us]."

Thou [Soma] art the best of the plants, to thee [all] trees are prostrate; may he be prostrate to us, who attacks us.

To Indra and the Maruts

The circumstationed [inhabitants of the three worlds] associate with [Indra], the mighty [Sun], the indestructive [fire], the moving [wind], and the lights that shine in the sky.

They [the charioteers] harness to his car his two desirable coursers, placed on either hand, bay-colored, high-spirited, chief-bearing.

Mortals, you owe your [daily] birth [to such an Indra], who, with the rays of the morning, gives sense to the senseless, and, to the formless, form.

Thereafter, verily, those who bear names invoked in holy rites [the Maruts], having seen the rain about to be engendered, instigated him to resume his embryo condition [in the clouds].

Associated with the conveying Maruts, the traversers of places difficult of access, thou, Indra, hast discovered the cows hidden in the cave.

The reciters of praises praise the mighty [troop of Maruts], who are celebrated and conscious of the power of bestowing wealth, in like manner as they [glorify] the counselor [Indra].

May you be seen, Maruts, accompanied by the undaunted Indra; [both] rejoicing, and of equal splendor.

This rite is performed in adoration of the powerful Indra, along with the irreproachable, heavenward-tending, and amiable bands [of the Maruts].

Therefore, circumambient [troop of Maruts], come hither, whether from the region of the sky or from the solar sphere; for in this rite [the priest] fully recites your praises.

We invoke Indra—whether he come from this earthly region, or from the heaven above, or from the vast firmament—that he may give [us] wealth.

Oblation to the Sun for the Cure of Paralysis

According to a Brahman legend, some demons, called *kalanga* built an altar to serve as a stairway to heaven, but were hurled to the depths below by Indra. During the fall, two of them escaped and were taken into heaven as celestial dogs, probably representing the sun and moon. However, some scholars believe they represent the galaxies and stars in general.

Through the air he flies, looking down upon all beings: with the majesty of the heavenly dog, with that oblation would we pay homage to thee!

The three kâlakânga that are fixed upon the sky like gods, all these I have called for help, to render this person exempt from injury.

In the waters is thy origin, upon the heavens thy home, in the middle of the sea, and upon the earth thy greatness. With the majesty of the heavenly dog, with that oblation would we pay homage to thee!

For Health and Long Life

This hymn, intended to tie the individual life to the cosmic life, belongs to the ritual initiating a young *arya* into the Brahman community. The first part indicates the principles of separation, and the second, the principles of identification and unity.

The gods are free from decrepitude; thou, O Agni, art removed from the demon of hostility. I free thee from all evil and disease, [and] unite thee with life.

[Vayu], the purifying [wind], shall free thee from misfortune, Sakra [Indra] from evil sorcery! I free thee from all evil and disease, [and] unite thee with life.

The tame [village] animals are separate from the wild [forest animals]; the water has flowed apart from thirst. I free thee from all evil and disease, [and] unite thee with life.

Heaven and earth here go apart; the paths go in every direction. I free thee from all evil and disease, [and] unite thee with life.

"Tvashtar is preparing a wedding for his daughter," thus [saying] does this whole world pass through. I free thee from all evil and disease, [and] unite thee with life.

Agni unites [life's] breaths, the moon is united with [life's] breath. I free thee from all evil and disease, [and] unite thee with life.

By means of [life's] breath the gods aroused the everywhere mighty sun. I free thee from all evil and disease, [and] unite thee with life.

Live thou by the [life's] breath of them that have life, and that create life; do not die! I free thee from all evil and disease, [and] unite thee with life.

Breathe thou with the [life's] breath of those that breathe; do not die! I free thee from all evil and disease, [and] unite thee with life.

Do thou [rise] up with life, unite thyself with life, [rise] up with the sap of the plants! I free thee from all evil and disease, [and] unite thee with life.

From the rain of Parganya we have risen up, immortal. I free thee from all evil and disease, [and] unite thee with life.

Against Sorcerers and Demons

May this oblation carry hither the sorcerers, as a river [carries] foam! The man or the woman who has performed this [sorcery], that person shall here proclaim himself!

This vaunting [sorcerer] has come hither: receive him with alacrity! O Brihaspati, put him into subjection; O Agni and Soma, pierce him through!

Slay the offspring of the sorcerer, O soma-drinking [Indra], and subject [him]! Make drop out the farther and the nearer eye of the braggart [demon]!

Wherever, O Agni Gâtavedas, thou perceivest the brood of these hidden devourers [atrin], do thou, mightily strengthened by our charm, slay them: slay their [brood], O Agni, piercing them a hundredfold!

Imprecation Against Enemies Thwarting Holy Work

This formula accompanies an enchantment which is carried out by following the footprints of the person who is to be struck down. It has also been interpreted as a hymn to accompany a trial by fire, a kind of judgment of God.

Heaven and earth, the broad atmosphere, the goddess of the field, and the wonderful far-striding [Vishnu]; moreover, the broad atmosphere guarded by Vâta [the wind]: may these here be inflamed when I am inflamed!

Hear this, O ye revered gods! Let Bharadvâga recite for me songs of praise! May he who injures this our plan be bound in the fetter [of disease] and joined to misfortune!

Hear, O soma-drinking Indra, what with burning heart I shout to thee! I cleave, as one cleaves a tree with an ax, him that injures this our plan.

With [the aid of] thrice eighty sâman-singers, with [the aid of] the Adityas, Vasus, and Angiras—may our father's sacrifices and gifts to the priests aid us—do I seize this one with fateful fervor.

May heaven and earth look after me, may all the gods support me! O ye Angiras, O ye fathers devoted to Soma, may he who does harm enter into misfortune!

He who perchance despises us, O ye Maruts, he who abuses the holy practice which is being performed by us, may his evil deeds be firebrands to him, may the heavens surround with fire the hater of holy practices!

Thy seven in-breathings and thy eight marrows, these do I cut for thee by means of my charm. Thou shalt go to the seat of Yama, fitly prepared, with Agni as thy guide!

I set thy footstep upon the kindled fire. May Agni surround thy body, may thy voice enter into breath!

Charm to Obtain a Husband

This hymn is accompanied by the following instructions: "In reciting the hymn the girl eats a preparation of rice and sesame. On an altar of clay that has come from a cavern inhabited by animals, the offerings of gold, bdellium, etc., are laid out. Then they are oiled with butter and presented at the doorstep of the young girl's house. After making a nocturnal sacrifice of rice and barley in a copper vase to Gami, the goddess of maternity, the girl withdraws and rubs herself with fat."

May, O Agni, a suitor after our own heart come to us, may he come to this maiden with our fortune! May she, agreeable to suitors, charming at festivals, promptly obtain happiness through a husband!

Agreeable to Soma, agreeable to Brahma, arranged by Aryaman, with the unfailing certainty of god Dhâtar, do I bestow upon thee good fortune, the acquisition of a husband.

This woman shall obtain a husband, since king Soma makes her lovely! May she, begetting sons, become a queen; may she, going to her husband, shine in loveliness!

As this comfortable cave, O Maghavan [Indra], furnishing a safe abode, hath become pleasing to animals, thus may this woman be a favorite of fortune [Bhaga], beloved, not at odds with her husband!

Do thou ascend the full, inexhaustible ship of Bhaga [fortune]; upon this bring hither the suitor who shall be agreeable [to thee]!

Bring hither by thy shouts, O lord of wealth, the suitor, bend his mind toward her; turn thou the right side of every agreeable suitor toward [her]!

This gold and bdellium, this balsam, and Bhaga [fortune], too; these have prepared thee for husbands, that thou mayest obtain the one that is agreeable.

Hither to thee Savitar shall lead the husband that is agreeable! Do thou, O herb, bestow [him] upon her!

Prayer at the Election of a King

This prayer is used in the ritual restoration of a king who had been deposed by a usurper or conqueror.

[Thy] kingdom hath come to thee: arise, endowed with luster! Go forth as the lord of the people, rule [shine] thou, a universal ruler! All the regions of the compass shall call thee, O king; attended and revered be thou here!

Thee the clans, thee these regions, goddesses five, shall choose for empire! Root thyself upon the height, the pinnacle of royalty: then do thou, mighty, distribute goods among us!

Thy kinsmen with calls shall come to thee; agile Agni shall go with them as messenger! Thy wives, thy sons shall be devoted to thee; being a mighty [ruler], thou shalt behold rich tribute!

The Asvins first, Mitra and Varuna both, all the gods, and the Maruts, shall call thee! Then fix thy mind upon the bestowal of wealth, then do thou, mighty, distribute wealth among us!

Hither hasten forth from the farthest distance; heaven and earth, both, shall be propitious to thee! Thus did this king Varuna [as if, "the chooser"] decree that; he himself did call thee: "Come thou higher!"

O Indra, Indra, come thou to the tribes of men, for thou hast agreed, concordant with the Varunas [as if, "the electors"]. He did call thee to thy own domain [thinking]: "Let him revere the gods, and manage, too, the people!"

The rich divinities of the roads, of manifold diverse forms, all coming together have given thee a broad domain. They shall all concordantly call thee; rule here, a mighty, benevolent [king], up to the tenth decade [of thy life]!

From the Ritual for Kings: Prayer for Glory

The oblation that yields glory, sped on by Indra, of thousandfold strength, well offered, prepared with might, shall prosper! Cause me, that offers the oblation, to continue long beholding [light], and to rise to supremacy!

[That he may come] to us, let us honor with obeisance glory-owning Indra, the glorious one with glory-yielding [oblations]! Do thou [the oblation] grant us sovereignty sped on by Indra; may we in thy favor be glorious!

Glorious was Indra born, glorious Agni, glorious Soma. Glorious, of all beings the most glorious, am I.

Prayer at the Building of a House

This hymn belongs to the complex ritual accompanying the construction of a new house. The central pillar is coated with butter, and as it is raised, the following is recited.

Right here do I erect a firm house: may it stand upon a [good] foundation, dripping with ghee! Thee may we inhabit, O house, with heroes all, with strong heroes, with uninjured heroes!

Right here, do thou, O house, stand firmly, full of horses, full of cattle, full of abundance! Full of sap, full of ghee, full of milk, elevate thyself unto great happiness!

A supporter art thou, O house, with broad roof, containing purified grain! To thee may the calf come, to thee the child, to thee the milch cows when they return in the evening!

May Savitar, Vayu, Indra, Brihaspati, cunningly erect this house! May the Maruts sprinkle it with moisture and with ghee; may king Bhaga let our plowing take root!

O mistress of dwelling, as a sheltering and kindly goddess thou wast erected by the gods in the beginning; clothed in grass, be thou kindly disposed; give us, moreover, wealth along with heroes!

Do thou, O crossbeam, according to regulation ascend the post, do thou, mightily ruling, hold off the enemies! May they that approach thee reverently, O house, not suffer injury, may we with all our heroes live a hundred autumns!

Hither to this [house] hath come the tender child, hither the calf along with [the other] domestic animals; hither the vessel [full] of liquor, together with bowls of sour milk!

Carry forth, O woman, this full jar, a stream of ghee mixed with ambrosia! Do thou these drinkers supply with ambrosia; the sacrifice and the gifts [to the Brahmans] shall it [the house] protect!

These waters, free from disease, destructive of disease, do I carry forth. The chambers do I enter in upon together with the immortal Agni [fire].

A Merchant's Prayer

Indra, the merchant, do I summon: may he come to us, may he be our van; driving away the demon of grudge, the waylayers, and wild beasts, may he, the possessor, bestow wealth upon me!

May the many paths, the roads of the gods, which come together between heaven and earth, gladden me with milk and ghee, so that I may gather in wealth from my purchases!

Desirous do I, O Agni, with firewood and ghee offer oblations [to thee] for success and strength; according to ability praising [thee] with my prayer, do I sing this divine song, that I may gain a hundredfold!

[Pardon, O Agni, this sin of ours (incurred upon) the far road which we have traveled!] May our purchases and our sales be successful for us; may what I get in barter render me a gainer! May ye two [Indra and Agni], in accord, take pleasure in this oblation! May our transactions and the accruing gain be auspicious to us!

The wealth with which I go to purchase, desiring, ye gods, to gain wealth through wealth, may Indra, Pragâpati, Savitar, Soma, Agni, place luster into it for me!

We praise with reverence thee, O priest [Agni] Vaisvânara. Do thou over our children, selves, cattle, and life's breath watch!

Daily, never failing, shall we bring [oblations to thee], O Gâtavedas, [as if fodder] to a horse standing [in the stable]. In growth of wealth and nutriment rejoicing, may we, O Agni, thy neighbors, not take harm!

Expiatory Formula for Sins

This hymn was used for various occasions, such as the expiatory rite at the death of a teacher, the discharging of debts, the death of a creditor, and the purification ceremonies of granaries.

From the sins which knowingly or unknowingly we have committed, do ye, all gods, of one accord, release us!

If awake, or if asleep, to sin inclined, I have committed a sin, may what has been, and what shall be, as if from a wooden post—release me!

As one released from a wooden post, as one in a sweat by bathing [is cleansed] of filth, as ghee is clarified by the sieve, may all [the gods] clear me from sin!

Prayer for Heaven After Remission of Sins

If air or earth and heaven, if mother or father we have injured, may this Agni Gârhapatya [household fire] without fail lead us out from this [crime] to the world of well-doing!

The earth is our mother; Aditi [the universe], our kin; the air, our protector from hostile schemes. May father sky bring prosperity to us from the world of the Fathers; may I come to my [departed] kin, and not lose heaven!

In that bright world where our pious friends live in joy, having cast aside the ailments of their own bodies, free from lameness, not deformed in limb, there may we behold our parents and our children!

Hymn to Goddess Earth

One of a series of marvelous cosmic and theosophic hymns of the Atharvan; it is fresher than any of the others, since it is free from that doctrinal and theological artificiality which one too often finds in Vedic poems. Its ritual use was quite frequent, particularly in the *âgrahâyanî* ceremonies dedicated to the serpent cult, in the *dridhikarmani* ceremonies giving stability to houses, villages, etc., and in the expiatory rites following earthquakes. Certain stanzas of the hymn, and particularly those referring to "fragrance," were used during the ceremonies bearing the name *gandhapravâdâh*, at which time the kings were rubbed with fragrant substances.

Truth, greatness, universal order [rita], strength, consecration, creative fervor [tapas], spiritual exaltation [Brahma], the sacrifice, support the earth. May this earth, the mistress of that which was and shall be, prepare for us a broad domain!

The earth that has heights, and slopes, and great plains, that supports the plants of manifold virtue, free from the pressure that comes from the midst of men, she shall spread out for us, and fit herself for us!

The earth upon which the sea and the rivers and the waters, upon which food and the tribes of men have arisen, upon which this breathing, moving life exists, shall afford us precedence in drinking!

The earth whose are the four regions of space, upon which food and the tribes of men have arisen, which supports the manifold breathing, moving things, shall afford us cattle and other possessions also!

The earth upon which the old, the first, men unfolded themselves, upon which the gods overcame the Asuras,[13] shall procure for us [all] kinds of cattle, horses, and fowls, good fortune and glory!

The earth that supports all, furnishes wealth, the foundation, the golden-breasted resting place of all living creatures, she that supports Agni Vaisvânara [the fire], and mates with Indra, the bull, shall furnish us with property!

The broad earth, which the sleepless gods ever attentively guard, shall milk for us precious honey, and, morever, besprinkle us with glory!

That earth which formerly was water upon the ocean [of space], which the wise [seers] found out by their skillful devices; whose heart is in the highest heaven, immortal, surrounded by truth, shall bestow upon us brilliancy and strength, [and place us] in supreme sovereignty!

That earth upon which the attendant waters jointly flow by day and night, unceasingly, shall pour out milk for us in rich streams, and, moreover, besprinkle us with glory!

The earth which the Asvins have measured, upon which Vishnu has stepped out, which Indra, the lord of might, has made friendly to himself; she, the mother, shall pour forth milk for me, the son!

Thy snowy mountain heights, and thy forests, O earth, shall be kind to us! The brown, the black, the red, the multicolored, the firm earth, that is protected by Indra, I have settled upon, not supressed, not slain, not wounded.

Into thy middle set us, O earth, and into thy navel, into the nourishing strength that has grown up from thy body; purify thyself for us! The earth is the mother, and I the son of the earth; Parganya is the father; he, too, shall save us!

The earth upon which they [the priests] enclose the altar [vedi], upon which they, devoted to all [holy] works, unfold the sacrifice, upon which are set up, in front of the sacrifice, the sacrificial posts, erect and brilliant, that earth shall prosper us, herself prospering!

Him that hates us, O earth, him that battles against us, him that is hostile toward us with his mind and his weapons, do thou subject to us, anticipating [our wish] by deed!

The mortals born of thee live on thee, thou supportest both bipeds and quadrupeds. Thine, O earth, are these five races of men, the mortals, upon whom the rising sun sheds undying light with his rays.

These creatures all together shall yield milk for us; do thou, O earth, give us the honey of speech!

Upon the firm, broad earth, the all-begetting mother of the plants, that is supported by [divine] law, upon her, propitious and kind, may we ever pass our lives!

A great gathering place, thou, great [earth], hast become; great haste, commotion, and agitation are upon thee. Great Indra protects thee unceasingly. Do thou, O earth, cause us to brighten as if at the sight of gold: not any one shall hate us!

Agni [fire] is in the earth, in the plants, the waters hold Agni, Agni is in the stones; Agni is within men, Agnis [fires] are within cattle, within horses.

Agni glows from the sky, to Agni, the god, belongs the broad air. The mortals kindle Agni, the bearer of oblations, that loveth ghee.

The earth, clothed in Agni, with dark knees, shall make me brilliant and alert!

Upon the earth men give to the gods the sacrifice, the prepared oblation; upon the earth mortal men live pleasantly by food. May this earth give us breath and life, may she cause me to reach old age!

The fragrance, O earth, that has arisen upon thee, which the plants and the waters hold, which the Gandharvas and Apsaras have partaken of, with that make me fragrant: not anyone shall hate us!

That fragrance of thine which has entered into the lotus, that fragrance, O earth, which the immortals of yore gathered up at the marriage of Surya, with that make me fragrant: not anyone shall hate us!

That fragrance of thine which is in men, the loveliness and charm that is in male and female, that which is in steeds and heroes, that which is in the wild animals with trunks [elephants], the luster that is in the maiden, O earth, with that do thou blend us: not anyone shall hate us!

The earth, upon whom the forest-sprung trees ever stand firm, the all-nourishing compact earth do we invoke.

Rising or sitting, standing or walking, may we not stumble with our right or left foot upon the earth!

To the pure earth I speak, to the ground, the soil that has grown through the Brahma [spiritual exaltation]. Upon thee, that holdest nourishment, prosperity, food, and ghee, we would settle down, O earth!

Purified, the waters shall flow for our bodies; what flows off from us, that do we deposit upon him we dislike; with a purifier, O earth, do I purify myself!

Thy easterly regions, and thy northern, thy southerly [regions], O earth, and thy western, shall be kind to me as I walk [upon thee]! May I that have been placed into the world not fall down!

Do not drive us from the west, nor from the east; not from the north, and not from the south! Security be thou for us, O earth: waylayers shall not find us, hold far away [their] murderous weapon!

As long as I look out upon thee, O earth, with Surya [the sun] as my companion, so long shall my sight not fail, as year followeth upon year!

When, as I lie, I turn upon my right or left side, O earth; when stretched out we lie with our ribs upon thee, pressing against [us], do not, O earth, that liest close to everything, there injure us!

What, O earth, I dig out of thee, quickly shall that grow again: may I not, O pure one, pierce thy vital spot, [and] not thy heart!

Thy summer, O earth, thy rainy season, thy autumn, winter, early spring, and spring; thy decreed yearly seasons, thy days and nights shall yield us milk!

The pure earth that starts in fright away from the serpent, upon whom were the fires that are within the waters, she that delivers [to destruction] the blasphemous Dasyus, she that takes the side of Indra, not of Vritra, [that earth] adheres to Sakra [mighty Indra], the lusty bull.

Upon whom rests the sacrificial hut [sadas] and the [two] vehicles that hold the soma [havirdhâne], in whom the sacrificial post is fixed, upon whom the Brahmanas praise [the gods] with riks and sâmans, knowing [also] the yagur-formulas; upon whom the serving-priests [ritvig] are employed so that Indra shall drink the soma;

Upon whom the seers of yore, that created the beings, brought forth with their songs the cows, they the seven active [priests], by means of the satra-offerings, the sacrifices, and [their] creative fervor [tapas];

May this earth point out to us the wealth that we crave; may Bhaga [fortune] add his help, may Indra come here as [our] champion!

The earth upon whom the noisy mortals sing and dance, upon whom they fight, upon whom resounds the roaring drum, shall drive forth our enemies, shall make us free from rivals!

To the earth upon whom are food, and rice and barley, upon whom live these five races of men, to the earth, the wife of Parganya, that is fattened by rain, be reverence!

The earth upon whose ground the citadels constructed by the gods unfold themselves, every region of her that is the womb of all, Pragâpati shall make pleasant for us!

The earth that holds treasures manifold in secret places, wealth, jewels, and gold shall she give to me; she that bestows wealth liberally, the kindly goddess, wealth shall she bestow upon us!

The earth that holds people of manifold varied speech, of different customs, according to their habitations, as a reliable milch cow that does not kick, shall she milk for me a thousand streams of wealth!

The serpent, the scorpion with thirsty fangs, that hibernating torpidly lies upon thee; the worm, and whatever living thing, O earth, moves in the rainy season, shall, when it creeps, not creep upon us: with what is auspicious [on thee] be gracious to us!

Thy many paths upon which people go, thy tracks for chariots and wagons to advance, upon which both good and evil men proceed, this road, free from enemies, and free from thieves, may we gain: with what is auspicious [on thee] be gracious to us!

The earth holds the fool and holds the wise, endures that good and bad dwell [upon her]; she keeps company with the boar, gives herself up to the wild hog.

Thy forest animals, the wild animals homed in the woods, the man-eating lions and tigers that roam; the ula, the wolf, mishap, injury [rikshîkâ], and demons [rakshasas], O earth, drive away from us!

The Gandharvas, the Apsaras, the Arâyas and Kimîdins; the Pisâkas and all demons [rakshasas], these, O earth, hold from us!

The earth upon whom the biped birds fly together, the flamingos, eagles, birds of prey, and fowls; upon whom Mâtarisvan, the wind, hastens, raising the dust and tossing the trees—as the wind blows forth and back, the flame bursts after;

The earth upon whom day and night jointly, black and bright, have been decreed, the broad earth covered and enveloped with rain, shall kindly place us into every pleasant abode!

Heaven and earth and air have here given me expanse; Agni, Surya, the waters, and all the gods together have given me wisdom.

Mighty am I, "Superior" [uttara] by name, upon the earth, conquering am I, all-conquering, completely conquering every region.

At that time, O goddess, when, spreading [prathamânâ] forth, named [prithiví, "broad"] by the gods, thou didst extend to greatness, then prosperity did enter thee, [and] thou didst fashion the four regions.

In the villages and in the wilderness, in the assembly halls that are upon the earth; in the gatherings and in the meetings, may we hold forth agreeably to thee!

As dust a steed did she, as soon as she was born, scatter these people, that dwelt upon the earth, she the lovely one, the leader, the guardian of the world, that holds the trees and plants.

The words I speak, honeyed do I speak them: the things I see, they furnish me with. Brilliant I am, and alert: the others that rush [against me] do I beat down.

Gentle, fragrant, kindly, with the sweet drink [kîlâla] in her udder, rich in milk, the broad earth together with [her] milk shall give us courage!

She whom Visvakarman [the creator of all] did search out by means of oblations, when she had entered the surging [flood of the] atmosphere, she, the vessel destined to nourish, deposited in a secret place, became visible [to the gods] and the [heavenly] mothers.

Thou art the scatterer of men, the broadly expanding Aditi that yields milk according to wish. What is wanting in thee Pragâpati, firstborn of the divine order [rita], shall supply for thee!

Thy laps, O earth, free from ailment, free from disease, shall be produced for us! May we attentively, through our long lives, be bearers of bali-offerings to thee!

O mother earth, kindly set me down upon a well-founded place! With [father] heaven co-operating, O thou wise one, do thou place me into happiness and prosperity!

Glorification of the Sun, or the Primeval Principle, as a Brahman Disciple

In this hymn's first stanza the sun is glorified as a Brahman disciple, the brahmachari, a solitary ascetic fulfilling his vows. The sun, taking on the powers and functions of the brahmachari, becomes the basis of a cosmic and theosophical story of the universe. This is an example of the exalted functions of the Brahmas caste, and also of the complicated theories which Hindu religious speculation sometimes formulates.

The Brahmachari moves, inciting both hemispheres of the world; in him the gods are harmonized. He holds the heavens and the earth, he fills the teacher with creative fervor [tapas].

The fathers, the divine folk, and all the gods severally follow the Brahmachari; the Gandharvas did go after him, six thousand three hundred and thirty-three. He fills all the gods with creative fervor.

When the teacher receives the Brahmachari as a disciple, he places him as a fetus inside [his body]. He carries him for three nights in his belly: when he is born, the gods gather about to see him.

This earth is [his first] piece of firewood; the heaven, the second; and the atmosphere also he fills with [the third] piece of firewood. The

Brahmachari fills the worlds with his firewood, his girdle, his asceticism, and his creative fervor.

Prior to the Brahma [spiritual exaltation] the Brahmachari was born; clothed in heat, by creative fervor he arose. From him sprung the Brahmanam [Brahmanic life] and the highest Brahma, and all the gods together with immortality [amrita].

The Brahmachari advances, kindled by the firewood, clothed in the skin of the black antelope, consecrated, with long beard. Within the day he passes from the eastern to the northern sea; gathering together the worlds he repeatedly shapes them.

The Brahmachari, begetting the Brahma, the waters, the world, Pragâpati Parameshthin (he that stands in the highest place), and Virâg, having become an embryo in the womb of immortality, having, forsooth, become Indra, pierced the Asuras.

The teacher fashioned these two hemispheres of the world, the broad and the deep, earth and heaven. These the Brahmachari guards with his creative fervor: in him the gods are harmonized.

This broad earth and the heaven the Brahmachari first brought hither as alms. Having made these into two sticks of firewood, he reveres them; upon them all beings have been founded.

Invocation to Vishnu

Vishnu, who has a limited place in Vedaism, is a dominant figure in the Hindu pantheon, along with Siva and Brahma. According to the avatar doctrine this god spoke through a great many ancient gods and heroes; as a result, certain ancient traditions of preceding epochs have made their way into Vaishnavism. Vishnu is fundamentally good and merciful. He is represented with four arms, holding a seashell, a disc, a bludgeon, and a lotus flower. Sometimes he is astride Garuda, a mythical creature, half man and half bird, and at other times, seated with Laksmi, his wife, on a serpent; the snake, twisting and curling its head about, forms a baldachin over the deity's head.

Om! Glory to Vasudeva. —Victory be to thee, Puńdaríkásha; adoration be to thee, Viśwabhávana; glory be to thee, Hŕishíkeśa, Mahápurusha, and Púrvaja.

May that Vishnu—who is the existent, imperishable Brahma; who is Ishvara; who is spirit[14]; who, with the three qualities, is the cause of creation, preservation, and destruction; who is the parent of nature, intellect, and the other ingredients of the universe;—be to us the bestower of understanding, wealth, and final emancipation.

Prayer to Vishnu

Parásara said: Glory to the unchangeable, holy, eternal, supreme Vishnu, of one universal nature, the mighty over all: to him who is Hiráñyagarbha, Hari, and Sankara, the creator, the preserver, and destroyer of the world: to Vasudeva, the liberator of his worshipers: to him whose essence is both single and manifold; who is both subtile and corporeal, indiscrete and discrete: to Vishnu, the cause of final emancipation.[15] Glory to the supreme Vishnu, the cause of the creation, existence, and end of this world; who is the root of the world, and who consists of the world.

Prayer to the Wild Boar

This is the prayer recited by the Yogis, or saints, in honor of Varaha, the divine wild boar who is an incarnation of Vishnu's. It sets forth the fusion of the god Narayan, or Brahma, with Varaha. The myth of the divine boar is probably indigenous, and was later absorbed by Hinduism: highly symbolic, it tells of the boar at the creation of the world, holding up the entire universe on his tusks.

Triumph, lord of lords supreme; Keśava, sovereign of the earth, the wielder of the mace, the shell, the discus, and the sword: cause of production, destruction, and existence. Thou art, O god: there is no other supreme condition but thou. Thou, lord, art the person of sacrifice: for thy feet are the Vedas; thy tusks are the stake to which the victim is bound; in thy teeth are the offerings; thy mouth is the altar; thy tongue is the fire; and the hairs of thy body are the sacrificial grass. Thine eyes, O omnipotent, are day and night; thy head is the seat of all, the place of Brahma; thy mane is all the hymns of the Vedas; thy nostrils are all oblations: O thou, whose snout is the ladle of oblation; whose deep voice is the chanting of the Sama-Veda; whose body is the hall of sacrifice; whose joints are the different ceremonies; and whose ears have the properties of both voluntary and obligatory rites: do thou, who art eternal, who art in size a mountain, be propitious. We acknowledge thee, who hast traversed the world, O universal form, to be the beginning, the continuance, and the destruction of all things: thou art the supreme god. Have pity on us, O lord of conscious and unconscious beings. The orb of the earth is seen seated on the tip of thy tusks, as if thou hadst been sporting amidst a lake where the lotus floats, and hadst borne away the leaves covered with soil. The space between heaven and earth is occupied by thy body,

O thou of unequaled glory, resplendent with the power of pervading the universe, O lord, for the benefit of all. Thou art the aim of all: there is none other than thee, sovereign of the world: this is thy might, by which all things, fixed or movable, are pervaded. This form, which is now beheld, is thy form, as one essentially with wisdom. Those who have not practiced devotion conceive erroneously of the nature of the world. The ignorant, who do not perceive that this universe is of the nature of wisdom, and judge of it as an object of perception only, are lost in the ocean of spiritual ignorance. But they who know true wisdom, and whose minds are pure, behold this whole world as one with divine knowledge, as one with thee, O god. Be favorable, O universal spirit: raise up this earth, for the habitation of created beings. Inscrutable deity, whose eyes are like lotuses, give us felicity. O lord, thou art endowed with the quality of goodness: raise up, Govinda, this earth, for the general good. Grant us happiness, O lotus-eyed. May this, thy activity in creation, be beneficial to the earth. Salutation to thee. Grant us happiness, O lotus-eyed.

Prayer to Sri[16]

I bow down to Sri, the mother of all beings, seated on her lotus-throne, with eyes like full-blown lotuses, reclining on the breast of Vishnu. Thou art Siddhi; thou art Swadhá and Swáhá; thou art ambrosia [Sudhá], the purifier of the universe; thou art evening, night, and dawn; thou art power, intellect, faith; thou art the goddess of letters [Sarasvati]. Thou, beautiful goddess, art knowledge of devotion, great knowledge, mystic knowledge, and spiritual knowledge, which confers eternal liberation. Thou art the science of reasoning, the three Vedas, the arts and sciences; thou art moral and political science. The world is peopled, by thee, with pleasing or displeasing forms. Who else than thou, O goddess, is seated on that person of the god of gods, the wielder of the mace, which is made up of sacrifice, and contemplated by holy ascetics? Abandoned by thee, the three worlds were on the brink of ruin: but they have been reanimated by thee. From thy propitious gaze, O mighty goddess, men obtain wives, children, dwellings, friends, harvests, wealth. Health and strength, power, victory, happiness are easy of attainment to those upon whom thou smilest. Thou art the mother of all beings; as the god of gods, Hari,[17] is their father: and this world, whether animate or inanimate, is pervaded by thee and Vishnu. O thou who purifiest all things, forsake not our treasures, our granaries, our dwellings, our dependents, our persons, our wives. Abandon not our children, our friends, our lineage, our jewels, O thou who abidest on the bosom of the god of gods. They whom thou desertest are forsaken by truth, by purity, and goodness, by every amiable and excellent quality; whilst the base and worthless upon whom thou lookest favorably become immediately endowed with all excellent qualifications, with families, and with power. He on whom thy countenance is turned is honorable, amiable, prosperous, wise, and of exalted birth, a hero of irresistible prowess. But all his merits and his advantages are converted into worthlessness, from whom, beloved of Vishnu, mother of the world, thou avertest thy face. The tongues of Brahma are unequal to celebrate thy excellence. Be propitious to me, O goddess, lotus-eyed; and never forsake me more.

The Preservative Karmas

The Rakshás, preservatives against charms, are represented by a piece of cotton or silk cloth tied around the wrist or arm, with an appropriate prayer. Usually the application of these preservatives is made to young maidens during Rákhí Púrnimá, the month of the full moon of Śrávaña (July-August) to protect them from demons.

May Hari, the lord of all beings [without reserve], protect you; he from the lotus of whose navel the world was developed, and on the tip of whose tusks the globe was upraised from the waters! May that Keśava, who assumed the form of a boar, protect thee! May that Keśava, who, as the man-lion, rent, with his sharp nails, the bosom of his foe, ever protect thee! May that Keśava, who, appearing, first as the dwarf, suddenly traversed, in all his might, with three paces, the three regions of the universe, constantly defend thee! May Govinda guard thy head; Keśava, thy neck; Vishnu, thy belly; Janárdana, thy legs and feet; the eternal and irresistible Náráyaña, thy face, thine arms, thy mind, and faculties of sense! May all ghosts, goblins, and spirits malignant and unfriendly ever fly thee; appalled by the bow, the discus, mace, and sword of Vishnu, and the echo of his shell! May Vaikuñtha guard thee in the cardinal points; and, in the intermediate ones, Madhusúdana! May Hŕishíkeśa defend thee in the sky; and Mahídhara, upon earth![18]

Brahman Prayers

a)

If a bird has befouled him with its excrements, he murmurs:

The birds that timidly fly together with the destroyers shall pour out on me happy, blissful splendor and vigor.

b)

If a drop of water unexpectedly falls down on him:

From the sky, from the wide air, a drop of water has fallen down on me, bringing luck. With my senses, with my mind, I have united myself, protected by the prayer that is brought forth by the righteous ones.

c)

If a fruit unexpectedly falls down on him:

If a fruit has fallen down from the top of a tree or from the air, it is Vayu [who has made it fall]. Where it has touched our bodies or the garment, [there] may the waters drive away destruction.

d)

When he comes to a crossroads:

Adoration to him who dwells at the crossroads, whose arrow is the wind, to Rudra! Adoration to Rudra who dwells at the crossroads!

e)

At a place that is frequented by serpents:

Adoration to him who dwells among the serpents, whose arrow is the wind, to Rudra! Adoration to Rudra who dwells among the serpents!

f)

Against a solitary jackal:

If thou raisest thy divine voice, entering upon living beings, drive away our enemies by the voice. O death, lead them to death!

g)

When the cows go away to their pasture ground:

May Indra and Agni make you go. May the two Asvins protect you. Brihaspati is your herdsman. May Pushan drive you back again.

Formula for the Matrimonial Rite

a)

Formula which accompanies the sacrifice celebrated by the bridegroom:

May Agni come hither, the first of gods. May he release the offspring of this wife from the fetter of death. That may this king Varuna grant, that this wife may not weep over distress [falling to her lot] through her sons. Svâhâ! May Agni Gârhapatya protect this woman. May he lead her offspring to old age. With fertile womb may she be the mother of living children. May she experience delight in her sons. Svâhâ!

May no noise that comes from thee, arise in the house by night. May the [she-goblins called] the weeping ones take their abode in another [woman] than thee. Mayest thou not be beaten at thy breast by [the she-goblin] Vikesî ["the rough-haired one"]. May thy husband live, and mayest thou shine in thy husband's world, beholding thy genial offspring! Svâhâ! May heaven protect thy back; Vayu, thy thighs; and the two Asvins, thy breast. May Savitri protect thy suckling sons. Until the garment is put on may Brihaspati guard, and the Visvedevas afterward. Svâhâ! Childlessness, the death of sons, evil and distress, I take [from thee], as a wreath [is taken] from the head, and [like a wreath] I put all evil on [the head of] our foes. Svâhâ! With this well-disposed prayer which the gods have created, I kill the Pisâkas that dwell in thy womb. The flesh-devouring death-bringers I cast down. May thy sons live to old age. Svâhâ!

b)

Adoration of the stars[19]:

The seven Rishis who have led to firmness she, Arundhatî, who stands first among the six Krittikâs:—may she, the eighth one, who leads the conjunction of the [moon with the] six Krittikâs, the first [among conjunctions] shine upon us!

c)

Adoration of the polar star:

Firm dwelling, firm origin.
The firm one art thou, standing on the side of firmness. Thou art the pillar of the stars; thus protect me against my adversary.

Adoration be to the Brahman, to the firm, immovable one! Adoration be to the Brahman's son, Pragâpati. Adoration to the Brahman's children, to the thirty-three gods! Adoration to the Brahman's children and grandchildren, to the Angiras! He who knows thee [the polar star] as the firm, immovable Brahman with its children and with its grandchildren, with such a man children and grandchildren will firmly dwell, servants and pupils, garments and woolen blankets, bronze and gold, wives and kings, food, safety, long life, glory, renown, splendor, strength, holy luster, and the enjoyment of food. May all these things firmly and immovably dwell with me!

I know thee as the firm Brahman. May I become firm in this world and this country.

I know thee as the immovable Brahman. May I not be moved away from this world and from this country. May he who hates me, my rival, be moved away from this world and from this country.

I know thee as the unshaken Brahman. May I not be shaken off from this world and from this country. May he who hates me, my rival, be shaken off from this world and from this country. I know thee as the unfalling Brahman. May I not fall from this world and from this country. May he who hates me, my rival, fall from this world and from this country. I know thee as the nave of the universe. May I become the nave of this country. I know thee as the center of the universe. May I become the center of this country. I know thee as the string that holds the universe. May I become the string that holds this country. I know thee as the pillar of the universe. May I become the pillar of this country. I know thee as the navel of the universe. May I become the navel of this country.

As the navel is the center of the Pranas, thus I am the navel. May hundred-and-onefold evil befall him who hates us and whom we hate; may more than hundred-and-onefold merit fall to my lot!

d)

Formula for expiatory oblations:

Agni! Expiation! Thou art expiation, I, the Brahmana, entreat thee, desirous of protection. What is terrible in her, drive that away from here. Svâhâ!

Vayu! Expiation! Thou art expiation. I, the Brahmana, entreat thee, desirous of protection. What is blameful in her, drive that away from here. Svâhâ!

Sun! Expiation! Thou art expiation. I, the Brahmana, entreat thee, desirous of protection. What dwells in her that is death-bringing to her husband, drive that away from here. Svâhâ!

e)

Husband's call to wife[20]:

May Vishnu make thy womb ready; may Twashtri frame the shape [of the child]; may Pragâpati pour forth [the sperm]; may Dhâtri give thee conception!

Give conception, Sinîvâlî; give conception Sarasvatî! May the two Asvins, wreathed with lotus, give conception to thee! The embryo which the two Asvins produce with their golden kindling-sticks: that embryo we call into thy womb, that thou mayest give birth to it after ten months.

As the earth is pregnant with Agni, as the heaven is with Indra pregnant, as Vayu dwells in the womb of the regions [of the earth], thus I place an embryo into thy womb. Open thy womb; take in the sperm; may a male child, an embryo, be begotten in the womb. The mother bears him ten months; may he be born, the most valiant of his kin.

May a male embryo enter thy womb, as an arrow the quiver; may a man be born here, thy son, after ten months. I do with thee [the work] that is sacred to Pragâpati; may an embryo enter thy womb. May a child be born without deficiency, with all its limbs, not blind, not lame, not sucked out by Pisâkas.

By the superior powers which the bulls shall produce for us, thereby become thou pregnant; may he be born, the most valiant of his kin.

Indra has laid down in the tree the embryo of the sterile cow and of the cow that prematurely produces; thereby become thou pregnant; be a well-breeding cow.

Ceremony of the Youth's Bath

From chronic disease, from destruction, from wile, from Varuna's fetter I release thee. I make thee guiltless before the Brahman; may both Heaven and Earth be kind toward thee.

May Agni together with the waters bring thee bliss, Heaven and Earth together with the herbs; may the air together with the wind bring thee bliss; may the four quarters of the heaven bring thee bliss.

Rightly have the gods released the sun from darkness and from the seizing demon; they have dismissed him from guilt; thus I deliver this boy from chronic disease, from curse that comes from his kin, from wile, from Varuna's fetter.

For the Preparation of the Domestic Fire

Unite ye two, and get ye on together, loving, radiant, well disposed, dwelling together for food and drink! Together have I brought your minds, together your rites, together your thoughts: O Agni Purîshya, be thou the overlord, and bestow thou food and drink upon our Sacrificer! O Agni, thou art the Purîshya, wealthy, prosperous: having made happy all the regions, seat thee here in thine own seat! Be ye two unto us of one mind, of one thought, without guile! Injure ye not the sacrifice, nor the lord of the sacrifice, and be ye propitious unto us this day, ye knowers of beings!

To Vishnu

Glory to thee, god of the lotus-eye! Glory to thee, most excellent of spiritual things! Glory to thee, soul of all worlds! Glory to thee, wielder of the sharp discus! Glory to the best of Brahmans; to the friend of Brahmans and of kine; to Krishna, the preserver of the world! To Govinda be glory! To him who, as Brahma, creates the universe; who, in its existence, is its preserver; be praise! To thee, who, at the end of the Kalpa,[21] takest the form of Rudra; to thee, who art triform; be adoration! Thou, Achyuta, art the gods, Yakshas, demons, saints, serpents, choristers and dancers of heaven, goblins, evil spirits, men, animals, birds, insects, reptiles, plants, and stones, earth, water, fire, sky, wind, sound, touch, taste, color, flavor, mind, intellect, soul, time, and the qualities [of nature]. Thou art all these, and the chief object of them all. Thou art knowledge and ignorance, truth and falsehood, poison and ambrosia. Thou art the performance and discontinuance of acts; thou art the acts which the Vedas enjoin. Thou art the enjoyer of the fruit of all acts, and the means by which they are accomplished. Thou, Vishnu, who art the soul of all, art the fruit of all acts of piety. Thy universal diffusion, indicating might and goodness, is in me, in others, in all creatures, in all worlds. Holy ascetics meditate on thee: pious priests sacrifice to thee. Thou alone, identical with the gods and the fathers of mankind, receivest burnt offerings and oblations. The universe is thy intellectual form, whence proceeded thy subtle form, this world. Thence art thou all subtle elements and elementary beings, and the subtle principle, that is called soul, within them. Hence the supreme soul of all objects, distinguished as subtle or gross, which is imperceptible, and which cannot be conceived, is even a form of thee. Glory be to thee, Purushottama! And glory to that imperishable form, which, soul of all, is another manifestation of thy might, the asylum of all qualities, existing in all creatures! I salute her, the supreme goddess, who is beyond the senses; whom the mind, the tongue, cannot define; who is to be distinguished alone by the wisdom of the truly wise. Om! Salutation to Vasudeva; to him who is the eternal lord; he from whom nothing is distinct; he who is distinct from all! Glory be to the great spirit, again and again; to him who is without name or shape; who, alone, is to be known by adoration; whom, in the forms manifested in his descents upon earth, the dwellers in heaven adore! For they behold not his inscrutable nature. I glorify the supreme deity Vishnu, the universal witness, who, seated internally, beholds the good and ill of all. Glory to that Vishnu, from whom this world is not distinct! May he, ever to be meditated upon as the beginning of the universe, have compassion upon me! May he, the supporter of all, in whom everything is warped and woven, undecaying, imperishable, have compassion upon me! Glory, again and again, to that being to whom all returns, from whom all proceeds; who is all, and in whom all things are; to him who I, also, am! For he is everywhere, and through whom all things are from me. I am all things. All things are in me, who am everlasting. I am undecayable, ever enduring, the receptacle of the spirit of the Supreme. Brahma is my name; the supreme soul, that is before all things, that is after the end of all.

To the Sun

Glory to the Sun, the gate of liberation, the fountain of bright radiance, the triple source of splendor, as the Ṙig-, the Yajur-, and the Sama-vedas! Glory to him, who, as fire and the moon, is one with the cause of the universe: to the sun, that is charged with radiant heat, and with the Sushumńa ray, [by which the moon is fed with light]: to him who is one with the notion of time, and all its divisions of hours, minutes, and seconds: to him who is to be meditated upon as the [visible] form of Vishnu, as the impersonation of the mystic Om: to him who nourishes the troops of the gods, having filled the moon with his rays: who feeds the Pitris with nectar and ambrosia, and who nourishes mankind with rain; who pours down, or absorbs, the waters, in the time of the rains, of cold, and of heat! Glory be to Brahma, the sun, in the form of the three seasons: him who alone is the dispeller of the darkness of this earth, of which he is the sovereign lord! To the god who is clad in the raiment of purity be adoration! Glory to the sun, until whose rising, man is incapable of devout acts, and water does not purify; and, touched by whose rays, the world is fitted for religious rites: to him who is the center and source of purification! Glory to Savitri, to Surya, to Bháskara, to Vivaswat, to Aditya, to the first-born of gods or demons. I adore the eye of the universe, borne in a golden car, whose banners scatter ambrosia.

For Oblations

A prayer which accompanies a domestic rite, that of oblation to ancestors, and consists in a triple libation of water and sesame. It is recited in secret for the benefit of all creatures.

May the gods, demons, Yakshas, serpents, Gandharvas, Rakshasas, Piśáchas, Guhyakas,[22] Siddhas, Kúshmáńdas, trees, birds, fish, all that people the waters, or the earth, or the air, be propitiated by the water I have presented to them! This water is given, by me, for the alleviation of the pains of all those who are suffering in the realms of hell. May all those who are my kindred, and not my kindred, and who were my relations in a former life, all who desire libations from me, receive satisfaction from this water! May this water and sesamum, presented by me, relieve the hunger and thirst of all who are suffering from those inflictions, wheresoever they may be!

To All Beings

The formula accompanies the offering of the *bali,* or the remains of food to be given to ascetics.

May gods, men, animals, birds, saints, Yakshas, serpents, demons, ghosts, goblins, trees, all that desire food given by me; may ants, worms, moths, and other insects, hungered and bound in the bonds of act; may all obtain satisfaction from the food left them by me, and enjoy happiness. May they who have neither mother, nor father, nor relations, nor food, nor the means of preparing it, be satisfied and pleased with the food presented for their contentment. Inasmuch as all beings, and this food, and I, and Vishnu are not different, I therefore give for their sustenance the food that is one with the body of all creatures. May all beings, that are comprehended in the fourteen orders of existent things,[23] be satisfied with the food bestowed by me for their gratification, and be delighted.

After the Repast

Like the foregoing, this is a domestic ceremony.

May fire, excited by air, convert this food into the earthly elements of this frame, and in the space afforded by the ethereal atmosphere cause it to digest, and yield me satisfaction! May this food, in its assimilation, contribute to the vigor of the earth, water, fire, and air of my body, and afford unmixed gratification! May Agasti, Agni, and submarine fire effect the digestion of the food of which I have eaten; may they grant me the happiness which its conversion into nutriment engenders; and may health [ever] animate my form! May Vishnu, who is the chief principle of all invested with bodily structure and the organs of sense, be propitiated by my faith in him, and influence the assimilation of the invigorating food which I have eaten! For verily Vishnu is the eater and the food and the nutriment: and through this belief may that which I have eaten be digested.

Prayer for the Practice of Yoga

The formulas included here are part of the daily rites of Yoga practitioners. Yoga, etymologically "conjoinment," "union," from the root *yug,* is distinguished in the antique *rāja-yoga,* a union obtained by means of minute attention to detail in its practice, and in *Hatha-yoga,* which is the acquisition of magic powers by means of physical activities designed to eliminate the individual from the cycle of existence. It should be considered as a complement of Samkhya, the philosophic system on which it is based.

Sprinkling himself with water, the worshiper says:
I desire the removal of all sins that have adhered to me.

Drinking water from the palm of his hand, he repeats: Oh, water, the source of all comfort, grant us food so that our senses may grow strong and give us joy. Make us recipients of your essence, which is the most blissful. May we obtain enough of that essence of yours, the existence of which within you makes you feel glad. Oh, waters, give us offspring. May the sun and anger, may the lords of anger, preserve me from my sins of pride and passion. Whatever the nightly sins of thought, word, deed, wrought by my mind, my speech, my hands, my feet; wrought through my appetite and sensual organs. Oh, radiant sun, I offer up myself, and this my guilt.

The midday service is as follows:
May the waters purify the earth by pouring down rain. May the

purified earth, thus purified, make us pure. May the waters purify my spiritual preceptor, and may the Veda purify me. Whatever leavings of another's food [his wife needs no purification for having eaten the scraps off his plate], and whatever impure things I have eaten; whatever I have received as a gift from the unworthy [no gift is refused, purification can always follow acceptance], may the waters destroy all that sin and purify me. For this purpose, I pour this sanctified water as a libation down my throat.

Angulimâla Paritta

This is one of the six parittas—prayers—promulgated by Buddha himself. Angulimâla was an ill-famed bandit named for his necklace of human fingers hacked from his victims' hands. Converted by Buddha, he became a wanderer from city to city, asking alms. When he was recognized as the bandit and mistreated, he recited this paritta to defend himself.

> O let my foes but hear the Norm as told to me,
> And hearing join with me to keep the Buddha's Rule!
> O let my foes but minister to men of peace,
> Who e'en have taken to their hearts that holy Norm!
> O let my foes from time to time but hear that Norm
> From them who tell of gentleness, and who commend
> Affection, and to what they hear, their actions suit!
> For such a foe would verily not work me harm,
> Nor any other creature wheresoever found.
> He would himself attain the peace ineffable,
> And thus attaining, cherish all, both bad and good.

Hymn of the Bidhicaryâvatâra

Through the blessing which comes to me for pondering upon the entrance into the Path of Enlightenment, may all beings be brightened by walking in Enlightenment. May all that are sick of body and soul in every region find oceans of bliss and delight through my merits. Whilst embodied life lasts on, may they never lack happiness, and forever may the world win the joy of the Sons of Enlightenment. In all the hells that are in the spheres of the universe may creatures rejoice in the delights of paradise. May they that are afflicted with cold find warmth, the heat-smitten be cooled in the oceans raining from the mighty clouds of the Son of Enlightenment. . . . May all skies be gracious to all wayfarers, and may they encompass as their purpose the enterprise for which they journey. May such as travel on ship achieve their desire, and come in happiness to shore and rejoice with their kindred. May they who stray amid wildernesses find company of travelers' troops, and journey on without dread of bandits and wild beasts. In the stress of sickness, wildernesses, and the like may the heavenly powers guard the slumbering, the distraught, and the heedless, the masterless, the young, and the aged. May they be forever saved from all mischance, dowered with faith, understanding, and tenderness, and possessed of goodly shape and virtue. May their storehouses never fail and their treasuries rise to the skies, and may they live in freedom, without strife or affliction. May beings of little strength win much strength, and the hapless creatures that are of ill form become goodly. May all women in the world become men; and to their estate may the humble come, and lose their vanity. Through this my merit may all beings cease from every sin, and everlastingly do righteousness, lacking not the Thought of Enlightenment, surrendering themselves to the Path of Enlightenment, withholding their hands from the works of the Tempter, and be taken into the arms of the Enlightened. May all creatures have boundless term of age; may they live forever in bliss, and the very name of death perish. May all regions become filled with Buddhas and Sons of the Buddhas, and lovely with groves of the Trees of Desire ravishing the heart with the sound of the Law. . . . As long as the heavens and the earth abide, may I continue to overcome the world's sorrows. May all the world's suffering be cast upon me, and may the world be made happy by all the merits of the Bodhisattva.

Glorification of the Buddha

> Great sage, who didst reject
> the sense-based-sophistries
> of three and sixty sects,
> thou soarest o'er life's gloom!
>
> Ending, transcending, Ills,
> Cankerless Arahat,
> thy insight, light, and lore
> have brought me safe "Across"!
>
> For marking my distress,
> for freeing me from doubt,
> I laud thee, sage benign,

consummate master-mind,
great Kinsman of the Sun!

The doubts I had are solved by thee, O Seer,
O All-Enlighten'd sage immaculate!

With ev'ry perturbation rooted up,
unfever'd, tranquil, strong in Truth art thou!

Great Victor! Paragon! Thy words rejoice
all gods, all Nâradâs, all Pábbatás.

I hail thee noblest, foremost of mankind;
nor earth nor heaven holds thy counterpart!

Enlighten'd Master! Over Mâra's hosts
triumphant! Sage, who, wrong propensities
uprooting, for thyself salvation found
and taught mankind to find salvation, too!

Thou hast surmounted all that breeds rebirth
and extirpated Canker-growths within!
With naught to bind thee thrall to life, thou 'rt free
as forest lion from all fears and dread.

E'en as a lotus fair to water gives
no lodgment, thou by good and bad alike
art unaffected. Stretch thou forth thy feet,
O Victor. I salute my Master's feet!

Notes

   1. Agni, the Fire, is the least anthropomorphic of all the divinities. He is represented as a licking flame and sybil for the fused butter that is thrown on the flame (ghi or ghee) Originally the sacrificial fire which devoured the offerings of the gods, he is presented as a triformity: Agni terrestrial—or fire—that issues forth from the wood of the two *arani;* Agni celestial, or of the sun; Agni of the waters, of thunderbolts, of the clouds and fires that are in the waters. As Agni celestial, he is reborn each day with the dawn. He is considered the god nearest to humans, the celestial messenger, present everywhere.
   2. Indra is the god exalted for strength and dexerity, always accompanied through space by the Wind (Vayu), drawn along by bay horses and gripping thunderbolts in his fist. In myths Indra frees the celestial and terrestrial waters from the demon Vritra, the "destroyer," and conquers the light of the world For that reason he is the god of storms. The conquest of the dawn and of

light is represented in the myth of the cows. He frees them from the Pani, the demons that had kept them hidden in a cave.

3. TwashTri is the builder-architect of the gods.

4. Brahmanaspati, "Lord of the Brahman" in the magic-sacred formula that has an effect on both gods and men, is the prototype of the priest who exercises his ministry to Indra.

5. The Maruts are young, powerful brothers who race about on chariots drawn by antelopes. They hurtle through the forests, causing all kinds of mishaps. They are Indra's faithful companions. According to the most reliable interpretations, they represent tempests, particularly during the autumnal monsoons.

6. Rudra, the Marut's father, is the "Wailer," a terrifying and evil god. He is invoked so that those praying will not be struck by his mortal arrows.

7. The only Rig-Vedic hymn directed to Mitra, the divine solar figure who acquires an enormous importance in Avestan religion and in the decadent Greek-Alexandrian cults (practices). In the Vedaic religion, Mitra is always with Varuna.

8. Prithiví is a relatively unimportant divinity in the Rig-Veda, along with Dyaus, the Sky. She is distinguished as the divinity of the visible earth and of the atmosphere. In this brief hymn, the only one dedicated to her, she is considered as the latter.

9. One of the very few Rig-Veda hymns conserving the memory of agricultural ceremonies. It was used on the return of the cows from the pastures, or possibly on the arrival of cows at a new farm. The last verse was accompanied by the administering of salt water, designed to prevent diseases and increase production.

10. Vishnu, though an important personage in Hindu belief, is given very little space in the Rig-Veda. He "carries out his three steps" on the earth, leaving three footprints there. According to some authorities, he represents, in the Rig-Veda phase, a solar myth, and the three steps allude to the dividing up of the universe into three parts: air, earth, and sky. Vishnu never abandons Indra, not even during his struggle with Vritra, when all the other deities desert him.

11. Soma is the sacred and deified drink. The entire prayer is directed against the occult and demonic forces of the earth (ráksas).

12. This hymn is in close relation with the *ekadhaná* water-drawing ceremonies for the soma sacrifice. According to the known ritual, which presumably differs little from that of the Rig-Vedic, the waters were taken from the *adhvaryú* to another stream sufficiently close to the sacrificial place for the voice of the *hótar* reciting the hymn to be heard.

13. Not much is known about the origins and nature of the Asuras, though they may have been connected with the *asu*, the vital spirit. They are gods of order and creation who crush out darkness and struggle against demons.

14. Brahma is the neuter and abstract force of the supreme spirit, whereas Ishvara is the divine active nature of that spirit. The three qualities of the divinity here referred to are: goodness of spirit, passion in the form of activity, and inertia as ignorance and obscurity.

15. The three hypostases of Vishnu: Hyranyagarbha, which is the name

of Brahma, Hari, who is Vishnu, and Sankara, who is Siva. They correspond to the divine triune of Creator, Preserver, and Destroyer.

16. A Hindu title of address, equivalent to the English mister.

17. Hari is Vishnu.

18. Names of incarnations of Vishnu.

19. This prayer is said by the groom at the appearance of the stars. First it pays homage to the Seven Rishis [Great Bear], then to the Krittikâs [Pleiades], and finally to the North Star.

20. This is uttered during the fourth night after the matrimonial ceremony. Before it is pronounced, the wife has taken a bath and once more dressed in her most beautiful clothes.

21. One of the epochs of the world.

22. The servants of Kubera, guards of the celestial treasure.

23. The fourteen classes of spirits, or eight species of divine creatures plus a species of human beings and five species of animals.

✳

Siam

SIAM

Evocation of the Kwun

Every young Siamese preserves a topknot until the age of puberty, when it is shaved off during an elaborate "ritual of passing"—rites which are a mixture of Buddhistic, indigenous, and Brahmanistic elements, and which continue for days. Kwun is a complex spirit that might be translated into Western language as "soul," "spirit," "guardian genius or tutor," or "Lady Fortune." It is thought that it abandons the body under certain conditions, particularly during the shaving of the topknot; this formula, of Brahman origin, is designed to prevent such an occurrence.

Benignant Kwun! Thou fickle being who art wont to wander and dally about! From the moment that the child wast conceived in the womb, thou hast enjoyed every pleasure, until ten [lunar] months have elapsed and the time of delivery arrived, thou hast suffered and run the risk of perishing by being born alive into the world. Gracious Kwun, thou wast at that time so tender, delicate, and wavering as to cause great anxiety regarding thy fate; thou wast exactly like a child, youthful, innocent, and inexperienced. The least trifle frightened thee and made thee shudder. In thy infantile playfulness thou wast wont to frolic and wander to no purpose. As thou didst commence to learn to sit, and, unassisted, to crawl totteringly on all fours, thou wast ever falling flat on thy face or on thy back. As thou didst grow up in years and couldst move thy steps firmly, thou didst then begin to run and sport thoughtlessly and rashly all round the rooms, the terrace, and bridging planks of traveling boat or floating house, and at times thou didst fall into the stream, creek, or pond, among the floating water weeds, to the utter dismay of those to whom thy existence was most dear. O gentle Kwun, come into thy corporeal abode; do not delay this auspicious rite. Thou art now full grown and dost form everybody's delight and admiration.

Let all the tiny particles of Kwun that have fallen on land or water assemble and take permanent abode in this darling little child. Let them all hurry to the site of this auspicious ceremony and admire the magnificent preparations made for them in this hall.

Formula of the Oath of Loyalty

This formula, given only in part, was used every two years in all the centers of Siam for swearing loyalty to the king. Every citizen confirmed his loyalty, in a public assembly, by reading an oath and being sprinkled with special sacred water prepared by the priest in the capital.

We beseech the powers of the deities to plague with poisonous boils that will rapidly prove fatal, and with all manner of terrible diseases, the dishonorable, perverse, and treacherous. May we be visited with untimely wretched and appalling deaths, that our disloyalty may be made manifest in the eyes of the whole world. When we shall have departed from this life upon earth, cause us to be sent to, and all to be born again in, that great hell where we shall burn with unquenchable fire through limitless transmigrations. And when we have expiated our penalties there, and are born again into any other world, we pray that we may fail to find the least happiness in any pleasurable enjoyments that may there abound. Let us not meet the god Buddha; let us not hear the sacred teachings; let us not come into contact with the sacred priests whose mission it is to be gracious to men and animals, and to help them to escape from misery, to attain a progressive succession of births and deaths, and finally to reach heaven itself. Should we by any chance meet with holy men or priests, let us receive therefrom no gracious helpful assistance.

Judiciary Oath

I, ——, who have been brought here as an evidencee in this matter,
do now in presence of the divine Buddha declare that I am wholly un-
prejudiced against either party, and uninfluenced in any way by the
opinions or advice of others, and that no prospects of pecuniary advantages or of advancement to office have been held out to me. I also
declare that I have not received any bribes on this occasion. If what I
have now spoken be false, or if in my further averments I should color
or pervert the truth so as to lead the judgment of others astray, may
the three holy existences before whom I now stand, together with the
glorious Devattas of the twenty-two firmaments, punish me.

If I have not seen, yet shall say that I have seen—if I shall say that
I know that which I do not know, then may I be thus punished. Should
innumerable descents of the Deity happen for the salvation and regeneration of mankind, may my erring and migrating soul be found beyond
the pale of their mercy. Wherever I go, may I be encompassed by
dangers and not escape from them, whether arising from murderers,
spirits of the ground, robbers, spirits of the forest, of the water, of
the air, or from all the angels, or from the gods of the four elements
and all other spirits. May blood flow out of every pore of my body, that
my crime may be made made manifest to the world. May all or any of
these evils overtake me three days hence. Or may I never stir from the
place on which I now stand; or may be "lash of the sky"[1] cut me in
twain, so that I may be exposed to the derision of the people; or if I
should be walking abroad, may I be torn in pieces by either of the four
preternaturally endowed lions, or destroyed by poisonous herbs or
venomous snakes. When in the waters of the river or ocean may alliga-
tors and large fishes devour me; or may the winds or waves overwhelm
me; or may the dread of such evils keep me during my life a prisoner at
home, estranged from every pleasure; or may I be afflicted by the in-
tolerable oppressions of my superiors; or may cholera cause my death,
after which may I be precipitated into hell, there to go through innumerable stages of torture; amongst which, may I be condemned to
carry water over the flaming regions, in open wicker baskets, to assuage
the heat felt by the judge of hell when he enters the infernal courts of
justice, and thereafter may I fall into the lowest pit of hell. Or if these
miseries should not ensue, may I after death migrate into the body of a
slave, and suffer all the hardships and pain attending the worst state
of such a being, during a period of years measured by the sands of the

four seas; or may I animate the body of an animal or beast during five hundred generations; or endure in the body of a deaf, blind, dumb, homeless beggar, every species of loathsome disease during the same number of generations, and then may I be hurried to the bottomless pit, there to be crucified by the king of hell.

Notes

1. Lightning.

✳

Egypt

EGYPT

Hymn to the Sun by Amenophis IV

This hymn is attributed to Pharaoh Amenophis IV and is engraved in many tombs of the necropolis of Khounauten (tombs of Tell-el-Amarna El-Amarna).

Beautiful is thy rising upon the horizon of heaven, when the living Disk
    hangs vibrant.
Thou it is that shineth upon the Eastern horizon, and every land is
    filled with thy beauty.
It is thy beauty, thy greatness, and thy splendor that cause praises to
    thee from every land when thy rays embrace their lands.
Thou compellest their love of thee, for though thou art far distant, yet
    do thy rays illumine the earth.
When thou takest thy rest in the Western Horizon, the land is in dark-
    ness, with thoughts of death.
They [mankind] sleep within their houses—their heads wrapped up,
    their noses covered up, while their eyes cannot distinguish one
    another; yea, should there be stolen all their possessions from under
    their head, they would not know it.

Every lion cometh out from its den; every insect stings them [the sleepers]; the land is silent, for their Maker is reposing in his Horizon.

Day breaks at thy appearance upon the Horizon, when thou givest light by means of the Disk by day; yea, darkness flees when thou sendest forth thy beams, and the Two Lands are in festal mood.

Awaking, they stand upon their two feet, for thou hast raised them up.

After their limbs are bathed, they seize their clothes; finally their arms are in a posture of adoration at thy dawning.

The whole land takes up its work. All cattle repose amidst their pasturage. Trees and herbage spring into life, and as for the birds within their retreats, their wings are spread in a posture of adoration to thy Ka. Each small beast leaps upon its feet, birds and all those things that flutter begin their life when thou appearest. The fish in the river leap up toward thy face, and thy rays pierce even the depths of the Sea.

Thou makest man to unite with woman, thou hast put a life-giving seed into humankind, making to live a son within the womb of its mother; quieting him when he crieth; nourishing him in the womb. O, Thou, who givest him breath in order that he may live, who takest him from the womb of his mother, the day he is born thou dost open his mouth so that he speaks, and thou makest him possessed of it [speech].

If there is a chicken speaking within the egg, thou givest it breath within its shell, so that it lives. Thou makest it to unite all its strength, so that it breaketh the egg, cometh forth from the shell, and calleth for its [mother] . . . . It walketh upon its two feet.

Thou hast created the Earth by thy mere wish when thou wast the only one; all men and animals, all that goeth upon their feet upon the Earth, and all that fly on high by means of their wings.

As for Caria, Cush, and Egypt, thou seest that each man is in his place and givest to him his necessity, each one hath his portion, and his duration of life is set.

Tongues are distinguished by speech, forms, and skins also; thou dost distinguish between foreigner and Egyptian.

Thou dost send the Nile from the Duat; thou hast sent him by thy will in order to keep alive mankind, for thou hast created them, and to thee they all belong.

Foreign lands are far distant, yet thou makest them to live. Thou givest the Nile from heaven; it falls for them; it maketh waves upon the hills even as doth the Mediterranean Sea, moistening their fields within their suburbs.

Oh, Hapi [Nile god] in heaven, when thou commandest all foreign
countries and wild beasts of the desert, they proceed upon their
feet. The god Hapi, art thou who comest from the Duat to Egypt.

A Hymn to Amen-Ra

Adoration of Amen-Ra,[1] the Bull Residing in Heliopolis,[2] chief of
all gods, the good god, the beloved, who gives life to all that is warm
and to all good cattle.

Hail to thee, Amen-Ra,
Lord of the Thrones of the Two Lands, Presiding over Karnak,
Bull of His Mother, Presiding over His Fields!
Far-reaching of stride, presiding over Upper Egypt,
Lord of the Madjoi and ruler of Punt,[3]
Eldest of heaven, first-born of earth,
Lord of what is, enduring in all things, enduring in all things.
UNIQUE IN HIS NATURE LIKE THE FLUID of the gods,
The goodly bull of the Ennead, chief of all gods,
The lord of truth and father of the gods.
Who made mankind and created the beasts,
Lord of what is, who created the fruit tree,
Made herbage, and gave life to cattle.
The goodly daemon whom Ptah[4] made,

(ii)

The goodly beloved youth to whom the gods give praise,
Who made what is below and what is above,
Who illuminates the Two Lands
And crosses the heavens in peace:
The King of Upper and Lower Egypt: Ra, the triumphant,
Chief of the Two Lands,
Great of strength, lord of reverence,
The chief one, who made the entire earth.
MORE DISTINGUISHED IN NATURE THAN any [other] god,
In whose beauty the gods rejoice,
To whom is given jubilation in the Per-wer,
Who is given ceremonial appearance in the Per-nezer.
Whose fragrance the gods love, when he comes from Punt,
Rich in perfume, when he comes down [from] Madjoi,
The Beautiful of Face who comes [from] God's Land.
The gods FAWN [at] his feet,

According as they recognize his majesty as their lord,
The Lord of fear, great of dread,
Rich in might, terrible of appearances,
Flourishing in offerings and making provisions.
Jubilation to thee who made the gods,
Raised the heavens and laid down the ground!
THE END

(iii)

He who awakes in health, Min-Amen,
Lord of eternity, who made everlastingness,
Lord of praise, presiding over [the Ennead],
Firm of horns, beautiful of face,
Lord of the uraeus-serpent, lofty of plumes,
Beautiful of diadem, and lofty of White Crown.
The serpent-coil and the Double Crown, these are before him,
The aromatic gum which is in the palace,
The Double Crown, the headcloth, and the Blue Crown.
Beautiful of face, when he receives the atef-crown,
He whom the crowns of Upper and Lower Egypt love,
Lord of the Double Crown, when he receives the ames-staff,
Lord of the mekes-scepter, holding the flail.[5]
THE GOODLY ruler, CROWNED WITH THE WHITE CROWN,
The lord of rays, who makes brilliance,
To whom the gods give thanksgiving,
Who extends his arms to him whom he loves,
[But] his enemy is consumed by a flame.
It is his Eye that overthrows the rebels,
That sends its spear into him that sucks up Nun,

(iv)

And makes the fiend disgorge what he has swallowed.
HAIL TO THEE, O Ra, lord of truth!
Whose shrine is hidden, the lord of the gods,
Khepri in the midst of his barque,
Who gave commands, and the gods came into being.
Atum, who made the people,
Distinguished their nature, made their life,
And separated colors, one from another.
Who hears the prayer of him who is in captivity,

Gracious of heart in the face of an appeal to him.
SAVING THE FEARFUL FROM THE TERRIBLE OF HEART,
Judging the weak and the injured.
Lord of Perception, in whose mouth Command is placed,
For love of whom the Nile has come,
Possessor of sweetness, greatly beloved;
When he comes, the people live.
He who gives scope to every eye that may be made in Nun,
Whose loveliness has created the light,

(v)

In whose beauty the gods rejoice;
Their hearts live when they see him.
THE END.

O RA, ADORED IN KARNAK,
Great of appearances in the House of the Benben,[6]
The Heliopolitan, lord of the New Moon Feast,
For whom the Sixth-Day and Quarter-Month feasts are celebrated.
The Sovereign—life, prosperity, health!—lord of all gods;
[They] behold him in the midst of the horizon,
The overlord of men of the silent land,
Whose name is hidden from his children,
In this his name of Amen.
HAIL TO THEE, WHO ART IN PEACE!
Lord of joy, terrible of appearances,
Lord of the uraeus-serpent, lofty of plumes,
Beautiful of diadem, and lofty of White Crown.
The gods love to see thee
With the Double Crown fixed upon thy brow.
The love of thee is spread throughout the Two Lands
When thy rays shine forth in the eyes.
The good of the people is thy arising;
The cattle grow languid when thou shinest.
The love of thee is in the southern sky;

(vi)

The sweetness of thee is in the northern sky.
The beauty of thee carries away hearts;
The love of thee makes arms languid;
Thy beautiful form relaxes the hands;

And hearts are forgetful at the sight of thee.
THOU ART the sole one, WHO MADE [ALL] THAT IS,
[The] solitary sole [one], who made what exists,
From whose eyes mankind came forth,
And upon whose mouth the gods came into being.
He who made herbage [for] the cattle,
And the fruit tree for mankind,
Who made that [on which] the fish in the river may live,
And the birds soaring in the sky.
He who gives breath to that which is in the egg,
Gives life to the son of the slug,
And makes that on which gnats may live,
And worms and flies in like manner;
Who supplies the needs of the mice in their holes,
And gives life to flying things in every tree.
HAIL TO THEE, WHO DID ALL THIS!
Solitary sole one, with many hands,

(vii)

Who spends the night wakeful, while all men are asleep,
Seeking benefit for his creatures.
Amen, enduring in all things, Atum and Har-akhti—
Praises are thine, when they all say:
"Jubilation to thee, because thou weariest thyself with us!
Salaams to thee, because thou didst create us!"
HAIL TO THEE FOR ALL BEASTS!
Jubilation to thee for every foreign country—
To the height of heaven, to the width of earth,
To the depth of the Great Green Sea!
The gods are bowing down to thy majesty
And exalting the might of him who created them,
Rejoicing at the approach of him who begot them.
They say to thee: "Welcome in peace!
Father of the fathers of all the gods,
Who raised the heavens and laid down the ground,
WHO MADE WHAT IS AND CREATED WHAT EXISTS;
Sovereign—life, prosperity, health!—and chief of the gods!

(viii)

"We praise thy might, according as thou didst make us.
Let [us] act for thee, because thou brought us forth.

We give thee thanksgiving because thou hast wearied thyself with us!"
HAIL TO THEE, WHO MADE ALL THAT IS!
Lord of truth and father of the gods,
Who made mortals and created beasts,
Lord of the grain,
Who made [also] the living of the beasts of the desert.
Amen, the bull beautiful of countenance,
The beloved in Karnak,
Great of appearances in the House of the Benben,
Taking again the diadem in Heliopolis,
Who judges the Two in the great broad hall,
The chief of the Great Ennead.
THE SOLITARY SOLE ONE, WITHOUT HIS PEER,
Presiding over Karnak,
The Heliopolitan, presiding over his Ennead,
And living on truth every day.
The horizon-dweller, Horus of the east,
From whom the desert creates silver and gold,
Genuine lapis lazuli for love of him,

(ix)

Benzoin and various incenses from Madjoi,
And fresh myrrh for thy nostrils—
Beautiful of face when coming [from] Madjoi!
Amen-Ra, Lord of the Thrones of the Two Lands,
Presiding over Karnak,
The Heliopolitan, presiding over his harem!
THE END.

The sole king, like the fluid of the gods,
With many names, unknown in number,
Rising in the eastern horizon,
And going to rest in the western horizon;
Who overthrows his enemies,
[RE]BORN EARLY EVERY DAY.
Thoth[7] lifts up his two eyes,
And satisfies him with his effective deeds.
The gods rejoice in his beauty,
He whom his apes exalt.
Lord of the evening barque and the morning barque;
They cross Nun in peace for thee.

Thy CREW IS IN JOY,
When they see the overthrow of the rebel,
His body licked up by the knife.

(x)

Fire has devoured him;
His soul is more consumed than his body.
That dragon, his [power of] motion is taken away.
The gods are in joy,
The crew of Ra is in satisfaction,
Heliopolis is in joy,
For the enemies of Atum are overthrown.
Karnak is in satisfaction, Heliopolis is in joy,
The heart of the Lady of Life is glad,
For the enemy of her lord is overthrown.
The gods of Babylon are in jubilation,
They who are in the shrines are salaaming,
WHEN THEY SEE HIM RICH IN HIS MIGHT.
The daemon of the gods,
The righteous one, Lord of Karnak,
In this thy name of Maker of Righteousness;
The lord of provisions, bull of offerings,
In this thy name of Amen, Bull of His Mother;
Maker of all mankind,
Creator and maker of all that is,

(xi)

In this thy name of Atum-Khepri.
Great falcon, festive of bosom,
Beautiful of face, festive of breast,
Pleasing of form, lofty of plume,
On whose brow the two uraei flutter.
To whom the hearts of mankind make approach,
To whom the people turn about;
Who makest festive the Two Lands with his comings forth.
Hail to thee, Amen-Ra, Lord of the Thrones of the Two Lands,
Whose city loves his rising!
IT HAS COME [TO ITS END]. . . .

Hymn to the Nile

This hymn was sung at the great annual feast at Silsileh during the summer solstice. After a sacrifice made in honor of the river, a papyrus was flung into the waters containing requests that the country receive certain benefits.

Hail to thee, Hapi![8]—who appearest in the land and comest—to give life to Egypt;—thou who dost hide thy coming in darkness—in this very day whereon thy coming is sung,—wave, which spreadest over the orchards created by Ra—to give life to all them that are arthirst—who refusest to give drink unto the desert—of the overflow of the waters of heaven; as soon as thou descendest—Sibû, the earth-god, is enamored of bread—Napri, the god of grain, presents his offering—Ptah maketh every workshop to prosper.

Lord of the fish! as soon as he passeth the cataract—the birds no longer descend upon the fields; creator of corn, maker of barley—he prolongeth the existence of temples. Do his fingers cease from their labors, or doth he suffer?—then are all the millions of beings in misery; —doth he wane in heaven? then the gods—themselves, and all men perish;

The cattle are driven mad, and all the world—both great and small, are in torment! But if, on the contrary, the prayers of men are heard at his rising—and [for them] he maketh himself Khnemû[9]—when he ariseth, then the earth shouts for joy—then are all bellies joyful—each back is shaken with laughter—and every tooth grindeth.

Bringing food, rich in sustenance,—creator of all good things—lord of all seeds of life, pleasant unto his elect,—if his friendship is secured —he produceth fodder for the cattle—and he provideth for the sacrifices of all the gods,—finer than any other is the incense which cometh from him;—he taketh possession of the two lands—and the granaries are filled, the storehouses are prosperous—and the goods of the poor are multiplied.

He is at the service of all prayers to answer them—withholding nothing. To make boats to be, that is his strength.[10] Stones are not sculptured for him—nor statues whereon the double crown is placed; he is unseen; no tribute is paid unto him and no offerings are brought unto him—he is not charmed by words of mystery; the place of his dwelling is unknown, nor can his shrine be found by virtue of magic writings;

There is no house large enough for thee—nor any who may penetrate within thy heart! Nevertheless, the generations of thy children rejoice in thee—for thou dost rule as a king—whose decrees are established for the whole earth, who is manifest in presence of the people of the South and of the North, by whom the tears are washed from every eye, and who is lavish of his bounties.

Where sorrow was, there doth break forth joy—and every heart rejoiceth. Sovkû, the crocodile, the child of Nît,[11] leaps for gladness; for the Nine gods who accompany thee have ordered all things, the overflow giveth drink unto the fields—and maketh all men valiant; one man taketh to drink of the labor of another, without charge being brought against him.[12]

If thou dost enter in the midst of songs to go forth in the midst of gladness—if they dance with joy when thou comest forth out of the unknown—it is that thy heaviness is death and corruption. And when thou art implored to give the water of the year, the people of the Thebaïd and of the North are seen side by side, each man with the tools of his trade, none tarrieth behind his neighbor; of all those who clothed themselves, no man clotheth himself [with festive garments]—the children of Thot, the god of riches, no longer adorn themselves with jewels— nor the Nine gods, but they are in the night! As soon as thou hast answered by the rising, each one anointeth himself with perfumes.

Establisher of true riches, desire of men, here are seductive words in order that thou mayest reply; if thou dost answer mankind by waves of the heavenly Ocean—Napri, the grain-god, presents his offering— all the gods adore [thee]—the birds no longer descend upon the hills; though that which thy hand formeth were of gold—or in the shape of a brick of silver—it is not lapis lazuli that we eat—but wheat is of more worth then precious stones.

They have begun to sing unto thee upon the harp—they sing unto thee, keeping time with their hands, and the generations of thy children rejoice in thee, and they have filled thee with salutations of praise;[13]— for it is the god of Riches who adorneth the earth, who maketh barks to prosper in the sight of man—who rejoiceth the heart of women with child—who loveth the increase of the flocks.

When thou art risen in the city of the Prince—then is the rich man filled—the small man [the poor] disdaineth the lotus—all is solid and of good quality—all herbage is for his children. Doth he forget to give food?—prosperity forsaketh the dwellings, and earth falleth into a wasting sickness.

Judgment of the Dead

The following three excerpts belong to the liturgy for burial, and were placed beside the mummified body so that it might be instructed on how to face the world beyond the tomb. According to certain fundamental beliefs, the dead person is received by the gods and goddesses that make up the court of Osiris: Anubis, Hathor (the cow), the Lady of Cemeteries, Nît, the two Maits who preside over justice and truth, plus the four sons of Horus. This escort of honor accompanies the dead person and his winged guide to an enormous room surrounded by columns of painted wood. There, at the end of the great room, Osiris is seated in a recess in the wall, the doors of which are fashioned so as to cast a dusky and mysterious light over him, mixing in a confusion of many colors his white sash with the red band and his green features, over which can be seen a green diadem with plumes at the sides. In his fists he clasps the emblems of his power, the lash and the hook. Behind him, Isis and Nephtis stand bare-breasted, their bodies wrapped tightly in silk, with upraised hands, protecting him. To the right and to the left, waiting in silence, are forty-two jurists, all, like their leader, dead and resuscitated. In silence they wait to be spoken to. The guiding spirit then advances up to the foot of the throne, bearing in his hands the images of his heart and eyes, agents and accomplices of sin and virtue. Humbly, he bows to smell the ground. Then, rising, he voices the profession of faith as given below in *A*. Next he turns to the supreme judge and recites the peroration *B*. Meanwhile, in the room the assessors weigh the actions and deeds of the dead person on a scale animated and furnished with a small human head. Truth is placed on one side of the scale, and Thoth (from the head of the Ibis) is on the other, the dead person's heart in his hand. Always merciful, he tips the scales slightly to the side of Truth. After having ascertained the absence of all sin, he pronounces in the presence of his father, Osiris, the judgment given in *C*.

a)

The profession of faith:

Hail unto you, ye lords of Truth! hail to thee, great god, lord of Truth and Justice! I have come before thee, my master; I have been brought to see thy beauties. For I know thee, I know thy name, I know the names of thy forty-two gods who are with thee in the Hall of the Two Truths, living on the remains of sinners, gorging themselves with their blood, in that day when account is rendered before Onnophris, the true of voice. Thy name which is thine is "the god whose two twins are the ladies of the two Truths"; and I, I know you, ye lords of the two Truths, I bring unto you Truth, I have destroyed sins for you. I have not committed iniquity against men! I have not oppressed the poor! I have not made defalcations in the necropolis! I have not laid labor upon any free man beyond that which he wrought for himself! I have not transgressed, I have not been weak, I have not defaulted, I have not committed that which is an abomination to the gods. I have not caused the slave to be ill treated of his master! I have not starved any man, I have not made any to weep, I have not assassinated any man, I have not caused any man to be treacherously assassinated, and I have not committed treason against any! I have not in aught diminished the supplies of temples! I have not spoiled the shrewbread of the gods! I have not taken away the loaves and wrappings of the dead! I have done no carnal act within the sacred enclosure of the temple! I have not blasphemed! I have in nought curtailed the sacred revenues! I have not pulled down the scale of the balance! I have not falsified the beam of the balance! I have not taken away the milk from the mouths of sucklings! I have not lassoed cattle on their pastures! I have not taken with nets the birds of the gods! I have not fished in their ponds! I have not turned back the water in its season! I have not cut off a water channel in its course! I have not put out the fire in its time! I have not defrauded the Nine Gods of the choice part of victims! I have not ejected the oxen of the gods! I have not turned back the god at his coming forth! I am pure! I am pure! I am pure! Pure as this Great Bonû of Heracleopolis is pure! . . . There is no crime against me in this land of the Double Truth! Since I know the names of the gods who are with thee in the Hall of the Double Truth, save thou me from them!

b)

The peroration to the supreme judge:

Hail unto you, ye gods who are in the Great Hall of the Double Truth, who have no falsehood in your bosoms, but who live on Truth in Aûnû, and feed your hearts upon it before the Lord God who dwelleth in his solar disc! Deliver me from the Typhon who feedeth on entrails, O chiefs! in this hour of supreme judgment; grant that the deceased may come unto you, he who hath not sinned, who hath neither lied, nor done evil, nor committed any crime, who hath not borne false witness, who hath done nought against himself, but who liveth on truth, who feedeth on truth. He hath spread joy on all sides; men speak of that which he hath done, and the gods rejoice in it. He hath reconciled the god to him by his love; he hath given bread to the hungry, water to the thirsty, clothing to the naked; he hath given a boat to the shipwrecked; he hath offered sacrifices to the gods, sepulchral meals unto the manes. Deliver him from himself, speak not against him before the Lord of the Dead, for his mouth is pure, and his two hands are pure!

c)

The verdict of Thoth:

Thus saith Thoth, lord of divine discourse, scribe of the Great Ennead, to his father Osiris, lord of eternity, "Behold the deceased in this Hall of the Double Truth, his heart hath been weighed in the balance in the presence of the great genii, the lords of Hades, and been found true. No trace of earthly impurity hath been found in his heart. Now that he leaveth the tribunal true of voice, his heart is restored to him as well as his eyes and the material cover of his heart, to be put back in their places, each in its own time, his soul in heaven, his heart in the other world, as is the custom of the "Followers of Horus." Henceforth let his body lie in the hands of Anubis,[14] who presideth over the tombs; let him receive offerings at the cemetery in the presence of Onnophris; let him be as one of those favorites who follow thee; let his soul abide where it will in the necropolis of his city, he whose voice is true before the Great Ennead."

Inscription on a Libation Table

This inscription is on the libation table on which water was offered to the dead warrior Outjahorsoun. Water represents the element of humidity that gives life and resurrection to the dead, whose mummified bodies have lost all liquids. In funerary libations, water was used from famous fonts, such as Horus of Heliopolis, reputed to have therapeutic and thaumaturgic powers.

Noble chief Outjahorsoun, whose good name is Raneferket neb pehti.[15] To you I offer these libations from the land of Heliopolis.

Through them the divine orders live in the temple of the fig tree of Heliopolis. I offer them to you; be peaceful in them; live; be happy; ask what you wish from them forever. Refresh your heart with them.

These libations, Osiris, these libations chief of the soldiers, Outjahorsoun, were poured by your son, poured by Horus. I come, I bring you the Eye of Horus,[16] refresh your heart through it. I bring it to your feet; I offer you the humidity it exudes: May your heart, due to this, never stop beating.

Spell for Bringing a Bone Forth from the Throat

I am he whose head reacheth the sky,
And whose feet reach the abyss,
Who hath awakened the crocodile of wax in Pe-zême of Thebes;
For I am So, Sime, Tamaho,[17]

This is my correct name.
Anuk, anuk!
For a hawk's egg is what is in my mouth,
An ibis's egg is what is in my belly.[18]
Therefore, bone of god,
Bone of man,
Bone of bird,
Bone of fish,
Bone of animal,
Bone of anything,
None being excepted;
Therefore, that which is in thy belly,
Let it come to thy chest!
That which is in thy chest,
Let it come to thy mouth!
That which is in thy mouth,
Let it come to my hand now!
For I am he who is in the seven heavens,
Who standeth in the seven sanctuaries,
For I am the son of the living god.

Spell Uttered Over the Bite of a Dog

The spell of Amen and Triphis thus:
I am this strong messenger,[19]
Shlamala, Malet,
The mysterious one who hath reached the most mysterious one,[20]
Greshei, Greshei,[21]
The lord of Rent, Tahne, Bahne.
This dog, this black one,
The dog, the mysterious one,
This dog of the four [bitch] pups,[22]
The wild dog, son of Ophoïs,
Son of Anubis,
Relax thy tooth,
Stop thy spittle!
Thou actest as the face of Set against Osiris,[23]
Thou actest as the face of "Apop against Ra."[24]
Horus, the son of Osiris, born by Isis,
Is he with whom thou didst fill thy mouth;
N.N., son of N.N.,

Is he with whom thou didst fill thy mouth.
Listen to this speech,
Horus, who healed burning,
Who went to the abyss,
Who founded the earth;
Listen, O Yaho-Sabaho,[25]
Abiaho[26] by name!

The Legend of Isis and the Scorpion

An example of the long mythological tales narrated by wizards to formu-
late an analogy with the desired magic effect, in this case against the bite of a
scorpion.

I, Isis, left the mansion in which my brother Set had placed me.
Thout, the great one, commander of justice in heaven and earth, spake
    to me:
"Come, O Isis, O goddess, for it is good to listen,
And one liveth when another acteth as guide.
Hide thyself with thy little son!
He will come to us when his limbs have grown,
And his full strength [hath developed].
Make him take his place then on the throne of his father,
Hand over to him the dignity of the ruler of both countries!"

I went forth at the time of evening.
Seven scorpions were my followers and furnished me aid;
Tefen and Ben were behind me;
mestet and mest-[yo]tef were near me;
Petet, Tetet, and Matet prepared the way for me.

I gave orders to them aloud, my voice found access to their ears thus:
"Know that obedience in worship . . .
Distinguisheth a son of somebody from a subject.
Let your face be below on the road
As companions and guides seeking for me!"

We reached the city of Psoïs and the City of the Two Sisters
At the beginning of the [Delta] marshes as far as the city of Deh.
I approached the houses of the most respectable woman.
The noblest saw me on my way;
She closed her door to me,

Suspicious of my companions,
These, therefore, took counsel,
They placed their poison all together on the tail of Tefen.
A poor woman opened her door for me,
I entered into her house.
Tefen secretly entered under the wings of the door,
She stung the son of the rich woman.
(Fire broke forth in the house of the rich woman;[27]
There was no water to quench it,
Neither was there rain against it in the house of the rich woman;
It was not the season for this.)

This was because she had not opened to me.
Her heart was in grief,
She knew not [how to save] his life;
She roamed around in her city, lamenting;
There was not one who came at her voice.

Therefore my heart was grieved for the sake of the child;
[Wishing] to restore the innocent being to life,
I called her: "To me! Come to me! Come to me!
Behold, my mouth holdeth life;
I am a daughter well known in her city,
Through whose word the bite is stilled.
[The word] which my father taught me,
That should be known;
I am his true daughter."

Isis put her hands on the child
To revive that which had no more breath:

"O poison, O Tefen, come!
Come forth on the ground! Go not on!
The poison shall not penetrate!

O Befnet, come!
Come forth on the ground!
I am Isis the goddess,
The mistress of magic who doth magic,
The best one to speak words.

Listen to me, ye reptiles of all kinds that bite!
Fall down, thou poison of Mestet!
The poison of Mest-[yo]tef shall run no farther,
The poison of Petet and Tetet shall not rise!
Thou shalt not enter, Matet!
Fall down, do not bite!"

To the Mysterious God

Probably the narrator of this hymn, by enumerating the attributes of many divinities, has tried to create an image of a superior god, one which does not actually exist in the Egyptian pantheon.

O thou dwarf of heaven,
Thou big-faced dwarf
With high back,
With weakly legs,
The great pillar which [reacheth] from heaven [to] the lower world!
O lord of the corpse which resteth in Heliopolis,
O great lord of life who resteth in Dêdet![28]
N.N., son of N.N., guard him by day,
Watch him by night;
Protect him as thou hast protected Osiris against (Sêt)
On that day of [his] burial in Heliopolis!

I am the lion in the ship of the Phoenix.
Thy form is that of a monkey
With the face of an old man.
There were witnesses when thou didst send [a message] to me,
[When] a resting place was taken in the wall [*i.e.* of Memphis]
Thus: may a chapel of one cubit be made for me!

"Art thou not a giant of seven cubits?"
I said to thee, "Thou canst not enter into this chapel of one cubit;
Art thou not a giant of seven cubits?"
[But] thou didst enter it and rest in it.

(Fall, O flames which know not the abyss!
Thou chapel, open, open thyself!
Thou who art in it with thy monkey face,

Woe! Woe! Fire! Fire!
Thou child of the maiden,
Thou baboon!)

To Thout

This very brief and incredible invocation is a reaction to the formalistic
prayers of Amenophis IV.

> Thou savest the silent, O Thout,
> Thou sweet well of water for him who is athirst in the desert!
> It is closed for the eloquent;
> It is open for the silent.
> When the silent cometh, he findeth the well;
> The one that burneth with heat, him dost thou refresh.

Prayer of a Perjurer

Inscription on a pillar erected by a man who swore falsely by the god of
the moon.

I am a man who had wrongly said,
"(As) he remaineth" to the moon concerning the barrier.
Then before the whole country he made me see how great his might is.
I report thy power to the fish in the river
And to the birds in the sky.
They [i.e. mankind] shall say to the children of their children,
"Beware of the moon, who can turn this [away] when he is appeased."

Prayer of a Blind Man

This prayer is recited by a man who, like the one above, dramatically implores pardon from the god to whom he attributes his blindness.

I am one who swore falsely by Ptah, the Lord of Justice;
He made me see darkness in daytime.
I shall tell his power to the one who knoweth him not, as well as to the
    one who knoweth,
To the small and to the great.
Beware of Ptah, the Lord of Justice!
Behold, he doth not overlook a [wrong] deed of any man.
Abstain from pronouncing Ptah's name wrongly!

Lo, he who pronounceth it wrongly,
Behold, he goeth to destruction.

He made me to be like a dog on the street;
I was in his hand.
He made me to be a spectacle for men and for gods
Since I have been a man who wrought abomination against his master.

Ptah, the Lord of Justice, is just to me;
He hath afflicted me with punishment.
Be merciful unto me!
I have seen that thou art merciful.

To Osiris

Praise to thee, Osiris, son of Nut![29] Lord of the horns; with tall atef-crown! To whom the crown was given [in] joy in the presence of the Ennead of gods.

He, the reverence for whom Atum[30] hath fashioned in the hearts of men and of gods, of the glorified and of the dead.

He to whom the lordship was given in Heliopolis; of great estate in Busiris;[31] fearful in the Two Places, terrible in Rosetau, revered in Ehnas, mighty in Tenent.

The greatly loved upon earth, of goodly memory in the gods' palace, that appeared in greatness at Abydos.[32]

He to whom justification was ascribed before the entire Ennead, for whom a slaughtering was made in the great hall at Herwer.

He of whom the great mighty ones were in terror, and before whom the great ones rose up from their mats.

Shu hath inspired fear of him, and Tefnet hath created reverence for him.

The two sanctuaries of Upper and Lower Egypt came making obeisance to him, because the fear of him is so great and the reverence for him, so immense.

Inscription on a Funerary Scarab

Stone and metal scarabs were placed in tombs, on the chest of the deceased, with recommendations to the infernal gods inscribed on them.

Oh heart that I have from my mother! Oh heart that belongs to my spirit, do not appear against me as witness, provide no opposition against me before the judges, do not contradict me before him who governs the balance; thou art my spirit that is in my body . . . do not suffer our name to stink . . . tell no lie against me before the god.

Glorification of the Dead Cannibal

The deceased is conceived as a hunter who captures stars and eats transfigured gods, a god who devours his fathers and mothers.

He it is who devours men and lives on gods. The Clasper of the Heads and the Emi-kehuu are they who capture them for him; he who is Splendid of Head guards them for him and drives them to him, the Heri-terut binds them for him, the runners with all knives stab them for him, and draw out their entrails. The Sheshnu cuts them up for him and cooks part of them in his evening caldrons. He it is who devours their magic and swallows their illuminated ones. The great ones among them are his morning meal, the middle ones are his evening meal, and the small ones, his night meal. The old men and women among them come into his oven. The great one in heaven casts fire on the caldron, which contains the thighs of their eldest. The inhabitants of heaven are his property, and what he shoots are caldrons with the limbs of their wives. This horrible fare is profitable to him, for he consumes their full entrails and enjoys therewith satiety; he devours their hearts and their crowns and thereby gains their powers, so that their magic is in his body; he swallows the understanding of every god.

Notes

1. Amen-Ra means "creator of all things" or "he who conceals his name." Represented as a king, with all regal majesties and powers of a Pharaoh, he was the god of Thebes, where two temples were dedicated to him. He was worshiped as the physical father of the Pharaoh; his wife was a vulture, Mut, and his son, the moon god Konsu.

2. Heliopolis, originally called On, was the capital of Lower Egypt during the period of the Pharaohs, and famous for the solar divinities worshiped there, such as Har-akhti, Atun and Riê.

3. Regions to the south and southeast of Egypt.

4. Ptah, one of the major gods, holds in his hands the scepter of Lord of the Two Countries. He had a temple at Memphis. He is probably a symbol of primordial matter which emerged from chaos, for which reason he bears the name of "first of the gods," "father of the gods." By his word, he created everything. He protects artists and workmen.

5. These are all symbols of regal power.

6. A sanctuary in Heliopolis.

7. Thoth, originally a moon god, reckons time and measures the earth,

substitutes the sun, invents scripture and magic books, and functions as a scribe in judgments of death. He is identified with the monkey, the crane, the ibis, and the palm. His cult is located in Hermopolis.

8. Hapi is the personification of the Nile, similarly represented in two figures, one red and one blue, one to preside over Lower Egypt and the other over Upper Egypt.

9. Khnemu, sovereign of Elephantine and Cataract, is a supreme Nile god who pasted the world together with a mixture of lime and water. The author of the hymn declares that when the Nile overflows its banks, it takes on the form of a *K,* in honor of the god who created the whole world with lime from its waters.

10. He provides so many riches that men are forced to build new ships in order to transport them.

11. The goddess Nît, the heifer born from the midst of the primordial waters, had two crocodiles as children. In monuments she is represented with her children hanging from her breasts.

12. Reference to the frequent arguments which arose during periods of drought regarding the allotment of water for irrigation.

13. Reference to the papyrus thrown in the river bearing laudatory hymns to the Nile god.

14. Anubis is the god-jackal, an inhabitant of the underworld, venerated in Heliopolis. He presided at embalming ceremonies and was an adept of the scales used for the dead at the infernal tribunal. According to tradition, he is a brother of Osiris, whose body he located by his sense of smell.

15. The first name of Psammethik II. Evidently the warrior had been authorized to use this name as a reward for services rendered.

16. Here the term "Horus's eye" is used in a generic sense to mean a product which beguiles by its suavity and sweetness.

17. Magic names in which a corruption of the Hebrew Yô (Yhvh) Sabaoth can be seen.

18. He possesses the sun (hawk's egg) and the moon (ibis's egg).

19. Probably in the sense of "angel."

20. Literally: "He who is great in secret."

21. Terms not interpreted.

22. Probable allusion to the children of Horus.

23. Set, who by origin is the okapi, is a patron, along with Hor, of the realm. He provokes storms and is identified with the Greek Typhoon. During the XII Dynasty he was named a persecutor of Osiris in the myth of the divine death, thus drawing down upon himself the reputation of personifying the evil life. Reference is made in the text to this last attribute.

24. Apop is the serpent personifying storm clouds that struggle against Ra, the sun.

25. Corruption of the Hebraic Yhvh Sabaoth.

26. Variation of ab-haho, father of Yhvh.

27. These four lines about the fire appear to have no significance. Their insertion may be explained by the reference in the text saying that these bites burned like fire.

28. The body lying in Heliopolis is Osiris, just as Osiris is the god of the city of Dêd(u), called Dêdet.

29. Nut is the feminine personification of the sky.

30. The king-god of Heliopolis, representing the evening sun, the old sun.

31. Busiris, Busiride, among other variations of the name, is the capital city of the IX *nomo* of Egypt, originally called Sete. The god of this city was similar to Osiris, since there also a tomb of the god had been uncovered and great festivals were held in honor of the resurrection. Here the author lists the places sacred to the god: Rosetau, Ehnas, Tenent.

32. Abydos also possessed a tomb of Osiris and was therefore the goal of pilgrims. During the festival, which was held in the form of sacred mysteries, the victory of Osiris over Set was celebrated.

✴

Mesopotamia

Hymn to the Moon God

O Lord, hero of the gods, who in heaven and earth is exalted in his
    uniqueness,
Father Nanna,[1] lord Anshar,[2] hero of the gods,
Father Nanna, great lord Anu,[3] hero of the gods,
Father Nanna, lord Sin,[4] hero of the gods,
Father Nanna, lord of Ur,[5] hero of the gods,
Father Nanna, lord of Egishshirgal,[6] hero of the gods,
Father Nanna, lord of the shining crown,[7] hero of the gods,
Father Nanna, who is grandly perfected in kingship, hero of the gods,
Father Nanna, who solemnly advances in garments of princeliness, hero
    of the gods,
Ferocious bull, whose horn is thick, whose legs are perfected, who is
    bearded in lapis, and filled with luxury and abundance,
Offspring which is self-created, full grown in form, pleasant to the
    sight, whose exuberance is unrestrained,
Womb that gives birth to everything, which dwells in a holy habitation
    with living creatures,

247

Begetter, merciful in his disposing, who holds in his hand the life of
the whole land,

O Lord, thy divinity fills the wide sea with awe, as well as the distant
heavens.

O progenitor of the land, who has founded temples, thou likewise dost
give them their names.

O father begetter of gods and men, who founds shrines and establishes
offerings,

Namer of kingships, giver of the scepter, thou dost determine destiny
unto distant days.

O mighty prince whose deep heart no one of the gods comprehends,

Swift colt whose knees do not tire, who opens the way for his brother
gods,

Whose light goes from the base of heaven to the zenith, who opens the
door of heaven and gives light to all people,

Father begetter, who looks favorably upon all living creatures. . . .

O Lord, decider of the destinies of heaven and earth, whose word no
one alters,

Who controls water and fire, leader of living creatures, what god is like
thee?

In heaven, who is exalted? Thou! Thou alone art exalted.

On earth, who is exalted? Thou! Thou alone art exalted.

Thou! When thy word is pronounced in heaven, the Igigi[8] prostrate
themselves.

Thou! When thy word is pronounced on earth, the Anunnaki[9] kiss the
ground.

Thou! When thy word drifts along in heaven like the wind, it makes
rich the feeding and drinking of the land.

Thou! When thy word settles down on the earth, green vegetation is
produced.

Thou! Thy word makes fat the sheepfold and the stall; it makes living
creatures widespread.

Thou! Thy word causes truth and justice to be, so that the people speak
the truth.

Thou! Thy word which is far away in heaven, which is hidden in the
earth, is something no one sees.

Thou! Who can comprehend thy word, who can equal it?

O Lord, in heaven as to dominion, on earth as to valor, among the gods
thy brothers, thou hast not a rival.

Hymn to Ramman

"Glorious Ramman"[10] is thy name, eminent god:
"Lord Ramman, gigantic steer and glorious," is thy name, eminent god:
"Ramman, child of Heaven, gigantic steer and glorious," is thy name,
    eminent god:
"Lord of Karkar, gigantic steer and glorious," is thy name, eminent god:
"Ramman, lord of plenty, gigantic steer and glorious," is thy name
    [eminent] god:
"Companion of the lord Ea,[11] gigantic steer and glorious,"
"Father Ramman, lord that rideth the storm," is thy name, eminent god:
"Father Ramman, that rideth the great storm," is thy name, eminent god:
"Father Ramman, that rideth the great lion," is thy name, eminent god:
"Ramman, lion of heaven, gigantic steer and glorious," is thy name,
    eminent god:
Thy name doth enthrall the land.
Thy splendor covers the land like a garment.
At thy thunder the great mountain father Enlil[12] is shaken.
At thy rumbling the great mother Ninlil[13] trembles.
Enlil addressed his son Ramman;
"Oh my child, spirit of wisdom with all-seeing eyes, spirit of wisdom
    with elevated vision;
Ramman, spirit of wisdom with all-seeing eyes, spirit of wisdom with
    elevated vision,
Spirit who, like Pleiades, art fraught with knowledge, spirit of wisdom
    with elevated vision;
Spirit, may thy sonorous voice give forth its utterance, spirit of wisdom
    with elevated vision;
The lightning thy messenger send forth, spirit of wisdom with elevated
    vision;
My son go forth, go up, who that cometh can strive [with thee]?
If the foe do evil, the father is over thee, who can strive with thee?
With the little hailstones, exceedingly cunning [art thou], who can
    strive with thee?
With the great hailstones, exceedingly cunning [art thou], who can
    strive with thee?
Thy little and great hailstones let be upon him.
Let thy right hand destroy the foe, thy seizing arm pluck him away."
Ramman gave ear to the words of the father who was over him,
The father Ramman who went from the house, spirit of sonorous voice,

Who from the house, from the dwelling, went up, the youthful lion,
Who from the dwelling took his way [?], the spirit of counsel.

Lamentation for Nirgal

O mighty lord, hero, first-born of NU.NAM.NIR![14]
Prince of the Anunnaki,[15] lord of the battle!
Offspring of KU.TU.SAR,[16] the mighty queen!
O Nirgal,[17] strong one of the gods, the darling of NIN.MIN.NA![18]
Thou treadest in the bright heavens, lofty is thy place!
Thou art exalted in the Underworld and art the benefactor of its . . .
With Ia[19] among the multitude of the gods inscribe thy counsel!
With Sin[20] in the heavens thou seekest all things!
And Bîl[21] thy father has granted thee that the black-headed race, all
    living creatures,
The cattle of Nirgal, created things, thy hand should rule!
I ——, the son of ——, am thy servant!
The . . . of god and goddess are laid upon me!
Uprooting and destruction are in my house! . . .
Since thou art beneficent, I have turned to thy divinity!
Since thou art compassionate, I have sought for thee!
Since thou art pitiful, I have beheld . . . !
Since thou art merciful, I have taken my stand before thee!
Truly pity me and hearken to my cries!
May thine angry heart have rest!
Loosen my sin, my offense . . .
O god and angry goddess . . .
Let me talk of thy greatness, let me bow in humility before thee!

Lamentation for Ishtar

I pray to thee,[22] O Lady of ladies, goddess of goddesses.
O Ishtar, queen of all peoples, who guides mankind aright,
O Irnini,[23] ever exalted, greatest of the Igigi,[24]
O most mighty of princesses, exalted is thy name.
Thou indeed art the light of heaven and earth, O valiant daughter of Sin.
O supporter of arms, who determines battle,
O possessor of all divine power, who wears the crown of dominion,
O Lady, glorious is thy greatness; over all the gods it is exalted.
O star of lamentation, who causes peaceable brothers to fight,
Yet who constantly gives friendship,

O mighty one, Lady of battle, who suppresses the mountains,

O Gushea,[25] the one covered with fighting and clothed with terror,

Thou dost make complete judgment and decision, the ordinances of heaven and earth.

Chapels, holy places, sacred sites, and shrines pay heed to thee.

Where is not thy name, where is not thy divine power?

Where are thy likenesses not fashioned, where are thy shrines not founded?

Where art thou not great, where art thou not exalted?

Anu, Enlil, and Ea have made thee high; among the gods they have caused thy dominion to be great.

They have made thee high among all the Igigi; they have made thy position pre-eminent.

At the thought of thy name heaven and earth tremble.

The gods tremble; the Anunnaki stand in awe.

To thine awesome name mankind must pay heed.

For thou art great and thou art exalted.

All the black-headed [people and] the masses of mankind pay homage to thy might.

The judgment of the people in truth and righteousness thou indeed dost decide.

Thou regardest the oppressed and mistreated; daily thou causest them to prosper.

Thy mercy! O Lady of heaven and earth, shepherdess of the weary people.

Thy mercy! O Lady of holy Eanna,[26] the pure storehouse.

Thy mercy! O Lady; unwearied are thy feet; swift are thy knees.

Thy mercy! O Lady of conflict [and] of all battles.

O shining one, lioness of the Igigi, subduer of angry gods,

O most powerful of all princes, who holdest the reins [over] kings,

[But] who dost release the bridles of all maidservants,

Who art exalted and firmly fixed, O valiant Ishtar, great is thy might.

O brilliant one, torch of heaven and earth, light of all peoples,

O unequaled angry one of the fight, strong one of the battle,

O firebrand which is kindled against the enemy, which brings about the destruction of the furious,

O gleaming one, Ishtar, assembler of the host,

O deity of men, goddess of women, whose designs no one can conceive,

Where thou dost look, one who is dead lives; one who is sick rises up;

The erring one who sees thy face goes aright.

I have cried to thee, suffering, wearied, and distressed, as thy servant.

See me, O my Lady; accept my prayers.

Faithfully look upon me and hear my supplication.

Promise my forgiveness and let thy spirit be appeased.

Pity! For my wretched body which is full of confusion and trouble.

Pity! For my sickened heart which is full of tears and suffering.

Pity! For my wretched intestines [which are full of] confusion and
trouble.

Pity! For my afflicted house which mourns bitterly.

Pity! For my feelings which are satiated with tears and suffering.

O exalted Irnini, fierce lion, let thy heart be at rest.

O angry wild ox, let thy spirit be appeased.

Let the favor of thine eyes be upon me.

With thy bright features look faithfully upon me.

Drive away the evil spells of my body [and] let me see thy bright light.

How long, O my Lady, shall my adversaries be looking upon me,

In lying and untruth shall they plan evil against me,

Shall my pursuers and those who exult over me rage against me?

How long, O my Lady, shall the crippled and weak seek me out?

One has made for me long sackcloth; thus I have appeared before thee.

The weak have become strong; but I am weak.

I toss about like flood-water, which an evil wind makes violent.

My heart is flying; it keeps fluttering like a bird of heaven.

I mourn like a dove night and day.

I am beaten down, and so I weep bitterly.

With "Oh" and "Alas" my spirit is distressed.

I—what have I done, O my god and my goddess?

Like one who does not fear my god and my goddess, I am treated;

While sickness, headache, loss, and destruction are provided for me;

So are fixed upon me terror, disdain, and fullness of wrath,

Anger, choler, and indignation of gods and men.

I have to expect, O my Lady, dark days, gloomy months, and years of
trouble.

I have to expect, O my Lady, judgment of confusion and violence.

Death and trouble are bringing me to an end.

Silent is my chapel; silent is my holy place;

Over my house, my gate, and my fields silence is poured out.

As for my god, his face is turned to the sanctuary of another.

My family is scattered; my roof is broken up.

[But] I have paid heed to thee, my Lady; my attention has been turned
to thee.

To thee have I prayed; forgive my debt.

Forgive my sin, my iniquity, my shameful deeds, and my offense.
Overlook my shameful deeds; accept my prayer;
Loosen my fetters; secure my deliverance;
Guide my steps aright; radiantly, like a hero, let me enter the streets
    with the living.
Speak so that at thy command the angry god may be favorable;
[And] the goddess who has been angry with me may turn again.
[Now] dark and smoky, may my brazier glow;
[Now] extinguished, may my torch be lighted.
Let my scattered family be assembled;
May my stable be enlarged.
Accept the abasement of my countenance; hear my prayers.
Faithfully look upon me and accept my supplication.
How long, O my Lady, wilt thou be angered so that thy face is turned
    away?
How long, O my Lady, wilt thou be infuriated so that thy spirit is
    enraged?
Turn thy neck which thou hast set against me; set thy face [toward]
    good favor.
Like the water of the opening up of a canal, let thy emotions be released.
My foes like the ground let me trample;
Subdue my haters and cause them to crouch down under me.
Let my prayers and my supplications come to thee.
Let thy great mercy be upon me.
Let those who see me in the street magnify thy name.
As for me, let me glorify thy divinity and thy might before the black-
    headed [people, saying],
Ishtar indeed is exalted; Ishtar indeed is queen;
The Lady indeed is exalted; the Lady indeed is queen.
Irnini, the valorous daughter of Sin, has no rival.

Accadian Prayer to Shamash

  This incantation is an excerpt from reconstructed fragments.

Magnified, perfect one, son of Nannar,
Who alone opens the sight of men, causing them to behold the light,
Shamash, guide to the dying and the living, controller of all things
    with names.
God, who is the light of heaven and earth, splendor of the lands,
Lord of Sippar, protection of Ebbarra,

Elder brother of Marduk, the help of Babylon.
The "Six Hundred" gods give heed to thy command.
The wide-dwelling peoples, they that are dark-headed, praise thy bravery.
Thou causest the lonely man to have a companion.
To the impotent thou givest an heir.
The fastening of the lock pin of heaven thou openest.
Unto him that sees not, thou providest light; thou readest the occult
    tablet, which is not revealed.
Thou writest omens on the innards of sheep, and providest a decision,
O judge of the gods, lord of the "Six Hundred" gods!
Shamash, lord of the fate of the lands and of concepts art thou, fix my
    fate, make happy my way.
May my omens be satisfactory,
    and my dreams be propitious.
The dream vision which I have seen make propitious.
May I walk righteously, and obtain a companion.
May there be good fortune in my days.
Send me pious thoughts.
May my speech in the market place be acceptable.
In joy and gladness may I pass my days.
May god, the unrivaled one, stand at my right, and the goddess . . .
    stand at my left.
May the god, who brings peace, go at my side.
May the guardian of peace behind me tarry not.
May Bunene, the prince, say to thee words [in my] favor.
May Aya, thy beloved wife, say to thee "be at peace" [with him].
O Shamash, first of the gods art thou, have mercy.
May heaven be glad of thee, and earth joyfully cry to thee.
May the gods of the universe adore thee.
May the great gods make merciful thy heart.

To Shamash

Shamash, when thou enterest into the midst of heaven,
May the bar of the shining heavens speak peace to thee.
May the door of heaven salute thee with prayer.
May Justice, thy beloved messenger, guide thee.
Make glorious thy fame in Ebarra, abode of thy lordship.
May Aja thy beloved spouse joyfully come to meet thee.
May thy heart repose in peace.
May the banquet of thy divinity be set for thee.

O heroic and strong Shamash, with one tongue may they praise thee.
O lord of Ebarra hasten, may thy path be straight.
O Shamash, direct thou thy way and walk in [thy] true course [until thou comest] to thy subterranean abode.
O Shamash, thou art the judge of the Land, of its counsel thou art its director.

To Shamash

Only the complete and reconstructed parts of this hymn are given.

Direct thou the laws of all men.
O god of justice, in heaven thou art steadfast.
O god of righteousness, in the lands thou art the sage.
Righteousness and wisdom in the lands thou art.
The true thou knowest, the wicked thou knowest.
O Shamash, Justice lifts her head to thee.
O Shamash, the wicked is lacerated before thee as with a flail.
Shamash, thou art the help of Anu and Enlil.
Shamash, thou art the far-famed judge of heaven and earth.
Shamash, thou art he who renders the judgment of the gods.
Shamash, the decrees of the Anunnaki thou decreest.
Shamash, far-famed judge, great lord of the lands art thou.
Lord of the creatures with the breath of life, merciful one of the lands, art thou.
O Shamash, this day make pure, make clean the king, son of his god.
May whatsoever causes the evil, which is in his body, be removed afar.
Like a stone ointment bowl wash him.
Like a stone butter bowl purify him.
Like copper which has been purified may he be pure.
Loosen his bonds.
As long as he lives may he speak of thy greatness.
And I, the magician, thy servant, will sing thy praises.

To Shamash

I have called unto thee, O Shamash, in the midst of the bright skies.
Sit thou in the shadow of the cedar.
Verily thy feet are set upon the hill of cypress.
The lands shout to thee, they rejoice for thee, O praised one!
All peoples behold thy light.

Thy great net overwhelms all lands.
Thou art Shamash, who knowest all of them,
Destroyer of the wicked, who givest effect to the rituals of expiation
    for evil signs and omens, for disturbing and harmful dreams,
Severing the cord of evil, which destroys people and land.
The evil workers of sorcery, witchcraft, poison, I have designed before
    thee;
I have fashioned images of them with pure millet,
Of them who have exercised sorcery, who have planned things unpro-
    pitious.
Their heart plotted, being full of wickedness.
Assist, O Shamash, light of the great gods.
May I be stronger than the worker of my witchcraft.
May the god, my creator, stand at my side.
The washing of my mouth, the right use of my hands,
Correctly direct, O lord, light of the universe, Shamash, the judge.

Fragments of a Penitential Psalm

Forgive me my sins, shower me with mercy,
Cause my woman to walk among pure women.
I feel thy chastisement,
Witness this supplicating hand of a servant who fears his God and
    Goddess.
O my God, be merciful!
O my Goddess, be not angry!
Hear my prayer, see my uplifted hands,
Turn thy face upon me.
Calm thy angry heart,
Calm thy wrath.
Be merciful.
I sing thy deeds, never forgetting them,
Throughout all lands and people.
My master's God created me and my name,
Watches over my soul, will care for my posterity.
O my wrathful God, calm thy stormy heart,
Be merciful toward me, O my angry Goddess.
Who, O my God, knows thy dwelling?
Never shall I know
Thy magnificent dwelling.
Like the weeping reed, NA-A, I bend in sadness.

O my God forgive me.
Turn not thy back on me.
Turn thy face full on me from thy splendid dwelling
In the sky, and make me strong.
May kind words fall from thy lips. Tell me I shall prosper.
Tell me with thy chaste tongue that I shall prosper!
Let me not be rent and stricken by tribulations.
I cry to thee:
Show me my destiny,
Lengthen my days, give me the gift of life.

To Samas

O Samas,[27]
Give me life.
Into the pure arms of my God and Goddess, hand me,
For my salvation and my life.
Bewitched!
O Samas, thou art king of earth and sky,
And govern all both high and low,
O Samas, who has power over life and death,
Free this prisoner.
Incorruptible judge of humanity thou art.
Illustrious son of an illustrious Lord of illustrious origins,
Powerful son, light of the land,
Sweep away these dark clouds from earth and sky, O Samas.
O Samas, the witchery which now for many days
Eats at me, is not yet ended.
In me are the corruption and blight of the flesh.
This witchery eats at me when I am among men,
When I am among animals in the fields, wherever I am
And with all that has a name,
And has filled me with sickness and loathing.
I am stricken by the corruption of this flesh and heart.
My days and nights are sleepless,
I am fallen on evil days, my soul in anguish.
Out of pain and lamentation have I grown weak.
I know not the source of my wretchedness,
Nor what crime I have committed.
It seems I have always sinned,
That I have broken my God's commandments.

O my Lord, arise and hear my prayer.
O Samas, arise and hear,
For the germ of my sickness has utterly destroyed me:
Whether the germ is an enchantment of my father,
An enchantment of my mother,
An enchantment of the seven branches of my father's house,
An enchantment of my caste and my male relatives,
An enchantment of my family and my female relatives,
An enchantment of life or death,
An enchantment of posterity and descendants,
Or whether for false swearing or failing to swear,
For having sworn in the name of father, mother,
Brother, sister, friend, companion, river or lake,
In the name of plain, in the name of weapons,
Or in the name of destruction,
Or for swearing without loyalty in the name of my God—
I know not.
I beseech thee, O Samas, great Lord,
In the name of humanity, the beasts in the fields,
And all that grows and has a name,
Strike down this sickness that weighs upon me.
May Marduk set my body right.
A malevolent spirit, an alu, an evil utukku,
An evil shedu, an evil rabisu, a namtaru,
A labasu, a labartu, an ahhazu,
A lilu, a lilitu, a servant of lilu,
That perhaps inhabits my body, my flesh, my articulation. . . .

Dedicatory Prayer to En-Me-Shar-Ra

Enchantment.
O EN-ME-SHAR-RA,[28] Lord of the land, Lord of Arallu,
Lord of the earth and the place from which no one returns,
Sovereign of the Anunnaki,
Thou who makest the laws of earth, who art the bridge
Between earth and sky,
Great Lord, without whom NIN-GIR-SU
Could not water the lands and fill the rivers
To make us prosperous in plants and seeds.
Lord of all creation, whose power dominates the earth,

Who consolidates all space, touches the extremity
Of the lower world,
Who gives throne and scepter to Anu and Bel,
By whose orders,
In whose presence,
This temple shall remain throughout all time.
May thy tower be glorified
As thy dwelling place on this earth.
Ever in it will Anu, Bel, and Ea dwell.
And I, N.N., the August one, thy servant,[29]
Bring before thy divine presence
A prosperous name in the eternity of our days.
The dwelling of the great gods dominates my land.
In a tranquil house live I.

Hymn to Gula

O Goddess NIN-DIN-DI-GA, "Sovereign who gives life to the dead,"
Sovereign who grants rest to all men,
Goddess NIN-KAR-RA-AG, sovereign of enchantment and witchery,
Sovereign of commerce and works of art,
The frowning one, powerful, imperious,
Goddess KUR-RIB-BA, who triumphs over evil, placates wrath,
Goddess ME-ME, who lights the day, O glorious ME-ME,
Broad-beamed as earth and sky,
Goddess DAGAL-SHU-HAL-BI, whose merciful words
Placate the body,
Good shedu, who makes the knife gleam, who grants a benign shedu,
Good lamassu, who forms the fundament of earth and sky, who grants
     a benign lamassu,
Goddess MAH, most exalted of goddesses,
Goddess MUR-TSA-KIN-NA, who gives light to new-born infants'
     eyes, . . .
Cleanses sin, rights error,
To her, foremost among sovereigns, I cast my plea.
Listen to the prayers of men, grant them life.
Grant the soothing enchantment, the enchantment of life.
Slice the hard ties, put down painful ills.
Thou canst do all:
Decide, cut, enchant, perform all things for men.
Gather them in, render them prosperous, guide them.

To Samas

To Lugalbanda the pure, born of the mountain,
I wish to lift my voice.
To him, the high spirit from which rises the sky,
To God, whose merciful spirit is never wrathful,
To God, whose counsels guide us,
To Samas, toward the sky I wish to lift mine eyes.
To him, as to the father, I wish to lift my voice,
On him whose merciful hands provide for me
I wish to gaze.
O God, shepherd of the land, father of the black-faced men,
Though thou slumberest, thine eye sleepeth not over the land.
Heroic Samas, lift thine eye, regard the land.
None other is like unto thee, Samas.
Crowned Lord, thou guidest him who is lost.
Thou art the companion of the Lord of the shining light.
Samas, thou art thrice times the perfect hero.

To Samas

Shining with thy splendor are the powerful mountains,
Resplendent in thy light the land.
Thou art powerful over the mountains,
Thou lookest at the land.
In the center of the sky, to the rim of earth, thou hangest,
To govern the numberless men,
To guide all things created by Ea, the king and counselor.
All living things together are guided by thee,
Thou art the shepherd of all on high and below.
Thou movest across the great sky-plain,
Over the raging sea, over the mountains, over all the earth and sky
Thou movest regularly from day to day.
The lower realms of Ea, Azagsud and the Anunnaki
Are guided by thee, as are the celestial realms.
Shepherd of celestial and supernal regions,
Light of the world thou art, O Samas!
Over the vast ocean thou movest,
Over the depths unknown by the Igigi.

O Samas, thy light penerates to the uttermost depths, to the unknown
    depths of the sea.
O Samas, thou clingest to all,
Thy shield covers all lands.
Never dost thou wear mourning dress
Nor ever is thy face in darkness.
At night thou seest, thou lightest the fire,
Down unknown trails thou movest over distant realms,
O Samas, thou rushest, moving by day, rising by night.
Not one among the Igigi can move without thee.
No god in all the universe is so powerful.
At thy rising, all the gods of the land unite,
Thy splendorous light showers down upon the earth.
From every corner, at the sound of any tongue,
Thou knowest their thoughts and guidest their steps.
In thy name all men rejoice, O Samas,
For the universe ardently desires thy light.
In the diviner's cup, in the cedar shell,
Augurers, thanks to thee, can hear explanations of their dreams.
Magic preparations kneel before thee,
Before thee kneel Good and Evil.

To Samas

Samas, Lord of earth and sky, founder of cities and houses!
In thy hands are things determined and destinies formed.
Thou givest order to life and formest destinies.
Words from thy mouth undergo no changes.
Whatever judgment thy lips pronounce will never be altered.
Samas,
In these days do this:
Bless the brick-god of this house
That N.N., son of N.N., has constructed.
Grant him a happy fate,
A happy destiny.
May this brick bring happiness to its builder,
And this house bring health to its founder.
May this house be made for life and sustenance to N.N., its master.
O Samas, to him who constructed this house
Grant, out of thy generous heart,
A happy fate,

A happy destiny.
May he thrive and know abundance,
And long may it stand, the house he has built.
May it stand long.
O Samas,
Grant for N.N., the master,
A glad future for his house.
In this house
May he have joy in his heart,
And day by day take pleasure.
Grant him what he asks
As he takes possession of his house.

To Samas

Thou art lawgiver to all men.
Just God of the sky art thou.
Truly art thou the God of Justice and Wisdom of all lands.
The pious acknowledge thee, the evil quake before thee.
Samas, before thee Justice stands with head raised high.
Samas, before thee the wicked will be torn to shreds.
Samas, thou art companion to Anu and Bel,
Samas, thou art the exalted judge of earth and sky.
O Samas, who pronounces godly laws,
Who decides august sentences of the gods.
Samas, thou art the exalted judge, great master of the land,
Lord of all creatures, and thou art compassionate.
Samas, in these times purify the king, the son of thy God.
May every evil spirit be driven from his body.
As a vase is washed with alum, let him be washed,
As a vase is laden with pure cream, let him be laden.
As a vase shines splendidly, let him shine.
Let him be no longer outcast.
As long as he has breath, he will praise thee.
And I, the singer of songs, thy servant, humbly wish to serve thee.

To Samas

Incantation.
O Lord who lights the shadows and opens out dark ways,
O God who lifts the hearts of the humble, who protects the weak,

In whose great light the gods themselves find hope,
All the Anunnaki are gazing at thee.
Thou art the word and the way.
With heads held high they watch the approaching sun,
And as soon as thou art present, they burst forth joyously.
Thou art the light of the illimitable sky,
Thou art the banner of all the earth.
Earth's numberless men look upon thee and rejoice.
All the great gods send thee their perfumes.
Niklite, Lord of all living creatures, returns to the earth,
To the swarming earth, the dark cloak of his grief.
Damu, the great enchanter, is purified in his senses.
Gula, the lady who wakes the dead, is placated by pure hands.
And thou, O Marduk, merciful Lord
Whose pleasure it is to call the dead to life,
Must recite the formula that calls back life.
Man, the son of God, is pure and clear and clean.
Like a splendid vase, he is washed,
Like a vase laden with pure cream, he is laden.
Samas, prince of the gods, preserve him.
Samas, prince of the gods, ask thy merciful God
To let him prosper.
Hear this incantation against tribulations and want,
Against spirits and specters.

Enchantment

> Burn the wizard and the witch:
> Devour my enemy, devour my evil.
> A furious tempest sweeps over them:
> Like cascading waters they are lost in the swirl,
> Like carved stone their fingers are sliced off.

Against Evil Spirits

> Away! Away!
> Fly! Fly!
> Shame! Shame! Fly away in shame!
> Depart! Away, fly, begone!
> Evil spirits, rise like smoke to the sky.
> Depart from my body; fly from my body.

Be ashamed of my body.
Fly from my body.
Arise from my body.
Begone from my body.
Return not to my body.
Gather not in my body.
Come not near my body.
Don't pass near my body!

Confession of Sins

a) *Priest examines the sinner's conscience*:
Have you turned the father against the son?
Have you turned the son against the father?
Have you turned the mother against the daughter?
Have you turned the daughter against the mother?
Have you turned friend against friend?
Have you refused freedom to the prisoner?
Have you refused to break the prisoner's chains?
Have you sinned against your God?
Have you sinned against your Goddess?
Have you said "yes" instead of "no"?
Have you used false scales of measurement?
Have you driven out an illegitimate son?
Have you taken in an illegitimate son?

b) *The confession*:
I have spoken rebellious words, and wicked words,
And words not peaceful, and done bad things.
I have eaten the fruit of my God,
I have set my foot on sacred ground; bad things have I done.
I have lifted up my face to my God's property,
To my master's precious silver have my desires inclined.
I have lifted my hand, my hand has touched untouchable things.
Impurely have I entered into the houses.
My angered heart has cursed the divinity.
O my God, how long wilt thy face be turned from me?
O my Goddess, Inninni, wilt not thy face regard me?
O my Lord, don't trample thy servant in the dust.
He is sinking in the waters; give him thy hand.
Turn my sin into goodness;

Carry my faults away on the wind.
Strip me, as if they were clothes, of my sins.

c) *The sinner's promise to God*:
Riches will I devote to thy sanctuary.
By me shall thy house be constantly cared for.
With oil, as freely were it water, will I cleanse thy door,
With oil will I leave the door shining.
Before thee will I place perfumed cedar,
All species of fruit, and the best grain.

To Marduk

The God Bel gave thee sovereignty:
What more dost thou need?
The God Sin gave thee pre-eminence:
What more dost thou need?
The God In-urta gave thee noble arms:
What more dost thou need?
The Goddess Istar assured thee victory in battle:
What more dost thou need?
The Gods Samas and Adad are thy protectors:
What more dost thou need?

Lament of the Flutes for Tammuz

When he is no more, a lament rises:
"O my loved one."
When he is no more, her lament rises:
"O my loved one."
When he is no more, her lament rises:
"O my enchanter!"
When he is no more, her lament rises:
Under the silvery cedar, vast-limbed and shady,
At Eanna, over mountains and dales, her lament rises.
The lament says that a home is rising to weep with her.
No longer does the grass have roots;
No longer does the grain have heads;
No longer is there joy in the dwelling.
She is a tired woman, a maiden, withered too soon.
The river weeps for the willow that no longer grows;

Fields weep for the herbs and grains that now grow not;
Swamps weep for the lake and the fish that have gone;
Forests weep for the glades that are parched;
Hills and plains weep for the cypress;
The vineyard weeps for the dead vine;
Pastures weep for the missing flowers;
The Palace weeps for the life that is no more.

The Vow of Puduhepa, a Hittite Queen

These are my words, the words of Puduhepa,
Great queen of Hittite lands, daughter of Kummanni:
To LELWANI, my Lady, for the health of the person
Who is "My Sun," I make this vow:
O Goddess, O My Lady, if for many long years
Thou wilt keep My Sun in good health and life,
Before thee, and on thee, O Goddess,
He will shine in splendor.

For the Pardoning of Sins

O sun Goddess of Arinna, thou art a venerated goddess;
Thy name is venerated above all others,
Thy divinity is venerated above all others.
Sun Goddess of Arinna, thou art the most venerated goddess;
Thou art grand, O sun Goddess of Arinna.
No divinity is more venerated or more great than thou;
Thou art our lady of justice,
Whose sovereignty is over land and sky,
Who fixes the limits of lands,
Who hears our supplications!
O sun Goddess of Arinna, thou art a benevolent goddess;
Humanity, O sun Goddess of Arinna, is dear to thee.
For thou forgivest, O sun Goddess of Arinna.

Notes

1. Nana is the Sumerian name of Sin, the moon god, who was also the protecting divinity of agriculture and science.
2. The god symbolizing the celestial world.
3. Anu is the sky, chief of the Mesopotamian gods.
4. Sin is the moon.

5. City.

6. Egishshirgal means "house of the great light" and "house of the oracle of the universe." It was the main temple of Ur, dedicated to the moon.

7. The images of the gods, resembling those of men, wore tiaras that distinguished them from kings by the greater number of horns.

8. 9. Igigi and Anunnaki are two divine groups forming the Babylonian pantheon: the former are gods of the sky and higher regions, while the latter are beneficent gods of the earth and the lower regions.

10. Ramman is the god of tempests, lightning, rain and thunder. The name probably means "the thunderer." Some also consider him a phallic god, since he brought rain and fecundity and had phallic attributes.

11. Lord of the ocean.

12. Enlil is the second god in the cosmic Babylonian triad. He presides over winds and hurricanes, carrying with him first destruction and then abundance. He also personifies the absolute master of the world, dominating the universe.

13. Ninlil, the wife of Enlil, dominates, with her husband, the sky and the earth.

14. A name given to Enlil.

15. An order of gods.

16. Kutusar is to be identified with Ninlil.

17. Nirgal is king of the lower regions, of war and destruction.

18. Ninmenna is Ninlil.

19. Ia is the third member of the cosmic triad, god of waters and oceans, of art and knowledge, first among sorcerers.

20. God of the moon.

21. God of hurricanes.

22. This prayer in lamentation form is directed to Ishtar, the Assyrian-Babylonian goddess of war and love. She is the most important of the figures in the feminine pantheon; the name Ishtar means "goddess."

23. Ishtar's title.

24. Gods of the sky and the higher regions.

25. Divinity with affinities to Ishtar and identified with her.

26. Temple.

27. Samas (Shamash, Babbar-Shamash) is one of the principal Babylonian and Assyrian deities, the god of the sun (the corresponding divinity of the Arabs, Shams, is feminine). He is the manifestation of the sun's beneficent activity, and also represents justice and all that is good and beautiful. The son of the moon god Sin-Nannar and of his wife, Ningal, he is sometimes referred to as "son of Anu." His wife is Aya. He, his father, Sin, and Ishtar, his sister, form the second Babylonian triad.

28. The god of foundations, of vegetations and abundance. One of the infernal gods.

29. At this point the officiant inserts his name. The term August reveals that it is a formula to be pronounced by the king.

∗

Iran

IRAN

Hymn to Haoma

Adoration to the Haoma![1]
Good is Haoma, well created is Haoma, rightly created is Haoma.
Well created and health bringing,
Gifted with good body, rightly acting,
Victorious, golden, with moist stalks.
He is very good when one eats him, and the surest for the soul.
Thy wisdom, O Golden, praise I;
Thy powers, thy victory,
Thy healthfulness, thy healing power,
Thy furtherance, thy increase,
Thy powers in the whole body, thy greatness in the whole form.
That I may go about in the world as Ruler, paining the tormentors,
    smiting the Drujas;
That I may torment all the torments, the tormenting Daevas[2] and men.
The Yâtus, Pairikas,[3] Câthras, Koyas, and Karafnas.[4]
The serpents with two feet, the very deadly two-footed [men], the
    wolves with four feet.
The armies with great masses, the running, rushing.—

For this, as the first favor, pray I thee, O Haoma, thou who art far from death: for the best place of the pure [Paradise], the shining, adorned with all brightness.

For this, as the second favor, I pray thee, O Haoma, thou who art far from death: for health for this body.

For this, as the third favor, I pray thee, O Haoma, thou who art far from death: for long life for the vital powers.

For this, as the fourth favor, I pray thee, O Haoma, thou who art far from death: that I may go about upon the earth joyous, strong, well fed, plaguing the tormentors, smiting the Drujas.

For this, as the fifth favor, I pray thee, O Haoma, thou who art far from death: that I may go about upon the earth victorious, smiting the bad, plaguing the tormentors, smiting the Drujas.

For this, as the sixth favor, pray I thee, O Haoma, thou who art far from death: May we first mark the thief, the robber, the wolf.

May no one mark him sooner than we; may we first mark him.

Haoma gives to those who, as mighty ones, make teams to hasten, horses, might, and strength.

Haoma gives to the women who wish to bear, brilliant children, pure posterity.

Haoma gives to those who recite the Nackas[5] as masters of houses, holiness and greatness.

Haoma makes manifest to those who are maidens and were long unwedded, a spouse, who quickly sues, and is endowed with good understanding.

Haoma has diminished the rule of Kerecâni, who had arisen eager after rule;

Who spake: Not hereafter shall an Âthrava,[6] a teacher, wander at will through my regions.

This [Kerecâni] would slay all increase, annihilate all increase.—

Hail to thee, thou who through thine own strength art illimitable ruler, O Haoma!

Hail to thee, thou who art acquainted with many pure-spoken speeches!

Hail to thee, thou who askest not for the pure-spoken speech!

To thee has Ahura-Mazda[7] first brought the girdle studded with stars, prepared in heaven according to the good Mazdayacnian law.

Begirt with this, thou tarriest on the heights of the mountains, to hold upright the commandments and precepts of the Mańthra.

Haoma is the lord of the house, of the clan, of the confederacy, of the region, through his holiness, [also] lord of wisdom.

I invoke thee, for strength, for victory, for the body, as very pure nourishment.

Bring us away from the plagues of the tormentors, away our spirit [from
the torments] of the poisoners.

What man in this house, this clan, this society, this region, is revenge-
ful?

From his feet take away strength,

Cast a shadow on his spirit,

Inflict a blow on his spirit.

May he not hasten forward with the feet, have no strength in the hands;

May he not see the earth with his eyes, not see the cattle with eyes,

Who hates our soul, who hates our body.

Against the serpent, the green, terrible, bringing forth poison,

Come hither with a remedy for the pure, to protect the body, O golden
Haoma.

Against the wicked, corrupt, tormenting, and plaguing [men],

Come hither with a weapon for the pure, to protect the body, O golden
Haoma.

Against the head of the wicked, profligate, hindering men,

Come hither with a weapon for the pure, to protect the body, O golden
Haoma.

Against the very wicked, impure destroyer of the world, who certainly
has in remembrance the words of this law, but does not perform,

Come hither with a weapon for the pure, to protect the body, O golden
Haoma.

Against the harlots,[8] endowed with magic art, causing concupiscence,
exciting to lust, whose spirit goes forward like a cloud driven by
the wind,

Come hither with a weapon for the pure, to protect the body, O golden
Haoma.

Yes, O golden Hoama, bring hither a weapon for the pure, to protect
the body.

Hymn to Ashi Vanguhi

Ashi[9] is fair; Ashi is radiant with joy; she is far-piercing with her
rays. Ashi gives good Glory unto those men whom thou dost follow,
O Ashi! Full of perfumes is the house in which the good, powerful
Ashi Vanguhi puts her . . . feet, for long friendship.

Those men whom thou dost attend, O Ashi! are kings of kingdoms,
that are rich in horses, with large tributes, with snorting horses, sound-

ing chariots, flashing swords, rich in aliments and in stores of food; well scented where the beds are spread and full of all the other riches that may be wished for. Happy the man whom thou dost attend! do thou attend me, thou rich in all sorts of desirable things and strong!

Those men whom thou dost attend, O Ashi Vanguhi! have houses that stand well laid up, rich in cattle, foremost in Asha, and long supported. Happy the man whom thou dost attend! Do thou attend me, thou rich in all sorts of desirable things and strong!

The men whom thou dost attend, O Ashi Vanguhi! have beds that stand well spread, well adorned, well made, provided with cushions and with feet inlaid with gold. Happy the man whom thou dost attend! Do thou attend me, thou rich in all sorts of desirable things and strong!

The men whom thou dost attend, O Ashi Vanguhi! have their ladies that sit on their beds, waiting for them: they lie on the cushions, adorning themselves, . . . , with square bored earrings and a necklace of gold: "When will our lord come? when shall we enjoy in our bodies the joys of love?" Happy the man whom thou dost attend! Do thou attend me, thou rich in all sorts of desirable things and strong!

The men whom thou dost attend, O Ashi Vanguhi! have daughters that sit . . .; thin is their waist, beautiful is their body, long are their fingers; they are as fair of shape as those who look on can wish. Happy the man whom thou dost attend! Do thou attend me, thou rich in all sorts of desirable things and strong!

The men whom thou dost attend, O Ashi Vanguhi! have horses swift and loud-neighing; they drive the chariot lightly, they take it to the battle, they bear a gallant praiser [of the gods], who has many horses, a solid chariot, a sharp spear, a long spear, and swift arrows, who hits his aim, pursuing after his enemies, and smiting his foes. Happy the man whom thou dost attend! Do thou attend me, thou rich in all sorts of desirable things and strong!

The men whom thou dost attend, O Ashi Vanguhi! have large-humped, burden-bearing camels, flying from the ground or fighting with holy fieriness. Happy the man whom thou dost attend! Do thou attend me, thou rich in all sorts of desirable things and strong!

The men whom thou dost attend, O Ashi Vanguhi! have hoards of silver and gold brought together from far distant regions; and garments of splendid make. Happy the man whom thou dost attend! Do thou attend me, thou rich in all sorts of desirable things and strong!

Do not turn thy look from me! turn thy mercy toward me, O great Ashi! thou art well made and of a noble seed; thou art sovereign at thy wish; thou art Glory in a bodily form.

Hymn to Souls

Here praise we now the soul and body of the Bull,
Then our souls, and the souls of the cattle, which desire to maintain us
    in life,
For whom these, who are for those.
The souls of those going afoot, and of the riders, praise we.
Then we praise the souls of the pure, who have ever been born, men
    and women,
Whose good laws one honors, will honor, and has honored.
Then we invoke the good men and women.
The Amesha-Spentas,[10] the ever living, ever profiting,
Who dwell together with Vohu-manu and the female [Genii] also.
As Thou, Ahura-Mazda, hast thought, spoken, done, and created what
    [is] good,
So we give to Thee, offer to Thee, praise Thee,
Pray to Thee, acknowledge ourselves as Thy debtors, Ahura-Mazda.

Professions of Faith

I drive away the Daevas, I profess myself a Zarathustrian, an expeller
of the Daevas, a follower of the teaching of Ahura,

A hymn-singer of the Amesha-Spentas, a praiser of the Amesha-
spentas.

To Ahura-Mazda, the good, endued with good wisdom, I offer all
good.

To the Pure, Rich, Majestic:

Whatever are the best goods to Him, to whom the cow, to whom
purity belongs, from whom arises the light, the brightness which is
inseparable from the lights.

Spenta-armaiti, the good, choose I, may she belong to me.

By my praise will I save the cattle from theft and robbery.

[To keep far off] hurt and affliction from the Mazdayacnian clans.

I promise to the heavenly free course, dwelling according to their
desire.

That they may dwell on this earth with the cattle.

With prayer to Ashi, with uplifted [Draona?] pray I as follows:

May I not hereafter bring harm and affliction on the Mazdayacnian
clans.

Not on account of love for the body, not for the love of life.

I deny rule to the bad, wicked, wandering in error, evil-witting Daevas,

The most lying of beings, the most wicked of beings, the most reprobate of beings.

I deny to the Daevas, to those possessed with Daevas, to the sorcerers, the possessed by sorcerers, to all evil beings:

I deny with thoughts, words, works, and tokens, rule to those that are bad and fearful.

Thus has Ahura-Mazda commanded Zarathustra,

In all questionings, in all meetings in which Ahura-Mazda and Zarathustra conversed with one another.

So also has Zarathustra renounced the rule of the Daevas,

In all questionings, in all meetings in which Ahura-Mazda and Zarathustra conversed with one another.

Thus I also, as a Mazdayacnian, a follower of Zarathustra, renounce the rule of the Daevas, as the pure Zarathustra has renounced them.

As the water, as the trees, as the well-created cow, as Ahura-Mazda who created the cow, who [created] the pure man.

Like Zarathustra, like Kava-vîstâcpa,[11] like Frashaoctra and Jamâcpa, like any one of the Profitable, open-working, pure, of such belief am I, too,

A Mazdayacnian. As a Mazdayacnian, a follower of Zarathustra, will I confess myself,

As a praiser, as a follower.

I praise the well-thought sentiment, the well-spoken speech, the well-performed action. I praise the good Mazdayacnian law, the free from doubt, removing strife.

[I praise] marriage between relations, the pure of the [women] who are, and are about to be, the best, greatest, fairest, the Ahurian, Zarathustrian.

To Ahura-Mazda I offer every good. Let this be the laud of the Mazdayacnian law.

Hymn to Sirius

We offer up libations unto Tistrya,[12] the bright and glorious star, that gives happy dwelling and good dwelling; the white, shining, seen afar, and piercing; the health-bringing, loud-snorting, and high, piercing from afar with its shining, undefiled rays; and unto the waters of the wide sea, the Vanguhi of wide renown, and the species of the Bull, made by Mazda, the awful kingly Glory, and the Fravashi of the holy Spitama Zarathustra.

We sacrifice unto Tistrya, the bright and glorious star, who is the seed of the waters, powerful, tall, and strong, whose light goes afar; powerful and highly working, through whom the brightness and the seed of the waters come from the high Apam Napât.

We sacrifice unto Tistrya, the bright and glorious star; for whom long flocks and herds and men, looking forward for him and deceived in their hope: "When shall we see him rise up, the bright and glorious star Tistrya? When will the springs run with waves as thick as a horse's size and still thicker? Or will they never come?"

We sacrifice unto Tistrya, the bright and glorious star; who flies, toward the sea Vouru-Kasha,[13] as swiftly as the arrow darted through the heavenly space, which Erekhsha, the swift archer, the Arya amongst the Aryas whose arrow was the swiftest, shot from Mount Khshaotha to Mount Hvanvant.

We sacrifice unto Tistrya, the bright and glorious star, whose rising is watched by men who live on the fruits of the year, by the chiefs of deep understanding; by the wild beasts in the mountains, by the tame beasts that run in the plains; they watch him, as he comes up to the country for a bad year, or for a good year [thinking in themselves]: "How shall the Aryan countries be fertile?"

We sacrifice unto Tistrya, the bright and glorious star, for whom long the standing waters, and the running spring-waters, the stream-waters, and the rain-waters:

"When will the bright and glorious Tistrya rise up for us? When will the springs with a flow and overflow of waters, thick as a horse's shoulder, run to the beautiful places and fields, and to the pastures, even to the roots of the plants, that they may grow with a powerful growth?"

We sacrifice unto Tistrya, the bright and glorious star, who washes away all things of fear, who stunts the growth of all . . ., and brings health to all these creations, being most beneficent when he has been worshiped with a sacrifice and propitiated, rejoiced, and satisfied.

Hymn to the Moon

Hail to Ahura-Mazda! Hail to the Amesha-Spentas! Hail to the Moon that keeps in it the seed of the Bull! Hail to thee when we look at thee! Hail to thee when thou lookest at us!

How does the moon wax? How does the moon wane?

For fifteen days does the moon wax; for fifteen days does the moon wane. As long as her waxing, so long is the waning; as long as her waning, so long is the waxing.

"Who is there but thee who makes the moon wax and wane?"

We sacrifice unto the Moon that keeps in it the seed of the Bull, the holy and master of holiness.

Here I look at the moon, here I perceive the moon; here I look at the light of the moon, here I perceive the light of the moon, The Amesha-Spentas stand up, holding its glory; the Amesha-Spentas stand up, pouring its glory upon the earth, made by Mazda.

And when the light of the moon waxes warmer, golden-hued plants grow on from the earth during the spring.

We sacrifice unto the new moons, the full moons, and the Vîshaptathas.

We sacrifice unto the new moon, the holy and master of holiness: We sacrifice unto the full moon, the holy and master of holiness; We sacrifice unto the Vîshaptatha, the holy and master of holiness.

I will sacrifice unto the Moon, that keeps in it the seed of the Bull, the liberal, bright, glorious, water-giving, warmth-giving, wisdom-giving, wealth-giving, riches-giving, thoughtfulness-giving, weal-giving, freshness-giving, prosperity-giving, the liberal, the healing.

For its brightness and glory, I will offer unto it a sacrifice worth being heard, namely, unto the Moon that keeps in it the seed of the Bull.

Hymn to Ardvi Sûra Anâhita

Then Ardvi Sûra Anâhita,[14] O Spitama Zarathustra! proceeded forth from the Maker Mazda. Beautiful were her white arms, thick as a horse's shoulder or still thicker;[15] beautiful was her . . ., and thus came she, strong, with thick arms.

Offer up a sacrifice, O Spitama Zarathustra! unto this spring of mine, Ardvi Sûra Anâhita. . . .

Strong and bright, tall and beautiful of form, who sends down by day and by night a flow of motherly waters as large as the whole of the waters that run along the earth, and who runs powerfully.

For her brightness and glory, I will offer her a sacrifice. . . .

Ardvî Sûra Anâhita, who stands carried forth in the shape of a maid, fair of body, most strong, tall-formed, high-girded, pure, nobly born of a glorious race, wearing along her . . . a mantle fully embroidered with gold;

Ever holding the baresma[16] in her hand, according to the rules, she wears square golden earrings on her pierced ears, and a golden necklace around her beautiful neck, she, the nobly born Ardvi Sûra Anâhita; and she girded her waist tightly, so that her breasts may be well shaped, that they may be tightly pressed.

Upon her head Ardvi Sûra Anâhita bound a golden crown, with a hundred stars, with eight rays, a fine . . ., a well-made crown, in the shape of a . . ., with fillets streaming down.

She is clothed with garments of beaver, Ardvi Sûra Anâhita; with the skin of thirty beavers of those that bear four young ones, that are the finest kind of beavers;[17] for the skin of the beaver that lives in water is the finest-colored of all skins, and when worked at the right time, it shines to the eye with full sheen of silver and gold.

Here, O good, most beneficent Ardvi Sûra Anâhita! I beg of thee this favor: that I, fully blessed, may conquer large kingdoms, rich in horses, with high tributes, with snorting horses, sounding chariots, flashing swords, rich in aliments, with stores of food, with well-scented beds; that I may have at my wish the fullness of the good things of life and whatever makes a kingdom thrive.

Through the strength of this sacrifice, of this invocation, O Ardvi Sûra Anâhita! come down from those stars, toward the earth made by Ahura, toward the sacrificing priest, toward the full boiling [milk]; come to help him who is offering up libations, giving gifts, sacrificing, and entreating that thou wouldst grant him thy favors.

Hymn to the Fravashis

I praise, I invoke, I meditate upon, and we sacrifice unto the good, strong, beneficent Fravashis[18] of the faithful. We worship the Fravashis of the masters of the houses, those of the lord of the boroughs, those of the lords of the towns, those of the lords of the countries, those of the Zarathustrôtemas; the Fravashis of those that are, the Fravashis of those that have been, the Fravashis of those that will be; all the Fravashis of all nations, and most friendly the Fravashis of the friendly nations;

Who maintain the sky, who maintain the waters, who maintain the earth, who maintain the cattle, who maintain in the womb the child that has been conceived, so that it does not die from the assaults of Vîdôtu, and develop in it the bones, the hair, the . . ., the entrails, the feet, and the sexual organs;

Who are much-bringing, who move with awfulness, well moving, swiftly moving, quickly moving, who move when invoked; who are to be invoked in the conquest of good, who are to be invoked in fights against foes, who are to be invoked in battles;

Who give victory to their invoker, who give boons to their lover, who give health to the sick man, who give good Glory to the faithful man that brings libations and invokes them with a sacrifice and words of propitiation;

Who turn to that side where are faithful men, most devoted to holiness, and where is the greatest piety, where the faithful man is rejoiced, and where the faithful man is not ill treated.

We worship the good, strong, beneficent Fravashis of the faithful, who are the mightiest of drivers, the lightest of those driving forward, the slowest of the retiring, the safest of all bridges, the least-erring of all weapons and arms, and who never turn their backs.

We worship the good, strong, beneficent Fravashis of the faithful; awful, overpowering, and victorious, smiting in battle, sorely wounding, blowing away [the foes], moving along to and fro, of good renown, fair of body, godly of soul, and holy; who give victory to their invoker, who give boons to their lover, who give health to the sick man;

Who give good glory to him who worships them with a sacrifice, as that man did worship them, the holy Zarathustra, the chief of the material world, the head of the two-footed race, in whatever struggle he had to enter, in whatever distress he did fear;

Who, when well invoked, enjoy bliss in the heavens; who, when well invoked, come forward from the heavens, who are the heads of that sky above, possessing the well-shapen Strength, the Victory made by Ahura, the crushing Ascendant, and Welfare, the wealth-bringing, boon-bringing, holy, well fed, worthy of sacrifice and prayer in the perfection of holiness.

They shed Satavaêsa between the earth and the sky, him to whom the waters belong, who listens to appeals and makes the waters flow and the plants grow up, to nourish animals and men, to nourish the Aryan nations, to nourish the five kinds of animals, and to help the faithful.

We worship the Fravashis of the holy men in the Aryan countries;

We worship the Fravashis of the holy women in the Aryan countries.

We worship the Fravashis of the holy men in the Turanian countries;

We worship the Fravashis of the holy women in the Turanian countries.

We worship the Fravashis of the holy men in the Sairimyan countries;

We worship the Fravashis of the holy women in the Sairimyan countries.

We worship the Fravashis of the holy men in the Sâini countries;

We worship the Fravashis of the holy women in the Sâini countries.

We worship the Fravashis of the holy men in the Dâhi countries;

We worship the Fravashis of the holy women in the Dâhi countries.

We worship the Fravashis of the holy men in all countries;

We worship the Fravashis of the holy women in all countries.[19]

We worship Zarathustra, the lord and master of all the material world, the man of the primitive law; the wisest of all beings, the best-ruling of all beings, the brightest of all beings, the most glorious of all beings, the most worthy of sacrifice amongst all beings, the most worthy of prayer amongst all beings, the most worthy of propitiation amongst all beings, the most worthy of glorification amongst all beings, whom we call well desired and worthy of sacrifice and prayer as much as any being can be, in the perfection of his holiness.

We worship this earth;

We worship those heavens;

We worship those good things that stand between [the earth and the heavens] and that are worthy of sacrifice and prayer and are to be worshiped by the faithful man.

We worship the souls of the wild beasts and of the tame.

We worship the souls of the holy men and women, born at any time, whose consciences struggle, or will struggle, or have struggled, for the good.

We worship the spirit, conscience, perception, soul, and Fravashi of the holy men and holy women who struggle, will struggle, or have struggled, and teach the Law, and who have struggled for holiness.

Hymn to the Waters

All waters, the fountains as well as those flowing down in streams, praise we.

All trees, the growing, adorned with tops, praise we.

The whole earth, praise we.

The whole heaven, praise we.

All Stars, the Moon and Sun, praise we.

All lights, without beginning, praise we.

All cattle, that which lives under the water, under the heaven, the birds, the wide-stepping, the beasts with claws, praise we.

All the good pure creatures, working well for Ahura-Mazda, praise we,

Through which He created fullness and blessings,

Which are to be praised and adored on account of the best purity.

All mountains which have a pure brightness, praise we.

All Varas, created by Mazda, praise we.

All fires, praise we.

All right-spoken sayings, praise we.

All these which are united with purity, with wisdom, praise we, for protection and shelter, rule and overseeing. May ye serve me for preparation:

The Gâthâs, the holy, the lords over the times, the pure, I invite and I praise, for protection, shelter, dominion, and supervision. May they serve me for preparation,

For me, for my own soul implore I and praise I, for protection, defense, dominion, supervision.

In Praise of Yima

Since on account of his rule men and cattle were immortal, water and trees not dried up,

The eatable food inexhaustible.

In the wide rule of Yima[20] there was no cold, no heat,

No old age and death, no envy created by the Daevas.

Father and son walked along, fifteen years old in countenance, each of the two,

So long as Yima of the good rule, the son of Vivanhao, governed.

To Fire

Offering and praise, good nourishment, fortunate nourishment, helpful nourishment, I vow to thee, O fire, son of Ahura-Mazda.

To thee it is to be offered, thou art to be praised, mayest thou [continually] be provided with offering and praise, in the dwellings of men.

Hail to the man who continually offers to thee,

Holding firewood in the hand, holding baresma in the hand, holding flesh in the hand, holding the mortar in the hand.

Mayest thou continually obtain right firewood, right fragrance, right nourishment, right increase.

Mayest thou be in complete aliment, in good aliment, O fire, son of Ahura-Mazda.

Mayest thou burn in this dwelling, ever mayest thou burn in this dwelling, mayest thou be in brightness in this dwelling, mayest thou be in increase in this dwelling:

Throughout the long time, until the perfect resurrection, the perfect good resurrection included.

Give me, O fire, son of Ahura-Mazda,

Swift brightness, swift nourishment, swift blessings of life,

Greatness in holiness, fluency for the tongue, but for the soul, sense and understanding, which afterward increases, not diminishes; then manly courage,

Activity, sleeplessness the third part of the night,[21] easy-going, watchfulness,

Well-nourished, heavenly posterity, which makes a circle, collects itself together,

Which grows up, is enduring, pure from crime, and manly,

Which can help me in the house, in the clan, in the confederacy, in the region, in the district.

Give me, O fire, son of Ahura-Mazda, what instructs me now and and for all time concerning the best place of the pure, the shining, wholly brilliant.

May I attain good reward, good renown, good sanctification for the soul.

Hymn to Mithra

We sacrifice unto Mithra,[22] the lord of wide pastures, who is truth-speaking, a chief in assemblies, with a thousand ears, well shapen, with ten thousand eyes, high, with full knowledge, strong, sleepless, and ever awake;

Whom the horsemen worship on the back of their horses, begging swiftness for their teams, health for their own bodies, and that they may watch with full success those who hate them, smite down their foes, and destroy at one stroke their adversaries, their enemies, and those who hate them.

We sacrifice unto Mithra, the lord of wide pastures, . . . sleepless and ever awake;

Who first of the heavenly gods reaches over the Hara[23], before the undying, swift-horsed sun; who, foremost in a golden array, takes hold of the beautiful summits, and from thence looks over the abode of the Aryans with a beneficent eye.

Where the valiant chiefs draw up their many troops in array; where the high mountains, rich in pastures and waters, yield plenty to the cattle; where the deep lakes, with salt waters, stand.

We sacrifice unto Mithra, the lord of wide pastures, . . . sleepless, and ever awake;

Who upholds the columns of the lofty house and makes its pillars solid; who gives herds of oxen and male children to that house in which he has been satisfied; he breaks to pieces those in which he has been offended.

Thou, O Mithra! art both bad and good to nations; thou, O Mithra! art both bad and good to men; thou, O Mithra! keepest in thy hands both peace and trouble for nations.

Thou makest houses large, beautiful with women, beautiful with chariots, with well-laid foundations, and high above their groundwork; thou makest that house lofty, beautiful with women, beautiful with chariots, with well-laid foundations, and high above its groundwork, of which the master, pious and holding libations in his hand, offers thee a sacrifice, in which thou art invoked by thy own name and with the proper words.

With a sacrifice, in which thou art invoked by thy own name, with the proper words, will I offer thee libations, O powerful Mithra!

With a sacrifice, in which thou art invoked by thy own name, with the proper words, will I offer thee libations, O most beneficent Mithra!

With a sacrifice, in which thou art invoked by thy own name, with the proper words, will I offer thee libations, O thou undeceivable Mithra!

We sacrifice unto Mithra, the lord of wide pastures, . . . sleepless, and ever awake;

Whose dwelling, wide as the earth, extends over the material world, large, unconfined, and bright, a far-and-wide-extending abode.

Whose eight friends sit as spies for Mithra, on all the heights, at all the watching places, observing the man who lies unto Mithra, looking at those, remembering those who have lied unto Mithra, but guarding the ways of those whose life is sought by men who lie unto Mithra, and, verily, by the fiendish killers of faithful men.

Helping and guarding, guarding behind and guarding in front, Mithra, the lord of wide pastures, proves an undeceivable spy and watcher for the man to whom he comes to help with all the strength of his soul, he of the ten thousand spies, the powerful, all-knowing, undeceivable god.

We sacrifice unto Mithra, the lord of wide pastures, . . . sleepless, and ever awake;

For whom the Maker, Ahura-Mazda, has built up a dwelling on the Hara Berezaiti, the bright mountain around which the many [stars] revolve, where come neither night nor darkness, no cold wind and no hot wind, no deathful sickness, no uncleanness made by the Daevas, and the clouds cannot reach up unto the Haraiti Bareza.

The cow driven astray invokes him for help, longing for the stables:

"When will that bull, Mithra, the lord of wide pastures, bring us back, and make us reach the stables? when will he turn us back to the right away from the den of the Durg where we were driven?"

And to him with whom Mithra, the lord of wide pastures, has been satisfied, he comes with help; and of him with whom Mithra, the lord of wide pastures, has been offended, he crushes down the house, the borough, the town, the province, the country.

Who first lifted up Haomas, in a mortar inlaid with stars and made of a heavenly substance. Ahura-Mazda longed for him, the Amesha-Spentas longed for him, for the well-shapen body of him whom the swift-horsed sun awakes for prayer from afar.

Hail to Mithra, the lord of wide pastures, who has a thousand ears and ten thousand eyes! Thou art worthy of sacrifice and prayer: mayest thou have sacrifice and prayer in the houses of men! Hail to the man who shall offer thee a sacrifice, with the holy wood in his hand, the baresma in his hand, the holy meat in his hand, the holy mortar in his hand, with his hands well washed, with the mortar well washed, with the bundles of baresma tied up, the Haoma uplifted, and the Ahuna Vairya sung through.

The holy Ahura-Mazda confessed that religion and so did Vohu-Manu, so did Asha-Vahista, so did Khshathra-Vairya, so did Spenta-Ârmaiti, so did Haurvatât and Ameretât; and all the Amesha-Spentas longed for and confessed his religion. The kind Mazda conferred upon him the mastership of the world; and [so did they] who saw thee amongst all creatures the right lord and master of the world, the best cleanser of these creatures.

So mayest thou in both worlds, mayest thou keep us in both worlds, O Mithra, lord of wide pastures! both in this material world and in the world of the spirit, from the fiend of Death, from the fiend Aêshma, from the fiendish hordes, that lift up the spear of havoc, and from the onsets of Aêshma, wherein the evil-doing Aêshma rushes along with Vîdôtu,[24] made by the Daevas.

We sacrifice unto Mithra, the lord of wide pastures, . . . sleepless, and ever awake;

A warrior with a silver helm, a golden cuirass, who kills with the poniard, strong, valiant, lord of the borough. Bright are the ways of Mithra, by which he goes toward the country, when, wishing well, he turns its plains and vales to pasture grounds.

And then cattle and males come to graze, as many as he wants.

May Mithra and Ahura, the high gods, come to us for help, when the poniard lifts up its voice aloud, when the nostrils of the horses quiver, when the poniards . . ., when the strings of the bows whistle and shoot sharp arrows; then the brood of those whose libations are hated fall smitten to the ground, with their hair torn off.

We sacrifice unto Mithra, the lord of wide pastures, who is truth-speaking, a chief in assemblies, with a thousand ears, well shapen, with a thousand eyes, high, with full knowledge, strong, sleepless, and ever awake.

We sacrifice unto the Mithra around countries;
We sacrifice unto the Mithra within countries;
We sacrifice unto the Mithra in this country;
We sacrifice unto the Mithra above countries;
We sacrifice unto the Mithra under countries;
We sacrifice unto the Mirtha before countries;
We sacrifice unto the Mithra behind countries.

We sacrifice unto Mithra and Ahura, the two great, imperishable, holy gods; and unto the stars, and the moon, and the sun, with the trees that yield up baresma. We sacrifice unto Mithra, the lord of all countries.

I bless the sacrifice and prayer, and the strength and vigor of Mithra, the lord of wide pastures, who has a thousand ears, ten thousand eyes, a Yazata[25] invoked by his own name; and that of Râma Hvâstra.[26]

Holiness is the best of all good. . . .

Hymn to Kingly Glory

For its brightness and glory, I will offer it a sacrifice worth being heard, namely, unto the awful kingly Glory. Unto the awful kingly Glory we offer up the libations, the Haoma and meat, the baresma, the wisdom of the tongue, the holy spells, the speech, the deeds, the libations, and the rightly spoken words.

We sacrifice unto the awful kingly Glory, made by Mazda; most conquering, highly working, that possesses health, wisdom, and happiness, and is more powerful to destroy than all other creatures;

That belongs to Ahura-Mazda, as [through it] Ahura Mazda made the creatures, many and good, many and fair, many and wonderful, many and prosperous, many and bright;

So that they may restore the world, which will [thenceforth] never grow old and never die, never decaying and never rotting, ever living and ever increasing, and master of its wish, when the dead will rise, when life and immortality will come, and the world will be restored at its wish;

When the creation will grow deathless—the prosperous creation of the Good Spirit—and the Durg shall perish, though she may rush on every side to kill the holy beings; she and her hundredfold brood shall perish, as it is the will of the Lord.

Ritual of the Haoma Sacrifice

I invite and announce to:[27] the Lords of the Heavenly, the Lords of the Earthly, the Lords of those who live in the Water, the Lords of those which live under Heaven, the Lords of the Winged, the Lords of the Wide-stepping, the Lords of the beasts with claws, the pure Lords of the pure.

I invite and announce to: the yearly feasts,[28] the lords of purity, Maidhyôzaremaya, the pure milk, lord of purity.

I invite and announce to: Maidhyôshema, the giver of pastures to the pure, lord of purity.

I invite and announce to: Paitish-hahya, the giver of corn to the pure, lord of purity.

I invite and announce to: Ayâthrema, the promoter, the distributor of manly strength to the pure, lord of purity.

I invite and announce to: Maidhyâirya, the pure, belonging to the year, lord of purity.

I invite and announce to: Hamaspathmaêdaya, the pure, provided with good works, lord of purity.

I invite and announce to: the future of the world, the pure, lord of purity, which being will bring forth.

I invite and announce to: the prayers, the praiseworthy, arranged-together, well-praised, pure, lords of purity.

I invite and announce to: the prayers, the praiseworthy, composed, well-praised, pure, the Myazdas of purity.

I invite and announce to: the Ahurian Question, the Ahurian Custom, the Ahurian Ruler, the Ahurian High-priest, the pure, lord of purity.

I invite and announce to: the habitation provided with fodder, the abundant beautiful fodder for the cow, and the cattle-breeding pure man.

I desire the priests, the soldiers, [and] the active husbandmen.

The lords of the houses, of the clan, of the society, the lords of the region.

The young man who thinks well, speaks well, acts well, who is devoted to the law, I desire. I desire the youth who utters the words. Those who have married amongst kindred I desire.

I invite the furtherers of the region, I desire the willing worshipers. I desire the mistresses of the house.

I desire the woman who especially thinks good, speaks good, does good, lets herself be commanded well, who obeys her lord, the pure. Cpenta-ârmaiti, and who [besides] are Thy women, O Ahura-Mazda. I desire the pure man, who especially thinks, speaks, and does good. Who knows the faith, does not know sins.

Through whose deeds the worlds increase in purity.

Then we call you, every lord of the Mazdayacnians, hither; we invite you, the lords.

The Amesha-Spentas and the profitable ones, the very wise.

The very wise-speaking [helpful] hastening hither, brilliant in understanding.

The greatest, powerful [followers] of the Mazdayacnian law, call we hither.

Priests, soldiers, and husbandmen.

To Ahura-Mazda announce we this Haoma, the uplifted,

The very profitable, [to Him] the Victorious, the Promoter of the world,

To Him the good Ruler, the pure; to Him the Ruler over the lords of purity.

To the Amesha-Spentas make we the Haomas known.

To the good waters we make the Haomas known.

To [our] own souls we make known the Haomas.

To the whole world of purity we announce the Haomas.

These Haomas, these Haoma-utensils,

These covers, these Myazdas.

These stones, the first among the creations,

These stone mortars, these brought hither, O golden Haoma.

These iron mortars, brought hither, O golden Haoma.

This Haoma-juice, this Baresma, which is bound together in holiness.

These bodies, these strengths, these flowing Zaothras.

This pure Haoma, this well-created cow, this pure man.

The heavenly souls of the pure, the heavenly souls of the profitable.

This flesh of living beings, uplifted with purity; this tree Hadhâ-naêpata,[29] uplifted with purity; these Zaothras of the good waters, those provided with Haoma, those provided with flesh, those provided

with Hadhâ-naêpata, lifted up with purity, of the good waters the
Haoma water, the stone mortars, the iron mortars, the Baresma branch,
the helpful prayer at the right time, the successful recitation and doing
of the good Mazdayacnian law, the singing of the Gâthâs, the helpful
right prayer to the pure lords of purity, this wood, these odoriferous
[woods] for thee, the fire, the son of Ahura-Mazda, all the acceptable
[things] created by Mazda, which have a pure origin, we give and
make them known.

Prayer to the Fravashis and to the World

The brilliant deeds of purity praise we,
At which the souls of the deceased rejoice, the Fravashis of the pure.
We praise the best place of the pure, the illumining, wholly brilliant.
Milk and fodder, the running water, the growing trees, praise we:
For resistance against Âzhi,[30] created by the Daevas, against the
  Pairika, the withstanding.
For the destroying, for the expelling
Of the hostile plagues,
And of the Ashemaogha, the impure, slaying, who is full of death.
We praise all waters, we praise all trees,
We praise all good men, we praise all good women.
We praise all heavenly Yazatas and all earthly, the well-created, pure.

Hymn of Praise to Waters and Liquids

This earth, together with the women, we praise,
Which bears us, which are Thy women, Ahura-Mazda,
Whose wishes arise from purity, these we praise.
Fullness, readiness, questioning, wisdom.
The good holiness [which arises] through them, the good wish,
The good fullness, the good blessing, the good Parendi, praise we.
The waters praise we, the dropping, flowing, forward-running,
The arising from Ahura, the well-working, having good fords,
The well-flowing, well-washing, desirable for both worlds.
Which names Ahura-Mazda has given to you, the good.
He the Giver of good, whatever He may have given, with these we
  praise you,
With these we invoke you, with these we pray to you, with these we
  confess ourselves as your debtors.
You, the waters Azi, Mâtaras, Agenayô, Dregudâya,

[You] the lords over all, will we invoke, the best, fairest, you, ye
  good, on account of offering.
[Who] with long arms lead [the body of the world] without creat-
  ing, without speaking: the Mâtarô jîtayô [milk].

Homage to the Gâthâs

The whole world: bodies together with bones, vital power and form,
  strength and consciousness, soul and Fravashi,
We give and make known. We make them known: to the holy Gâthâs,[31]
  the lords over the times, the pure.
Which Gâthâs are ruling and protecting for us, heavenly food.
Which are for our soul both: food and raiment.
These Gâthâs it is who govern and protect us, our heavenly food.
These Gâthâs are for our soul both: food and raiment.
May they bring us good reward, much reward, pure reward.
For the next world, after the separation of the vital powers and con-
  sciousness.

Exorcism for Cutting Fingernails[32]

With the nails [of both hands] dig a hole beyond the house;
As deep as the top joint of the longest finger.
Thither carry them.
Then speak these words, the victorious, O Zarathustra.
Ashâ vôhû, etc.[33]
With the knife make circles, three, six, or nine.
Speak the Ahuna-vairya[34] three, six, or nine times; [afterward]:
"To thee, O Bird Ashô-zusta,[35] I show these nails;"
"These nails I devote to thee."
May these nails, O Bird Ashô-zusta, be thy lances, swords, bows, thine
  arrows the swift flying, thy sling-stones which are to be employed
  against the Mazanian Daevas.[36]
If they do not announce these nails, then they belong afterward to the
  Mazanian Daevas; the lances, swords, bows, these swift-flying
  arrows and these sling-stones which should be employed against the
  Mazanian Daevas.
All those are evil and noxious Drujas, who do not head the Faith.
All have not the Faith who do not hear it.
All hear it not who are unclean.
All are unclean who are sinners.

Exorcism for Obtaining Rain and Keeping Sickness Away

Praise be to thee, O holy bull,[37] praise to thee, well-created cow, praise to
thee, thou who multipliest, praise to thee, thou who makest to in-
crease, praise to thee, gift of the Creator, for the best pure, for
the pure yet unborn.
Whom Jahi slays, the very hurtful, unclean, and wicked man, the godless.
The cloud gathers, it gathers
The water up, the water down.
Down to the water it rains, as thousandfold, ten thousandfold rain—
speak, O pure Zarathustra;
For the driving away of sickness, for the driving away of death;
For the driving away of the sickness which smites [kills], for the driv-
ing away of death which smites;
For the driving away of illness.
If it slays in the evening, then may it [the cloud] heal in the clear day.
If it slays in the clear day, then may it heal in the night.
If it slays in the night, then may it heal in the morning dawn.
It shall rain down,
With the rain,
Fresh water, fresh earth, fresh trees, fresh remedies, fresh preparations
of remedies.
As the sea Vouru-kasha is the meeting of the waters.
Lift up thyself; go from the air to the earth,
From the earth to the air.
Lift up thyself, arise,
Thou, for the sake of whose birth and increase Ahura-Mazda has created
the air,
Go up, O shining Sun, with thy swift steeds over Haraberezaiti, and
illumine the creatures.
Lift up thyself thus if thou art worthy of honor,
On the way which Ahura-Mazda has created; in the air which the
Baghas have created, on that created [way] abounding with water.

Exorcism Against Evil Spirits

I combat the Aeshma,[38] I combat the Nacu.[39]
I combat uncleanness, the direct and the indirect.
I combat Bushyańcta[40] the yellow.
I combat Bushyańcta dareghô-gava.

I combat the Pairika who goes there to the fire, to the water, to the earth, to the cattle, and to the trees.

I combat the uncleanness which goes there to the fire, to the water, to the earth, to the cattle, and to the trees.

I combat thee, O evil Anra-mainyus[41] [away] from the dwelling, from the fire, from the water, from the earth, from the cattle, from the trees, from the pure man, from the pure woman, from the stars, from the moon, from the sun, from the lights without beginning, from all the good things which Ahura has made which have a pure origin.

In Praise of Dogs

A dog has eight characters.

One like an Âthrava, one like a warrior, one like a husbandman, one like a villager, one like a thief, one like a wild beast, one like a courtesan, one like a child.

He eats what is offered him like an Âthrava.

He is contented like an Âthrava.

He is patient like an Âthrava.

He needs only a little bread like an Âthrava.

These are his qualities like those of an Âthrava.

He goes forward like a warrior.

He kills the well-created cow like a warrior.

He is before and behind the dwelling like a warrior.

These are his qualities like those of a warrior.

From his watchfulness he does not take sleep enough, like a husbandman.

He is before and behind the dwelling like a husbandman.

He is behind and before the dwelling like a husbandman.

These are his qualities like those of a husbandman.

He is friendly like a villager.

Wounding when near like a villager.

House and food are the chiefest to him, as to a villager.

These are his qualities like those of a villager.

He loves darkness like a thief.

He runs about in the night like a thief.

He eats undressed [food] like a thief.

He is given to rapine like a thief.

These are his qualities like those of a thief.

He loves darkness like a beast of prey.

He runs about in the night like a beast of prey.

He eats raw [meat] like a beast of prey.
He is given to rapine like a beast of prey.
These are his qualities like those of a beast of prey.
He is friendly like a courtesan.
Wounding from close by like a courtesan.
To be found on the way like a courtesan.
House and treasure are chiefest to him as to a courtesan.
These are his qualities like those of a courtesan.
He loves sleep like a child.
He is fawning like a child.
He has a long tongue (*i.e.* he cries often) like a child.
He runs forward like a child.
These are his qualities like those of a child.
If two [dogs] come to this my dwelling, they shall not drive them away.
Namely, the dog which belongs to the cattle and to the village.
For the dwellings would not stand fast on the earth, created by Ahura-
Mazda, if there were not dogs which pertain to the cattle and the
village.

The Principal Prayer of the Yezidiz

The Yezidiz are a religious sect whose principal group live east of Mossul and in Gebel Singar. They are erroneously referred to as "worshipers of the Devil." Their religion is monotheistic, recognizing the action of certain beings who act as mediators between God and man; these beings are of a divine or semidivine nature. The religion is not too far removed in spirit from the great pre-Islamic religions of Asia. It has undergone considerable Christian influence. What distinguishes the Yezidiz is the adoration they hold for a being called Melek Ta'us, which means "King" or "Peacock Angel," which corresponds in Christianity and Islam with Devil, but which should be interpreted to correspond with the Arimane of the Avesta. Melek Ta'us is essentially a good God, because, by substituting for the true God, he assumes care of the world and sees to its salvation. In a sense he is the Christ of the Yezidiz.

Amen, Amen, Amen!
Through the intermediation of Sams-ad-Dîn,
Fahr-ad-Dîn, Nasir-ad-Dîn,
Sajad ad-Dîn, Seih Sin (Husein),
Seih Bakr, Kâdir ar-Rahmân.[42]
Lord, thou art gracious, thou art merciful;
Thou art God, king of kings and lands,

King of joy and happiness,
King of good possession [eternal life].
From eternity thou art eternal.
Thou art the seat of luck [happiness] and life;
Thou art lord of grace and good luck.
Thou art king of jinns and human beings,
King of the holy men [saints],
Lord of terror and praise,
The abode of religious duty and praise,
Worthy of praise and thanks.
Lord! Protector in journeys,
Sovereign of the moon and of the darkness,
God of the sun and of the fire,
God of the great throne,
Lord of goodness.
Lord! No one knows how thou art.
Thou hast no beauty; thou hast no height.
Thou hast no going forth; thou hast no number.
Lord! Judge of kings and beggars,
Judge of society and of the world,
Thou hast revealed the repentance of Adam.
Lord, thou hast no house; thou hast no money;
Thou hast no wings, hast no feathers;
Thou hast no voice, thou hast no color.
Thou hast made us lucky and satisfied.
Thou hast created Jesus and Mary.
Lord, thou art gracious,
Merciful, faithful.
Thou art Lord; I am nothingness.
I am a fallen sinner,
A sinner by thee remembered.
Thou hast led us out of darkness into light.
Lord! My sin and my guilt,
Take them and remove them.
O God, O God, O God, Amen!

Poem in Praise of Seih 'Adi

This hymn of praise to Seih 'Adi, in which the Angel Peacock exalts himself, is the fundamental religious text of the sect. The Yezidiz hold this poem
as sacred, and all their prayers are fragments of it.

My understanding surrounds the truth of things,
And my truth is mixed up in me,
And the truth of my descent is set forth by itself,
And when it was known it was altogether in me.
And all that are in the universe are under me,
And all the habitable parts and deserts,
And everything created is under me,
And I am the ruling power preceding all that exists.
And I am he that spoke a true saying,
And I am the just judge and the ruler of the earth.
And I am he that men worship in my glory,
Coming to me and kissing my feet.
And I am he that spread over the heavens their height.
And I am he that cried in the beginning.
And I am he that of myself revealeth all things,
And I am he to whom came the book of good tidings
From my Lord, who burneth the mountains.
And I am he to whom all created men come
In obedience to kiss my feet.
I bring forth fruit from the first juice of early youth
By my presence, and turn toward me my disciples.
And before this light the darkness of the morning cleared away.
I guide him that asketh for guidance.
I am he that caused Adam to dwell in Paradise
And Nimrod to inhabit a hot burning fire.
And I am he that guided Ahmed the Just,[43]
And led him into my path and way.
And I am he unto whom all creatures
Come for my good purposes and gifts.
And I am he that visited all the heights,
And goodness and charity proceed from my mercy.
And I am he that made all hearts to fear
My purpose, and they magnify the majesty and power of my awfulness.
And I am he to whom the destroying lion came
Raging, and I shouted against him and he became stone.
And I am he to whom the serpent came,
And by my will I made him dust.
And I am he that struck the rock and made it tremble,[44]
And made to burst from its sides the sweetest of waters.
And I am he that sent down the certain truth;
For me is the book that comforteth the oppressed.

And I am he that judged justly,
And when I judged it was my right
And I am he that made the springs to give water,
Sweeter and pleasanter than all waters.
And I am he that caused it to appear in my mercy,
And by my power I called it the pure.
And I am he to whom the Lord of heaven hath said,
Thou art the just Judge and Ruler of the earth.
And I am he that disclosed some of my wonders,
And some of my virtues are manifested in that which exists.
And I am he that caused the mountains to bow,
To move under me and at my will.
And I am he before whose majesty the wild beasts cried;
They turned to me, worshiping, and kissed my feet.
And I am 'Adî as-Sâmî, the son of Musâfir.
Verily the All-Merciful has assigned unto me names,
The heavenly throne, and the seat, and the [seven] heavens, and the
     earth.
In the secret of my knowledge there is no God but me.
These things are subservient to my power.
O mine enemies, why do you deny me?
O men, deny me not, but submit.
In the day of judgment you will be happy in meeting me.
Who dies in my love, I will cast him
In the midst of Paradise, by my will and pleasure;
But he that dies unmindful of me
Will be thrown into torture in misery and affliction.
I say I am the only one and the exalted;
I create and make rich those whom I will.
Praise it to myself, for all things are by my will,
And the universe is lighted by some of my gifts.
I am the king that magnifies himself,
And all the riches of creation are at my bidding.
I have made known unto you, O people, some of my ways.
Who desireth me must forsake the world.
And I can also speak the true saying,
And the garden on high[45] is for those who do my pleasure.
I sought the truth and became a confirming truth;
And by the like truth shall they, like myself, possess the highest place.

Notes

1. Haoma, corresponding to the Vedaic soma, is the main offering of the Avestan cult. It was taken from the flowering yellow part of an unidentified plant, though probably the *asclepias acida* or the *cynanchum viminale,* both common in Iran. The preparation of the haoma was the occasion for a special ceremony. The stalks of the plant were pressed in a sacred mortar, and the juice obtained was mixed with sacred water and milk, then used as a sacramental libation by the priests. The entire ceremony also had a profound cosmic significance, because the *haoma bitter* of this world is a reflection of the *haoma white* from the gaokorena tree, from which was extracted the nectar of immortality. The vegetable offering of the haoma was known as parahaoma.

2. Daevas are those beneficent and illuminating gods in Vedaic mythology that become, in Avestan mythology, the princes of evil and of the lower world.

3. Yâtus and Pairikas, enchanters and enchantresses, though often linked together in the texts, are of completely different natures. Yâtu, the same as the Persian *jadû,* "witch," seems to be applied to masculine beings and connected with the followers of Ahriman, the negative prince. Pairika, the beautiful and dangerous fata morgana, always indicates a supernatural creature who deceives men by her wiles.

4. Koyas and Karafnas are names of families who were adversaries of Zarathustra.

5. Parts of the Avesta that the faithful must recite.

6. Priest of fire.

7. The supreme god representing the beneficent principle of the universe.

8. Jahika—the courtesan. In the Bundahishi the Jahika personifies the genius of dissolute practices; on earth, she is the bad woman.

9. Ashi Vanguhi, the good Ashi, symbolizes the richness that flows from virtue. She brings to virtuous men all the richness of earth, water, and air. Since she was the genius of growth, no sterile person could take part in the ceremonies of her cult, no babies, eunuchs, virgins, courtesans or impotent persons.

10. The Amesha-spentas, "immortal saints," which are frequently mentioned in these hymns, are an array of ministers who follow the orders of Mazda. They are distinguished as follows: Vohu Manah (or Manu), the "Good Thought," the Good Mind, the well-arranged Intelligence; Asa Vahista, the "Best of Laws," right and justice being in conformity to moral order; Xsadra Vairya, the "Elect Sovereignty," the realm of God; Spenta Armatay, the "Sacred Piety," humble devotion; Haurvatat, the "Integrity," well-being; Ameretat, the "Immortality."

11. Kava-vîstâcpa is the mythical king with whom Zarathustra stayed during his wanderings. He is identified by legend with Istapse, the father of Darius I. Frasaostra and Gamaspa, of the Hvogva family, are ministers of the pious king, also converted by Zarathustra.

12. Tistrya (Tir, Sirio, Sirius) is the guiding star in the battle that the

astrals waged against the demons in favor of Ahura. It is the angel of rain and the adversary of drought.

13. Vouru-Kasha is not actually a sea, but rather the source and reserve of all waters. There is nothing in the texts that permits us to localize it. It is therefore the general term implying the source of waters and the return of waters to that source. It is also the seat of several supernatural beings, the Haoma White, which gives immortality to the dead at the moment of resurrection, the Tree of all Seeds, and the bird Saema, that disperses the seeds to the winds, as well as the three-footed Ass that purifies the water of the sea, etc.

14. Ardi Sûra Anâhita, a feminine divinity, is the incarnation of all waters (*âpo*), a marvelous font located in the regions of the stars, at the top of a celestial mountain, from which come flowing all the rivers of the earth. Later, under the influence of Hellenism, she was blended with Aphrodite.

15. The arms are rippling streams of water coming from the celestial font to flow out across the earth.

16. Baresma is an important ritual accessory, being formed of small branches of trees which are the incarnation of virtue in the vegetable world. The number of branches varies according to the service. Twenty-one branches are used for the Yasna, while thirty-three are used for the Vispered and the Vendidad.

17. Born in good condition because the beaver regularly gives birth to four.

18. The Fravashis correspond roughly to the Hands. Man is made up of five elements: body, life, soul, form, and Fravashis. When man dies, the body returns to the earth, life (breath) to the wind, the form dissolves in the sun, but the soul attaches itself indissolubly to the Fravashis, an immortal element, and rises up to Ahura. When Ahura created this element, even before material creation, she gave it the choice of dwelling forever in the spiritual world with the other angels or taking form and descending to the earth to struggle against demons. The Fravashis chose the struggle which, thanks to their great strength, must culminate in the eventual triumph of good.

19. This part of the hymn gives important proof of the universality of the Avestan religion.

20. Yima is a god-hero, the son of Vivanhant, to whom Ahura-Mazda revealed religion, that he might proclaim it to men. He held the task to be greater than his strength, and dedicated himself to the lighter task of increasing the human species, wishing to establish a realm of perfect happiness. This is the mythical golden age, of which there is an echo in the piece given here. That age was destroyed by a glacial epoch, during which Yima saved couples of animals in his retreat, a variant of the Biblical Ark.

21. A third of the night. The explanation of this is found elsewhere in the Vendidad: "The Fire that belongs to me, the Fire of Ahura-Mazda, implores the aid of the head of the household for the first third of the night, and speaks thusly to him: Arise, dress thyself in thy garments, cleanse thy hands, go forth and seek a burning brand, deposit it on me, and, with purified hands, light a flame of pure wood. Otherwise, Azi will come to assault me. She wishes to take my life from me."

22. Mithra has characteristics quite similar to those of Ahura-Mazda, the

supreme god. He becomes, however, a figure of a more heroic kind, since, in addition to being the sun god, he is also the champion of truth and justice who strikes down violators of pacts and contracts.

23. Hara is the Elburz, the chain of high-topped mountains south of the Caspian Sea. The Elburz is the limit of mythological geography in Iran; it surrounds the earth and ascends to the sky. The sun, the moon, and the stars cross over it each day. From this mountain all other mountains detach themselves and spread out, like limbs from a tree.

24. Aêshma and Vîdôtu are demons. Aêshma is one of the liveliest demons in all Avestan mythology, and passes into Christianity under the name of Asmodeo (Aêshma deva).

25. Yazata signifies "worshipful," but means angel in current Avestan nomenclature.

26. Râma Hvâstra is the genius of air and taste; it gives flavor to food and is identified with the wind.

27. To be noted here and in successive verses is the characteristic division of the universe into various orders, as was imagined by the wizards. Over each order there presides a chief: Ahura-Mazda is chief of celestial beings; Zarathustra is chief of terrestrial beings; Kâro presides over aquatic beings, while Karshipta is the bird who presides over all other birds.

28. These are the genii of the seasons (Gahanbar), corresponding to festivals that assumed a cosmic significance, because they were related to the six ages of the world and of creation. Precisely these feasts are: Maidhyoizaremaya, the festival of spring, commemorative of the creation of the sky, from May 1 to 15; Maidhyoi-shema, festival of the great summer, commemorative of the creation of the waters, from June 31 to July 4; Paitish-hahya, festival of the end of reaping, commemorative of the creation of the earth, from September 12 to 16; Ayathrima, festival of the great summer, commemorative of the creation of plants, from October 12 to 16; Maidhyâirya, festival of the middle of high-winter, commemorative of the creation of animals, from December 31 to January 4; and, finally, the Hamaspathmaêdaya, which seems to be the only festival having no relation with natural events. It is referred to as the festival "where sacrifices are held," and takes place during the final ten days of the Iranian year. It honors the Fravashis of forebears.

29. The Hadhâ-naêpata is the pomegranate. Included in the offering were pomegranates, palms, rice, perfumes, and scented plants.

30. Âzhi is one of the druje, a malign feminine spirit.

31. The Gâthâs are liturgical hymns of the Avesta, five of them altogether. The calendar is divided into twelve months of thirty days each. At the end of the year five days are added to bring the total to three hundred and sixty-five. Each of these complementary days is a *gâh,* which means that it is consecrated to one of the Gâthâs.

32. A certain formula must be recited while cutting the fingernails, otherwise the spirits will be contrary.

33. One of the more common formulas of prayer.

34. This is also a common prayer form.

35. Ashô-zusta is one of the various wise birds recorded in the Avesta, perhaps the owl.

36. Mazanian Daevas are the demons of Mazana, a rough region around the Caspian Sea which tradition held to be inhabited by demons.

37. The primordial bull, the first creature created by Ahura-Mazda.

38. See preceding note.

39. Nacu is the vilest of the druje, the black fly of putrefaction that deposits its eggs on dead flesh; it belongs to the species of *Calliphora erytrocephala.*

40. Bushyañcta presides over abusive sleep and laziness. He plunges men into lethargy, thus keeping them from religious and professional duties. Bushyañcta has long slender hands and a yellowish complexion, in the manner of one who has slept constantly and lazily.

41. Anra-mainyus is the most ancient name of Ahriman, the spirit of evil.

42. The names of the seven angels between the prayer and the Peacock.

43. Ahmed may be Mohammed.

44. An allusion to the sacred water Zemzem which flows through the national sanctuary and was set in motion by Seih 'Adi. He did this by uttering the words *zem zem,* meaning "murmuring, gurgling, abundantly."

45. The garden on high is Paradise.

The Hebrews

THE HEBREWS

Offering of the First Fruits

And thou shalt speak and say before the Lord thy God: "A wandering Aramean was my father, and he went down into Egypt and sojourned there, few in number; and he became there a nation, great, mighty, and populous. And the Egyptians dealt ill with us, and afflicted us, and laid upon us hard bondage. And we cried unto the Lord, the God of our fathers and the Lord heard our voice, and saw our affliction, and our toil, and our oppression. And the Lord brought us forth out of Egypt with a mighty hand, and with an outstretched arm, and with great terribleness, and with signs, and with wonders. And He hath brought us into this place, and hath given us this land, a land flowing with milk and honey. And now, behold, I have brought the first of the fruit of the land, which Thou, O Lord, hast given me. And thou shalt set it down before the Lord thy God, and worship before the Lord thy God.

Offering of the Tenth Part

When thou hast made an end of tithing all the tithe of thine increase in the third year, which is the year of tithing, and hast given it unto the Levite, to the stranger, to the fatherless, and to the widow, that they may eat within thy gates, and be satisfied, then thou shalt say before the Lord thy God: I have put away the hallowed things out of my house, and also have given them unto the Levite, and unto the stranger, to the fatherless, and to the widow, according to all Thy commandment which Thou hast commanded me; I have not transgressed any of Thy commandments, neither have I forgotten them. I have not eaten thereof in my mourning, neither have I put away thereof, being unclean, nor given thereof for the dead; I have hearkened to the voice of the Lord my God, I have done according to all that Thou hast commanded me. Look forth from Thy holy habitation, from heaven, and bless Thy people Israel, and the land which Thou has given us, as Thou didst swear unto our fathers, a land flowing with milk and honey.

The Song of Moses

The following was sung by Moses and the Israelites when crossing over the Red Sea.

Then sang Moses and the children of Israel this song unto the Lord,
    and spoke, saying:
I will sing unto the Lord, for He is highly exalted.
The horse and his rider hath He thrown into the sea.
The Lord is my strength and song
And He is become my salvation;
This is my God, and I will glorify Him;
My father's God, and I will exalt Him.
The Lord is a man of war,
The Lord is His name.
Pharaoh's chariots and his host hath He cast into the sea.
And his chosen captains are sunk in the Red Sea.
The deeps cover them—
They went down into the depths like a stone.
Thy right hand, O Lord, glorious in power,
Thy right hand, O Lord, dasheth in pieces the enemy.
And in the greatness of Thine excellency Thou overthrowest them that
    rise up against Thee;
Thou sendest forth Thy wrath, it consumeth them as stubble.
And with the blast of Thy nostrils the waters were piled up—
The floods stood upright as a heap;
The deeps were congealed in the heart of the sea.

The enemy said:

I will pursue, I will overtake, I will divide the spoil;

My lust shall be satisfied upon them;

I will draw my sword, my hand shall destroy them.

Thou didst blow with Thy wind, the sea covered them;

They sank as lead in the mighty waters.

Who is like unto Thee, O Lord, among the mighty?

Who is like unto Thee, glorious in holiness,

Fearful in praises, doing wonders?

Thou stretchedst out Thy right hand—

The earth swallowed them.

Thou in Thy love hast led the people that Thou hast redeemed;

Thou hast guided them in Thy strength to Thy holy habitation.

The peoples have heard, they tremble;

Pangs have taken hold on the inhabitants of Phillistia.

Then were the chiefs of Edom affrighted;

The mighty men of Moab, trembling taketh hold upon them;

All the inhabitants of Canaan are melted away.

Terror and dread falleth upon them;

By the greatness of Thine arm they are as still as a stone;

Till Thy people pass over, O Lord,

Till the people pass over that Thou hast gotten.

Thou bringest them in, and plantest them in the mountain of Thine inheritance,

The place, O Lord, which Thou has made for Thee to dwell in,

The sanctuary, O Lord, which Thy hands have established.

The Lord shall reign for ever and ever.

Song of Moses

This is the song that Moses delivered to the Israelites before his death,
that they might hold it in perpetual memory. Divinely inspired, the song
uses historical facts to demonstrate that God had kept his promise and would
continue to keep them for the chosen people.

Give ear, ye heavens, and I will speak;

And let the earth hear the words of my mouth.

My doctrine shall drop as the rain

My speech shall distill as the dew;

As the small rain upon the tender grass,

And as the showers upon the herb.

For I will proclaim the name of the Lord;
Ascribe ye greatness unto our God.

The Rock, His work is perfect;
For all His ways are justice;
A God of faithfulness and without iniquity,
Just and right is He.
Is corruption His? No; His children's is the blemish;
A generation crooked and perverse.
Do ye thus requite the Lord,
O foolish people and unwise?
Is not He thy father that hath gotten thee?
Hath He not made thee, and established thee?

Remember the days of old,
Consider the years of many generations;
Ask thy father, and he will declare unto thee,
Thine elders, and they will tell thee.
When the Most High gave to the nations their inheritance,
When He separated the children of men,
He set the borders of the peoples
According to the number of the children of Israel.
For the portion of the Lord is His people,
Jacob the lot of His inheritance.

He found him in a desert land,
And in the waste, a howling wilderness;
He compassed him about, He cared for Him,
He kept him as the apple of His eye.
As an eagle that stirreth up her nest,
Hovereth over her young,
Spreadeth abroad her wings, taketh them,
Beareth them on her pinion—
The Lord alone did lead him,
And there was no strange god with Him.

He made him ride on the high places of the earth,
And he did eat the fruitage of the field;
And He made him to suck honey out of the crag,
And oil out of the flinty rock;
Curd of kine, and milk of sheep,
With fat lambs
And rams of the breed of Bashan, and he-goats,

With the kidney-fat of wheat;
And of the blood of the grape thou drankest foaming wine.

But Jeshurun waxed fat, and kicked—
Thou didst wax fat, thou didst grow thick, thou didst become gross—
And he forsook God who made him,
And contemned the Rock of his salvation.
They roused Him to jealousy with strange gods,
With abominations did they provoke Him.
They sacrificed unto demons, no-gods,
Gods that they knew not,
New gods that came up of late,
Which your fathers dreaded not.
Of the Rock that begot thee thou wast unmindful,
And didst forget God that bore thee.

And the Lord saw, and spurned.
Because of the provoking of His sons and His daughters.
And he said: I will hide My face from them,
I will see what their end shall be,
For they are a very forward generation,
Children in whom is no faithfulness,
They have roused Me to jealousy with a no-god;
They have provoked Me with their vanities;
And I will rouse them to jealousy with a no-people;
I will provoke them with a vile nation.
For a fire is kindled in My nostril,
And burneth unto the depths of the nether-world,
And devoureth the earth with her produce,
And setteth ablaze the foundations of the mountains.

I will heap evils upon them;
I will spend Mine arrows upon them;
The wasting of hunger, and the devouring of the fiery bolt,
And bitter destruction;
And the teeth of beasts will I send upon them,
With the venom of crawling things of the dust.
Without shall the sword bereave,
And in the chambers terror;
Slaying both young man and virgin,
The suckling with the man of gray hairs.

I thought I would make an end of them,
I would make their memory cease from among men;
Were it not that I dreaded the enemy's provocation,
Lest their adversaries should misdeem,
Lest they should say: Our hand is exalted,
And not the Lord hath wrought all this.

For they are a nation void of counsel,
And there is no understanding in them.
If they were wise, they would understand this,
They would discern their latter end.
How should one chase a thousand,
And two put ten thousand to flight,
Except their Rock had given them over,
And the Lord had delivered them up?
For their rock is not as our Rock,
Even our enemies themselves being judges.
For their vine is of the vine of Sodom,
And of the fields of Gomorrah;
Their grapes are grapes of gall,
Their clusters are bitter;
Their wine is the venom of serpents,
And the cruel poison of asps.

Is not this laid up in store with Me,
Sealed up in My treasuries?
Vengeance is Mine, and recompense,
Against the time when their foot shall slip;
For the day of their calamity is at hand,
And the things that are to come upon them shall make haste.

For the Lord will judge His people,
And repent Himself for His servants;
When He seeth that their stay is gone,
And there is none remaining, shut up or left at large.
And it is said: Where are their gods

The rock in whom they trusted;
Who did eat the fat of their sacrifices,
And drank the wine of their drink-offering?
Let him rise up and help you,
Let him be your protection.

See now that I, even I, am He,
And there is no god with Me;
I kill and I make alive;
I have wounded, and I heal;
And there is none that can deliver out of My hand.
For I lift up My hand to heaven,
And say: As I live for ever,
If I whet My glittering sword,
And My hand take hold on judgment;
I will render vengeance to Mine adversaries,
And will recompense them that hate Me.
I will make Mine arrows drunk with blood.
And My sword shall devour flesh;
With the blood of the slain and the captives
From the long-haired heads of the enemy.

Sing aloud, O ye nations, of His people;
For He doth avenge the blood of His servants,
And doth render vengeance to His adversaries,
And doth make expiation for the land of His people.

The Benediction of Moses

After the first two verses, there follows the benedictions of the twelve tribes of Israel.

And this is the blessing, wherewith Moses the man of God blessed the children of Israel before his death. And he said:

The Lord came from Sinai
And rose from Seir unto them;
He shined forth from Mount Paran,
And He came from the myriads holy,
At His right hand was a fiery law unto them.
Yea, He loveth the peoples,
All His holy ones—they are in Thy hands;
And they sit down at Thy feet,
Receiving of Thy words.
Moses commanded us a law,
An inheritance of the congregation of Jacob.
And there was a king in Jeshurun,
When the heads of the people were gathered,
All the tribes of Israel together.

The Song of Anne

Anne was the first wife of Elcan.

My heart exulteth in the Lord,
My horn is exalted in the Lord;
My mouth is enlarged over mine enemies;
Because I rejoice in Thy salvation.
There is none holy as the Lord;
For there is none beside Thee;
Neither is there any rock like our God.
Multiply not exceeding proud talk;
Let not arrogancy come out of your mouth;
For the Lord is a God of knowledge,
And by Him actions are weighed.
The bows of the mighty men are broken,
And they that stumbled are girded with strength.
They that were full have hired out themselves for bread;
And they that were hungry have ceased;
While the barren hath borne seven,
She that had many children hath languished.

The Lord killeth, and maketh alive;
He bringeth down to the grave, and bringeth up.
The Lord maketh poor, and maketh rich;
He bringeth low, He also lifteth up.
He raiseth up the poor out of the dust,
He lifteth up the needy from the dunghill,
To make them sit with princes,
And inherit the throne of glory;
For the pillars of the earth are the Lord's
And He hath set the world upon them.
He will keep the feet of His holy ones,
But the wicked shall be put to silence in darkness;
For not by strength shall man prevail.
They that strive with the Lord shall be broken to pieces;
Against them will He thunder in heaven;
The Lord will judge the ends of the earth;
And He will give strength unto His king,
And exalt the horn of His anointed.

The Song of David

This is the song composed by David on the day he was liberated by Saul.

The Lord is my rock, and my fortress, and my deliverer;
The God who is my rock, in Him I take refuge;
My shield, and my horn of salvation, my high tower, and my refuge;
My saviour, Thou savest me from violence.
Praised, I cry, is the Lord,
And I am saved from mine enemies.

For the waves of Death compassed me.
The floods of Belial assailed me.
The cords of Sheol surrounded me;
The snares of Death confronted me.
In my distress I called upon the Lord,
Yes, I called unto my God;
And out of His temple He heard my voice,
And my cry did enter into His ears.
Then the earth did shake and quake,
The foundations of heaven did tremble;
They were shaken, because He was wroth.
Smoke arose up in His nostrils,
And fire out of His mouth did devour;
Coals flamed forth from Him.
He bowed the heavens also, and came down;
And thick darkness was under His feet.
And He rode upon a cherub, and did fly;
Yea, He was seen upon the wings of the wind.
And he made darkness pavilions round about Him,
Gathering of waters, thick clouds of the skies.
At the brightness before Him
Coals of fire flamed forth.
The Lord thundered from heaven,
And the Most High gave forth His voice.
And He sent out arrows, and scattered them;
Lightning, and discomfited them.
And the channels of the sea appeared,
The foundations of the world were laid bare,
By the rebuke of the Lord,
At the blast of the breath of His nostrils.

He sent from on high, He took me;
He drew me out of many waters;
He delivered me from mine enemy most strong.
From them that hated me, for they were too mighty for me.
They confronted me in the day of my calamity;
But the Lord was a stay unto me:
He brought me forth also into a large place;
He delivered me, because He delighted in me.
The Lord rewarded me according to my righteousness;
According to the cleanness of my hands hath He recompensed me.

For I have kept the ways of the Lord
And have not wickedly departed from my God.
For all His ordinances were before me;
And as for His statutes, I did not depart from them.
And I was single-hearted toward Him,
And I kept myself from mine iniquity.
Therefore hath the Lord recompensed me according to my righteousness,
According to my cleanness in His eyes.

With the merciful Thou dost show Thyself merciful,
With the upright man Thou dost show Thyself upright;
With the pure Thou dost show Thyself pure;
And with the crooked Thou dost show Thyself subtle.
And the afflicted people Thou dost save;
But thine eyes are upon the haughty, that Thou mayest humble them.

For Thou art my lamp, O Lord;
And the Lord doth lighten my darkness.
For by Thee I run upon a troop;
By my God do I scale a wall.
As for God, His way is perfect;
The word of the Lord is tried;
He is a shield unto all them that take refuge in him.

For who is God, save the Lord?
And who is a Rock, save our God?
The God who is my strong fortress,
And who letteth my way go forth straight;
Who maketh my feet like hinds,
And setteth me upon my high places;
Who traineth my hands for war,
So that mine arms do bend a bow of brass.

Thou hast also given me Thy shield of salvation;
And Thy condescension hath made me great.
Thou hast enlarged my steps under me,
And my feet have not slipped.

I have pursued mine enemies, and destroyed them;
Neither did I turn back till they were consumed.
And I have consumed them, and smitten them through, that they can-
    not arise;
Yea, they are fallen under my feet.
For Thou hast girded me with strength unto the battle;
Thou hast subdued under me those that rose up against me;
Thou hast also made mine enemies turn their backs unto me;
Yea, them that hate me, that I might cut them off.
They looked, but there was none to save;
Then I did beat them small as the dust of the earth,
I did stamp them as the mire of the streets, and did tread them down.
Thou also hast delivered me from the contentions of my people;
Thou hast kept me to be the head of the nations;
A people whom I have not known serve me.
The sons of the stranger dwindle away before me;
As soon as they hear of me, they obey me.
The sons of the stranger fade away,
And come halting out of their close places.

The Lord liveth, and blessed be my Rock;
And exalted be the God, my Rock of salvation;
Even the God that executeth vengeance for me,
And bringeth down peoples under me,
And that bringeth me forth from mine enemies;
Yea, Thou liftest me up above them that rise up against me;
Thou deliverest me from the violent man.
Therefore I will give thanks unto Thee, O Lord, among the nations,
And will sing praises unto Thy name.
A tower of salvation is He to His king;
And showeth mercy to His anointed,
To David and to his seed, for evermore.

Confession of Sin

And I prayed unto the Lord my God, and made confession, and said:
"O Lord, the great and awful God, who keepest covenant and mercy

with them that love Thee and keep Thy commandments, we have sinned, and have dealt iniquitously, and have done wickedly, and have rebelled, and have turned aside from Thy commandments and from Thine ordinances, neither have we hearkened unto Thy servants the prophets, that spoke in Thy name to our kings, our princes, and our fathers, and to all the people of the land. Unto Thee, O Lord, belongeth righteousness, but unto us confusion of face, as at this day; to the men of Judah, and to the inhabitants of Jerusalem, and unto all Israel, that are near, and that are far off, through all the countries whither Thou hast driven them, because they dealt treacherously with Thee. O Lord, to us belongeth confusion of face, to our kings, to our princes, and to our fathers, because we have sinned against Thee. To the Lord our God belong compassions and forgiveness; for we have rebelled against Him; neither have we hearkened to the voice of the Lord our God, to walk in His laws, which He set before us by His servants the prophets. Yea, all Israel have transgressed Thy law and have turned aside, so as not to hearken to Thy voice; and so there hath been poured out upon us the curse and the oath that is written in the Law of Moses, the servant of God; for we have sinned against Him. And He hath confirmed His word, which He spoke against us, and against our judges that judged us, by bringing upon us a great evil; so that under the whole heaven hath not been done as hath been done upon Jerusalem. As it is written in the Law of Moses, all this evil is come upon us; yet have we not entreated the favor of the Lord our God, that we might turn from our iniquities and have discernment in Thy truth. And so the Lord hath watched over the evil, and brought it upon us; for the Lord our God is righteous in all His works which He hath done, and we have not hearkened to His voice. And now, O Lord our God, that hast brought Thy people forth out of the land of Egypt with a mighty hand, and hast gotten Thee renown, as at this day; we have sinned, we have done wickedly. O Lord, according to all Thy righteousness, let Thine anger and Thy fury, I pray Thee, be turned away from Thy city Jerusalem, Thy holy mountain; because for our sins, and for the iniquities of our fathers, Jerusalem and Thy people are become a reproach to all that are round about us. Now therefore, O our God, hearken unto the prayer of Thy servant and to his supplication and cause Thy face to shine upon Thy sanctuary that is desolate for the Lord's sake. O my God, incline Thine ear, and hear; open Thine eyes, and behold our desolations, and the city upon which Thy name is called; for we do not present our supplications before Thee because of our righteousness, but because of Thy great compassions. O Lord, hear, O Lord forgive, O Lord, attend and do, defer not; for Thine own sake, O my God, because Thy name is called upon Thy city and Thy people.

Solomon's Prayer for the Dedication of the Temple

O Lord, the God of Israel, there is no God like Thee, in heaven above or on earth beneath; who keepest covenant and mercy with Thy servants, that walk before Thee with all their heart; who hast kept with Thy servant David, my father, that which Thou didst promise him; yea, Thou spokest with Thy mouth, and hast fulfilled it with Thy hand, as it is this day. Now therefore O Lord, the Lord of Israel, keep with Thy servant David, my father, that which Thou hast promised him, saying: There shall not fail thee a man in My sight to sit on the throne of Israel, if only thy children take heed to their way, to walk before Me as thou hast walked before Me. Now therefore, O God of Israel, let Thy word, I pray Thee, be verified, which Thou didst speak unto Thy servant David my father.

But will God in very truth dwell on the earth? behold, heaven and the heaven of heavens cannot contain Thee; how much less this house that I have builded! Yet have Thou respect unto the prayer of Thy servant, and to his supplication, O Lord my God, to hearken unto the cry and to the prayer which Thy servant prayeth before Thee this day; that Thine eyes may be open toward the place whereof Thou hast said: My name shall be there; to hearken unto the prayer which Thy servant shall pray toward this place. And hearken Thou to the supplication of Thy servant, and of Thy people Israel, when they shall pray toward this place. And hearken Thou to the supplication of Thy servant, and of Thy people Israel, when they shall pray toward this place; yea, hear Thou in heaven Thy dwelling place; and when Thou hearest, forgive.

If a man sin against his neighbor, and an oath be exacted of him to cause him to swear, and he come and swear before Thine altar in this house; then hear Thou in heaven, and do, and judge Thy servants, condemning the wicked, to bring his way upon his own head; and justifying the righteous, to give him according to his righteousness.

When Thy people Israel are smitten down before the enemy, when they do sin against Thee, if they turn again to Thee, and confess Thy name, and pray and make supplication unto Thee in this house; then hear Thou in heaven, and forgive the sin of Thy people Israel, and bring them back unto the land which Thou gavest unto their fathers.

When heaven is shut up, and there is no rain when they do sin against Thee; if they pray toward this place, and confess Thy name, and turn from their sin, when Thou dost afflict them; then hear Thou in heaven, and forgive the sin of Thy servants, and of Thy people Israel, when Thou teachest them the good way wherein they should walk; and send rain upon Thy land, which Thou hast given to Thy people for an inheritance.

If there be in the land famine, if there be pestilence, if there be blasting or mildew, locust or caterpillar; if their enemy besiege them in the land of their cities; whatsoever plague, whatsoever sickness there be; what prayer and supplication soever be made by any man of all Thy people Israel, who shall know every man the plague of his own heart, and spread forth his hands toward this house; then hear Thou in heaven, Thy dwelling place, and forgive, and do, and render unto every man according to all his ways, whose heart Thou knowest—for Thou, even Thou only, knowest the hearts of all the children of men —that they may fear Thee all the days that they live in the land which Thou gavest unto our fathers.

Moreover, concerning the stranger that is not of Thy people Israel, when he shall come out of a far country for Thy name's sake—for they shall hear of Thy great name, and of Thy mighty hand, and of Thine outstretched arm—when he shall come and pray toward this house; hear Thou in heaven, Thy dwelling place, and do according to all that the stranger calleth to Thee for; that all the peoples of the earth may know Thy name, to fear Thee, as doth Thy people Israel, and that they may know that Thy name is called upon this house which I have built.

If Thy people go out to battle against their enemy, by whatsoever way Thou shalt send them, and they pray unto the Lord toward the city which Thou hast chosen, and toward the house which I have built for Thy name; then hear Thou in heaven their prayer and their supplication, and maintain their cause. If they sin against Thee—for there is no man that sinneth not—and Thou be angry with them, and deliver them to the enemy, so that they carry them away captive unto the land of the enemy, far off or near; yet if they shall bethink themselves in the land whither they are, carried captive, and turn back and make supplication unto Thee in the land of them that carried them captive, saying: We have sinned, and have done iniquitously, we have dealt wickedly; if they return unto Thee with all their heart and with all their soul in the land of their enemies, who carried them captive, and pray unto Thee toward their land, which Thou gavest unto their fathers, the city which Thou hast chosen and the house which I have built for

Thy name; then hear Thou their prayer and their supplication in heaven, Thy dwelling place, and maintain their cause; and forgive Thy people who have sinned against Thee, and all their transgressions wherein they have transgressed against Thee; and give them compassion before those who carried them captive that they may have compassion on them; for they are Thy people, and Thine inheritance, which Thou broughtest forth out of Egypt, from the midst of the furnace of iron; that Thine eyes may be open unto the supplication of Thy servant, and unto the supplication of Thy people Israel, to hearken unto them whensoever they cry unto Thee. For Thou didst set them apart from amongst all the peoples of the earth, to be Thine inheritance, as Thou didst speak by the hand of Moses Thy servant, when Thou broughtest our fathers out of Egypt, O Lord God.

Benediction of Solomon

Blessed be the Lord, that hath given rest unto His people Israel, according to all that He promised; there hath not failed one word of all His good promise, which He promised by the hand of Moses His servant. The Lord our God be with us, as He was with our fathers; let Him not leave us, nor forsake us; that He may incline our hearts unto Him, to walk in all His ways, and to keep His commandments, and His statutes, and his ordinances, which He commanded our fathers. And let these my words wherewith I have made supplication before the Lord be nigh unto the Lord our God day and night, that He maintain the cause of His servant, and the cause of His people Israel, as every day shall require; that all the peoples of the earth may know that the Lord, He is God; there is none else. Let your heart therefore be whole with the Lord our God, to walk in His statutes, and to keep His commandments, as at this day.

Song of David

O give thanks unto the Lord, call upon His name;
Make known His doings among the peoples.
Sing unto Him, sing praises unto Him;
Speak ye of all His marvelous works.
Glory ye in His holy name;
Let the heart of them rejoice that seek the Lord.
Seek ye the Lord and His strength;
Seek His face continually.

Remember His marvelous works that He hath done,
His wonders, and the judgments of His mouth;
O ye seed of Israel His servant,
Ye children of Jacob, His chosen ones.
He is the Lord our God;
His judgments are in all the earth.
Remember His covenant for ever,
The word which He commanded to a thousand generations;
The covenant which He made with Abraham,
And His oath unto Isaac;
And He established it unto Jacob for a statute,
To Israel for an everlasting covenant;
Saying: "Unto thee will I give the land of Canaan,
The lot of your inheritance."

When ye were but a few men in number,
Yea, very few, and sojourners in it,
And when they went about from nation to nation,
And from one kingdom to another people,
He suffered no man to do them wrong,
Yea, for their sake He reproved kings:
Touch not Mine anointed ones,
And do My prophets no harm.

Sing unto the Lord, all the earth;
Proclaim His salvation from day to day.
Declare His glory among the nations,
His marvelous works among all the peoples.
For great is the Lord, and highly to be praised;
He also is to be feared above all gods.
For all the gods of the peoples are things of naught;
But the Lord made the heavens.
Honor and majesty are before Him;
Strength and gladness are in His place.
Ascribe unto the Lord, ye kindreds of the peoples,
Ascribe unto the Lord the glory and strength.
Ascribe unto the Lord the glory due unto His name;
Bring an offering, and come before Him;
Worship the Lord in the beauty of holiness.
Tremble before Him, all the earth;
The world also is established that it cannot be moved.
Let the heavens be glad, and let the earth rejoice;

And let them say among the nations: "The Lord reigneth."
Let the sea roar, and the fullness thereof;
Let the field exult, and all that is therein;
Then shall the trees of the wood sing for joy,
Before the Lord, for He is come to judge the earth.
O give thanks unto the Lord; for He is good;
For His mercy endureth for ever.
And say ye: "Save us, O God of our salvation,
And gather us together and deliver us from the nations,
That we may give thanks unto Thy holy name,
That we may triumph in Thy praise.
Blessed be the Lord, the God of Israel,
 From everlasting even to everlasting."
And all the people said: "Amen," and praised the Lord.

The Lament of Isaiah

And we are all become as one that is unclean,
And all our righteousnesses are as a polluted garment;
And we all do fade as a leaf,
And our iniquities, like the wind, take us away.
And there is none that calleth upon Thy name,
That stirreth up himself to take hold of Thee;
For Thou hast hid Thy face from us,
And hast consumed us by means of our iniquities.

But now, O Lord, Thou art our Father;
We are the clay, and Thou art our potter,
And we all are the work of Thy hand.
Be not wroth very sore, O Lord,
Neither remember iniquity for ever;
Behold, look, we beseech Thee, we are all Thy people.
Thy holy cities are become a wilderness,
Zion is become a wilderness,
Jerusalem a desolation.
Our holy and our beautiful house,
Where our fathers praised Thee,
Is burned with fire;
And all our pleasant things are laid waste.
Wilt Thou refrain Thyself for these things, O Lord?
Wilt Thou hold Thy peace, and afflict us very sore?

Jonah's Cry from the Belly of the Whale

I called out of mine affliction
Unto the Lord, and He answered me;
Out of the belly of the netherworld cried I,
And Thou heardest my voice.
For Thou didst cast me into the depth,
In the heart of the seas,
And the flood was round about me;
All Thy waves and Thy billows
Passed over me.
And I said: "I am cast out
From before Thine eyes;
Yet I will look again
Toward Thy holy temple.
The waters compassed me about, even to the soul;
The deep was roundabout me;
The weeds were wrapped about my head.
I went down to the bottoms of the mountains;
The earth with her bars closed upon me for ever;
Yet hast Thou brought up my life from the pit,
O Lord my God.
When my soul fainted within me,
I remembered the Lord;
And my prayer came in unto Thee,
Into Thy holy temple.
They that regard lying vanities
Forsake their own mercy.
But I will sacrifice unto Thee
With the voice of thanksgiving;
That which I have vowed I will pay.
Salvation is of the Lord"
And the Lord spoke unto the fish, and it vomited
    out Jonah upon the dry land.

O Lord, Many Are Mine Enemies

A psalm of David, when he fled from Absalom his son.

Lord how many are mine adversaries become!
Many are they that rise up against me.

Many there are that say of my soul:
"There is no salvation for him in God."
> Selah

But Thou, O Lord, art a shield about me;
My glory, and the lifter up of my head.
With my voice I call unto the Lord,
And he answereth me out of His holy mountain.
> Selah

I lay me down, and I sleep;
I awake, for the Lord sustaineth me.
I am not afraid of ten thousands of people,
That have set themselves against me round about.

Arise, O Lord; save me, O my God;
For Thou hast smitten all mine enemies upon the cheek,
Thou hast broken the teeth of the wicked.
Salvation belongeth unto the Lord;
Thy blessing be upon Thy people.
> Selah

The Lord Is My Shepherd
A PSALM OF DAVID

The Lord is my shepherd; I shall not want.
He maketh me to lie down in green pastures;
He leadeth me beside the still waters.
He restoreth my soul;
He guideth me in straight paths for His name's sake.
Yea, though I walk through the valley of the shadow of death,
I will fear no evil,
For Thou art with me;
Thy rod and Thy staff, they comfort me.
Thou preparest a table before me in the presence of mine enemies;
Thou hast anointed my head with oil; my cup runneth over.
Surely goodness and mercy shall follow me all the days of my life;
And I shall dwell in the house of the Lord for ever.

The Lord Is My Light and My Salvation
A PSALM OF DAVID

The Lord is my light and my salvation; whom shall I fear?
The Lord is the stronghold of my life; of whom shall I be afraid?

When evil-doers came upon me to eat up my flesh,
Even mine adversaries and my foes, they stumbled and fell.
Though a host should encamp against me,
My heart shall not fear;
Though war should rise up against me,
Even then will I be confident.

One thing have I asked of the Lord, that will I seek after:
That I may dwell in the house of the Lord all the days of my life,
To behold the graciousness of the Lord, and to visit early in His temple.
For he concealeth me in His pavilion in the day of evil;
He hideth me in the covert of His tent;
He lifteth me up upon a rock.
And now shall my head be lifted up above mine enemies round about me;
And I will offer in His tabernacle sacrifices with trumpet-sound;
I will sing, yea, I will sing praises unto the Lord.

Hear, O Lord, when I call with my voice,
And be gracious unto me, and answer me.
In Thy behalf my heart hath said: "Seek ye My face";
Thy face, Lord, will I seek.
Hide not Thy face from me;
Put not Thy servant away in anger;
Thou hast been my help;
Cast me not off, neither forsake me, O God of my salvation,
For though my father and my mother have forsaken me,
The Lord will take me up.

Teach me Thy way, O Lord;
And lead me in an even path,
Because of them that lie in wait for me.
Deliver me not over unto the will of mine adversaries;
For false witnesses are risen up against me, and such as breathe out
    violence.
If I had not believed to look upon the goodness of the Lord
In the land of the living!—
Wait for the Lord—
Be strong, and let thy heart take courage;
Yea, wait thou for the Lord.

Rejoice in the Lord, O Ye Righteous

>Rejoice in the Lord, O ye righteous,
>Praise is comely for the upright.
>Give thanks unto the Lord with harp,
>Sing praises unto Him with the psaltery of ten strings.
>Sing unto Him a new song;
>Play skillfully amid shouts of joy.
>
>For the word of the Lord is upright;
>And all His work is done in faithfulness.
>He loveth righteousness and justice;
>The earth is full of the loving kindness of the Lord.
>By the word of the Lord were the heavens made;
>And all the host of them by the breath of His mouth.
>He gathereth the waters of the sea together as a heap;
>He layeth up the deeps in storehouses.
>
>Let all the earth fear the Lord;
>Let all the inhabitants of the world stand in awe of Him.
>For He spoke, and it was;
>He commanded, and it stood.
>The Lord bringeth the counsel of the nations to nought;
>He maketh the thoughts of the peoples to be of no effect.
>The counsel of the Lord standeth for ever,
>The thoughts of His heart to all generations.
>
>Happy is the nation whose God is the Lord;
>The people whom He hath chosen for His own inheritance.
>The Lord looketh from heaven;
>He beholdeth all the sons of men;
>From the place of His habitation He looketh intently
>Upon all the inhabitants of the earth;
>He that fashioneth the hearts of them all,
>That considereth all their doings.
>A king is not saved by the multitude of a host;
>A mighty man is not delivered by great strength.
>A horse is a vain thing for safety;
>Neither doth it afford escape by its great strength.
>Behold, the eye of the Lord is toward them that fear Him,
>Toward them that wait for His mercy;

To deliver their soul from death,
And to keep them alive in famine.

Our soul hath waited for the Lord;
He is our help and our shield.
For in Him doth our heart rejoice,
Because we have trusted in His holy name.
Let Thy mercy, O Lord, be upon us,
According as we have waited for Thee.

O Clap Your Hands All Ye Peoples

For the Leader; a psalm of the sons of Korah.

O clap your hands, all ye peoples;
Shout unto God with the voice of triumph.
For the Lord is most high, awful;
A great King over all the earth.
He subdueth peoples under us,
And nations under our feet.
He chooseth our inheritance for us.
The pride of Jacob whom He loveth.
           Selah
God is gone up amidst shouting,
The Lord amidst the sound of the horn.
Sing praises to God, sing praises;
Sing praises unto our King, sing praises.
For God is the King of all the earth;
Sing ye praises in a skillful song.
God reigneth over the nations;
God sitteth upon His holy throne.

The princes of the peoples are gathered together,
Sing ye praises in a skillful song.
God reigneth over the nations;
God sitteth upon His holy throne.

The princes of the peoples are gathered together,
The people of the God of Abraham;
For unto God belong the shields of the earth;
He is greatly exalted.

O God, Thou Art My God

A psalm of David when he was in the wilderness of Judah.

O God, Thou art my God, earnestly will I seek Thee;
My soul thirsteth for Thee, my flesh longeth for Thee,
In a dry and weary land, where no water is.
So have I looked for Thee in the sanctuary,
To see Thy power and Thy glory.

For Thy loving-kindness is better than life;
My lips shall praise Thee.
So will I bless Thee as long as I live;
In Thy name will I lift up my hands.

My soul is satisfied as with marrow and fatness;
And my mouth doth praise Thee with joyful lips;
When I remember Thee upon my couch,
And meditate on Thee in the night watches.

For Thou hast been my help,
And in the shadow of Thy wings do I rejoice.
My soul cleaveth unto Thee;
Thy right hand holdeth me fast.

But those that seek my soul, to destroy it,
Shall go into the nethermost parts of the earth.
They shall be hurled to the power of the sword;
They shall be a portion for foxes.
But the king shall rejoice in God;
Every one that sweareth by Him shall glory;
For the mouth of them that speak lies shall be stopped.

God Bless Us and Have Pity on Us

For the Leader; with string music. A psalm.

God be gracious unto us, and bless us;
May He cause His face to shine toward us;
Selah
That Thy way may be known upon earth,
Thy salvation among all nations.

Let the peoples give thanks unto Thee, O God;
Let the peoples give thanks unto Thee, all of them.
O let the nations be glad and sing for joy;
For Thou wilt judge the peoples with equity,
And lead the nations upon earth.
Selah
Let the peoples give thanks unto Thee, O God;
Let the peoples give thanks unto Thee, all of them.
The earth hath yielded her increase;
May God, our own God, bless us.
May God bless us;
And let all the ends of the earth fear him.

For Yom Kippur

Kippur is a fast, a ceremony of mortification which, originally was intended to expiate transgressions of the people, as, for example, on the eve of a battle. Later it became a solemn fast which fell on the tenth day of the year, according to the calendar which begins the year in autumn.

Thou hast chosen us from all peoples, thou has loved us and taken pleasure in us, and hast exalted us above all tongues; thou hast hallowed us by thy commandments and brought us near unto thy service, O our King, and hast called us by thy great and holy Name.

And thou has given us in love, O Lord our God, this Day of Atonement for pardon, forgiveness, and atonement, that we may obtain pardon thereon for all our iniquities; an holy convocation, as a memorial of the departure from Egypt.

Our God and God of our fathers! May our remembrance rise and come and be accepted before thee, with the remembrance of our fathers, of Messiah the son of David thy servant, of Jerusalem thy holy city, and of all thy people the house of Israel, bringing deliverance and well-being, grace and loving-kindness and mercy, life and peace on this Day of Atonement. Remember us, O Lord our God, thereon for our well-being; be mindful of us for blessing, and save us unto life: by thy promise of salvation and mercy, spare us and be gracious unto us; have mercy upon us and save us; for our eyes are bent upon thee, because thou art a gracious and merciful God and King.

Our God and God of our fathers, pardon our iniquities on this Day of Atonement; blot out our transgressions and our sins, and make them pass away from before thine eyes; as it is said, I, even I, am he that blotteth out thy transgressions for mine own sake; and I will not remember thy sins. And it is said, I have blotted out, as a cloud, thy transgressions, and, as a mist, thy sins: return unto me, for I have redeemed thee. And it is said, For on this day shall atonement be made for you, to cleanse you; from all your sins shall ye be clean before the Lord. Sanctify us by thy commandments, and grant our portion in thy Torah; satisfy us with thy goodness, and gladden us with thy salvation; and purify our hearts to serve thee in truth; for thou art the Forgiver of Israel and the Pardoner of the tribes of Jeshurun in every generation, and beside thee we have no king who pardoneth and forgiveth. Blessed art thou, O Lord, thou King who pardonest and forgivest our iniquities and the iniquities of thy people, the house of Israel, who makest our transgressions to pass away year by year, King over all the earth, who hallowest Israel and the Day of Atonement.

Prayers Following Torah Reading

The following prayer, Av Harahamim, is a dirge composed after the dreadful massacre in 1096, in the Rhineland.

May the Father of mercies who dwelleth on high, in his mighty compassion, remember those loving, upright, and blameless ones, the holy congregations, who laid down their lives for the Sanctification of the divine Name. Beloved and faithful were they in life and in death were not separated; swifter than eagles and stronger than lions to do the will of their Master and the desire of their Rock. May our God remember them for good with the other righteous of the world, and avenge the blood of the people which hath been shed; as it is written in the Torah: "Sing aloud, O ye nations, for God doth bring to judgment those who shed the blood of His servants." Wherefore should the nations say: "Where is their God?" Let the retribution of Thy servants' blood be made known among the nations in our sight. God will judge among the nations and He will emerge triumphant.

Happy are they who dwell in Thy house; forever shall they praise Thee. Happy the people who thus fare; happy the people whose God is the Eternal.

> I will extol Thee, My God, O King;
> And praise Thy Name for ever and ever.
> Every day will I bless Thee;
> And I will praise Thy name for ever and ever.

Great is the Lord and greatly to be praised,
And his greatness is without end.
>One generation shall laud Thy works to another,
>And shall declare Thy mighty acts.

I will speak of the splendor of Thy glorious majesty,
And tell of Thy wonders.
>And men shall proclaim the might of Thy acts;
>And I will declare Thy greatness.

They shall make known the fame of Thy great goodness,
And shall joyously proclaim Thy righteousness.
>The Lord is gracious and full of compassion;
>Slow to anger and abundant in kindness.

The Lord is good to all;
And His love is over all His works.
>All whom Thou hast made shall give thanks unto
>   Thee, O Lord;
>And Thy faithful ones shall bless Thee.

They shall declare the glory of Thy kingdom,
And tell of Thy power;
>To make known to the sons of men Thy mighty acts,
>And the glorious splendor of thy kingdom.

Thy kingdom is an everlasting kingdom,
And Thy dominion endureth throughout all generations.
>The Lord upholdeth all who fall,
>And raiseth up all who are bowed down.

The eyes of all hopefully look to Thee,
And thou givest them their food in due season.
>Thou openest Thy hand,
>And satisfiest every living thing with favor.

The Lord is righteous in all His ways,
And gracious in all His works.
>The Lord is near unto all who call upon Him,
>To all who call upon Him in truth.

Morning Prayer for Yom Kippur

O my God, the soul which thou gavest me is pure; thou didst create it, thou didst form it, thou didst breathe it into me. Thou preservest it within me, and thou wilt take it from me, but wilt restore unto me hereafter. So long as the soul is within me, I will give thanks unto thee, O Lord my God and God of my fathers, Sovereign of all words, Lord of all souls! Blessed art thou, O Lord, who restorest souls unto the dead.

Blessed art thou, O Lord our God, King of the universe, who hast given to the mind understanding to distinguish between day and night.

Blessed art thou, O Lord our God, King of the universe, who hast not made me a heathen.

Blessed art thou, O Lord our God, King of the universe, who hast not made me a bondman.

(Men say:)

Blessed art thou, O Lord our God, King of the universe, who hast not made me a woman.

(Women say:)

Blessed art thou, O Lord our God, King of the universe, who hast made me according to thy will.

Blessed art thou, O Lord our God, King of the universe, who openest the eyes of the blind.

Blessed art thou, O Lord our God, King of the universe, who clothest the naked.

Blessed art thou, O Lord our God, King of the universe, who settest free them that are bound.

Blessed art thou, O Lord our God, King of the universe, who raisest up them that are bowed down.

Blessed art thou, O Lord our God, King of the universe, who spreadest forth the earth above the waters.

Blessed art thou, O Lord our God, King of the universe, who providest my every want.

Blessed art thou, O Lord our God, King of the universe, who hast made firm the steps of man.

Blessed art thou, O Lord our God, King of the universe, who girdest Israel with might.

Blessed art thou, O Lord our God, King of the universe, who crownest Israel with glory.

Blessed art thou, O Lord our God, King of the universe, who givest strength to the weary.

Blessed art thou, O Lord our God, King of the universe, who removest sleep from mine eyes and slumber from mine eyelids.

Praise

> O give thanks unto the Lord, for he is good,
> For His mercy endureth for ever.

O give thanks unto the God of gods,
For His mercy endureth forever.
O give thanks unto the Lord of lords,
For His mercy endureth for ever.

To Him who alone doeth great wonders,
For His mercy endureth for ever.
To Him that by understanding made the heavens,
For His mercy endureth for ever.
To Him that spread forth the earth above the waters,
For His mercy endureth for ever.
To Him that made great lights,
For His mercy endureth for ever;
The sun to rule by day,
For His mercy endureth for ever;
The moon and stars to rule by night,
For His mercy endureth for ever.
To Him that smote Egypt in their first-born,
For His mercy endureth for ever;
And brought out Israel from among them,
For His mercy endureth for ever;
With a strong hand, and with an outstretched arm,
For His mercy endureth for ever.
To Him who divided the Red Sea in sunder,
For His mercy endureth for ever;
And made Israel to pass through the midst of it,
For His mercy endureth for ever;
But overthrew Pharaoh and his host in the Red Sea,
For His mercy endureth for ever.
To him that led His people through the wilderness,
For His mercy endureth for ever.

To Him that smote great kings;
For His mercy endureth for ever;
And slew mighty kings,
For His mercy endureth for ever.
Sihon king of the Amorites,
For His mercy endureth for ever;
And Og king of Bashan,
For His mercy endureth for ever;
And gave their land for a heritage,
For His mercy endureth for ever;

Even a heritage unto Israel His servant,
For His mercy endureth for ever.

Who remembered us in our low estate,
For His mercy endureth for ever;
And hath delivered us from our adversaries,
For His mercies endureth for ever.
Who giveth food to all flesh,
For His mercy endureth for ever.
O give thanks unto the God of heaven,
For His mercy endureth for ever.

Evening Service—Yom Kippur
KOL NIDRE

> Kol Nidre—chant of ages,
> Chant of Israel, chant of sorrow,
> Measuring off the throbbing heartbeats
> Of a people bowed in anguish,
> Crushed by tyrants, thwarted, broken,
> Wand'ring ever—homeless, weary,
> Generations set your motif
> Out of trials, hopes, and yearnings,
> Added each its variations
> To your theme and to your cadence.
> Diverse lands and diverse periods
> Poured their soul into your music.
> When we hearken with our hearts tuned,
> We can hear the lamentations
> Through time's corridor resounding.
> We can see revealed before us
> Heroes, martyrs, saints and scholars,
> Loyal steadfast sons of Israel
> Sanctifying God, their Father.

KOL NIDRE

> Kol Nidre—chant of ages,
> Chant of pain and chant of pathos,
> Mingles with your notes of sorrow
> Vibrant measures trill and quiver,

Rising to a great crescendo
With the Jew's undying spirit
As he raises 'loft his Torah,
Symbol of his faith and vigor.
Notes of joyous exultation
Crept into your dirgeful music
As with fortitude he cherished
All his fathers held most sacred.
While our hearts beat to your rhythm.
Stir us with new consecration
To our fathers' God, to serve Him
With our heart and soul and fervor.

KOL NIDRE

Kol Nidre—chant of ages,
Chant of grief and chant of triumph,
Echoing, this night of mem'ries,
In the ears and heart of Israel,
Once again you draw together
All dispersed and all God's faithful
To return and humbly seek Him—
Suppliants for His grace and pardon.
Faced by grim, appalling forces
In these days of woeful living,
Do we plead before God's mercy
For His strength, His help, His guidance.
With your plaintive chant, Kol Nidre,
Rise our prayers to heaven ascending,
For a surcease of man's sorrows,
For the dawn of peace and freedom,
When all hearts are purged of hatred,
Passions, lusts that rend asunder.
Then all men will stand together
To acknowledge God, their Father.

Kaddish

Mourner's prayer.

Magnified and sanctified be his great Name in the world which he hath created according to his will. May be established his kingdom during your life and during your days, and during the life of all the house of Israel, even speedily and at a near time, and say ye, Amen.

Let his great Name be blessed for ever and to all eternity.

Blessed, praised and glorified, exalted, extolled and honored, magnified and lauded be the Name of the Holy One, blessed be he; though he be high above all the blessings and hymns, praises and consolations, which are uttered in the world; and say ye, Amen.

May there be abundant peace from heaven, and life for us and for all Israel; and say ye, Amen.

He who maketh peace in his high places, may he make peace for us and for all Israel; and say ye, Amen.

Amida

Morning Service: The Eighteen Benedictions.

O Lord, open thou my lips, and my mouth shall declare thy praise.

Blessed art thou, O Lord our God and God of our fathers, God of Abraham, God of Isaac, and God of Jacob, the great, mighty, and revered God, the most high God, who bestowest loving-kindnesses, and art Master of all things; who rememberest the pious deeds of the patriarchs, and in love wilt bring a redeemer to their children's children for Thy Name's sake.

O King, Helper, Saviour and Shield. Blessed art thou, O Lord, the shield of Abraham.

Thou, O Lord, art mighty for ever, thou revivest the dead, thou art mighty to save.

Thou sustainest the living with loving-kindness, revivest the dead with great mercy, supportest the falling, healest the sick, freest the bound, and keepest thy faith to them that sleep in the dust. Who is like unto thee, Lord of mighty acts, and who resembleth thee, O King, who orderest death and restorest life, and causest salvation to spring forth?

Yea, faithful art thou to revive the dead. Blessed art thou, O Lord, who revivest the dead.

We will sanctify thy Name in the world even as they sanctify it in the highest heavens, as it is written by the hand of thy prophet: And they called one unto the other and said,

Holy, Holy, Holy is the Lord of Hosts: the whole earth is full of his glory.

Those over against them say, Blessed—

Blessed by the glory of the Lord from his place.

And in thy Holy Words it is written, saying,

The Lord shall reign for ever, thy God, O Zion, unto all generations. Praise ye the Lord.

Unto all generations we will declare thy greatness, and to all eternity we will proclaim thy holiness, and thy praise, O our God, shall not depart from our mouth for ever, for thou art a great and holy God and King. Blessed art thou, O Lord, the holy God.

Thou art holy, and thy Name is holy, and the holy praise thee daily.

Selah

Blessed art thou, O Lord, the holy God.

Thou favorest man with knowledge, and teachest mortals understanding. O favor us with knowledge, understanding, and discernment from thee. Blessed art thou, O Lord, gracious Giver of knowledge.

Cause us to return, O our Father, unto thy Torah; draw us near, O our King, unto thy service, and bring us back in perfect repentance unto thy presence. Blessed art thou, O Lord, who delightest in repentance.

Forgive us, O our Father, for we have sinned; pardon us, O our King, for we have transgressed; for thou dost pardon and forgive.

Blessed art thou, O Lord, who art gracious, and dost abundantly forgive.

Look upon our affliction and plead our cause, and redeem us speedily for thy Name's sake; for thou art a mighty Redeemer. Blessed art thou, O Lord, the Redeemer of Israel.

Heal us, O Lord, and we shall be healed; save us, and we shall be saved; for thou art our praise. Grant a perfect healing to all our wounds; for thou, almighty King, art a faithful and merciful Physician. Blessed art thou, O Lord, who healest the sick of thy people Israel.

Bless this year unto us, O Lord our God, together with every kind of the produce thereof, for our welfare; give a blessing upon the face of the earth. O satisfy us with thy goodness, and bless our year like other good years. Blessed art thou, O Lord, who blessest the years.

Sound the great horn for our freedom; raise the ensign to gather our exiles, and gather us from the four corners of the earth. Blessed art thou, O Lord, who gatherest the dispersed of thy people Israel.

Restore our judges as in former times, and our counselors as at the beginning; remove from us sorrow and sighing; reign thou over us, O Lord, thou alone, in loving-kindness and tender mercy, and clear us in judgment. Blessed art Thou, O Lord, the King who lovest righteousness and judgment.

And for slanders let there be no hope, and let all wickedness perish as in a moment; let all thine enemies be speedily cut off, and the dominion of arrogance do thou uproot and crush; cast down and humble speedily in our days. Blessed art thou, O Lord, who breakest the enemies and humblest the arrogant.

Toward the righteous and the pious, toward the elders of thy people the house of Israel, toward the remnant of their scribes, toward true proselytes, and toward us also may thy tender mercies be stirred, O Lord our God; grant a good reward unto all who faithfully trust in thy Name; set our portion with them for ever, so that we may not be put to shame; for we have trusted in thee. Blessed art thou, O Lord, the stay and trust of the righteous.

And to Jerusalem, thy city, return in mercy, and dwell therein as thou hast spoken; rebuild it soon in our days as an everlasting building, and speedily set up therein the throne of David. Blessed art thou, O Lord, who rebuildest Jerusalem.

Speedily cause the offspring of David, thy servant, to flourish, and lift up his glory by thy divine help because we wait for thy salvation all the day. Blessed art thou, O Lord, who causest the strength of salvation to flourish.

Hear our voice, O Lord our God; spare us and have mercy upon us, and accept our prayer in mercy and favor; for thou art a God who hearkenest unto prayers and supplications: from thy presence, O our King, turn us not empty away; for thou hearkenest in mercy to the prayer of thy people Israel. Blessed art thou, O Lord, who harkenest unto prayer.

Accept, O Lord our God, thy people Israel and their prayer; restore the service to the inner sanctuary of thy house; receive in love and favor both the offerings of Israel and their prayer; and may the worship of thy people Israel be ever acceptable unto thee.

Our God and God of our fathers! May our remembrance ascend, come and be accepted before thee, with the remembrance of our fathers, of Messiah the son of David thy servant, of Jerusalem thy holy city, and of all thy people, the house of Israel, bringing deliverance and well-being, grace, loving-kindness and mercy, life and peace on this day.

Remember us, O Lord our God, thereon for our well-being; be mindful of us for blessing, and save us unto life; by thy promise of salvation and mercy, spare us and be gracious unto us; have mercy upon us and save us; for our eyes are bent upon thee, because thou art a gracious and merciful God and King.

And let our eyes behold thy return in mercy to Zion. Blessed art thou, O Lord, who restorest thy divine presence unto Zion.

We give thanks unto thee, for thou art the Lord our God and the

God of our fathers for ever and ever; thou art the Rock of our lives, the Shield of our salvation through every generation. We will give thanks unto thee and declare thy praise for our lives which are committed unto thy hand, and for our souls which are in thy charge, and for thy miracles, which are daily with us, and for thy wonders and thy benefits, which are wrought at all times, evening, morn, and noon. O thou who art all-good, whose mercies fail not; thou, merciful Being, whose loving-kindnesses never cease, we have ever hoped in thee.

And everything that liveth shall give thanks unto thee for ever, and shall praise thy Name in truth, O God, our salvation and our help.

Selah

Blessed art thou, O Lord, whose Name is All-good, and unto whom it is becoming to give thanks.

Grant peace, welfare, blessing, grace, loving-kindness and mercy unto us and unto all Israel, thy people. Bless us, O our Father, even all of us together, with the light of thy countenance; for by the light of thy countenance thou has given us, O Lord our God, the Torah of life, loving-kindness and righteousness, blessing, mercy, life and peace; and may it be good in thy sight to bless thy people Israel at all times and in every hour with thy peace. Blessed art thou, O Lord, who blessest thy people Israel with peace.

O my God! Guard my tongue from evil and my lips from speaking guile; and to such as curse me let my soul be dumb, yea, let my soul be unto all as the dust. Open my heart to thy Torah, and let my soul pursue thy commandments. If any design evil against me, speedily make their counsel of no effect, and frustrate their designs. Do it for the sake of thy Name, do it for the sake of thy power, do it for the sake of thy holiness, do it for the sake of thy Torah. In order that thy beloved ones may be delivered, O save by thy power, and answer me. Let the words of my mouth and the meditation of my heart be acceptable before thee, O Lord, my Rock and my Redeemer. He who maketh peace in his high places, may he make peace for us and for all Israel, and say ye, Amen.

May it be thy will, O Lord our God and God of our fathers, that the temple be speedily rebuilt in our days and grant our portion in thy Torah. And there we will serve thee with awe, as in the days of old, and as in ancient years. Then shall the offering of Judah and Jerusalem be pleasant unto the Lord, as in the days of old, and as in ancient years.

AMIDAH: SHORTENED FORM

Give us understanding, O Lord our God, to know thy ways; open our hearts to fear thee, and forgive us so that we may be redeemed.

Keep us far from sorrow; satisfy our needs on the produce of thy land, and gather our scattered ones from the four corners of the earth. Let them that go astray be judged according to thy will, and bring thy hand upon the wicked. Let the righteous rejoice in the rebuilding of thy city, and in the establishment of thy temple, and in the flourishing of the might of David thy servant, and in the clear shining light of the son of Jesse, thine anointed. Even before we call, do thou answer. Blessed art thou, O Lord, who hearkenest unto prayer.

Evening Service—Yom Kippur

A Piyyut, emphasizing man's dependence on his Maker and pleading for God's mercy.

As clay are we, as soft and yielding clay
That lies between the fingers of the potter.
At his will he molds it thick or thin,
And forms its shape according to his fancy.
So are we in Thy hand, God of love;
 Thy covenant recall and show Thy mercy.

As stone are we, inert, resistless stone
That lies within the fingers of the mason.
At his will he keeps it firm and whole,
Or at his pleasure hews it into fragments.
So are we in Thy hand, God of life;
 Thy covenant recall and show Thy mercy.

As iron are we, as cold and rigid iron
That lies within the fingers of the craftsman.
At his will he forges it to shape,
Or draws it boldly forth to lie unbended.
So are we in Thy hand, God who saves;
 Thy covenant recall and show Thy mercy.

As glass are we, as thin, transparent glass
That lies within the fingers of the blower.
At his will, he blows it crystal clear,
Or melts it down to suit his whim or notion
So are we in Thy hand, gracious God;
 Thy covenant recall and show Thy mercy.

As cloth are we, as formless, graceless cloth
That lies within the fingers of the draper.

At his will he shapes its lines and folds,
Or leaves it unadorned to hand unseemly.
So are we in Thy hand, righteous God;
    Thy covenant recall and show Thy mercy.

As silver are we, with metal dross alloyed
That lies within the fingers of the smelter.
At his will he fuses or refines,
Retains the slag or keeps it pure and precious.
So are we in Thy hand, healing God;
    Thy covenant recall and show Thy mercy.

Thou sittest on Thy Judgment seat
    Enthroned on high,
And one by one man's trespasses
    In penance pass Thee by.
Almighty King, Thy governing
With tender love replete.
Absolve we pray, our fears allay,
With mercy judgment mete.

Thou dwellest high, our Rock and Shield,
    Enthroned in might,
And pardonest each one his sins,
    From scarlet mak'st Thou white.
O Ruler wise, before Thine eyes,
Our frailties stand revealed.
Thy judgment be with charity,
Thy might with mercy wield.

Thou taughtest us Thy attributes
    Thirteen to say.
Remember then Thy covenant
    With us unto this day.
O living Fount, on Sinai's mount
Did'st plant Thy nation's roots.
The truth, Thy seal, didst Thou reveal,
And none Thy word refutes.

Thou stoodest in a heavenly glow
    With Moses there.
Invoked he then Thy Name, O God
    And thus didst Thou declare;

"A gracious Lord, compassionate Lord,
To wrath and anger slow,
Forgiving sin, men's hearts to win,
To thousands mercy show."

From the Sabbath Ritual: Lechoh Dod

A Sabbath hymn wherein the holy day is represented as a bride.

Come my beloved, with chorus of praise,
Welcome Bride Sabbath, the Queen of the days,
"Keep and Remember"!—in One divine Word
He that is One, made His will heard;
One is the name of Him, One is the Lord!
　　His are the fame and the glory and praise!
Sabbath, to welcome thee, joyous we haste;
Fountain of blessing from ever thou wast—
First in God's planning, thou fashioned the last,
　　Crown of His handiwork, chiefest of days.
City of holiness, filled are the years;
Up from thine overthrow! Forth from thy fears!
Long hast thou dwelt in the valley of tears,
　　Now shall God's tenderness shepherd thy ways.
Rise, O my folk from the dust of the earth,
Garb thee in raiment beseeming thy worth;
Nigh draws the hour of the Bethlehemite's birth,
　　Freedom who bringeth, and glorious days.
Wake and bestir thee, for come is thy light!
Up! With thy shining, the world shall be bright;
Sing! For thy Lord is revealed in His might—
　　Thine is the splendor His glory displays!
Be not ashamed, saith the Lord, nor distressed;
Fear not and doubt not. The people oppressed,
Zion, My city, in thee shall find rest—
　　Thee, that anew on thy ruins I raise.
Those that despoil thee shall plundered be,
Routed all those who showed no ruth;
God shall exult and rejoice in thee,
　　Joyful as bridegroom with bride of youth.
Stretch out thy borders to left and to right;
Fear but the Lord, Whom to fear is delight—

The man, son of Perez shall gladden our sight,
　　And we shall rejoice to the fullness of days.
Come in thy joyousness, Crown of thy lord;
Come, bringing peace to the folk of the Word;
Come where the faithful in gladsome accord,
　　Hail thee as Sabbath-Bride, Queen of the days.
Come where the faithful are hymning thy praise,
Come as a bride cometh, Queen of the days!

Shema

The Shema was written on door posts, parchments, and carried in the phylacteries.

Hear, O Israel: The Lord our God, The Lord is one, And thou shalt love the Lord thy God with all thy heart, and with all thy soul, and with all thy might. And these words, which I command thee this day, shall be upon thy heart; and thou shalt teach them diligently unto thy children, and shalt talk of them when thou sittest in thy house, and when thou walkest by the way, and when thou liest down, and when thou risest up. And thou shalt bind them for a sign upon thy hand, and they shall be for frontlets between thine eyes. And thou shalt write them upon the door posts of thy house, and upon thy gates.

Ha-Mavdil

Ha-Mavdil means separation and is the form used to consecrate the closing of the Sabbath.

He who marks the holy from the profane,
May he also pardon our transgressions;
May he multiply our seed as the sand,
And as the stars that appear in the night.

The day has declined like the shade of a palm;
I call upon God who fills all my needs;
The watchman-prophet has said: Morning comes,
Bright morning comes after a gloomy night.

Thy righteousness is like Mount Tabor high;
O condone and pardon my transgressions;
May they be like the flight of yesterday,
Or like the watch-hours passing in the night.

Gone is the time when I made offerings;
Oh, that again I had my place of rest!
I am worn out because of my moaning;
I flood my bed with tears every night.

Let not my supplication be repelled;
Open heaven's exalted gate for me,
Seeing that my head is drenched with the dew,
My locks are wet with the drops of the night.

Revered God, O respond to my prayer;
I call for thy help, O grant redemption,
In the twilight, the evening of the day,
And in the profound blackness of the night.

I call upon thee, O Lord, O save me;
Do thou reveal to me the path of life;
Do thou deliver me from privation,
Within the twilight, between day and night.

O cleanse the impurity of my deeds,
So that those who provoke me may not say:
"Where, then, is the God who created you,
He who inspires you to sing in the night?"

We are but like potter's clay in thy hand;
Pardon our transgressions, both light and grave;
Day after day proclaims the Lord's wonders,
His powers are revealed night after night.

For the Conclusion of Sabbath

At the close of the day of rest,
O grant relief to thy people;
Send Elijah to the distressed,
That grief and sighs may flee away.

It behooves thee, my Creator,
To gather my scattered people
From amidst a cruel nation
That is digging pitfalls for me.

O God, do thou arouse thy love,
To save a people that asks to see

Thy grace when a redeemer comes
To thy dispersed, unhappy flock.

Proclaim freedom to a noble people,
Thou who art worshiped by myriads;
May this coming week be given
To deliverance and relief.

The bereaved city of Zion,
Held today in utter contempt,
May she soon be populated—
A happy mother of children.

The fountains shall be aflow;
Those freed by the Lord shall return;
They shall draw water that saves,
The trouble shall soon be forgotten.

Merciful Father, guide thy people;
A people, unbereft, say
That the word of God is faithful,
When thou wilt have kept thy promise.

Thy loved ones, escaping ruin,
Will break into vigorous song—
Without alarm, without havoc,
No surrender and no panic.

May the vision of the great seer
Jeremiah come to pass this month;
May in this household be heard
The sound of mirth and gladness.

May God fulfill our petitions,
The Almighty do what we ask;
May He prosper all our efforts,
And send us blessings and success.

At the close of the joyous day,
Send Elijah to thy chosen people,
Thou whose deeds are awe-inspiring;
Send relief, mirth, and a release.

Then shall our lips joyfully chant:
O Lord, save us; O Lord, prosper us.

The Lord said to Jacob:
   Fear not, my servant Jacob.
The Lord has chosen Jacob.
   Fear not, my servant Jacob.
The Lord has redeemed Jacob.
   Fear not, my servant Jacob.
A star has risen from Jacob.
   Fear not, my servant Jacob.
Then shall Jacob take root.
   Fear not, my servant Jacob.
Out of Jacob shall one rule.
   Fear not, my servant Jacob.
Remember this, O Jacob.
   Fear not, my servant Jacob.
Joyous triumph shall Jacob have.
   Fear not, my servant Jacob.
Goodly are your tents, O Jacob.
   Fear not, my servant Jacob.
Thy laws are taught to Jacob.
   Fear not, my servant Jacob.
There is no sorcery with Jacob.
   Fear not, my servant Jacob.
None has seen iniquity in Jacob.
   Fear not, my servant Jacob.
Who has counted Jacob's masses?
   Fear not, my servant Jacob.
The Lord has made promise to Jacob.
   Fear not, my servant Jacob.
O pardon the sins of Jacob.
   Fear not, my servant Jacob.
Bring now back the captivity of Jacob.
   Fear not, my servant Jacob.
The Lord redeems Jacob.
   Fear not, my servant Jacob.
Command the salvation of Jacob.
   Fear not, my servant Jacob.
The voice is the voice of Jacob.
   Fear not, my servant Jacob.
Sing with gladness for Jacob.
   Fear not, my servant Jacob.

> The Lord restores the pride of Jacob.
> Fear not, my servant Jacob.
> Thou wilt grant kindness to Jacob.
> Fear not, my servant Jacob.

The Havdolah Service

A religious ceremony that marks the end of the Sabbath.

Behold thus shall the man be blessed that feareth the Lord. May the Lord bless thee out of Zion: mayest thou see the good of Jerusalem all the days of thy life. Yea, mayest thou see thy children's children. Peace be upon Israel.

Behold, God is my salvation; I will trust, and will not be afraid: for God the Lord is my strength and song, and he is become my salvation. Therefore with joy shall ye draw water out of the wells of salvation. Salvation belongeth unto the Lord; thy blessing be upon thy people.
    Selah
The Lord of hosts is with us; the God of Jacob is our refuge.
    Selah
The Jews had light and joy and gladness and honor.
    So be it with us.
I will lift the cup of salvation, and call upon the Name of the Lord.
Blessed art thou, O Lord our God, King of the universe, who createst
    the fruit of the vine.
Blessed art thou, O Lord our God, King of the universe, who createst
    divers kinds of spices.
Blessed art thou, O Lord our God, King of the universe, who createst
    the light of the fire.

> May He who sets the holy and profane
> Apart blot our our sins before His sight,
> And make our numbers as the sand again,
>   And as the stars of night.
>
> The day declineth like the palm-tree's shade,
> I call on God, who leadeth me aright.
> The morning cometh—thus the watchman said—
>   Although it now be night.
>
> Thy righteousness is like Mount Tabor vast;
> O let my sins be wholly put to flight,
> Be they as yesterday, for ever past,
>   And as a watch at night.

The peaceful season of my prayers is o'er,
Would that again had rest my soul contrite,
Weary am I of groaning ever more,
    I melt in tears each night.

Hear thou my voice, be it not vainly sped,
Open to me the gates of lofty height;
For with the evening dew is filled my head,
    My locks with drops of night.

O grant me Thy redemption, while I pray,
Be Thou entreated, Lord of power and might,
In twilight, in the evening of the day,
    Yea, in the gloom of night.

Save me, O Lord, my God, I call on Thee!
Make me to know the path of life aright,
From sore and wasting sickness snatch Thou me,
    Lead me from day to night.

We are like clay within Thy hand, O Lord,
Forgive us all our sins both grave and light,
And day shall unto day pour forth Thy word,
    And night declare to night.

Sovereign of the Universe, Father of mercy and forgiveness, grant that we begin the working days which are drawing nigh unto us, in peace; freed from all sin and transgression; cleansed from all iniquity, trespass, and wickedness; and clinging to the study of thy Teaching, and to the performance of good deeds. Cause us to hear in the coming week tidings of joy and gladness. May there not arise in the heart of any man envy of us, nor in us envy of any man. O, our King, our God, Father of mercy, bless and prosper the work of our hands. And all who cherish toward us and thy people Israel thoughts of good, strengthen and prosper them, and fulfill their purposes; but all who devise against us, and thy people Israel, plans which are not for good, O frustrate them and make their designs of none effect; as it is said, "Take counsel together, and it shall be brought to naught; speak the word, and it shall not stand; for God is with us." Open unto us, Father of mercies and Lord of forgiveness, in this week and in the weeks to come, the gates of light and blessing, of redemption and salvation, of heavenly help and rejoicing, of holiness and peace, of the study of thy Torah and of prayer. In us also let the Scripture be fulfilled: How beautiful upon the mountains are the feet of him that

bringeth good tidings, that announceth peace, the harbinger of good
tidings, that announceth salvation; that saith unto Zion, Thy God
reigneth! Amen. Selah

A Song

A psalm of the sons of Korah.

Great is the Lord, and highly to be praised,
In the city of our God, His holy mountain,
Fair in situation, the joy of the whole earth;
Even mount Zion, the uttermost parts of the north,
The city of the great King.
God in her palaces
Hath made Himself known for a stronghold.

For, lo, the kings assembled themselves,
They came onward together.
They saw, straightway they were amazed;
They were affrighted, they hasted away.
Trembling took hold of them there,
Pangs, as of a woman in travail.
With the east wind
Thou breakest the ships of Tarshish.
As we have heard, so have we seen
In the city of the Lord of hosts, in the city of our God—
God establish it for ever. Selah

We have thought on Thy loving-kindness, O God,
In the midst of Thy temple.
As in Thy name, O God,
So is Thy praise unto the ends of the earth;
Thy right hand is full of righteousness.
Let mount Zion be glad,
Let the daughters of Judah rejoice,
Because of Thy judgments.
Walk about Zion, and go round about her;
Count the towers thereof.
Mark ye well her ramparts,
Traverse her palaces;
That ye may tell it to the generation following.
For such is God, our God, for ever and ever;
He will guide us eternally.

Blessing on the Appearance of the New Moon

Blessed art thou, O Lord our God, King of the universe, by whose word the heavens were created, and by the breath of whose mouth all their host. Thou didst assign them a statute and a season, that they should not deviate from their appointed charge. They are glad and rejoice to do the will of the Master, the truthful Worker whose work is truth, who bade the moon renew itself, a crown of glory, unto those that have been upborne by him from the womb who in the time to come will themselves be renewed like it, to honor their Creator for his glorious kingdom's sake. Blessed art thou, O Lord, who renewest the months.

Morning Service

> The living God we praise, exalt, adore!
> He was, He is, He will be ever more!
> No unity like unto His can be:
> Eternal, inconceivable is He.
> No form, or shape has the incorporeal One,
> Most Holy He, past all comparison.
> He was, ere aught was made in heaven, or earth,
> But His existence has no date, or birth.
> Lord of the Universe is He proclaimed,
> Teaching His power to all His hand has framed.
> He gave His gift of prophecy to those
> In whom He gloried, whom He loves and chose.
> No prophet ever yet has filled the place
> Of Moses, who beheld God face to face.
> Through him (the faithful in His house) the Lord
> The law of truth to Israel did accord.
> This Law God will not alter, will not change
> For any other through time's utmost range.
> He knows and heeds the secret thoughts of man:
> He saw the end of all ere aught began.
> With love and grace doth He the righteous bless,
> He metes out evil unto wickedness.
> He at the last will His anointed send,
> Those to redeem, who hope, and wait the end.

God will the dead to life again restore.
Praised be His glorious Name for ever more!

Lord of the world, He reigned alone
While yet the universe was naught,
When by His will all things were wrought,
Then first His sovereign name was known.
And when the All shall cease to be,
In dread lone splendor He shall reign,
He was, He is, He shall remain
In glorious eternity.
For He is one, no second shares
His nature or His loneliness;
Unending and beginningless,
All strength is His, all sway He bears.
He is the living God to save,
My Rock while sorrow's toils endure,
My banner and my stronghold sure,
The cup of life whene'er I crave.
I place my soul within His palm
Before I sleep as when I wake,
And though my body I forsake,
Rest in the Lord in fearless calm.

In the Tabernacle

To be said in the Tabernacle on the first night of the Festival of Succah.

May it be thy will, O Lord my God and God of my Fathers, to let thy divine Presence abide among us. Spread over us the canopy of thy peace in recognition of the precept of the Tabernacle which we are now fulfilling, and whereby we establish in fear and love the unity of thy holy and blessed Name. O surround us with the pure and holy radiance of thy glory, that is spread over our heads as the eagle over the nest he stirreth up: and thence bid the stream of life flow in thy servant. And seeing that I have gone forth from my house abroad, and am speeding the way of thy commandments, may it be accounted unto me as though I had wandered far in thy cause. O wash me thoroughly from mine iniquity, and cleanse me from my sin. Keep me in life, O Lord; bestow upon me the abundance of thy blessings; and to such as are hungry and thirsty, give bread and water unfailingly. Make me worthy to dwell trustingly in the covert of thy shadowing wings at the time when I depart this world. O deal graciously with us in the decree to which thou settest thy seal, and make us worthy to dwell many days upon the land, the holy land, ever serving and fearing thee. Blessed be the Lord for ever. Amen and Amen.

Blessed art thou, O Lord our God, King of the universe, who hast hallowed us by thy commandments, and hast commanded us to dwell in the Tabernacle.

Blessed art thou, O Lord our God, King of the universe, who hast kept us in life, and hast preserved us, and enabled us to reach this season.

Prayer for the Welfare of the State of Israel
BY THE CHIEF RABBINATE OF ISRAEL

Our Father who art in heaven, Protector and Redeemer of Israel, bless thou the State of Israel which marks the dawn of our deliverance. Shield it beneath the wings of thy love; spread over it thy canopy of peace; send thy light and thy truth to its leaders, officers and counselors, and direct them with thy good counsel.

O God, strengthen the defenders of our Holy Land; grant them salvation and crown them with victory. Establish peace in the land and everlasting joy for its inhabitants.

Remember our brethren, the whole house of Israel, in all the lands of their dispersion. Speedily let them walk upright to Zion thy city, to Jerusalem thy dwelling place, as it is written in the Torah of thy servant Moses: "Even if you are dispersed in the uttermost parts of the world, from there the Lord your God will gather and fetch you. The Lord your God will bring you into the land which your fathers possessed, and you shall possess it."

Unite our heart to love and revere thy name, and to observe all the precepts of thy Torah. Shine forth in thy glorious majesty over all the inhabitants of thy world. Let everything that breathes proclaim: "The Lord God of Israel is King; his majesty rules over all." Amen.

Hoshanna Rabbah
SEVENTH CIRCUIT, IN MEMORY OF DAVID

Save us now! O save us!

O thou who didst cause seven things to precede the creation of the world, who didst arrange the creation in seven days; and expand the seven heavens, and stretch out the seven countries, save us on the celebration of the seventh day, and when making the seventh circuit. Remember, we beseech thee, the father, to whom thou didst promise the inheritance of the countries of seven nations: who built a house to wisdom; framed its seven pillars, and made a convenant with a prince by the presentation of seven lambs.

Save us now! O save us!

Remember, we beseech thee, the only son, the tidings of whose birth was announced at the end of seven wonders; who was offered on the most eminent of the seven mountains; and rejoiced when he found water, and called the well Shibah.

Save us now! O save us!

Remember, we beseech thee, the perfect man, who bowed himself to the earth seven times: to fulfill what is written, "A just man falleth seven times, and riseth up again": whom thou didst prove with seven years of plenty, and seven of famine.

Save us now! O save us!

O thou who didst cause us to inherit the sabbath on the seventh day; the year of release on the seventh year; and the year of the jubilee at the end of seven times seven.

Save us now! O save us!

O thou who didst ordain the festival of our freedom to consist of seven days: and the feast of the first fruits to be at the end of seven weeks; and the use of the lulab, the celebration of the feast of tabernacles, and the tabernacle, and the pouring out of water for a drink-offering, to continue seven days; save us on the celebration of the seventh day, and when making the seventh circuit.

Save us now! O save us!

O remember the prince, who played upon the ten-stringed instrument and the psaltery: with whose songs and psalms mankind praise thee throughout the universe; who was anointed unto thee, and bowed himself unto thee, to bear the yoke and burden of thy law: and redeem those who are wounded, and who are called thy lot and inheritance; reveal also thyself from thy exalted throne, to save and grant them rest.

For the merit of David, the beloved, who was sealed with the crown of thy kingdom, have compassion, and comfort thy people and thy inheritance. For his merit show to the wounded people the construction of thy house and dwelling; and remember, we pray thee, from heaven, the merit of the patriarchs to thy congregation; and bear and exalt them for the merit of thy seven perfect men. Remember unto us, O our God! the merit of David the son of Jesse; and from his stem call forth the rod who is to gather my captives: and through his merit collect my dispersed ones, my wives and children: and then we will rejoice in thy kingdom, and will recount thy wonders. O Lord! remember us, thy people, in thy favor.

O most merciful! remember favorably unto us thy covenant made with David thy anointed.

O most merciful! cause thy splendor to rest upon us.

O most merciful! seek a justification for our deeds.

O most merciful! vouchsafe to seal us in the book of life.

O most merciful! vouschsafe to seal us in the book of mercy.

O most merciful! vouchsafe to seal us in the book of the righteous.

O most merciful! vouchsafe to seal us in the book of the upright and perfect.

O most merciful! vouchsafe to seal us in the book of good maintenance and sustenance.

O most merciful! vouchsafe to open the gates of heaven to our supplications.

O most merciful! turn from thy anger.

O most merciful! dismiss us not empty from thy presence.

"Hear, O Israel, the Lord our God, the Lord is One."

"The Lord he is God. The Lord he is God."

The Lord reigneth; the Lord hath reigned: "the Lord shall reign for ever and ever."

Our God who art in heaven, remember us with a good memorial before thee.

Our God who art in heaven, have compassion upon us, our children, and our sucklings.

Our God who art in heaven, vouchsafe to seal us in the book of happy life.

Our God who art in heaven, vouchsafe to seal us in the book of the righteous.

Our God who art in heaven, vouchsafe to seal us in the book of the upright and perfect.

Our God who art in heaven, vouchsafe to seal us in the book of sustenance and good maintenance.

Hear us, O thou who art the Shield of David, and answer us. Hear us, O God, who dwellest in the midst of thy angels, and answer us. Hear us, O thou who art merciful and gracious, and answer us.

O Lord! bless our bread and water.

O remember us, and seal us in the book of life.

O Lord! grant our request for the sake of thy name.

And have compassion upon thy people Israel.

O Lord! grant our request for the sake of thy sweet psalmist.

O Lord, grant our request for the sake of the king, who built a temple to thy name.

O Lord! grant our request for the sake of those who have been slain and burnt for testifying the UNITY of thy holy name.

May he who answered David, and Solomon his son, in Jerusalem, answer us. May he who answered the righteous, pious, and virtuous of every generation, answer us.

Save us now! O save us now, we beseech thee.

I beseech thee, direct the people who come on Hoshanna Rabbah to praise thee in love, O God of my salvation! Hasten our redemption, O thou who art tremendous and awful, I beseech thee, and grant that we may praise thee in Jerusalem, as we do on this seventh day; O save us now. O save us now, we beseech thee. I beseech thee, utterly destroy the kingdom of false worship; then will I sing on the flute, on my festival of delight. Cause my redemption, thou who hast triumphed gloriously, that in the ensuing year, we may praise thee in Jerusalem on the seventh day; O save us now. O save us now, we beseech thee. I beseech thee, rebuild the gate of song, that I may sing unto thee there, and offer a present unto thee, O thou God of my rest! when thou wilt gather from the most distant places those who suffer; and erect thy tabernacle, that we may praise thee on the seventh day: O save us now. O save us now, we beseech thee. I beseech thee, be favorable unto us, and raise the desolate mountain; exalt thy tower, and reveal the period of my salvation. Show thy greatness to the distressed people, that they may appear in thy presence: and we will praise thee on the seventh day; O save us now. O save us now, we beseech thee. O satisfy thy beloved people with thy goodness, and extend thy glory over them: then will I declare thy goodness amidst the people that thou hast saved. Cause Zion to be filled with this people, that there we may pray unto thee; and we will praise thee this seventh day; O save us now. O save us now, we beseech thee. O cause thy army to inherit the walls and ramparts; may their adversaries be humbled low, and cause my salvation to spring forth. Establish my congregation, and I will teach mankind thy goodness, and sing praise to thy name; and we will praise thee this seventh day; O save us now. O save us now, we beseech thee.

O thou who art the same eternally, save us, we beseech thee.

As thou didst save thy beloved people from the hands of those who held them in subjection, and didst wound the Egyptians, who hastened to humble me; so save those who are loaded with affliction, and who praise thee with their whole heart, even with the citron, which resembles the heart: and as we praise thee this seventh day, so save us now.

As thou didst save and help those who were wounded, and didst gird thyself with armor to judge those who ill-used me; so save the scattered residue, who carry round thy law, bearing the lulab, which resembles the spine: and as we praise thee this seventh day, so save us now. As thou didst save those who were bound in chains, who groaned with anguish; whom thou didst load with spoil, sinking those who endeavored to sink me: so save those who in their encampments, in the time of the constellation Libra, perform their circuits with the myrtle, which resembles the eyes: and as we praise thee this seventh day, so save us now. As thou didst save the redeemed of thy people by the hand of the Prophet and of the Priest, and didst put those to shame, who thought to overwhelm me; so save those who open the gates to celebrate thy praise on the cymbals, with the willow which resembles the lips: and as we praise thee this seventh day, so save us now.

O thou who art the same eternally, save us, we beseech thee.

O God! save us now, and help us, we beseech thee.

O God! we beseech thee, set open the abode of thy good treasure, that the earth may give her fruit. Save us now, and help us, we beseech thee. O God! we beseech thee, to satiate the grass and herbage with liberal drops, so that the threshing may reach unto the vintage.

O God! we beseech thee, be entreated to bless the fruit of the earth, that we may eat, be satisfied, and leave thereof.

O God! we beseech thee, to seal it this day with thy seal: and bless the wheat, barley, and millet.

O God! we beseech thee to cause the north wind to bring forth liberal showers; and bless the oats and rye.

O God! we beseech thee, furnish a sufficiency for every month; and bless the rice, peas, beans, and lentils.

O God! we beseech thee, that this year may be free from briars and thorns; and bless the oil and the olive tree.

O God! we beseech thee to satiate with rain the waste places of the desert; and bless the wine, fig, and pomegranate trees.

O God! we beseech thee to exalt thy assembly, and rear the tender children! and bless the nut, date, and apple trees.

O God! we beseech thee to stretch out thy hand, and multiply the lightnings of heaven; and bless the nuts, almonds, and pomegranates.

O God! we beseech thee to withdraw not thy righteousness from thy people; and bless the filberts, quinces, and peaches.

O God! we beseech thee to deliver the congregation which pant around thee; and bless the mulberries, hazel nuts, and citrons.

O God! we beseech thee to proclaim plenty by means of the heavenly rains; and bless every specie of greens and vegetables.

O God! save us now, and send us prosperity, we beseech thee.

O God! we beseech thee, step forth for our redemption, and deliver from their oppressors the wounded; even the vine thou didst bring forth from Egypt.

O God! thou didst lead its stem from Noph, and cause its pruned shoots to bloom; thou didst drive out the nations, and plant it.

O God! thou didst cause its tender grapes to shoot vigorously forth: thou didst prepare the ground for it, casting out the seven nations with thy mighty power; thou didst cause it to take deep root, and it filled all the land.

O God! thou didst cause its shoots to bloom with fruit, and plentifully adorn them with thy goodness, so that it sent its branches to the sea.

O God! verily thou hast planted and guarded it, and of old protected and preserved it: wherefore hast thou then broken down its fences?

O God! who art holy, and great in might, we beseech thee, look down from heaven, and visit this vine.

O God! we beseech thee, reveal thy goodness to those who have been upheld by thee from the womb with thy goodness; satisfy those who inherit thy law which was reserved till two thousand years after the creation: and cause them to draw water from the springs of salvation.

O God! save us now, and grant us enlargement, we beseech thee, for thou art our Father.

O God! we beseech thee, for the sake of the patriarch who strengthened himself against those who set the flood at defiance; in thy shadow shielded thou didst deliver him from the overflowing waters: because of him didst thou swear not to deluge the world with water, withhold not water.

O God! we beseech thee, for the sake of the patriarch who said, let a little water now be brought; who drew the perfidious to thy worship, O God! who hast measured the waters in the hollow of thy hand; who overcame the strangers who worshiped the fire and water, withhold not water.

O God! we beseech thee, for the sake of the son who was bound for a sacrifice, and who dug a well of water; and when he sojourned in Gerar, was opposed on account of the water, whose servants brought him the tidings, saying, We have found water, withhold not water.

O God! we beseech thee for the sake of the perfect man, who rolled the stone from the well of water; who drew water to water the flock of Laban, and who set the rods in the water troughs, withhold not water.

O God! we beseech thee for the sake of the chosen one who was drawn out of the water, who caused thy heritage to pass through the waves of water, who opened the rock, and there gushed forth water, withhold not water.

O God! we beseech thee, heal us, pardon us, save us, and help us now, for thou art our Father.

For the sake of the patriarch who was visited and proved in the destruction of the ill-savored generation, as it is said, "But Noah found grace"; receive in favor the praise of those who address their prayer unto thee. For the sake of the faithful patriarch, whose fortitude never faltered, and whom thou didst deliver from all obstruction, and who planted a grove, entirely forgive this day those who praise thee with the complete Hallel. For the sake of the only son who thou didst call for, and who thou, O God! who seest all, didst bless at the well of Lachay Roee, let those who say the additional service be acceptable to thee. For the sake of him who slept in the center of the earth, and dreamt of the hidden secret, as it is said, And he dreamed, and there was a ladder, bless thy people, who make seven circuits. For the sake of the pious man whose countenance and eyes shone with splendor, and who was the meekest of men, bless this year, for those who proclaim aloud Hoshaana. For the sake of him who destroyed the evil-doers, and whom thou didst reward with peace, and a covenant of an everlasting priesthood, diminish the haughty pride of the nations, and cause us to hear good tidings from the joyful messenger.

Save us, O our Saviour; for unto thee do we lift up our eyes, and come for our salvation.

O thou, who existest eternally; awful and tremendous One! strengthen those who this day carry round thy law, and grant that this may be a year of light. Exalt those, who call upon thee with a contrite spirit, poured out when they perform the seven circuits, and grant that this year may be for a blessing. O shield this year from every disease, and grant rain and dew to fertilize it; so that it may be a year of joy. Open thy doors wide to a people, beautiful as Tirzah, who supplicate thee with eloquent speech; and grant that this may be a year of gladness. For unto thee do we lift up our eyes, and come for our salvation.

O God of our salvation! with thy loving-kindness save the people, who have often been saved by thee, O Lord! We wait for thee, O Lord! for we hope in thy salvation. For thou, O Lord! savest man and beast.

Open the earth, and let salvation bloom to a people whom thou hast redeemed from transgression on the day of their atonement; for thou, O Lord! hearest the desire of the meek. Satisfy thy people abundantly from thy full stream, as in the day when thou didst go forth for the salvation of thy people, even the day on which it was said, "And the Lord saved the people." We beseech thee to be our salvation, O thou Rock! Who answerest in time of distress: cause also my redemption to draw nigh, for thy power is not circumscribed; behold, I have longed for thy salvation, O Lord! Save him that is in chains who crieth from his prison-house: be thou present to his cry, O thou Rock! who workest wonderfully; open the full stream, that the trees of the Lord may be satisfied. Incline thy ear; hear now, and save, we beseech thee, the souls who are wearied with the length of their supplication: whose lips continually speak of the Lord's salvation. Accept the supplication of those who languish; who hope for thy salvation, and request their sustenance of thee, on the day that they take the lulab; grant them rain and dew to distill from their habitations: and cause them speedily to go free, as the redeemed of the Lord.

A voice announceth the joyful tidings, announceth and saith.

I will exalt the beautiful climate with the vision of my testimony; that mount Zion may rejoice, and the daughters of Judah be glad. The messenger announceth and saith, I will raise up the pillars of thy dwelling, and enlarge thy border; for the Lord shall be thy everlasting light: and the days of thy mourning shall be ended. The messenger announceth and saith, Walk about Zion, go round about it, and number the towers thereof: be exceeding joyful with her, all ye that mourn over her. Suddenly will I cast my shoes over Edom: burst forth into joy, shout together ye ruins of Jerusalem. The period of my salvation will I hasten for thee, from my heavenly abode: I have caused my justice to draw nigh, it is not far off. Rouse thyself from the east, and come from the west to mount Zion, for on the north side is the city of the great king.

As it is written, "How beautiful appear on the mountains the feet of the joyful messenger; of him that announceth peace; of the joyful messenger of good tidings; of him that announceth salvation! of him that sayeth unto Zion, Thy God reigneth!" And it is said, "Thy watchmen lift up their voice; with a loud voice they shout together; for face to face shall they see, when the Lord returneth to Zion." And it is said, "Burst forth into joy, shout together, ye ruins of Jerusalem! for the

Lord hath comforted his people: he hath redeemed Jerusalem." And it is said, "For the Lord hath consoled Zion; he hath consoled all her desolations; and he hath made her wilderness like Eden, and her desert like the garden of the Lord: joy and gladness shall be found in her, thanksgiving, and the voice of psalmody." And it is said, "Sing aloud, O ye heavens! and rejoice, O earth! ye mountains, burst forth into song! for the Lord hath comforted his people, and will have compassion on his afflicted." And it is said, "And many people shall go, and shall say, Come ye, and let us go up to the mountain of the Lord; to the house of the God of Jacob; and he shall teach us his ways: and we will walk in his paths; for from Zion shall go forth the law: and the word of the Lord from Jerusalem." And it is said, "And the ransomed of the Lord shall return; they shall come to Zion in triumph, and perpetual gladness shall crown their heads: joy and gladness shall they obtain, and sorrow and sighing shall flee away." And it is said, "The Lord hath made bare his holy arm, in the sight of all the nations; and all the ends of the earth shall see the salvation of our God." And it is said, "And let these my words wherewith I have made supplication before the Lord, be nigh unto the Lord our God, day and night, that he maintain the cause of his servant, and the cause of his people Israel in their daily necessities. That all the people of the earth may know that the Lord is God, and that there is none else."

Prayer for Rain

Blessed art thou, Lord our God and God of our fathers, God of Abraham, God of Isaac and God of Jacob; great, mighty, and revered God, sublime God, who bestowest loving-kindness, and art Master of all things; who rememberest the good deeds of our fathers, and who wilt graciously bring a redeemer to their children's children for the sake of thy name. O King, Supporter, Saviour and Shield!
Af-Bri is the title of the prince of rain,
Who gathers the clouds and makes them drop rain,
Water to adorn the earth with verdure.
Be it not held back because of unpaid debts;
O shield faithful Israel who prays for rain.
Blessed art thou, O Lord, Shield of Abraham.
Thou, O Lord, art mighty forever; thou revivest the dead; thou art
powerful to save.
May he send rain from the heavenly source,
To soften the earth with its crystal drops.

Thou hast named water the symbol of thy might;
Its drops refresh all that have breath of life,
And revive those who praise thy powers of rain.
    Our God and God of our fathers,
Remember Abraham who followed thee like water,
Whom thou didst bless like a tree planted near streams of water;
Thou didst shield him, thou didst save him from fire and water;
Thou didst care for him when he sowed by all streams of water.
    For his sake, do not refuse water.
Remember Isaac, whose birth was foretold over a little water;
Thou didst tell his father to offer his blood like water;
Isaac was heedful in pouring out his heart like water;
Digging wells, he did discover water.
    For his righteousness' sake, grant abundant water.
Remember Jacob who, staff in hand, crossed the Jordan's water;
His heart trusted when he rolled the stone of the well of water,
When he wrestled with the prince of fire and water,
Thou didst promise to be with him through fire and water.
    For his sake, do not refuse water.
Remember Moses in an ark of papyrus reeds drawn out of the water;
They said: He drew water for us and provided the flock with water;
And when thy chosen people thirsted for water,
He struck the rock and there gushed out water.
    For his righteousness' sake, grant abundant water.
Remember the Temple-priest who bathed five times in water;
He removed sins when he washed his hands with sanctified water;
He read from the Scriptures when he sprinkled purifying water;
He was kept at a distance from a people as turbulent as water.
    For his sake, do not refuse water.
Remember the twelve tribes thou didst bring across the water;
Thou didst sweeten for them the bitterness of the water;
For thy sake was the blood of their descendants spilt like water;
Turn to us, for our life is encircled by foes like water.
    For their righteousness' sake, grant abundant water.

For thou art the Lord our God, who causest the wind to blow and the
    rain to fall.

For a blessing and not a curse.   Amen.
For life and not for death.   Amen.
For plenty and not for scarcity.   Amen.

Service at a Circumcision

Upon the arrival of the Child who is to be initiated into the Covenant of Abraham, those present at the ceremony rise and say:

Blessed be he that cometh.

Father:

I am here ready to perform the affirmative precept to circumcise my son, even as the Creator, blessed be he, hath commanded us, as it is written in the Torah, And he that is eight days old shall be circumcised among you, every male throughout your generations.

Mohel:

This is the throne of Elijah: may he be remembered for good!

For thy salvation I have waited, O Lord, I have hoped, O Lord, for thy salvation; and have done thy commandments. I have hoped for thy salvation, O Lord. I rejoice at thy word, as one that findeth great spoil. Great peace have they who love thy Torah; and there is no stumbling for them. Happy is he whom thou choosest, and causest to approach, that he may dwell in thy courts.

All:

O let us be satisfied with the goodness of thy house, thy holy temple.

Mohel, before performing circumcision:

Blessed art thou, O Lord our God, King of the universe, who hast hallowed us by thy commandments, and hast given us command concerning the Circumcision.

Father, after circumcision:

Blessed art thou, O Lord our God, King of the universe, who hast hallowed us by thy commandments, and has commanded us to make our sons enter into the covenant of Abraham our father.

All:

Even as this child has entered into the covenant, so may he enter into the Torah, the nuptial canopy, and into good deeds.

Mohel:

Blessed art thou, O Lord our God, King of the universe, who createst the fruit of the vine.

Blessed art thou, O Lord our God, King of the universe, who didst sanctify Isaac the well-beloved from birth, setting thy statute in his flesh, and sealing his offspring with the sign of the holy covenant. On this account, O living God, our Portion and our Rock, give command to deliver from destruction thy dearly beloved People, for the sake of the covenant thou has set in our bodies. Blessed art thou, O Lord, who dost establish thy covenant.

Our God and God of our fathers, preserve this child to his father and to his mother, and let his name be called in Israel —— the son of ——. Let the father rejoice in his offspring, and the mother be glad with the fruit of her body; as it is written, Let thy father and thy mother rejoice, and let her that bore thee be glad: and it is said, And I passed by thee, and I saw thee weltering in thy blood, and I said unto thee, In thy blood live. Yea, I said unto thee, In thy blood live. And it is said, He hath remembered his covenant for ever, the word which he commanded to a thousand generations; [the covenant] which he made with Abraham, and his oath unto Isaac, and established it unto Jacob for a statute to Israel for an everlasting covenant. And it is said, And Abraham circumcised his son Isaac when he was eight days old, as God had commanded him. O give thanks unto the Lord; for he is good; for his loving-kindness endureth for ever. This little child ——, may he become great. Even as he has entered into the covenant, so may he enter into the Torah, the nuptial canopy, and into good deeds.

Grace After the Meal Following a Circumcision

Let us say grace.
Blessed be the Name of the Lord from this time forth and for ever.
We will give thanks unto thy Name in the midst of the faithful: blessed are ye of the Lord.

With the sanction of the awful and revered God, who is a refuge in times of trouble, the God girt with strength, the Lord mighty on high, we will give thanks unto thy Name in the midst of the faithful: blessed are ye of the Lord.
With the sanction of the holy Torah, pure and clear, which Moses the servant of the Lord commanded us to be an heritage, we will give thanks unto thy Name in the midst of the faithful: blessed are ye of the Lord.
With the sanction of the priests and Levites I will call upon the God of the Hebrews, I will declare his glory in every region, I will bless the Lord. We will give thanks unto thy Name in the midst of the faithful: blessed are ye of the Lord.
With the sanction of those present I will open my lips with song, yea, my whole body shall declare, Blessed is he that cometh in the Name of the Lord. We will give thanks unto thy Name in the midst of the faithful: blessed are ye of the Lord.
May the All-merciful bless the father and mother of the child; may

they live to rear him, to initiate him in the precepts of the Torah, and to train him in wisdom: from this eighth day and henceforth his entrance into the covenant finds acceptance, and may the Lord his God be with him.

May the All-merciful bless the master of this festivity who has observed the covenant of Circumcision, and rejoiced exceedingly to perform this deed of piety; may God reward and advance him for his act with a full recompense.

May the All-merciful bless the tender infant that has been circumcised on his eighth day; may his hands and heart be firm with God, and may he live to appear before the Divine Presence three times in the year.

May the All-merciful bless him who has performed the circumcision, duly fulfilling each part of the precept. The service would be invalid of one who is timid and faint-hearted, or who failed to carry out the three essentials of the ceremony.

May the All-merciful, regardful of the merit of them that are akin by the blood of the circumcision, send us the righteous anointed one to bring good tidings and consolation to the people that is scattered and dispersed among the nations.

May the All-merciful send us the righteous priest, who remains withdrawn in heaven until a throne, bright as the sun and radiant as the diamond, shall be prepared for him, the Prophet who covered his face with his mantle and wrapped himself therein, with whom is God's covenant of life and of peace.

Service for the Redemption of the First-Born

The first-born child, if a male, must be redeemed on the thirty-first day of his birth.

Father:

This is my first-born son, is the first-born of his mother, and the Holy One, blessed be he, hath given command to redeem him, as it is said, And those that are to be redeemed of them from a month old shalt thou redeem, according to thine estimation, for the money of five shekels, after the shekel of the sanctuary, the shekel being twenty gerahs; and it is said, Sanctify unto me all the first-born, whatsoever openeth the womb among the children of Israel, both of man and of beast: it is mine.

Cohen:

Which wouldst thou rather, give me thy first-born son, the first-born of his mother, or redeem him for five selaim, which thou art bound to give according to the Torah?

Father:

I desire rather to redeem my son, and here thou hast the value of his redemption, which I am bound to give according to the Torah.

Blessed art thou, O Lord our God, King of the universe, who hast hallowed us by thy commandments, and given us command concerning the redemption of the first-born son.

Blessed art thou, O Lord our God, King of the universe, who hast kept us in life, and hast preserved us, and enabled us to reach this season.

Cohen:

This is instead of that, this in commutation for that, this in remission of that. May this child enter into life, into the Torah and the fear of Heaven. May it be God's will that even as he has been admitted to redemption, so may he enter into the Torah, the nuptial canopy, and into good deeds. Amen.

God make thee as Ephraim and Manasseh. The Lord bless thee, and keep thee: the Lord make his face to shine upon thee, and be gracious unto thee: the Lord turn his face unto thee, and give thee peace.

The Lord is thy guardian: the Lord is thy shade upon thy right hand. For length of days, and years of life and peace shall they add to thee. The Lord shall guard thee from all evil; he shall guard thy soul. Amen.

A Hymn to "Zoharariel, Adonai, God of Israel"

His throne radiates before Him and His palace is full of splendor.
His Majesty is becoming and His Glory is an adornment for Him.
His servants sing before Him and proclaim the might of his wonders,
    as King of all Kings and master of all masters, encircled by rows
    of crowns, surrounded by the ranks of the princes of splendor.
With a gleam of His ray he encompasses the sky and His splendor
    radiates from the heights.
Abysses flame from His mouth and firmaments sparkle from His body.

*

The Greeks and Romans

THE GREEKS AND ROMANS

To Earth, Mother of All

    I sing the earth, the firmly founded earth,
The honor'd nurse that tends us from our birth.
The dwellers of the air, the sea, the field,
Live on the treasures that she joys to yield.
Oh Earth! Thy generous deeds are greatly done,
Thine are good fruits and many a gallant son,
'Tis thine the springs of life to stop or move;
But happy, happy he who claims thy love.
Upon his flow'ry fields will flocks abound,
While his long vineyards teem their wealth around;
Honor and bliss will stand before his eyes,
And full of splendor will his halls arise.
Mild laws shall round them twine their silky chain,
In peaceful towns where beauteous damsels reign,
His sons in glowing youth will bloom divine,
His daughters at the choral banquet shine;
And all the boons creation can bestow,
Around that happy man will plenteous flow.

Parent of Gods, the starry heaven's rich wife,
Oh grant me for my song a happy life;
And Oh, whene'er I touch the vocal string,
I'll think of thee, and of another sing.

To the Moon

Ye skillful Muses, that from Jove arise,
Whose ev'ry breath in rapturous numbers dies,
Teach me to sing the Moon, the Moon that springs
Up from the wave on broad and silvery wings;
From whose immortal curls rich splendors fall,
whose radiance from the heav'ns envelops all,
The gloomy air throws off its sable gown,
Refresh'd and lighted by her golden crown,
When, rising beauteous from her blushing bath,
She walks in majesty the heavenly path.

Yoking the long neck'd coursers in her car,
On each half month her splendors shine afar,
The silver globe receives them as they fall,
At vesper hour—be this a sign to all.

Once in her arms reposed high-thundering Jove,
Pandea came the offspring of their love—
A charming girl, with soul and eye of fire,
And beauteous even amid the starry choir.
Hail, bright-haired, silent, snowy-wristed Moon;
Goddess, from thee I'll strike the anthem soon
Of demigods, whose praise the poets choose,
The favor'd priests of every lovely Muse.

A Chorus from the Dionysiac Mysteries

O happy to whom is the blessedness given
To be taught in the Mysteries sent from heaven,
Who is pure in his life, through whose soul the unsleeping
        Revel goes sweeping!
Made meet by the sacred purifying
For the Bacchanal rout o'er the mountains flying,
For the orgies of Cybele mystery-folden,
        Of the Mother olden,
Wreathed with the ivy sprays,

The thyrsus on high doth he raise,
Singing the Vine-god's praise—
        Come, Bacchanals, come!
The Clamor-king, child of a God,
O'er the mountains of Phrygia who trod,
Unto Hellas's highways broad
        Bring him home, bring him home!

The God whom his mother—when anguish tore her
Of the travail resistless that deathward bore her
On the wings of the thunder of Zeus down-flying—
        Brought forth at her dying,
An untimely birth, as her spirit departed,
Stricken from life by the flame down-darted:
But in birth-bowers new did Zeus Cronion
        Receive his scion;
    For, hid in a cleft of his thigh,
    By the gold-clasps knit, did he lie
    Safe hidden from Hera's eye
        Till the Fates's day came;
    Then a God bull-horned Zeus bare,
    And with serpents entwined his hair:
    And for this do his Maenads wear
        In their tresses the same.

Thebes, nursing-town of Semele, crown
        With the ivy thy brows, and be
All bloom, embowered in the starry-flowered
        Lush green of the briony,
While the oak and pine thy tresses entwine
        In thy bacchanal-ecstasy.
And thy fawn-skin flecked, with a fringe be it decked
        Of wool white-glistering
In silvery tassels;—O Bacchus's vassals,
        High-tossed let the wild wands swing!
One dancing band shall be all the land
        When, led by the Clamor-king,
His revel-rout fills the hills—the hills
        Where thy women abide till he come
Whom the Vine-god chasing, in frenzy racing,
        Hunted from shuttle and loom.

O cavern[1] that rang when Curetès sang,
    O bower of the Babe Zeus's birth,
Where the Corybants, dancing with helm-crests glancing
    Through the dark halls under the earth,
This timbrel sound whose hide-stretched round
    We smite, and its Bacchanal mirth
They blent with the cry ringing sweet and high
    From the flutes of the Phrygian land,
And its thunder, soaring o'er revel-shouts' roaring,
    They gave unto Rhea's hand;
But the gift passed on from the Mother, was won
    By the madding Satyr-band;
And to Semele's child gave the woodfolk wild
    The homage he holdeth dear,
When to feet white-flashing the timbrels clashing
    Are wedded in each third year.

O trance of rapture, when, reeling aside
    From the Bacchanal rout o'er the mountains flying,
One sinks to the earth, and the fawn's flecked hide
      Covers him lying
With its sacred vesture, wherein he hath chased
The goat to the death for its blood—for the taste
    Of the feast raw-reeking,[2] when over the hills
Of Phrygia, of Lydia, the wild feet haste,
    And the Clamor-king leads, and his "Evoë!" thrills
      Our hearts replying!

Flowing with milk is the ground, and with wine is it flowing, and flowing
    Nectar of bees; and a smoke as of incense of Araby soars;
And the Bacchant, uplifting the flame of the brand of the pine ruddy-
    glowing,
    Waveth it wide, and with shouts, from the point of the wand as it
      pours,
Challengeth revelers straying, on-racing, on-dancing, and throwing
    Loose to the breezes his curls, while clear through the chorus that
      roars
    Cleaveth his shout, "On, Bacchanal-rout,
On, Bacchanal maidens, ye glory of Tmolus the hill gold-welling,
Blend the acclaim of your chant with the timbrels thunder-knelling,
    Glad-pealing the glad God's praises out

With Phrygian cries and the voice of singing,
 When upsoareth the sound of the melody-fountain,
Of the hallowed ringing of flutes far-flinging
  The notes that chime with the feet that climb
   The pilgrim-path to the mountain!"
And with rapture the Bacchanal onward racing,
  With gambolings fleet
As of foals round the mares in the meads that are grazing,
  Speedeth her feet.

To Apollo

In this hymn, given here complete except for the final strophe, the poet affirms the Cyrenians' faith and loyalty to the Egyptian monarchy. It was written for the festival of Karna, honoring Apollo, which went on for nine days at the end of August.

 Lo, how have Apollo's bay boughs shaken stormily!
How hath his whole fane shivered! Afar, ye unhallowed ones, flee!
Lo, clasheth the door at the coming of Phoebus' radiant feet—
Dost mark not? The Delian palm breathed sudden odors sweet!
O hearken!—the swan in the clear air ravishingly doth sing!
O bolts, by no hands touched do ye suddenly backward spring,
And ye, O locks! Full nigh in this hour is the God, I trow.
O youthful choir, for the song and the dance make ready now!
Apollo appears not to all, to the good alone and the brave.
Who hath seen him, great man is he; who hath seen not, to sin is he
  slave.
We will look upon thee, Far-worker, to sin will we never be thrall.
Never hushed be the voice of thy lyre, nor unheard be thy footstep's fall.
When Phoebus descendeth amidst of his children awhile to abide,
When they fain would accomplish a bridal, or mourn for the old which
  have died,
Or establish on ancient foundations a city's ramparts strong,
Happy I count them. The lyre for thy sons is not silent long.
Break forth into praise, ye who hear them acclaim Apollo in song.
Yea, the sea breaks forth into praise, when bards of the God's lyre sing,
Or the bow, which Lycorean Phoebus about his shoulders doth sling.
Yea, Thetis forbeareth her woeful wail for Achilles slain
When she heareth "Iê Paiêon!" the chanted Paean's refrain.
Yea, and the Crag of Weeping³ the load of its anguish doth cast,
The tear-streaming rock that in Phrygia-land is established fast,

The woman made marble, whose parted lips from lament never rest—
Sing loud the refrain of the Paean! Ill is it to strive with the Blest!
Whoso fighteth against the Blessèd, against my king let him fight:
Whoso fighteth against my king, let him brave Apollo's might!
Apollo shall honor his chorus, for sweet to his soul is their strain,
And he can, for throned on high at Zeus's right hand doth he reign.
Nor the chorus shall sing the praises of Phoebus one only day;
It hath store of hymns. Who would chant not gladly to Phoebus the lay?
Of gold is Apollo's vesture, the brooch whereby 'tis upcaught,
His lyre and his Lyctian bow, and his quiver arrow-fraught;
And of gold be his sandals; for gold-abounding Apollo is,
And exceeding wealthy: from Pytho thou mightest divine all this.
Ever lovely he is, ever young: his cheeks as a woman's are fair
And smooth; never came the down, not in smallest measure, there.
The oil from his tresses that streams the plain with its fragrance fills:
No earthly unguent is that from Apollo's locks that distills,
But the true Panacea it is. In the city whose ways are besprayed
With its dewdrops as earthward they fall, incorruptible all things are
    made.
He is lord over many a craft—there is none like Apollo the King—
His vassal the archer is, he inspireth the bard to sing,
For Phoebus's prerogative is it the bow and the lay to teach:
Of him divination and prophecy are: from Phoebus the leech
Learneth the lore of healing and holding death at bay.
The Lord of the Pastures we name him withal; they be his for aye
Since the days when he nurtured the yoke-bearing steeds on Amphrysia's
    plain,
What time for the love of Admetus the young his spirit was fain.
Ah, well might it prosper, the feeding of cattle: and multiplied fast
Were the offspring of bleating goats, over which Apollo cast
His glance as they pastured, nor ever the fountains of milk would run
Dry in the udders of ewes, and barren among them was none;
But she that had borne one lamb was suddenly mother of two.
By Phoebus's guidance the builders the lines of their town-walls drew;
For Phoebus delighteth ever the cities of men to raise.
Like the webs of a weaver, himself their broad foundations lays.
He established a city's foundations first in the God's fourth year
In Ortygia the lovely: it stands yet nigh to the rounded mere.
The heads of Cynthian goats the Huntress Artemis brought
To her brother in plenty: an altar therewith Apollo wrought;
For he buildeth its base with their horns, and he fashioned the altar
    throughout

Of horns, and with walls of horns did he compass his altar about.
Thus Phoebus devised how the first foundations of cities should stand:
By him taught, Battus founded my city mid fertile land.
As they entered Libya, in form as a raven at his right hand
Was he guide to his people and founder; and unto our kings he swore
To give walled cities: Apollo keepeth his oaths evermore.
O Apollo, nany there be that name thee the Driver of Kine,
And the Clarian many: in all lands many a name is thine.
But I—the Carneian, I call thee; mine ancestors so named thee.
Sparta is thine, O Carneian; by thee first founded was she.
The second was Thera, the third was Cyrene. The sixth in descent
Of Oedipus's line with thee at his side from Sparta went
Forth to the founding of Thera. From Thera the vehement-souled
Aristoteles brought to Asbystian soil thine image of gold.
And a royal temple and fair did he rear thee, and there did ordain
In the city a yearly feast where bulls full many are slain
In this the latest of thine abodes, O Archer-king.
"Iê!" Carneian of many a prayer! Thine altars in spring
Bear burdens of garlanded flowers, all flowers of manifold hue
That the Hours lure forth into bloom when the West-wind breatheth
    dew,
And in winter the crocus sweet. The fire thereon burns aye,
And never the ashes smother the brands of yesterday.
Greatly did Phoebus rejoice when the War-queen's belted band
Danced with the daughters golden-haired of Libya-land,
When the Feast Carneian returned in the season due of the year.
Not then to the Fountain of Kyrê could Dorian men draw near,
But these in Azilis with glens deep-furrowed were dwelling then;
And my King in Kyrene beheld them, and showed to its Nymph the men
As he stood on Myrtusa's horn-crest, where towering full-height he had
    slain
The lion that long had been of Eurypylus's oxen the bane.
No goodlier dance than that had Apollo looked upon.
On no city he showered such constant boons as Kyrene won,
For he ever remembered that woodland spoil: and of Battus's line
Was none more honored than Phoebus of all the Powers divine.
"Iê! Iê Paion!"—we hear it, the hymnal shout
Which first unto thee from the lips of the Delphian folk rang out
When thou showedst forth the far-flying range of thy golden bow.
At thy coming to Pytho there met thee the monster, the Gods' grim foe,
The terrible serpent. Thou slewest him: shaft upon keen shaft came
From thy bowstring raining on him, and the people raised the acclaim—

"Iê Paiêon! Speed thou the arrow! Thy mother bore
Truly a Helper in thee!" So hymned art thou since evermore.

To Pallas Athena

This hymn was composed for the annual festival at which the image of
Pallas Athena was carried to the river for a ritualistic purifying bath. Only
a few strophes are given.

Fare forth, O Athena, Destroyer of towns, with thine helmet of gold,
Thou who lovest the tramp of the war horse, the clang of the shield
    array!
Here dip not your vessels today, water-bearers. O Argos, beware
That not from our river today thou drink, but where fountains flow.
Today, ye handmaids, to Physadeia your pitchers bear,
Or to Amymone, the fountain of Danaus, shall ye go.
For with mingled gold and blossoming flowers shall the waters run
Of Inachus as he floweth adown from the pasture-clad hill
To Athena bringing her beautiful bath. But, Argos's son,
Beware lest thou look on our Queen—yea, even against thy will.
The man who on Pallas disrobed Burg-warder turneth his eye,
He for the last time of all upon this our Argos shall gaze.
O fare thou forth, Queen-lady Athena, the while that I
Tell these a story not mine, a tradition from olden days.

To Demeter

It is not known for what occasion this hymn was composed, though it is
of particular importance during the procession of the calathus, the basket
containing the symbols of Demeter of Ephesus, which were essentially sexual
and could be viewed only by the initiated.

The Maund-procession goes forth: with you women's acclaim be it
    hymned!
O Sustainer of Nations, all hail, Demeter of corn-measures brimmed!
When returneth the Maund—O profane ones, be your eyes earthward
    cast—
Nor from roof nor from tower look ye down as the Mystery goeth past,
O boy, O woman, O maiden whose locks o'er thy shoulders float.
And let none dare fasting to void the phlegm from a thirst-parched
    throat.[4]

In his hour of return hath Hesperus forth of his cloud-veils burst,
He who alone prevailed on Demeter to quench her thirst
When she sped on the vanished tracks of her child from the green earth
    torn.
Queen, how could thy feet bear thee to the setting sun's far bourne,
To the dark-skinned folk and to where the golden apples glow?
Thou didst drink not nor eat nor bathe while wandered thy feet to and
    fro.
Thrice o'er Achelous the silver-swirling thy feet had gone,
And thrice over each ever-flowing stream in thy path that shone.
To the island Kalliste's mid-point Enna thrice didst thou race:
By the well-head of Kallichorus thrice sat'st thou to rest for a space,
Yet didst slake not thy burning thirst, nor didst eat nor bathe.
Hymn her, ye maidens! Ye mothers, acclaim her with shouts ringing far!
Hail, Feeder of Nations, Demeter, O thou of the measure brimmed o'er!
And while thine holy basket is drawn of the white steeds four,
O wide-dominioned Goddess, with blessings to us draw nigh
Of a radiant spring and summer, a kindly winter's sky
And a bounteous autumn. Preserve us to greet a glad new year.
And as now unsandaled, uncoifed, we tread thy city here,
So ever unscathed be our feet and the light on our heads undimmed.
As the bearers carry thy golden winnowing-maunds full-brimmed,
Even so may we win of the gold thou bestowest enough and to spare.
So far as our burg's town hall may the initiate share
In this our festal procession; and matrons of years threescore
With this our assembly shall fare to the Goddess's very door.[5]
But the eld-bowed ones, and the travailing wives, and the racked with
    pain,
For these it sufficeth to kneel in prayer, and these shall obtain
All boons in abundance of Deo,[6] as though in her temple they prayed.
Hail, Goddess! O save thou our city! In concord may she be upstayed
And prosperity! Grant to us increase of all seed sown in the field.
Foster our kine; bring us fruits and a bountiful harvest yield.
O foster our peace, that the sower may reap from the paths of the plow.
O thrice-petitioned, be gracious, most queenly of Goddesses thou!

For the Dedication of a Bow

This bow, resting from tearful war, hangs here under the roof of
Athene's temple. Often mid the roar of battle, in the struggle of men,
was it washed in the blood of Persian cavaliers.

For the Dedication of Fishing Tackle

The patron god invoked is Pan, or possibly Hermes.

Diophantus the fisherman, as is fit, dedicates to the patron of his craft these relics of his old calling, his hook, easily gulped down, his long poles, his line, his reels, this weel, device of sea-faring netsmen for trapping fishes, his sharp trident, weapon of Poseidon, and the two oars of his boat.

Dedication of Three Hunters

Huntsman Pan, the three brothers dedicated these nets to thee, each from a different chase: Pigres, these from fowl; Damis, these from beast; and Clitor, his from the denizens of the deep. In return for which, send them easily caught game, to the first through the air, to the second through the woods, and to the third through the shore-water.

For a Mirror

The accuser referred to in the epigram is the mirror that Lais dedicated to Venus.

Lais took captive by her beauty Greece, which had laid in the dust the proud shield of Persia. Only old age conquered her, and the proof of her fall, the friend of her youth, she dedicates to thee, Cyrpis. She hates to see even the shadowy image of those gray hairs, whose actual sight she cannot bear.

Dedication of a Shepherd

This skin did Teleso stretch on the woodland plane tree, an offering to goat-hoofed Pan the goat-treader, and the crutched, well-pointed staff, with which he used to bring down red-eyed wolves, the cheese pails, too, and the leash and collars of his keen-scented hounds.

Dedication of a Young Bride

Artemis is venerated as the goddess of fecundity in many localities of the Peloponnesus.

Timareta, the daughter of Timaretus, before her wedding, hath dedicated to thee, Artemis of the lake, her tambourine and her pretty ball, and the caul that kept up her hair, and her dolls, too, and their dresses; a virgin's gift, as is fit to virgin Dian. But, daughter of Leto, hold thy hand over the girl, and purely keep her in her purity.

Dedication of a Young Bride

Hippe, the maiden, has put up her abundant curly hair, brushing it from her perfumed temples, for the solemn time when she must wed has come, and I, the snood that used to rest, there require in my wearer the grace of virginity. But, Artemis, in thy loving kindness grant to Lycomedes's child, who has bidden farewell to her knucklebones, both a husband and children.

Dedication of a Hunter

Caves of the Nymphs with many springs, from which such abundance of water trickles down this winding slope; and thou, echoing shrine of Pan crowned with pine leaves, the home that is his at the foot of the woodland rock; ye stumps of the ancient juniper, holy to hunters,[7] and thou, stone-heap raised in Hermes's honor,[8] be gracious unto us and accept the spoil of fortunate Sosander's swift chase of the deer.

Inscription on the Petelia Tablet

This inscription is from one of the Orphic tablets that were meant to instruct the dead about their journey beyond the tomb. It was discovered at Petelia, near Strongoli, and dates back to between the fourth and third centuries B.C. The springs referred to are Lethe on the left and Mnemosyn on the right. The former extinguishes remembrance of the divine origin, the latter revives this memory. The traveler must tell the guardians of the font of his divine initiation.

Thou shalt find to the left of the House of Hades a Wellspring,
And by the side thereof standing a white cypress.
To this Wellspring approach not near.
But thou shalt find another by the Lake of Memory,
Cold water flowing forth, and there are Guardians before it.
Say: "I am a child of Earth and of Starry Heaven;
But my race is of Heaven [alone]. This ye know yourselves.
And lo, I am parched with thirst and I perish. Give me quickly
The cold water flowing forth from the Lake of Memory."
And of themselves they will give thee to drink from the holy Wellspring,
And thereafter among the other Heroes thou shalt have lordship. . . .

Inscription from Eleuthernae

This inscription is also from an Orphic fragment, dating from about the second century B.C., which is now in the Athens Museum. The dialogue takes place between the soul of the Orphic, the divine font, and its custodians.

I am parched with thirst and I perish.—Nay, drink of Me,
The Wellspring flowing forever on the Right, where the Cypress is.
Who art thou? . . .
Whence art thou?—I am son of Earth and of Starry Heaven.

Inscriptions of Thurii

Pure, I come from the pure, O queen of the lower regions,
O Eukles and Eubuleo, and all you other immortal gods:
For I also glory in being of your divine stock;
But I was struck down by the god of the stars.
Only by flying did I escape the painful trials.[9]
I was saved by the desired crown,[10]
And descended into the lap of the nether queen.
"Thou, beatified and happy, shall from a man be made a god."
I, little goat, scampered through milky realms.[11]

Prescriptions of the Orphic Liturgy

O son of the woman of Tyre, of Phoenecian birth,
Offspring of Europa and mighty Zeus,
You who lorded it over Crete of the hundred cities,
Here I am at last,
After having departed the sacred temple,
Whose cypress, born there, and cut with a sturdy blade,
Makes such solid beams, and,
When joined together with hardy sap,
Welds the connections solidly.
A purer life I lead since becoming a follower of Zeus.
As a follower of Zagreo
I have assisted at the feasts
And carried the torch for the mother of Ida.
They have pressed down upon me the title of Bacchus.
I have avoided the perils of mortals,
Which are birth and the tomb,
And dead animals no longer do I feast upon.

To Heaven
THE FUMIGATION FROM FRANKINCENSE

Great Heav'n, whose mighty frame no respite knows,
Father of all, from whom the world arose:
Hear, bounteous parent, source and end of all,
Forever whirling round this earthly ball;
Abode of Gods, whose guardian pow'r surrounds
Th' eternal World with ever during bounds;
Whose ample bosom and encircling folds
The dire necessity of nature holds.
Ethereal, earthly, whose all-various frame
Azure and full of forms, no power can tame.
All-seeing Heav'n, progenitor of Time,
Forever blessed, deity sublime,
Propitious on a novel mystic shine,
And crown his wishes with a life divine.

To Ether
THE FUMIGATION FROM SAFFRON

Ether (Air), with Chaos and Erebus, was the raw material out of which
Cronus generated the cosmic egg.

O ever untam'd Ether, rais'd on high
In Jove's dominions, ruler of the sky;
Great portion of the Stars and lunar light,
And of the Sun, with dazzling luster bright;
All-taming pow'r, ethereal shining fire,
Whose vivid blasts the heat of life inspire;
The world's best element, light-bearing pow'r,
With starry radiance shining, splendid flow'r;
O hear my suppliant pray'r, and may thy frame
Be ever innocent, serene, and tame.

To the Sun
THE FUMIGATION FROM FRANKINCENSE AND MANNA

Hear golden Titan, whose eternal eye
With broad survey, illumines all the sky:
Self-born, unwearied in diffusing light,

And to all eyes the mirror of delight:
Lord of the seasons, with thy fiery car
And leaping coursers, beaming light from far:
With thy right hand the course of morning light,
And with thy left the father of the night.
Agile and vig'rous, venerable Sun,
Fiery and bright around the heav'ns you run.
Foe to the wicked, but the good man's guide,
O'er all his steps propitious you preside:
With various-sounding, golden lyre, 'tis thine
To fill the world with harmony divine.
Father of ages, guide of prosp'rous deeds,
The world's commander, borne by lucid steeds,
Immortal Jove, all-searching, bearing light,
Source of existence, pure and fiery bright:
Bearer of fruit, almighty lord of years,
Agile and warm, whom ev'ry pow'r reveres.
Great eye of Nature and the starry skies,
Doom'd with immortal flames to set and rise:
Dispensing justice, lover of the stream,
The world's great despot, and o'er all supreme.
Faithful defender, and the eye of right,
Of steeds the ruler, and of life the light:
With sounding whip four fiery steeds you guide,
When in the car of day you glorious ride.
Propitious on these mystic labors shine,
And bless thy suppliants with a life divine.

To the Moon
THE FUMIGATION FROM AROMATICS

Hear, Goddess queen, diffusing silver light,
Bull-horn'd and wand'ring through the gloom of Night.
With stars surrounded, and with circuit wide
Night's torch extending, through the heav'ns you ride:
Female and Male with borrow'd rays you shine,
And now full-orb'd, now tending to decline.
Mother of ages, fruit-producing Moon,
Whose amber orb makes Night's reflected noon:
Lover of horses, splendid, queen of Night,
All-seeing pow'r bedeck'd with starry light.

Lover of vigilance, the foe of strife,
In peace rejoicing, and a prudent life:
Fair lamp of Night, its ornament and friend,
Who giv'st to Nature's works their destin'd end.
Queen of the stars, all-wise Diana hail!
Deck'd with a graceful robe and shining veil;
Come, blessed Goddess, prudent, starry, bright,
Come moon-lamp with chaste and splendid light,
Shine on these sacred rites with prosp'rous rays,
And pleas'd, accept thy suppliant's mystic praise.

To Nature
THE FUMIGATION FROM AROMATICS

Nature, all-parent, ancient and divine,
O much mechanic mother, art is thine;
Heav'nly, abundant, venerable queen,
In ev'ry part of thy dominion seen.
Untam'd, all taming, ever splendid light,
All ruling, honor'd, and supremely bright.
Immortal, first-born, ever still the same,
Nocturnal, starry, shining, powerful dame.
Thy feet's still traces in a circling course,
By thee are turn'd, with unremitting force.
Pure ornament of all the Pow'rs divine,
Finite and infinite alike you shine;
To all things common, and in all things known,
Yet incommunicable and alone.
Without a father of thy wondrous frame,
Thyself the father whence thy essence came;
Mingling, all-flourishing, supremely wise,
And bond connective of the earth and skies.
Leader, life-bearing queen, all various nam'd,
And for commanding grace and beauty fam'd.
Justice, supreme in might, whose general sway
The waters of the restless deep obey.
Ethereal, earthly, for the pious glad,
Sweet to the good, but bitter to the bad:
All-wise, all-bounteous, provident, divine,
A rich increase of nutriment is thine;
And to maturity whate'er may spring,

You to decay and dissolution bring.
Father of all, great nurse, and mother kind,
Abundant, blessed, all-spermatic mind:
Mature, impetuous, from whose fertile seeds
And plastic hand this changing scene proceeds.
All-parent pow'r, in vital impulse seen,
Eternal, moving, all-sagacious queen.
By thee the world, whose parts in rapid flow,
Like swift descending streams, no respite know,
On an eternal hinge, with steady course,
Is whirl'd with matchless, unremitting force.
Thron'd on a circling car, thy mighty hand
Holds and directs the reins of wide command:
Various thy essence, honor'd, and the best,
Of judgment, too, the general end and test.
Intrepid, fatal, all-subduing dame,
Life everlasting, Parca, breathing flame.
Immortal Providence, the world is thine,
And thou art all things, architect divine.
O, blessed Goddess, hear thy suppliants' pray'r,
And make their future life thy constant care;
Give plenteous seasons and sufficient wealth,
And crown our days with lasting peace and health.

To Pan

THE FUMIGATION FROM VARIOUS ODORS

Strong past'ral Pan, with suppliant voice I call,
Heav'n, sea, and earth, the mighty queen of all,
Immortal fire; for all the world is thine,
And all are parts of thee, O pow'r divine.
Come, blessed Pan, whom rural haunts delight,
Come, leaping, agile, wand'ring, starry light.
Thron'd with the Seasons, Bacchanalian Pan,
Goat-footed, horn'd, from whom the world began;
Whose various parts, by thee inspir'd, combine
In endless dance and melody divine.
In thee a refuge from our fears we find,
Those fears peculiar to the humankind.
Thee, shepherds, streams of water, goats rejoice,
Thou lov'st the chase and Echo's secret voice:

The sportive Nymphs thy ev'ry step attend,
And all thy works fulfill their destin'd end.
O all-producing pow'r, much-fam'd, divine,
The world's great ruler, rich increase is thine.
All-fertile Paean, heavenly splendor pure,
In fruits rejoicing, and in caves obscure.
True serpent-horned Jove, whose dreadful rage,
When rous'd, 'tis hard for mortals to assuage.
By thee the earth wide-bosom'd, deep and long,
Stands on a basis permanent and strong.
Th' unwearied waters of the rolling sea,
Profoundly spreading, yield to thy decree.
Old Ocean, too, reveres thy high command,
Whose liquid arms begird the solid land.
The spacious air, whose nutrimental fire
And vivid blasts the heat of life inspire;
The lighter frame of fire, whose sparkling eye
Shines on the summit of the azure sky,
Submit alike to thee, whose gen'ral sway
All parts of matter, various form'd, obey.
All natures change through thy protecting care,
And all mankind thy lib'ral bounties share;
For these, where'er dispers'd through boundless space,
Still find thy providence support their race.
Come, Bacchanalian, blessed pow'r, draw near,
Enthusiastic Pan, thy suppliants hear,
Propitious to these holy rites attend,
And grant our lives may meet a prosp'rous end;
Drive panic fury, too, wherever found,
From humankind to earth's remotest bound.

To Pluto
A HYMN

Pluto, magnanimous, whose realms profound
Are fix'd beneath the firm and solid ground,
In the Tartarean plains remote from sight,
And wrapt forever in the depths of night.
Terrestrial Jove, thy sacred ear incline,
And, pleas'd, accept these sacred rites divine.
Earth's keys to thee, illustrious king, belong,

Its secret gates unlocking, deep and strong.
'Tis thine abundant annual fruits to bear,
For needy mortals are thy constant care.
To thee, great king, all-sov'reign Earth's assign'd,
The seat of Gods and basis of mankind.
Thy throne is fix'd in Hades's dismal plains,
Distant, unknown to rest, where darkness reigns;
Where, destitute of breath, pale specters dwell,
In endless, dire inexorable hell;
And in dread Acheron, whose depths obscure,
Earth's stable roots eternally secure.
O mighty daemon, whose decision dread,
The future fate determines of the dead,
With captive Proserpine, through grassy plains,
Drawn in a four-yok'd car with loosen'd reins,
Rapt o'er the deep, impell'd by love, you flew
Till Eleusina's city rose to view:
There, in a wondrous cave, obscure and deep,
The sacred maid secure from search you keep,
The cave of Atthis, whose wide gates display
An entrance to the kingdoms void of day.
Of works unseen and seen thy power alone
To be the great dispensing source is known.
All-ruling, holy God, with glory bright,
Thee sacred poets and their hymns delight,
Propitious to thy mystics' works incline,
Rejoicing come, for holy rites are thine.

To the Clouds

THE FUMIGATION FROM MYRRH

Aerial Clouds, through heav'n's resplendent plains
Who wander, parents of prolific rains;
Who nourish fruits, whose wat'ry frames are hurl'd,
By winds impetuous, round the mighty world.
Loud-sounding, lion-roaring, flashing fire,
In Air's wide bosom bearing thunders dire:
Impell'd by each sonorous stormy gale,
With rapid course along the skies ye sail.
With gentle gales your wat'ry frames I call,
On mother Earth with fruitful show'rs to fall.

To the Mother of the Gods

THE FUMIGATION FROM A VARIETY OF ODORIFEROUS SUBSTANCES

Mother of Gods, great nurse of all, draw near,
Divinely honor'd, and regard my pray'r.
Thron'd on a car, by lions drawn along,
By bull-destroying lions, swift and strong,
Thou sway'st the scepter of the pole divine,
And the world's middle seat, much fam'd, is thine.
Hence earth is thine, and needy mortals share
Their constant food, from thy protecting care.
From thee at first both Gods and men arose;
From thee the sea and ev'ry river flows.
Vesta and source of wealth thy name we find
To mortal men rejoicing to be kind;
For ev'ry good to give thy soul delights.
Come, mighty pow'r, propitious to our rites,
All-taming, blessed, Phrygian Saviour, come,
Saturn's great queen, rejoicing in the drum.

To Bacchus

THE FUMIGATION FROM STORAX

Bacchus I call, loud-sounding and divine,
Fanatic God, a twofold shape is thine:
Thy various names and attributes I sing,
O, first-born, thrice begotten, Bacchic king:
Rural, ineffable, two-form'd, obscure,
Two-horn'd, with ivy crown'd, pure:
Bull-fac'd, and martial, bearer of the vine,
Endu'd with counsel prudent and divine:
Triennial, whom the leaves of vines adorn,
Of Jove and Proserpine, occultly born.
Immortal daemon, hear my suppliant voice,
Give me in blameless plenty to rejoice;
And listen gracious to my mystic pray'r,
Surrounded with thy choir of nurses fair.

To Ceres

THE FUMIGATION FROM STORAX

O Universal mother, Ceres fam'd
August, the source of wealth, and various nam'd:
Great nurse, all-bounteous, blessed and divine,
Who joy'st in peace, to nourish corn is thine:
Goddess of feed, of fruits abundant, fair,
Harvest and threshing are thy constant care;
Who dwell'st in Eleusina's seats retir'd,
Lovely, delightful queen, by all desir'd.
Nurse of all mortals, whose benignant mind,
First plowing oxen to the yoke confin'd;
And gave to men, what nature's wants require,
With plenteous means of bliss which all desire.
In verdure flourishing, in honor bright,
Assessor of great Bacchus, bearing light:
Rejoicing in the reaper's sickles, kind,
Whose nature lucid, earthly, pure, we find.
Prolific, venerable, Nurse divine,
Thy daughter loving, holy Proserpine:
A car with dragons yok'd, 'tis thine to guide,
And orgies singing round thy throne to ride:
Only-begotten, much-producing queen,
All flowers are thine and fruits of lovely green.
Bright Goddess, come, with Summer's rich increase
Swelling and pregnant, leading smiling Peace;
Come, with fair Concord and imperial Health,
And join with these a needful store of wealth.

To the Divinity of Dreams

THE FUMIGATION FROM AROMATICS

Thee I invoke, blest pow'r of dreams divine,
Angel of future fates, swift wings are thine.
Great source of oracles to humankind,
When stealing soft, and whisp'ring to the mind,
Thro' sleep's sweet silence, and the gloom of night,
Thy pow'r awakes th' intellectual sight;
To silent souls the will of heaven relates,

And silently reveals their future fates.
Forever friendly to the upright mind,
Sacred and pure, to holy rites inclin'd;
For these with pleasing hope thy dreams inspire:
Bliss to anticipate, which all desire.
Thy visions manifest of fate disclose,
What methods best may mitigate our woes;
Reveal what rites the Gods immortal please,
And what the means their anger to appease;
Forever tranquil is the good man's end,
Whose life thy dreams admonish and defend.
But from the wicked turn'd averse to bless,
Thy form unseen, the angel of distress;
No means to check approaching ill they find,
Pensive with fears, and to the future blind.
Come, blessed pow'r, the signatures reveal
Which heav'n's decrees mysteriously conceal,
Signs only present to the worthy mind,
Nor omens ill disclose of monstrous kind.

First Hymn to Love by Proclus

In our hymns we celebrate the famous shining wave-born divinity,
The great royal fountain from which the Immortals produced all the
     Cupids, the winged ones,
Of these, some hit souls with intelligible arrows,
So that, driven upward by the thorns of educative, anagogical desires,
They may ardently desire to behold the shining Halls of the Mother.
OTHERS again, by the counsel of the Father, protect from all evils,
     which they drive away,
Desiring to increase the immense world with generation,
And spurred on souls with the desire of terrestrial life.
OTHERS besides, are ever meditating on the sweet hymns of the
     marriage rite,
How they may transform the mortal race of pain-enduring men
Into a race immortal—all these are a care to the Cytherian Love-divinity
Who produces labors of love.

NOW, Goddess, for indeed thy ear is listening everywhere,
Whether thou art wandering around the majestic heaven, where, they
     say,

Thou art producing the divine Soul of the eternal World,
OR whether thou, who dwellest in the ether above the cycles of the
      seven spheres,
Infusing into our race indomitable virtue—
LISTEN, O venerable Deity, and with thy justest rays
Do thou direct the wearisome career of my life,
Destroying the bitter and pains-producing host of my unsanctified de-
      sires!

Hymn to the Gods by Proclus

Listen, Divinities, you who hold the reins of sacred wisdom.
Who set men's souls on fire with flames indomitable,
Drawing them, through the cloudy depths, far up to the Immortals,
Purging us with mystic rites of indescribable hymns;
Listen, great saviors! from divine books
Grant me the innocent, blameless light that dissipates the clouds,
So I may discover the truth about Man, and the immortal Divinity!
Neither let the Evil-working Spirit restrain me under the Lethean waters
      of Oblivion,
Ever far from the Blessed; for my soul
Would no longer continue to stray,
Nor suffer the cruel pains of imprisonment in the bands of life!

Nay, Gods of high and illustrious wisdom,
Masters and Leaders, hear me, the hastener
Along the Upward Way! Initiate me into the orgiac mysteries
And reveal them by the ceremonies of sacred words!

To Apollo
THE FUMIGATION FROM MANNA

> Blest Paean, come, propitious to my pray'r,
> Illustrious pow'r, whom Memphian tribes revere,
> Slayer of Tityus, and the God of health,
> Lycorian Phoebus, fruitful source of wealth:
> Spermatic, golden-lyr'd, the field from thee
> Receives its constant rich fertility.
> Titanic, Grunian, Smythian, thee I sing,
> Python-destroying, hallow'd, Delphian king:
> Rural, light-bearer, and the Muses' head,

Noble and lovely, arm'd with arrows dread:
Far-darting, Bacchian, twofold, and divine,
Pow'r far diffus'd, and course oblique is thine.
O Delian king, whose light-producing eye
Views all within, and all beneath the sky;
Whose locks are gold, whose oracles are sure,
Who omens good reveal'st, and precepts pure;
Hear me entreating for the human kind,
Hear, and be present with benignant mind;
For thou survey'st this boundless ether all,
And ev'ry part of this terrestrial ball
Abundant, blessed; and thy piercing sight
Extends beneath the gloomy, silent night;
Beyond the darkness, starry-ey'd, profound,
The stable roots, deep-fix'd by thee, are found.
The world's wide bounds, all-flourishing, are thine,
Thyself of all the source and end divine.
'Tis thine all Nature's music to inspire
With various-sounding, harmonizing lyre:
Now the last string thou tun'st to sweet accord,
Divinely warbling, now the highest chord;
Th' immortal golden lyre, now touch'd by thee,
Responsive yields a Dorian melody.
All Nature's tribes to thee their diff'rence owe,
And changing seasons from thy music flow:
Hence, mix'd by thee in equal parts, advance
Summer and Winter in alternate dance;
This claims the highest, that the lowest string,
The Dorian measure tunes the lovely spring:
Hence by mankind Pan royal, two-horn'd nam'd,
Shrill winds emitting through the syrinx fam'd;
Since to thy care the figur'd seal's consign'd,
Which stamps the world with forms of ev'ry kind.
Hear me, blest pow'r, and in these rites rejoice,
And save thy mystics with a suppliant voice.

Delphic Paean to Dionysus

Come! O dithyrambic Bacchus,
Bearer of the thyrsus, O reveler,

Come to the sacred feast of spring.
    Hail to Bacchus! Hail to Apollo!
You were sired by Jove in happy Thebes.
Stars danced at your birth and mortals feasted.
    Hail to Bacchus! Hail to Apollo!
In those days it was a true bacchanal
In the land of renowned Cadmus
And at the Minoan Gulf and Aulis.
    Hail to Bacchus! Hail to Apollo!
All was feasting and laughter at Delphi,
All sounded of songs and dancing.
And you, O God, showing yourself to the city,
Slipped away to Parnassus with comely Delphic maidens.
    Hail to Bacchus! Hail to Apollo!
Lifting the foaming cup on high,
Inspired by divine enthusiasm,
You came to the flowery niches of Elysium.
    Hail to Bacchus! Hail to Apollo!
There everyone on Hellenic soil familiarly
Called you "Bacch."
During the ninth year of the sacred orgies,
You flung into the river of forgetfulness
All human pain and suffering.
    Hail to Bacchus! Hail to Apollo!
In the choral songs that lasted through the night . . .
Turning then to that famous land
Which brought down the wrath of Olympus
And led to the famous exile.
    Hail to Bacchus! Hail to Apollo!
And then the virgin muses, laurel wreaths
On their heads,
Sang immortal and eternal hymns—
And Apollo led them all.
    Hail to Bacchus! Hail to Apollo!

A Song of the Brothers Arvall

Help us, O Lares, help us!
Help us, O Lares, help us,
Help us, O Lares, help us.
Nor you, O Mars, wreak destruction, but leave us. . . .

Nor you, O Mars, wreak destruction, but leave us. . . .
Nor you, O Mars, wreak destruction, but leave us. . . .
Be wise, rude Mars, go out of the land to fight.
Be wise, rude Mars, go out of the land to fight.
Be wise, rude Mars, go out of the land to fight.
Each will alternately invoke his gods,
Each will alternately invoke his gods,
Each will alternately invoke his gods.
Help us, O Mars, help us,
Help us, O Mars, help us,
Help us, O Mars, help us.
Triumph, triumph, triumph, triumph, triumph.

Expiatory Formula

In front of the Trebulan Gate three bulls are offered up to Jove Grabovin.[12] The following words are spoken: "I call thee, I have called thee, Jove Grabovin, in the name of the *fisian* bastion [*arce*—citadel], in the name of the "iguvina"[13] city, in the name of the one and the name of the other. Be benevolent, be propitious, to the citadel, to the city, to the one and to the other. I call thee, I have called thee, Jove Grabovin, with faith in this dedication. I call thee, I have called thee, Jove Grabovin.

Jove Grabovin, I commit myself to thee through this "profane" bull; may it serve as expiation for the citadel and the city, for the one and the other.

Jove Grabovin, if by this sacred act, lightning should strike the citadel or the city, if in the citadel or the city the assembly of priests is unduly broken up, let it be known that it is unwanted.

Jove Grabovin, if in the ceremonies to thee there is some transgression, some vice or sin, deception or plotting, some defect either visible or invisible, O Jove Grabovin, if it is right to do so, make the deceits and transgressions pure through the expiatory offering of this "profane" bull.

Jove Grabovin, purify the citadel, purify the city. Jove Grabovin, purify the citadel, purify the city. Purify their names. Purify the leaders, the priests, the men, the beasts, the crops. Be benevolent and propitious by showering down peace on the citadel and the city, on the name of the one and the other.

Jove Grabovin, serve well the citadel, serve well the city. Jove Grabovin, serve and preserve the citadel and the name of the city. Preserve the leaders, the priests, the men, the beasts, the crops. Serve and preserve. Be benevolent and propitious by bringing peace to the citadel and the city, to the name of the one and the other.

Jove Grabovin, I commit myself to thee by offering up this "profane" bull for the citadel and the city, for the one and the other.

Jove Grabovin, if by this sacred act, thunderbolts should strike the citadel, should the assembly of priests be broken up in the city, let it be known that it is unwanted.

Jove Grabovin, if in this ceremony to thee there is something deceitful, something sinful, some transgression or violation, some defect either visible or invisible, if it is permissible, O Jove Grabovin, purify it through the expiatory act of this second "profane" bull.

Jove Grabovin, purify the citadel and the city. Purify the name of the citadel and the name of the city. Purify the leaders, the priests, the men, the beasts, the crops. Be benevolent and propitious with the citadel and the city, with the name of the one and the other.

Jove Grabovin, serve and preserve the citadel, serve and preserve the city. Serve and preserve the name of the citadel and the name of the city. Serve and preserve the leaders, the priests, the men, the beasts, the crops. Be benevolent and propitious. Bring peace to the citadel, to the city, to the name of the one and the other.

Jove, Grabovin, I hereby offer up this second "profane" bull as an expiatory act for the citadel and the city, for the name of the one and the other.

Jove Grabovin, I call thee.

Jove Grabovin, I pledge myself to offer thee a third "profane" bull as an expiatory act for the citadel and the city, for the name of the one and the other.

Jove Grabovin, if in this sacred act a thunderbolt should strike the citadel and the city, if the assembly of priests should be broken up, let it be known that it is unwanted.

Jove Grabovin, if in the ceremony there is some transgression, some sin, vice, deceit or violation, some defect either visible or invisible, O Jove Grabovin, if it is permissible, let this third "profane" bull serve to expiate all sins and purify.

Jove Grabovin, purify the citadel, purify the city. Purify the name of the citadel and the name of the city. Purify the leaders, the priests, the men, the beasts, the crops. Be benevolent and propitious. Bring peace to the citadel and the city, to the name of the one and the other.

Jove Grabovin, serve and preserve the citadel and the city. Serve and preserve the name of the citadel and the city. Serve and preserve the leaders, the priests, the men, the beasts, the crops. Be benevolent, be propitious. Bring peace to the citadel and the city, to the name of the one and the other.

Jove Grabovin, I hereby offer thee this third "profane" bull as an expiatory act for the citadel and the city, for the name of the one and the other.

Jove Grabovin, I pledge myself to thee through the offering of the trinity of "profane" bulls as expiation for the citadel and the city, for the name of the one and the other.

O Jove Grabovin, I call thee!

Before Gathering the Grain

Before harvest the sacrifice of the *porca praecidanea* should be offered in this manner: Offer a sow as *porca praecidanea* to Ceres before harvesting spelt, wheat, barley, beans, and rape seed; and address a prayer, with incense and wine, to Janus, Jupiter, and Juno, before offering the sow.

Make an offering of cakes to Janus, with these words: "Father Janus, in offering these cakes, I humbly beg that thou wilt be gracious and merciful to me and my children, my house and my household."

Then make an offering of cake to Jupiter with these words: "In offering this cake, O Jupiter, I humbly beg that thou, pleased by this offering, wilt be gracious and merciful to me and my children, my house and my household."

Then present the wine to Janus, saying: "Father Janus, as I prayed humbly in offering the cakes, so wilt thou to the same end be honored by this wine placed before thee."

And then pray to Jupiter thus: "Jupiter, wilt thou deign to accept the cake; wilt thou deign to accept the wine placed before thee."

Then offer up the *porca praecidanea*.

The Purification of Land

The following is the formula for purifying land: Bidding the suovetaurilia to be led around, use the words: "That with the good help of the gods success may crown our work, I bid thee, Manius, to take care to purify my farm, my land, my ground, with this suovetaurilia, in whatever part thou thinkest best for them to be driven or carried around."

Make a prayer with wine to Janus and Jupiter, and say: "Father

Mars, I pray and beseech thee that thou be gracious and merciful to me, my house, and my household; to which intent I have bidden this suovetaurilia to be led around my land, my ground, my farm; that thou keep away, ward off, and remove sickness, seen and unseen, barrenness and destruction, ruin and unseasonable influence; and that thou permit my harvests, my grain, my vineyards, and my plantations to flourish and to come to good issue, preserve in health my shepherds and my flocks, and give good health and strength to me, my house, and my household. To this intent, to the intent of purifying my farm, my land, my ground, and of making an expiation, as I have said, deign to accept the offering of these suckling victims; Father Mars, to the same intent deign to accept the offering of these suckling offering."

Before Thinning a Grove

The following is the Roman formula to be observed in thinning a grove:

A pig is to be sacrificed, and the following prayer uttered: "Whether thou be god or goddess to whom this grove is dedicated, as it is thy right to receive a sacrifice of a pig for the thinning of this sacred grove, and to this intent, whether I or one at my bidding do it, may it be rightly done. To this end, in offering this pig to thee, I humbly beg that thou wilt be gracious and merciful to me, to my house and household, and to my children. Wilt thou deign to receive this pig which I offer thee to this end."

Proclamation of the Ver Sacrum

If the Republic of the Roman people, the Quirites, shall be preserved for the next five years—I would wish it preserved—in these wars, to wit, the war of the Roman People with the People of Carthage and the wars with the Gauls on this side of the Alps, let the Roman People, the Quirites, offer up in indefeasible sacrifice to Jupiter what the spring shall have produced of swine, sheep, goats, and cattle—which shall not have been consecrated to some other deity—beginning with the day which the senate and the People shall have designated. Let him who shall make a sacrifice do so at such time and by such rite as shall seem good to him; in what manner soever he does it, let it be accounted duly done. If the animal which he ought to sacrifice dies, let it be deemed unconsecrate and let no guilt attach to him; if any shall hurt it or slay it unawares, let it be no sin; if any shall steal it, let no guilt attach to the People nor to him from whom it shall have been stolen; if he shall sacrifice unwittingly on a black day, let the sacrifice be deemed to have been duly made; by night or by day, if slave or freeman perform the sacrifice, let it be deemed to have been duly made; if sacrifice shall be performed before the senate and the People shall have ordered it to be performed, let the People be absolved therefrom and free of obligation.

A Prayer of Romulus

This prayer was uttered by Romulus at the time the Sabines were occupying the city.

O Jupiter, it was thy omen that directed me when I layed here on the Palatine the first foundations of my City. The fortress is already bought by a crime and in the possession of the Sabines, whence they are come, sword in hand, across the valley to seek us here. But do thou, father of gods, and men, keep them back from this spot at least; deliver the Romans from their terror, and stay their shameful flight! I here vow to thee, Jupiter the Stayer, a temple, to be a memorial to our descendants how the City was saved by thy present help.

Dedication of the Spoils of War

Romulus dedicates the spoils taken from the King of the Cenninesi.

Jupiter Feretrius, to thee I, victorious Romulus, myself a king, bring the panoply of a king, and dedicate a sacred precinct within the bounds which I have even now marked off in my mind, to be a seat for the spoils of honor which men shall bear hither in time to come, following my example, when they have slain kings and commanders of the enemy.

Sacramental Formula for Pacts

In concluding the treaty between Alba and Rome, the fetial was Marcus Valerius; he made Spurius Fusius pater patratus, touching his head and hair with the sacred sprig. The pater patratus is appointed to pronounce the oath, that is, to solemnize the pact. . . . The conditions being then recited, he cries, "Hear, Jupiter; hear, pater patratus of the Alban People: hear ye, People of Alba: From these terms, as they have been publicly rehearsed from beginning to end, without fear, from these tablets, or this wax, and as they have been this day clearly understood, the Roman People will not be the first to depart. If it shall first depart from them, by general consent, with malice, aforethought, then on that day do thou so smite the Roman People as I shall here today smite this pig: and so much the harder smite them as thy power and thy strength are greater."

When Spurius had said these words, he struck the pig with a flint.

Invocation of Publius Valerius Publicolus

Father Romulus, grant thou to thy descendants that spirit in which thou didst aforetime regain thy Citadel from these same Sabines, when they had captured it with gold; bid them advance by that road where thou didst lead and thy army followed. Lo, I, the consul, will be the first, so far as mortal can emulate a god, to follow in thy footsteps!

Prayer of Voculas

I pray and beseech thee, Jupiter, most good and great, to whom we have rendered the honor of so many triumphs during eight hundred and twenty years, and thee, Qurinus, father of Rome, that, if it has not been your pleasure that this camp be kept pure and inviolate under my leadership, at least you will not allow it to be defiled and polluted by a Tutor and a Classicus; give to Roman soldiers either innocence or repentance, prompt and without disaster.

For the Republic

O Jupiter Capitolinus, and Mars Gradivus, author and stay of the Roman name, Vesta, guardian of the eternal fire, and all other divinities who have exalted this great empire of Rome to the highest point yet reached on earth! On you I call, and to you I pray in the name of this people: guard, preserve, protect the present state of things, the peace which we enjoy, the present emperor, and when he has filled his last post of duty—and may it be the longest granted to mortals—grant him successors until the latest time, but successors whose shoulders may be as capable of sustaining bravely the empire of the world as we have found his to be: foster the pious plans of all good citizens and crush the impious designs of the wicked.

Prayer of Scipio Africanus

When the day dawned, Scipio on his flagship, after silence had been secured by a herald, prayed: "Ye gods and goddesses who inhabit seas and lands, I pray and beseech you that whatever under my authority has been done, is being done, and shall henceforth be done, may prosper for me, for the Roman people and the commons, for allies and Latins who by land, by sea, and by rivers follow the lead, authority and auspices of the Roman people and of myself; and that ye lend your kind aid to all those acts and make them bear good fruit; that when the foe has been vanquished, ye bring the victors home with me, safe and sound, adorned with spoils, laden with booty, and in triumph; that ye grant power to punish opponents and enemies; and that ye bestow upon the Roman people and upon me the power to visit upon the state of the Carthaginians the fate that the people of Carthage have endeavored to visit upon our state."

The Devotionis Carmen

The pontiff bade him don the purple-bordered toga, and with veiled head and one hand thrust out from the toga and touching his chin, stand upon a spear that was laid under his feet, and say as follows: "Janus, Jupiter, Father Mars, Quirinus, Bellona, Lares, divine Novensiles, divine Indigites, ye gods in whose power are both we and our enemies, and you, divine Manes—I invoke and worship you, I beseech and crave your favor, that you prosper the might and the victory of the Roman People of the Quirites, and visit the foes of the Roman People of the Quirites with fear, shuddering, and death. As I have pronounced the words, even so in behalf of the republic of the Roman People of the Quirites, and of the army, the legions, the auxiliaries of the Roman People of the Quirites, do I devote the legions and auxiliaries of the enemy, together with myself, to the divine Manes and to Earth."

Dedication of the City and the Armies

Father Jove, Javeus, O Powerful, or by whatever name it is meet to invoke thee, I pray to all thy names and titles that thou fillest with terror, fright and quaking this city of Carthage and the army of which I speak.

May these men, these enemies, this armed force that hurls itself against our legions, may their cities, their fields, those who inhabit their lands and houses, all be routed by thee and deprived of heavenly light.

Let these enemy armies, their cities, their fields of which I wish to speak, let the heads of individuals of every age be offered up to thee and consecrated according to the rites of consecration established by thee regarding great and powerful armies and enemies.

By virtue of the power vested in me, I offer them votively in our place, and turn them over as substitutes for the Roman people, for our legions and our armies, that in the hazardous undertaking to follow thou wilt preserve my person, my dignity, my power, our legions and our armies.

If I am made by some sign to know, feel, and understand that thou hast heard me favorably, then whoever anywhere has pledged a votive offering of three black sheep to thee is obliged to carry out the offering.

In the name of our beloved land, O Jove, I hold thee witness.

To Sylvanus

> O great one among gods, Sylvanus,
> Most powerful and sacred shepherd
> Who looks after the woods of Ida
> And the peak-perched Roman castles.
> As to thee the honey clings, and the sweet
> Fluted reed in its melody sings,
> So only a step from this plaque
> Does the stream cling and sing
> As it gurgles, silvery, over the rocks.
> Thou, O Sylvanus, by bringing to this place
> A tender uprooted cypress,
> Can, O my favored one, shower thy
> Divine power down upon this spot,
> Since I have, to gain thy favors,
> Here consecrated an altar in thy name.
> This I have done for the salvation
> Of my master and myself,
> For my loved ones who dutifully
> Pray and lead a life inspired to service.
> Assist me, O benevolent one,
> While I present these gifts
> To the altar as a votive offering;
> Loosen my stumbling tongue
> While I choose those things to be
> Inscribed upon the altar in my name.
> And now, O men, gladly do all things,
> Restore the body and wish that it shall always be so.

To Priapus

Hail to sacred Priapus, father of all, hail!
Grant me eternally flowering youthfulness,
That young men and beautiful maidens
I might please and charm:
During endless feasts and joys
Keep far from my sparkling soul
The destructive weariness,
Nor hound me with excessive decrepitude
Or fears of old age,
Nor flay me with fear of some unhappy death
That will drag me to that land
Where the king tosses the souls of the dead
About so playfully for amusement,
As if they were no more than wispy fables,
That land from which none returns.
Hail to sacred Priapus, father Priapus, hail!
Up and away, O joyous throng,
However many you may be,
Up and away, run,
You who venerate the sacred wood,
You young maids who venerate the sacred waters,
Run, all of you, to gracious Priapus,
And say in your charming voices:
Hail, O sacred Priapus, father of all, hail!
It is he, in fact, who, while far away
And busily engaged in striking down the wicked,
Permits you to frolic in wood and glen,
To splash safely in the waters:
He keeps the wicked at a distance,
Those who would irreverently defile the streams.
And so now say to him:
O Priapus, O divine one, be propitious!
Hail to Priapus, O sacred Priapus, hail!
O Priapus, powerful friend, hail,
And may it please thee to be called
Generator and Author of the world,
Of the Universe itself, of Pan.

For in truth, out of thy lusty vigor
Were earth and air and sea conceived and filled.
Therefore hail! O Priapus, hail O saint!
Jove himself, when thou orderest, lays down
His destructive thunderbolts
And, overflowing with more gentle desires,
Rises from his luminous throne.
Beautiful Venus herself, and Cupid as well,
Venerate thee,
While Grace, with her dancing sisters,
The givers of joy, likewise venerate thee.
Without thee, Venus succeeds not in her charms,
Is indeed no longer beautiful,
And the Graces become Disgraces unholy,
As do Bacchus and Cupid.
O Priapus, powerful friend, hail!
Pure maidens invoke thee
To snap their protective belts.
The bride invokes thee,
That her husband will forever possess gleaming virile
      potency.
Hail, O sacred father Priapus, hail!

To the Parcae

O Parcae, in accordance with the prescriptions
Of the Sibylline Books,
And to gain the best of fortune for the Roman Quirites,
Accept this sacrificial offering of nine lambs and kids.
I ask and beseech you that, in war and peace,
You make grow and prosper the Empire
And the Roman Quirites,
That you protect the Latin Name,
That you grant perpetual safety, victory, and health
To the Roman Quirites,
That you be favorably disposed toward
The Roman Quirites and the legions,
That you preserve the republic of
The Roman Quirites,
And that you always show yourself benevolently disposed
To the Roman Quirites,

To the Collegio dei Quindecemviri, to me, my family
And my home.
Accept this sacrifice of nine lambs and kids
Now offered up to you in accordance
With the ritual.
In addition to the sacrifice,
Further accept this extra lamb
And be favorably inclined toward the Roman Quirites,
Towards the Collegio, toward me, my home, and my family.

Tablet of Malediction: To Proserpina

O piteous and beautiful Proserpina, wife of Pluto—or should I call thee Sage One?—strip the good health, the limbs, the color, the strength, the flesh and the virtue from Plozio. Turn him over to Pluto, thy husband. Cunning though he is, he cannot escape Pluto. Call a ruinous fever down upon him, rack him with miserable agues and fitful fevers that he cannot outconnive. Strike him down, crush him, until his very soul is squeezed out. And for that service I offer thee this victim, O Proserpina—or should I call thee Acheron?—call forth thy three-headed dog, that it might rip Plozio's black heart out with its teeth. I promise to give him three offerings: dates, figs, and one black hog, if, to be sure, he has done his work prior to the month of March. And to thee, O sagacious Proserpina, when thou hast heard and granted, I oblige myself to give as follows: I will give thee the head of Plozio Avonia. O sagacious Proserpina, I will give thee his brow. O sagacious Proserpina, I will give thee his eyebrows. O sagacious Proserpina, I will give thee his eyelashes. O sagacious Proserpina, I will give thee his eyeballs. O sagacious Proserpina, I will give thee his nostrils, his lips, his ears, his nose, his tongue, his teeth, that Plozio may not even utter his agony. I will give thee Plozio's neck, shoulders, arms, fingers, which in truth will be of no further use to him. I will give thee his chest, entrails, heart, liver and lights, that he may not even feel where he agonizes. I will give thee all his guts, bowels, umbilical cord, his loins, vitals, that he may not sleep on his back. I will give thee his shoulder blades, that he may not sleep on his back. I will give thee his bladder, that he may not urinate, his cheeks, his anus, his thigh bone, his knees, his calves, his fibia, his feet, his heels, his ankles, his toes and his toenails, that he may not stand upright.

Whether I have given thee too much here, or too little, I know not; but, according to the book, one must confide all in thee. And so, according to the rites, I hereby consign Plozio to thee, on the condition that, prior to the end of February, thou causest him to fall victim to a horrible fever. Ruin him utterly! Crush him! Hurl him to the devils! I consign him to thee; I put him in thy care, that he be not permitted to see, feel, or in any manner enjoy one more single month of life.

Tablet of Malediction: To Dis, for Rodine

In the manner that the dead soul resting here in this tomb can neither speak nor converse, let Rodine be dead for Marcus Lycinius Faustus, that he may never again converse with him. And since the dead are revolting to both gods and men, so let Marcus Lycinius be as revolting as the dead soul entombed here. O father Dis, I consign thee Rodine, that he may be made revolting in the eyes of Marcus Lycinius Faustus. Likewise let it be with Marcus Edius Anfione, with Gaius Popilus Apollonius, as well as with Vennonia Ermiona, and Sergia Glicinna.

Enchantment

Quintus Letinius Lupus, known as Caucadius, son of Salustia Venaria or Veneriosa, I offer up sacrifices to the divinities, that they, Gods of Boiling Waters, or Nymphs, or whatever their names are, will crush the life out of you within the current year.

Enchantment of Love

I request . . . the great God and Cupid, and the divinity whose emblem is the hawk, and the seven stars, that, from the moment I compose this enchantment, Sestilio, son of Dionisia, be not permitted to sleep again, but that he burn with desire and madness, that he find no rest, that his tongue refuse to speak, that he have fixed constantly in his mind me, Settimia, daughter of Amena. May he burn with love and madness for me, Settimia, daughter of Amena.

And so . . . cause Sestilio, son of Dionisia, to flame with passion and desire for me; make his heart burn, and, with it, all the members of his body, the body of Sestilio, son of Dionisia.

And if that not happen, I shall descend to the impenetrable regions of Osiris, open the tomb, and have him carried away on the current. For I am close to the great God Achrammachalae.

To Helios

Quite often during these feasts the gods permit me to honor and sanctify, particularly Helios, the universal king. He, out of eternal realms, proceeded to deal with the generative substance of Good; he dwells in the midst of gods gifted with great intellect, which gods themselves have an intermediate place in the arrangement; he has filled them with a cohesive spirit, with infinite beauty and harmony, exuberant reproductive force, perfect reasoning powers, with all benefits regardless of time or space; even now he lights up his place as he moves from eternal realms through the sky; he causes all the visible world to participate in the beauty of intelligence; he has populated the sky with such a multitude of gods, as many as one can intellectually comprehend, gods that in themselves are indivisibly multiplied around him, and yet uniformly conjoined; sublunar regions he keeps united by ties of perpetual generation that come from the celestial bodies; he provides for all the human race and most particularly for our city, just as out of the eternal realms he previously called forth our souls. He appointed me his follower. What little I have said, may he enlarge upon: in his benignity, may he guide the state and assure it, if possible, eternal life.

Regarding me, as long as he shall let me live, I hope to prosper in human and divine matters, to live by consecrating myself to the good of the state; as long as it please him, it shall be good for me and for the Romans. . . .

For the third time, therefore, as a reward for my zeal, I ask Helios the universal king to shower his blessings down on me, to give me a good life, a more perfect wisdom, an inspired mind, and, at the proper moment, the departure from this life as ruled by destiny.

Then I may rise to meet him and dwell near him, possibly for eternity, though should that be too long a time to presume on the simple merits of my life, at least for many years of long duration.

To the Mother of the Gods

O Mother of gods and men, you who share the throne with Zeus, O fount of the gods, gifted with intelligence, you who walk with the immaculate substance of the intelligent gods and from them have transmitted intellect to other gods, O generative goddess of life, you who counsel and provide, O creator of our souls, you who loved the great Dionysus and saved the Attic realm, you who are the guide to gods of intellect, who fills and refills all the visible world and touches all things with grace and goodness: give to all men happiness, the awareness of the gods, give to the Roman people the power to fend off the pest of impiety. May a happy destiny govern the future of the empire and accompany it for many hundreds of years.

As for me, for the fruit of my devotion to you, grant me the possession of truth regarding the doctrine of the gods, the perfection of religious practices; in whatever work I undertake, military or political, grant me virtue and good fortune, so the end of my life may be glorious and without pain, rich in the hope that I might, O god, rise to dwell with you.

A Litany

O August Claudius, may the gods keep thee for us! (*repeated 60 times*)
O August Claudius, always we hoped for thee as our emperor, or for one like thee! (*40 times*)
O August Claudius, the republic needed thee! (*40 times*)
O August Claudius, thou art brother, friend, good senator, thou art truly the first among us! (*80 times*)
O August Claudius, who liberated us from Aureolus! (*50 times*)
O August Claudius, avenge us against the Palmyrians! (*5 times*)
O August Claudius, avenge us against Zenobia and Vittoria! (*7 times*)
O August Claudius, Tetrico did nothing! (*7 times*)

To the Great Mother

This was the prayer of Lucius.

O blessed queen of heaven, whether Thou be the Dame Ceres which art the original and motherly nurse of all fruitful things in the earth, who, after the finding of Thy daughter Proserpine, through the great joy which Thou didst presently conceive, didst utterly take away and abolish the food of them of old time, the acorn, and madest the barren and unfruitful ground of Eleusis to be plowed and sown, and now givest men a more better and milder food; or whether Thou be the celestial Venus, who, in the beginning of the world, didst couple together male and female with an engendered love, and didst so make an eternal propagation of humankind, being now worshiped within the temples of the Isle Paphos; or whether Thou be the sister of the god Phoebus, who hast saved so many people by lightening and lessening with thy medicines the pangs of travail and art now adored at the sacred places of

Ephesus; or whether Thou be called terrible Proserpine, by reason of the deadly howlings which Thou yieldest, that hast power with triple face to stop and put away the invasion of hags and ghosts which appear unto men, and to keep them down in the closures of the Earth, which dost wander in sundry groves and art worshiped in divers manners; Thou, which dost luminate all the cities of the earth by Thy feminine light; Thou, which nourishest all the seeds of the world by Thy damp heat, giving Thy changing light according to the wanderings, near or far, of the sun: by whatsoever name of fashion or shape it is lawful to call upon Thee, I pray Thee to end my great travail and misery and raise up my fallen hopes, and deliver me from the wretched fortune which so long time pursued me. Grant peace and rest, if it please Thee, to my adversities, for I have endured enough labor and peril.

To Isis

Holy and blessed dame, the perpetual comfort of humankind, who by Thy bounty and grace nourishest all the world, and bearest a great affection to the adversities of the miserable as a loving mother, Thou takest no rest, night or day, neither art Thou idle at any time in giving benefits and succoring all men as well on land as sea; Thou art she that puttest away all storms and dangers from Men's life by stretching forth Thy right hand, whereby likewise Thou dost unweave even the inextricable and tangled web of fate, and appeasest the great tempests of fortune, and keepest back the harmful course of the stars. The gods supernal do honor Thee, the gods infernal have Thee in reverence; Thou dost make all the earth to turn, Thou givest light to the sun, Thou governest the world, Thou treadest down the Power of hell. By Thy means the stars give answer, the seasons return, the gods rejoice, the elements serve: at Thy commandment the winds do blow, the clouds nourish the earth, the seeds prosper, and the fruits do grow. The birds of the air, the beasts of the hill, the serpents of the den, and the fishes of the sea do tremble at Thy majesty: but my spirit is not able to give Thee sufficient praise, my patrimony is unable to satisfy Thy sacrifices; my voice hath no power to utter that which I think of Thy majesty, no, not if I had a thousand mouths and so many tongues and were able to continue forever. Howbeit, as a good religious person, and according to my poor estate, I will do what I may: I will always keep Thy divine appearance in remembrance, and close the imagination of Thy most holy godhead within my breast.

Incantation for Becoming Invisible

I invoke thee, I invoke thee alone, I invoke thee who alone ordered all that exists in the world for gods and men, I invoke thee who transformed thyself by sacred metamorphosis, and who from nothing raised up being, and from being raised up nothing, Thayt, the sacred one, whose true face no god is capable of looking upon.

Make me become in the eyes of others a wolf, a dog, a lion, fire, a tree, vulture, wall, water, or whatever thou wishest—for thou art powerful.

Sorcery

Fisio, Iâo . . . [magic terms follow], I pray that during this day, that during this same hour, the sun and light appear to this youth—Osiris, Isis—and Anubi, servant of the gods, and cause this youth to fall into a trance and see the gods that come to give the oracle, all of them.

May you also appear in the oracle, magnanimous god, Hermes Trismegistus, who seems to me the one who created the four parts of the sky and the four fundaments of earth. Come to me, you who are in the sky; come to me, you who were born of an egg.

I entreat you in the name of him who is at Tapsati, that in my eyes will appear the gods who are your escort, O Thath! The first god is called Sô, the second, Aph.

The prayer recited:

Come to me, spirit that flies through the air, you whom I call by means of symbols and ineffable words and names, come to this sorcery that I work, and enter into the soul of this youth, that he may represent the immortal form in a powerful light, for I call you in my incantation, Iâo, Elôai. Come to me, master, carried by the pure light, come without deceit or anger to me and to your small one, this youth—appear!

Incantation for Contests of Love, by Astrapsoukos

Come to me, O master Hermes, like a baby to its mother's breast. To me, ——, come, O master Hermes, and grant me favors, nourishment, victories, prosperity, happiness, fortune in love, beauty of countenance and that strength which buoys up all men and women. Your names are written in the sky. These are the names you carry to the four corners of all space. I know your forms: they are, in the east, the sacred ibis; in the west, the baboon; in the north, the serpent; and in the south, the wolf. Your vine is the grape, which in your realm is the olive. I also know your wood, which is ebony. I, O Hermes, know who you are, from whence you came and your city: Hermopolae.

Come to me, master Hermes, you of the many names, who know of things hidden under black celestial poles and under the earth itself. To me, ——, come, Hermes, be benevolent to me, O benefactor of the world. Hear my prayer, gain me consideration in the eyes of all species of beings on the earth. For me, open the hands of givers of gifts, and permit me to receive what they clutch in their hands.

I also know your barbarian name . . . such are your barbarian names. If it is true that Isis, greatest of all divinities, invoked you to serve her in every place against the gods, against men, demons and beasts that dwell on land and sea, and if she gained your favor and your victories over gods, men, and all animals of land and sea, why then can't I, ——, invoke you to come to me? Also grant me favors, a fair mien, beauty. Hear my prayer, O Hermes, benefactor, inventor of love potions, let me speak easily with you, hear me in the same manner as you listened to your Ethiopian baboon, he who belongs to those who dwell beneath the earth.

Cause everyone to hold sweet sentiments for me. Grant me vigor, a fair countenance [*your votive offerings, as usual*], and may they bring me gold and silver and every form of nourishment in inexhaustible quantities. Keep me always safe from poisoners, from ambuscades and the long knives, from every attack of the evil eye and wicked tongue, from being possessed by demons, from the anger of gods and men.

May these offerings bring me favors, victories, all manner of success and prosperity. Because you are me and I am you. Your name is mine and mine is yours, for I am your portrait.

If some accident strikes me down during this year or during this month or this day or hour, it shall also strike the great Akkemen Estroph, whose name is inscribed on the prow of the sacred ship.

Your name is written on the sacred pillar of the temple in the city of your name where you were born. Your true name is: Osergariach Nomaphi. That is your name, the fifteen-lettered name in which the letters correspond to the number of days contained in the phase of the crescent moon; your second name counts seven letters with the Dominators of the world, and your cipher is 365, as the days in the year. Yes, you are truly Abrasax.

I know you, Hermes, and you know me. I am you. You are me. Gain
for me all the good things and shower me with good fortune and good
demons. Now, now, quickly, quickly!

Incantation of the Ring of Thoth-Hermes

I am Thoth, inventor and creator of potions and letters. Come to me,
you who are underground; awaken for me, powerful demons! I am the
illustrious Heron, the egg of the ibis, the egg of the falcon, the egg of
the phoenix that rises in air. Under my tongue is the clay of Em; I am
cloaked from the spoils of Keph.

If I do not succeed in knowing how much is in everyone's soul,
Egyptians, Greeks, Syrians, Ethiopians, every race and every people, if
I do not succeed in knowing their past and their future, their art, their
occupations, their activities and their way of life, as well as that of their
fathers, mothers, brothers, friends both dead and alive, then I shall
slop blood from the black god with the dog's head into a new kettle
that has never been used, and I will hang it over a new brazier, while
under it I will burn the bones of the Esies, and, at the anchorage of
Busiride, I will shout out the name of him who remained three days
and nights in the river Esies, of him who was carried by the current
to the ocean and swept under by waves and storms.

Your stomach will be food for fishes, and I shan't cause the fish not
to devour your cadaver, nor will the fish close their mouths.

I will seize the fatherless child from the mother, cause the supporting
vault of heaven to crash, and two mountains will become one. I will
hurl against you the Opening and it will rage as it pleases. I will never
consent that gods and goddesses grant oracles of any kind until I, ——,
do not know profoundly how much there is in the souls of men, all men,
Egyptians, Syrians, Greeks, Ethiopians, every race and people, all who
question me and present themselves to my eyes, all who speak or remain silent, in order that I may announce to them all life past, present,
future, and know their art and ways of life, their occupations and their
every act, the names of the living and dead, and, generally speaking, all
about everything and everyone, and know how to read a sealed letter
and can reveal everything in conformity with the truth.

A Prayer for Dreams

O Hermes, dominant sovereign of the world, thou who art in the
heart, circle of the moon, thou who art round and square, originator of

the articulated word, defender of the cause of justice, thou who wearest the soldier's cloak, god of the winged sandals, thou who traversest all regions, from the airy spaces to the lower depths, guide of the spirit, eye of the sun, foremost, originator of the word that all can utter, thou who with thy light dost bring joy to those below, in the depths of Tartarus, while those mortals who have ended their existence call thee "He who foretells destinies" and "Divine dream," thou who by night and day dost bring us oracles.

Cure the suffering of all mortals with thy remedies. Come, O blessed, most worthy son of Memory that achieves its designs.

Show thyself in thy favorable form, rise up favorably for a pious man; let me, ——, see thy favorable form, so that I may receive thee in the oracles that express thy powerful virtue. I beseech thee, my Lord, be favorably disposed: show thyself without deceit and speak the oracle.

Prayer to the Supreme God, Ayion

I invoke thee, who art the greatest of all, who created all, who generated it from thyself, who sees all and is never seen. Thou hast given to the sun its glory and its power, to the moon hast thou granted the right to wax and wane and follow a regular course, without having robbed anything from other regions, but having been equal with all. For at thy appearance the world came into being and there was light. All things bowed down before thee, whom no one can contemplate in thy true form, who changes form, who remains the invisible Ayion of the Ayion.

Cosmic Prayer

Come to me, thou who comest from the direction of the four winds, O sovereign master god, thou who gave life to men, master of all that is beautiful in the world, O hear me, Lord, whose name is hidden, ineffable, at the sound of which the demons tremble out of fear, the Sun . . . the earth turns about in a circle, the River Ade moves, the flames, seas, swamps, and fountains coagulate to form a whole, the head of which is the sky, the ether is the body and the earth the feet. The water around thee is the ocean, Good Demon. Thou art the master who generates and makes all things grow.

Who modeled the forms of animals? Who laid out the pathways? Who produced the fruit, who lifted up the mountains? Who commanded the winds to do their work? Ayion, who nourishes Ayion, who reigns over Ayion. The only God, immortal God. Thou givest life to all beings, givest souls to them, reignest over all, king and lord of the Ayion, before whom all things quake—the mountains, the plains, the waters, the depths of the earth, the winds, all living things. The brilliant sky above quakes in thy presence, as does every sea, O Lord, sovereign master, head saint of all creatures. Out of thy power all things grow, all things take a pattern: the sun, the moon, the night, the day, the air on earth, the water, vapor, and fire.

To thee belongeth the eternal feast room, where, like a sacred image, thy name riseth up in accordance with the seven vowel sounds that correspond to the twenty-four phases of the moon.

From thee descend the favorable influence of the astrals, Demons, Fortunes, and Destinies. Thou bestowest wealth, happy old age, fecundity, vigor, nutriment. O master of life, who reigns over regions above and below, whose justice knows no obstacles, whose illustrious name is chanted lovingly by angels, who possesses truth without deceit, O hear me, consecrate my plea, that this power in me may be preserved in every place, throughout all time, without undergoing damages, without becoming fatigued or unclean.

Yes, O Lord, for all things are at thy will, god of the sky, let no demon or spirit come between me and my desire, for I invoke thy name, and still again I invoke thee, according to the Egyptian Phnô, according to the Hebrew Adonai, Saboath, according to universal Greek kings, lone Monarch, according to the great priests of the hidden God, the invisible God, who watches over all, according to the most potent Ouertô. Consecrate and fill with magic power this operation for all the days of my life.

Cosmic Prayer: Secret Text

Hail! system of the spirit of the air, hail! Breeze that penetrates all things of earth and sky, all things from the sky to the earth to the abyss, hail! Hail O breeze that enters into me and takes possession of me, then separates from me, in accordance with the will of God.

Hail, beginning and end of nature, hail, turbulent elements that never tire of doing their work, hail splendid sunlight at the service of the world, hail, round-rimmed moon that glows in darkness, hail, all breeze-demons of the air, hail to you who are permitted to play your joyous eulogies like devoted brothers and sisters. O vast, incomprehensible plan of the world! Celestial winds, ether inside the sky, vapor inside the ether; terrestrial, luminous wind, sparks, shadows, light, humidity, cold!

I laud thee, God of gods, who harmonized the parts of the world, who gathered up the waters from the abyss of their invisible fundament, who separated earth and sky, who covered the sky on one side with golden wings, and tied the earth to its fundaments, who suspended the ether in high regions, who cast winds on the world to move by themselves, who surrounded the earth with a belt of water, who hurls forth hurricanes, thunders, lightning, rain, who shakes the very earth itself and all creatures on it—God of Ayion. Thou art truly grand, sovereign of the universe!

Prayer to the Sun

A useful text for every purpose, also as a liberation from death. Seek not the secret.

Unique and happiest among the Ayion, father of the Cosmos, I invoke thee with a cosmic prayer. Come to me, thou who breathed life into the universe, who suspended the fire in the ocean of the sky, who separated land from water; hear me, O form, spirit, earth, sea, word, divine Necessity, and receive my prayer as if it were spoken with tongues of fire, for I am a man [or the "man"] of God, of all creatures the most beautiful, born of wind, dew, earth.

Open, O sky, and receive my plea. Listen, O Helios, father of the world. I invoke thee with thy name . . . [magic terms] . . . thy name is strong and healthy, a name sanctified by all the angels. Preserve me, ———, keep me from arrogance and from unworthy actions.

Yes, do that, O Lord, God of gods . . . [magic terms], creator of the world, who created all, Lord, God of gods . . . [magic terms].

I have called by name thy insuperable Glory, O creator of gods, archangels, and deacons. Myriads of angels flock to thee and sing to the sky of thy wisdom, which is Ayion.

I invoke thy name of a hundred letters, that pierces the depths of the earth. Save me, for it is that which gives thee the greatest joy, to save one of thine . . . [magic terms]. I invoke thee on the golden leaf, thee for whom the inextinguishable light shines, the great God that appears throughout the universe entire, who shines at Jerusalem, Lord Iaô! Prosper, O Lord!

Prayer to the Sun

I invoke thee, O greatest of the gods, constant Lord, dominator of the world, thou who art over and under the world, powerful dominator of the sea, who shines on the waters, who, for the world entire, rises up in the east and goes to sleep in the west. Come to me, thou who goest where the four winds go, gracious Agutodemone, whose festive rooms are the sky entire.

I invoke thy sacred names, great and hidden names, that are a joy to hear. Under thy rays the earth decks itself in flowers, plants bear fruit beneath thy smiles, and winds by thy command generate other living things. Give glory, honor, favor, success, and magic power to this rock with which I carry out the consecration against ———. I invoke thee, who art great in the sky . . . [magic terms], Sabaoth, Adonai, God . . . [magic terms], sparkling Helios who shines on all the earth. Thou art the great serpent that marches at the head of the gods, thou art accorded first place in Egypt, last of inhabited lands, thou who were generated in the ocean, Psoi, God of gods, thou art he who shows his face each day, setting in the northwest, rising out of the southwest.

Yes, Lord Kmeph . . . [magic terms]. I entreat the earth and sky, the light and shadows, asking the great God who created everything, Sarousis, Great Genius, to assist me. Grant me full success in this endeavor with the ring and the stone.

A Prayer for the Secret of Immortality

Generation before my generation, first Beginning of my beginning, Breeze of the breeze, of the breeze that in me first blew, Fire that, out of the mixtures inside me, was struck by God to make me, of the fire that in me was the first fire, Water of the water, of the water that in me was the first water, Substance of earth, prototype of the substance inside me, Body of mine so perfect, modeled by a glorious hand and immortal arm in a lightless and luminous world, in an animate and inanimate world, if it is your wish to give me immortal birth, me who am yet tied to my natural condition, that I might, after the violent constriction of the imminent Fatality, contemplate the immortal principle, thanks to the immortal breath, to the immortal water, to the solid air, that I might be regenerated in spirit and the sacred wind, that I might admire the sacred fire, see the abyss in the east, the frightening waters, and have the life-giving ether, so be it—for I, born a mortal from a mortal mother, must now contemplate my exalted and omnipotent force, thanks to the immortal breeze which blew across me, thanks to immortal Ayion, sovereign with the fiery diadem, saintly sanctified by the saintly purification, thus taking from me a little of my psychic human nature, which I will re-take once more, in no way diminished, after the sad constriction of the imminent Fatality. So shall it be with me, ———, someone's son, in accordance with the immutable decree of God. For it is not possible for me, born a mortal, to elevate myself with the golden rays of inextinguishable clarity: be tranquil, O perishing nature of mortals and [re-take me] safe and sound after the cruel constriction of the harsh Fatality. For I am the Son.

A Prayer for the Secret of Immortality

Hear me, listen to my prayer, the prayer of ———, someone's son, O Lord, thou who with thy breath hast closed the fire-lock of the fourth zone, guardian of fire, Creator of light, God of the breeze of fire, God of the heart of fire, Spirit of light, whom fire loveth, splendor of light, Ayion, Sovereign of light, God with a body of fire, as strong as light, thou who dost stir the fire, who mixest the light, who dost brandish lightning bolts, glory of light, thou who causest light to grow, who keepest the light by fire, dominator of the astrals.

Open to me, for I invoke thee, because of the cruel and relentless Fatality so imminent, give me the names that human tongues have not yet uttered, that have not found their places in human nature, names, sounds, voices of mortals, names eternally living and glorious.

Benediction of the Divine Father

Holy is God the Father of all, who is before the first beginning;
holy is God, whose purpose is accomplished by his several Powers;
holy is God, who wills to be known, and is known by them that are his
    own.
    Holy art Thou, who by thy word hast constructed all that is;
holy art Thou, whose brightness nature has not darkened;
holy art Thou, of whom all nature is an image.
    Holy art Thou, who art stronger than all domination;
holy art Thou, who art greater than all pre-eminence;
holy art Thou, who surpassest all praises.
    Accept pure offerings of speech from a soul and heart uplifted to thee,
        Thou of whom no words can tell, no tongue can speak, whom
        silence only can declare.
    I pray that I may never fall away from that knowledge of thee which
        matches with our being; grant Thou this my prayer. And put power
        into me, that so, having obtained this boon, I may enlighten those
        of my race who are in ignorance, my brothers and thy sons.

Wherefore I believe and bear witness that I enter into Life and Light.
Blessed art thou, Father; thy Man seeks to share thy holiness, even as
    Thou hast given him all authority.

Secret Hymn

Let every bar of the universe be flung open to me;
    and let all nature receive the sound of my hymn.
Be thou opened, O Earth, and ye trees, wave not your boughs;
    I am about to sing the praise of Him who is both the All and the One.
Be ye opened, ye heavens, and ye winds, be still;
    let the immortal sphere of heaven receive my utterance.
For I am about to sing the praise of Him who created all things,
    who fixed the earth, and hung heaven above;
who made the sweet water flow from Ocean into the lands wherein men
    dwell,
    that it might serve for the sustenance of all mankind,
and gave command that fire should come forth,
    to be used by gods and men in all their works.
Let us all with one accord give praise to Him,
    who is seated high upon the heavens, creator of all that is.
It is He that is the eye of my mind;
    May He accept the praise sung by my Powers.
Ye Powers that are within me, praise ye the One and the All;
    sing ye in concord with my will, all ye Powers that are within me.
O holy Knowledge, by thee am I illumined,
    and through thee do I sing praise to the incorporeal Light.
. . . I rejoice in joy of mind;
    rejoice with me, all ye Powers.
        And do thou, O Continence, sing praise;
        (And thou, Endurance;)
        and thou, my Justice, praise the Just through me;
        thou, my Unselfishness, praise the All through me;
        O Truth, sing praise to Truth.
O Good that is in me, praise the Good;
    O Life and Light, from you comes the song of praise, and to you does
    it go forth.
I give thanks to thee, O Father, who workest in my Powers;
    I give thanks to thee, O God. . . .
Thus crying, the Powers that are in me accomplish thy will;
    praising the All, they fulfill thy purpose.

It is thy Word that through me sings thy praise;
   for by thee, O Mind, is my speech shepherded.
Through me accept from all an offering of speech;
   for the All is from thee, and to thee returns the All.
O Light, illumine thou the mind that is in us;
   O Life, keep my soul alive.
Thy man cries thus to thee by means of the things thou hast made;
   but he has got from thine eternity the praises which he utters.
I have seen that which I seek;
I have found rest according to thy purpose;
by thy will I am born again.

Notes

1. According to the legend, Zeus was taken by Rhea from his father Cronus and hidden away in a cave in Crete; at the entrance to the cave, Rhea's priests struck their swords against their shields in order that passers-by might not hear and detect the presence of the child.

2. Eating goat meat was a rite for the Maenads because they believed that by this means they communicated with god.

3. Niobe.

4. Reference to the power of spit and saliva.

5. According to the ritual there was a different itinerary for the initiated women and the uninitiated.

6. Demeter.

7. They were used for hanging the skins of the animals killed in the hunt.

8. Ermakes or Ermaia, stone walls limiting property, later replaced by stone columns.

9. This is a reference to the cycle of rebirth; the soul cannot liberate itself until it has shed the body.

10. This crown is the prize of virtue.

11. This line can be interpreted in a variety of ways. It might mean that the Orphic initiate, by uttering the words, intends to declare that he has returned to his divine origins, since the Milky Way is held to be the dwelling place of the gods. It might also refer to a ritual immersion in milk or some similar liquid, or a return to a life of innocence and purity, similar to the life of the infant Dionysius, who was transformed into a goat by Hera to save him from the anger of Zeus.

12. The expiatory ceremony is composed of a series of "stations" honoring various divinities in the Ivuginae hierarchy. The station honoring Jove Grabovin or Jove of the Oak, the formula of which we give, is the first of the entire ritual. It is designed to liberate the city from ominous consequences brought about by transgressions of ceremonies, and is held near the Trebulana Gate (the southeast gate). The sacrifice is made through the medium of three bulls—"profane" bulls, since they come from unblessed and nonsacred

herds. There are three victims and three parts to the prayer, if one excludes the dedication to the sacrifice. This perfection of numbers and the repeating of the invocations will repair any eventual ritual violation or omission, and the divinities will be committed to protect the city.

13. *Arce* (*okri-*) and city (*tota*) distinguish the sacred and the civil parts of the city-state.

＊

Christianity

CHRISTIANITY

Jesus Prays

I thank thee, O Father, Lord of heaven and earth, that thou hast hid these things from the wise and prudent, and hast revealed them unto babes: even so, Father; for so it seemed good in thy sight.

All things are delivered to me of my Father: and no man knoweth who the Son is, but the Father; and who the Father is, but the Son, and he to whom the Son will reveal him.

Jesus Prays: the Farewell Prayer

Father, the hour is come; glorify thy Son, that thy Son also may glorify thee:

As thou hast given him power over all flesh, that he should give eternal life to as many as thou hast given him.

And this is life eternal, that they might know thee, the only true God, and Jesus Christ, whom thou hast sent.

I have glorified thee on the earth: I have finished the work which thou gavest me to do.

And now, O Father, glorify thou me with thine own self, with the glory which I had with thee before the world was.

417

I have manifested thy name unto the men which thou gavest me out of the world: thine they were, and thou gavest them me; and they have kept thy word.

Now they have known that all things whatsoever thou hast given me are of thee.

For I have given unto them the words which thou gavest me; and they have received them, and have known surely that I came out from thee, and they have believed that thou didst send me.

I pray for them: I pray not for the world, but for them which thou hast given me; for they are thine.

And all mine are thine, and thine are mine; and I am glorified in them.

And now I am no more in the world, but these are in the world, and I come to thee. Holy Father, keep through thine own name those whom thou hast given me, that they may be one, as we are.

While I was with them in the world, I kept them in thy name: those that thou gavest me I have kept, and none of them is lost, but the son of perdition; that the scripture might be fulfilled.

And now come I to thee; and these things I speak in the world, that they might have my joy fulfilled in themselves.

I have given them thy word; and the world hath hated them, because they are not of the world, even as I am not of the world.

I pray not that thou shouldest take them out of the world, but that thou shouldest keep them from the evil.

They are not of the world, even as I am not of the world.

Sanctify them through thy truth: thy word is truth.

As thou hast sent me into the world, even so have I also sent them into the world.

And for their sakes I sanctify myself, that they also might be sanctified through the truth.

Neither pray I for these alone, but for them also which shall believe on me through their word;

That they all may be one; as thou, Father, art in me, and I in thee, that they also may be one in us: that the world may believe that thou hast sent me.

And the glory which thou gavest me I have given them; that they may be one, even as we are one;

I in them, and thou in me, that they may be made perfect in one; and that the world may know that thou hast sent me, and hast loved them, as thou hast loved me.

Father, I will that they also, whom thou hast given me, be with me where I am; that they may behold my glory, which thou hast given me: for thou lovedst me before the foundation of the world.

O righteous Father, the world hath not known thee: but I have known thee, and these have known that thou hast sent me.

And I have declared unto them thy name, and will declare it: that my love wherewith thou hast loved me may be in them, and I in them.

In Praise of Charity

Though I speak with the tongues of men and of angels, and have not charity, I am become as sounding brass, or a tinkling cymbal.

And though I have the gift of prophecy, and understand all mysteries, and all knowledge; and though I have all faith, so that I could remove mountains, and have not charity, I am nothing.

And though I bestow all my goods to feed the poor, and though I give my body to be burned, and have not charity, it profiteth me nothing.

Charity suffereth long, and is kind; charity envieth not; charity vaunteth not itself, is not puffed up,

Doth not behave itself unseemly, seeketh not her own, is not easily provoked, thinketh no evil;

Rejoiceth not in iniquity, but rejoiceth in the truth;

Beareth all things, believeth all things, hopeth all things, endureth all things.

Charity never faileth: but whether there be prophecies, they shall fail; whether there be tongues, they shall cease; whether there be knowledge, it shall vanish away.

For we know in part, and we prophesy in part.

But when that which is perfect is come, then that which is in part shall be done away.

When I was a child, I spake as a child, I understood as a child, I thought as a child: but when I became a man, I put away childish things.

For now we see through a glass, darkly; but then face to face: now I know in part; but then shall I know even as also I am known.

And now abideth faith, hope, charity, these three; but the greatest of these is charity.

The Magnificat

My soul doth magnify the Lord,
And my spirit hath rejoiced in God my Saviour.

For he hath regarded the low estate of his handmaiden: for, behold, from henceforth all generations shall call me blessed.

For he that is mighty hath done to me great things; and holy is his name.

And his mercy is on them that fear him from generation to generation.

He hath shewed strength with his arm; he hath scattered the proud in the imagination of their hearts.

He hath put down the mighty from their seats, and exalted them of low degree.

He hath filled the hungry with good things; and the rich he hath sent empty away.

He hath holpen his servant Israel, in remembrance of his mercy;

As he spake to our fathers, to Abraham, and to his seed for ever.

A Prayer of Saint Paul

Saint Paul prays that the Ephesians may receive the strength to withstand the many tribulations resulting from their confessing to the Christian faith.

For this cause I bow my knees unto the Father of our Lord Jesus Christ,

Of whom the whole family in heaven and earth is named,

That he would grant you, according to the riches of his glory, to be strengthened with might by his Spirit in the inner man;

That Christ may dwell in your hearts by faith; that ye, being rooted and grounded in love,

May be able to comprehend with all saints what is the breadth, and length, and depth, and height;

And to know the love of Christ, which passeth knowledge, that ye might be filled with all the fullness of God.

Now unto him that is able to do exceeding abundantly above all that we ask or think, according to the power that worketh in us,

Unto him be glory in the church by Christ Jesus throughout all ages, world without end.

Christian Amulet

This inscription appears on a bronze plaque found at Reggio Calabria.

In the name of the Father, the Son, and the Holy Ghost.
I am the bearer of the sacred Spirit.
I am cloaked in the garments of the only son.

I call curses down on every malign spirit.

Fly from this servant of the Saviour, O evil spirit of restlessness, oppressive weight, fount of pride, error and impurity.

Fly before the power of the body and blood of our Lord Jesus Christ.

Christian Amulet

This inscription is on a marble plaque of the second century, now in the Museum of Bucharest.

I invoke the wrath of all-powerful God, master of spirits and of every creature of flesh, against those who did secretly kill or poison unhappy Eraclea, unjustly spilling his innocent blood.

May the same end come to those who killed or poisoned, to them and to their offspring.

O Lord, you who see all things, and O ye angels of the Lord, know that every soul is humbly prostrate before you, imploring vengeance for this innocent blood. Be quick with vengeance.

Basilian Amulet

This is inscribed on a silver amulet, dating from the second or third century.

In the great and sacred name of the living God,
And in the names of Damnameneo, Adonai, Jao, Sabaoth,
I cast a curse down on all demons having the form of a serpent, and on all demons of fever, epilepsy, hydrophobia.

The Thanksgiving (Eucharist)

Now concerning the Thanksgiving [Eucharist], thus give thanks. First, concerning the cup: We thank thee, our Father, for the holy vine of David Thy servant, which Thou madest known to us through Jesus Thy Servant; to Thee be the glory for ever. And concerning the broken bread: We thank Thee, our Father, for the life and knowledge which Thou madest known to us through Jesus Thy Servant; to Thee be the glory for ever. Even as this broken bread was scattered over the hills, and was gathered together and became one, so let Thy Church be gathered together from the ends of the earth into Thy kingdom; for Thine is the glory and the power through Jesus Christ for ever. But let no one eat or drink of your Thanksgiving [Eucharist], but they who have been baptized into the name of the Lord; for concerning this also the Lord hath said, Give not that which is holy to the dogs.

Prayer After Communion

But after ye are filled, thus give thanks; We thank Thee, holy Father, for Thy holy name which Thou didst cause to tabernacle in our hearts, and for the knowledge and faith and immortality, which Thou madest known to us through Jesus Thy Servant; to Thee be the glory for ever. Thou, Master almighty, didst create all things for Thy name's sake; Thou gavest food and drink to men for enjoyment, that they might give thanks to Thee; but to us Thou didst freely give spiritual food and drink and life eternal through Thy servant. Before all things we thank Thee that Thou art mighty; to Thee be the glory for ever. Remember, Lord, Thy Church, to deliver it from all evil and to make it perfect in Thy love, and gather it from the four winds, sanctified for Thy kingdom which Thou hast prepared for it; for Thine is the power and the glory for ever. Let grace come, and let this world pass away. Hosanna to the God [Son] of David! If any one is holy, let him come; if any one is not so, let him repent. Maranatha. Amen. But permit the prophets to make Thanksgiving as much as they desire.

The Most Ancient Consecration

This prayer of liturgical consecration was taken from a document known as "First Ecclesiastical Regulation," or "The Egyptian Constitution."

In memory of the death and the resurrection, we offer thee the bread and the chalice, thanking thee for having considered us worthy of standing in thy presence and offering thee our service.

And we ask thee to send thy sacred Spirit to sustain thy sacred Church. Throughout the human fraternity, to all those who receive thee, grant an abundance of the sacred Spirit, that all might be confirmed in the truth, that they might praise gloriously in song the Son, for which may there be glory to the Father, to the Son and to the Holy Ghost, in thy sacred Church, now and forever more. So be it.

Invocation on Papyrus

Angels and archangels, ye who rule cataracts from the sky, who light the world entire,
since I am writhing in a struggle with a headless hound, dominate him, when he comes.

Free me through the power of the Father, the Son and the Holy Ghost.
So be it.
Mother of God, inviolate, immaculate, mother of Christ, remember these
     things I have told thee.
Once more cure him who wears this amulet.
So be it.

Morning Prayer

From a papyrus conserved in Berlin, probably containing an entire second-
century collection.

Benefactor of all who look to thee, light of those who dwell in darkness, creator of every seed, caretaker of every spiritual plant, have pity
on me, O my Lord, and make of me a spotless temple.

Judge me not according to my sins. For, if you weigh my faults, no
longer could I stand in your presence. Out of your immense compassion
and infinite mercy, cleanse me in the name of our Lord Jesus Christ, the
only Son, most sacred curer of our souls.

And through Him may you know every glory, power, honor, magnificence, in the ages of the ages that never die, that never grow old.
Amen.

Benediction of the First Fruits

We thank thee, O God, and offer thee the first fruits which thou hast
given us. Thou produced them by means of thy word, commanding the
earth to bring forth every kind of fruit for the joy and nutriment of all
men and beasts.

We praise thee, O Lord, for thy gifts, for giving us the entire creation
of many fruits through thy Son, Jesus Christ, our Saviour.

Through Him shalt thou be held glorious for endless centuries. Amen!

A Prayer in Praise of God's Various Creation

Thou art blessed, O Lord, the King of ages, who by Christ hast made
the whole world, and by Him in the beginning didst reduce into order
the disordered parts; who dividedst the waters from the waters by a
firmament, and didst put into them a spirit of life; who didst fix the
earth, and stretch out the heaven, and didst dispose every creature by
an accurate constitution. For by Thy power, O Lord, the world is
beautified, the heaven is fixed as an arch over us, and is rendered illustrious with stars for our comfort in the darkness. The light also and

the sun were begotten for days and the production of fruit, and the moon for the change of seasons, by its increase and diminutions; and one was called Night, and the other Day. And the firmament was exhibited in the midst of the abyss, and Thou commandest the waters to be gathered together, and the dry land to appear. But as for the sea itself, who can possibly describe it, which comes with fury from the ocean, yet runs back again, being stopped by the sand at Thy command? For Thou hast said: "Thereby shall her waves be broken." Thou hast also made it capable of supporting little and great creatures, and made it navigable for ships. Then did the earth become green, and was planted with all sorts of flowers, and the variety of several trees; and the shining luminaries, the nourishers of those plants, preserve their unchangeable course, and in nothing depart from Thy command. But where Thou biddest them, there do they rise and set for signs of the seasons and of the years, making a constant return of the work of men. Afterward the kinds of the several animals were created—those belonging to the land, to the water, to the air, and both to air and water; and the artificial wisdom of Thy providence does still impart to every one a suitable providence. For as He was not unable to produce different kinds, so neither has He disdained to exercise a different providence toward every one. And at the conclusion of the creation Thou gavest direction to Thy Wisdom, and formedst a reasonable creature as the citizen of the world, saying, "Let us make man after our image, and after our likeness"; and hast exhibited him as the ornament of the world, and formed him a body out of the four elements, those primary bodies, but hadst prepared a soul out of nothing, and bestowdest upon him his five senses, and didst set over his sensations a mind as the conductor of the soul. And besides all these things, O Lord God, who can worthily declare the motion of the rainy clouds, the shining of the lightning, the noise of the thunder, in order to the supply of proper food, and the most agreeable temperature of the air? But when man was disobedient, Thou didst deprive him of the life which should have been his reward. Yet didst Thou not destroy him for ever, but laidst him to sleep for a time; and Thou didst by oath call him to a resurrection, and loosedst the bond of death, O Thou reviver of the dead, through Jesus Christ, who is our hope.

A Christian's Prayer

Make haste to protect me against the sharp claws of the dog and the
    horn of the unicorn.

In the presence of my brothers, in the midst of the assembly, I will sing
  to thee, my God.
Aided by thy martyrs Sabbatios, Propatios, and Kyriakos, care for thy
  servant, O God of goodness.
Free her soul from all forms of weakness.
Yes, in the name of the Lord and the living God is to be found salvation.

Spirit of Receiving Jesus

Let us prepare and cleanse our hearts, that our Lord Jesus may enter
joyously into our hearts and ask hospitality there.

To Him all glory and power during centuries of centuries! Amen.

For the Soul's Repose

Let us pray that the spirit of Jesus reign in us, that our lands be
freed from war, that we be no more assailed by lusts of the flesh. And
then that each may repose in the shade of his vineyard, his fig and olive
trees.

Under the wings of the Father, the Son, and the Holy Ghost, reposes
the soul that has gained peace of the spirit and the flesh.

All glory to God throughout centuries of centuries! Amen.

Christian Reawakening

Originally a night prayer.

The hushed breath of day sings of coming light. Already, the Christ
who reawakens minds invites us to the work of life.

He cries to us: Arise, O negligent ones, from the lethargy of your beds!
With chaste feelings and sobriety, awake! For I am near.
Let us, in supplicating voices and in honest prayer, invoke Jesus.
It is not meet for a pure heart, meant for prayer, to lie abed.
O Christ, shake us from our beds, break the ties of night, wipe out the
ancient sin and bring us new light!

Hymn in Adoration of the Holy Cross
BY VENANZIO FORTUNATO

The ensign of the King advances, splendid shines the mystery of the
  Cross, where the creator of all flesh, becoming Himself flesh, was
  suspended from the scaffold.

Bones split by nails, hands riven, marks of redemption, here Grace was the victim.

Here as well, where the cruel lance pierced, outflowed blood and water to cleanse us of our sins.

Here was fulfilled the prophecy of David, the one he announced in the psalm, when he foretold the people:

Out of wood God reigneth.

O venerated and splendid tree, ornate with the King's crimson blood, chosen out of the most noble trunks to touch the sacred limbs, in the midst of whose limbs didst hang suspended the world's salvation; there the divine body hung, robbing the Tartar of his prey; from thy bark comes a perfume sweeter than the sweetest nectar, thy limbs yield fertile fruit, signs of the noble triumph.

Hail, O altar, hail, O victim, hail to the glory of the passion, thanks to which Life escaped from death and, through death, brought back life.

Hail, O Cross, the only hope! Instil mercy in the faithful during this period of Passion, and forgive the kings their iniquities.

Every spirit praises thee, O Trinity, fount of health.

Reward them to whom thou givest the victory of the Cross.

Hail! Star of the Sea!

It is not certain who the author of this prayer was; some believe him to be Saint Bernard, others, Venanzio Fortunato.

Hail, star of the sea, mother of God, shining virgin, bright door of Heaven!

Hearkening to that cry from the lips of Gabriel, assure us peace, altering the name of Eve.

Loosen the kings from their chains, bring light to the blind, keep us from sickness, bring us good things.

Show us thou art truly the Mother. By thy intercession cause Him who was born for us to receive our prayers.

O unique virgin, more than all else, after having freed us from sin, make us chaste and sweet.

Give us a pure life, prepare for us the Way, that we may live always with the eternal vision of Jesus before us.

Praise to the Father, glory to the high Christ and to the Holy Spirit.

To the three let there be equal honor.

Festival of Saintly Innocents

God keep you, O finest flowers of martyrs, who, at the dawn of life, were crushed by the persecutor of Christ and flung like petals before a furious wind.

You, the first to die for Christ, tender flocks of martyrs, now dance before the altar, now laugh candidly with your palms and garlands.

Epistle of Ignatius of Antioch to the Romans
ALLOW ME TO FALL A PREY TO THE WILD BEASTS

I write to the Churches, and impress on them all, that I shall willingly die for God, unless ye hinder me. I beseech of you not to show an unreasonable good will toward me. Suffer me to become food for the wild beasts, through whose instrumentality it will be granted me to attain to God. I am the wheat of God, and let me be ground by the teeth of the wild beasts, that I may be found the pure bread of Christ. Rather entice the wild beasts, that they may become my tomb, and may leave nothing of my body; so that when I have fallen asleep [in death], I may be no trouble to any one. Then shall I truly be a disciple of Christ, when the world shall not see so much as my body. Entreat Christ for me, that by these instruments I may be found a sacrifice [to God]. I do not, as Peter and Paul, issue commandments unto you. They were apostles; I am but a condemned man: they were free, while I am, even until now, a servant. But when I suffer, I shall be the freedman of Jesus, and shall rise again, emancipated in Him. And now, being a prisoner, I learn not to desire anything worldly or vain.

Gnostic Canticle of Christ

Glory to thee, O Father!
(and turning we replied:) Amen!
Glory to thee, O Word; glory to thee, O Grace. Amen.
Glory to thee, Holy Spirit; glory to thy glory. Amen.
We praise thee, O Father, we thank thee, O light undimmed by any
    darkness. Amen.
(While we give thanks, he speaks:)
I wish to save and be saved. Amen.
I wish to unbind and be unbound. Amen.
I wish to crumble and be crumbled. Amen.

I wish to birth and be born. Amen.

I wish to eat and be eaten. Amen.

I wish to hear and be heard. Amen.

I wish to be understood, understanding all. Amen.

I wish to cleanse and be cleansed. Amen.

Grace dances, I wish to dance; dance all of you. Amen.

I wish to utter lamentation; strike your breasts, all. Amen.

An octet sings with you. Amen.

And all who can dance, dance. Amen.

The number twelve dances on high. Amen.

And all who can dance, dance. Amen.

Who fails to dance is blind to the imminent event. Amen.

I wish to escape and I wish to stay. Amen.

I wish to adore and be adored. Amen.

I wish to unite and be united. Amen.

No houses have I, and houses I have. Amen.

No chairs have I, and chairs I have. Amen.

No temples have I, and temples I have. Amen.

I belong to the lamp that shines on me. Amen.

I belong to the mirror that understands me. Amen.

I belong to the door that closes. Amen.

I belong to the street of the vagabond.

Reply to my dance.

Find thyself in my words, watch my actions, seal in silence my mysteries,

O dancer, understand my work: this passion of humanity

I must affront is thine.

Never could'st thou have understood remotely what I suffer, had I not
    been sent to thee as the Word of the Father.

Thou who hast seen how I suffer, what I suffer, and at the sight remained
    not unmoved, but was deeply moved, moved to know.

Thou hast me as a bed: repose upon me.

Who am I? Thou shalt know when I have gone.

What I now appear to be, I am not: what I really am, thou shalt later see.

Had thou known suffering, thy capacity for suffering would have been
    decreased.

Know suffering and thou shalt be able not to suffer.

What thou doest not, I shall teach thee.

I am thy God, not a betrayed one.

I wish to vibrate rhythmically with all the force of my soul.

In me is to be found the word of knowledge.

Again be with me: Glory to thee, O Father; glory to thee,

O Word; glory to thee, O Holy Spirit.

And now, regarding me, if thou would'st know who I am, I speak.

In a word: one time I instilled everything with the spirit of a child, and was never ashamed.

I leaped: now all is known; and knowing all, say: Glory to thee, O Father. Amen.

Gnostic Prayer from the Acts of Thomas

O Jesus Christ, most merciful thought; O peace and solitude, now speaking also to unreasoning animals; O restoring mystery that reveals itself through miracles, our Saviour and provider, who cares for us and restores us also [while we are] in strange bodies; Saviour of our soul; sweet and perpetual fount of goodness, never disturbed; who aids His servants in their battles, drives out the enemy and keeps him far, who has struggled mightily and many battles won for us, who wins over all; our true and insuperable athlete; our sacred leader and gainer of victories; glorious and uncorrupted joy that knows no tribulations; good shepherd who gave thyself for thy flock, who kept the wolf away and watched after thy sheep, bringing them to the flowery pastures: we glorify thee and lift our voices in a hymn to thy invisible Father, to thy Holy Spirit [which is also] the mother of all things.

A Chinese Manichean Hymn to Christ

The following strophes were found in the caves of Tungshan. Here the followers of Manes direct their words to Jesus.

I am, O Great Saint, a lamb of the Light; tears I wept;

I suffered, wept, and trembled for the oppression, and was finally assailed by the wolf and all the other fierce quadrupeds, who bound me and carried me far from the good family of the Light.

I am, O Great Saint, a perfumed seed of the Light, hurled by the wind into a thick forest of thorns: Be merciful; gather me in and bring me under the shelter of the law, deposit me in the Light.

And I am, O Great Saint, a vine, once planted in a pure vineyard, in the garden of the law, of righteousness, but was later choked by the ugly growth, which stripped my strength from me and left me to waste and wither.

And I am, O Great Saint, a rich and fertile soil in which the Demon planted five poisonous trees. I pray thee, seize thy spear, thy sharpened blade, the sickle of law, and strike down the poison plants. Give me purity.

I am, O Great Saint, a new and marvelous garment that was rendered slimy and filthy by the demons. I pray thee, wash me in the waters of the law and cleanse me afresh, that I may have a pure and joyous body and limbs.

Thou art, O Great Saint, the eternal life, the ever-living tree that gives life, wisdom, inspiration—the pure eternal tree, vigilant. Yes, thou art the king of wisdom and can distinguish all. With powerful desire and rectitude, I invoke the omniscient King of Law, Christ Jesus, to bring peace to this carnal body and render it spotlessly pure.

A Hymn to Christ the Saviour
COMPOSED BY SAINT CLEMENT

I

Bridle of colts untamed,
  Over our wills presiding;
Wing of unwandering birds,
  Our flight securely guiding.
Rudder of youth unbending,
  Firm against adverse shock;
Shepherd, with wisdom tending
  Lambs of the royal flock:
Thy simple children bring
In one, that they may sing
In solemn lays
Their hymns of praise
With guileless lips to Christ their King.

II

King of saints, almighty Word
Of the Father highest Lord;
Wisdom's head and chief;
Assuagement of all grief;
Lord of all time and space,
Jesus, Saviour of our race;
Shepherd, who dost us keep;
  Husbandman, who tillest,
Bit to restrain us, Rudder
  To guide us as Thou willest;

Of the all-holy flock celestial wing;
Fisher of men, whom Thou to life dost bring;
From evil sea of sin,
And from the billowy strife,
Gathering pure fishes in,
Caught with sweet bait of life:
Lead us, Shepherd of the sheep,
Reason-gifted, holy One;
King of youths, whom Thou dost keep,
So that they pollution shun:
Steps of Christ, celestial Way;
Word eternal, Age unending;
Life that never can decay;
Fount of mercy, virtue-sending;
Life august of those who raise
Unto God their hymn of praise,
Jesus Christ!

III

Nourished by the milk of heaven,
To our tender palates given;
Milk of wisdom from the breast
Of that bride of grace exprest;
By a dewy spirit filled
From fair Reason's breast distilled;
Let us sucklings join to raise
With pure lips our hymns of praise
As our grateful offering,
Clean and pure, to Christ our King.
Let us, with hearts undefiled,
Celebrate the mighty Child.
We, Christ-born, the choir of peace;
We, the people of His love,
Let us sing, nor ever cease,
To the God of peace above.

Inscription of Pectorius of Autun

Epitaph found in 1839 at Autun.

O divine race of the celestial Ichthys, accept, with heart-filled respect, immortal life in the midst of mortals.

Let thy soul grow younger, dear friend, in the divine waters of eternal wisdom.

Accept the sweet nourishment like honey from the Saviour of saints.

Eat as thou wishest, drink as thou wishest, for thou hast the Ichthys in the palm of thy hand. Find nutriment, therefore, through the master and Saviour, in the Ichthys. I pray that my mother may rest in peace, O Light of the dead. O Aschandius, father mine, in the name of my sweet mother and my brothers, with all the gratitude my heart is capable of, I pray thee: In the peace of the Ichthys, do not forget Pectorius.

Laymen's Benediction

May the hand of life and purity, may the hand of the only Son, the hand that relieves every illness, that brings sanctity and protection, may this hand rest on the inclined heads of this people.

May on this people fall the benediction of the Spirit, the benediction of Heaven, of the prophets and apostles. May bodies be kept pure and chaste, may souls be kept always aware of the mystery.

May all of us be blessed through the Son, Jesus Christ, and through Him may the Sacred Spirit be rendered glorious now and throughout all the coming centuries. Amen.

The Glory Hymn of the Codex Alexandrinus

Glory to God on high! Peace on earth! Good will to men!

We praise thee, bless thee, adore thee, glorify thee, thank thee, for thy great glory, O Lord, celestial king, omnipotent God, Saviour, only Son, Jesus Christ and the Holy Spirit!

O God the master, lamb of God, Son of the Father, thou who cleansest the sins of the world, have mercy on us. Hear our prayer. Thou, who sittest to the right of the Father, have mercy on us!

Yes, for thou alone art holy, thou alone art the Master, Jesus Christ, to the glory of God, the Father. Amen.

The Universal Prayer of Cyprian of Carthage

Let us supplicate the Lord with an open heart and in common accord; let us implore Him with trembling and with tears, as is befitting for creatures stricken with heavy hearts and sadness; let us lacerate our breasts, the faithful among other faithful who in their turn fear to fall, in the midst of a great throng of wounded and in the midst of a small group standing yet on their feet.

Let us ask that peace be brought quickly, that aid arrive to help us in this hour of darkness, that the desired manifestation be brought about, which is: the restoration of the Church of God, our souls' nutriment. After darkness comes the light, after the storm comes serenity.

Let us ask for paternal solicitude, that the prodigious works of His are carried out, that the curses and vileness of His persecutors be thrown to the winds, that those who have strayed be returned, and that those who have kept the faith be crowned in glory.

To Mine Own Soul

GREGORIO NAZIANZENO; POEMS ABOUT HIMSELF.

Now it is time, truly it is time, O my soul, to know thyself and thy destiny; from whence comest thou and wherefore would'st thou repose; if this which we live is truly life or if we may expect something better. Look to thyself, O my soul! Thou must purify thy life. Seek God and His mysteries, seek to know what there was prior to the world, what the world means to thee, from whence thou comest and what thy destiny may be.

Look to thyself, O my soul! Thou must purify thy life.

How does God guide and govern the universe? Why is there movement here, and none there? We are dragged along relentlessly on the current of life. Look to thyself, O my soul! Look only to God!

That which was once my pride is now my shame. What is my purpose with life? What is the end? Illumine my spirit, dissipate every error.

Look to thyself, O my soul! Yield not to fatigue!

A Prayer of Simeon Bar Sabbae, Persian Martyr

Simeon Bar Sabbae was Bishop of Seleucid, Persia. He and some companions were put to death during the persecutions of Sapor II, between 339 and 340.

O my Lord, press down on me the crown. Thou knowest well how much I do desire it, for I love thee with all my heart and soul. I shall be glad to come face to face with thee, for thou wilt give me rest. As things stand now, I shall live no longer on this earth, nor have to watch the sufferings of my people, see the churches devastated, the altars wrecked, the clergy sorely tried, the weak contaminated, the pusillanimous driven far from the truth, nor see my people, once so numerous, wiped out by bloody persecutions.

I shall no longer be forced to watch my friends become my enemies and assassins, nor watch old and trusted friends become disloyal in the face of slaughters by the proud ones against our people.

However it may be, I wish to bear heroic witness to the way of righteousness, to persevere in my vocation and courageously carry out my work so as to be an example to all the people of the Orient.

I have eaten at the head of the table, and now I wish to die at the head of my brothers, and mix my blood with theirs. With them I wish to come to know the life that holds neither suffering nor pain, that knows not tyranny or victims. In that life I shan't be flayed by the threats of kings or the terrors of prefectures. Nor will anyone be able to drag me before the tribunal or make me tremble out of fear. In thee shall I correct the errors of my past, O life of truth, in thee my weary limbs will find repose, O Christ, sacred oil of our unction. In thee all my sad soul-hurts vanish, for thou art truly the cup of my salvation. Thou shalt dry these tears from my eyes, O consolation and joy!

Hymn

> Hail to thee who carried in thy womb
> the guide for all the erring;
> Hail to thee who begot
> the liberator of servants;
> Hail to thee who begot the just Judge;
> Hail, pardon for those who denied and repented;
> Hail, refuge for lost ones;
> Hail, love above every desire;
> Hail, spotless bride!
> In gazing upon the unearthly birth,
> we become strangers to the world
> and must turn our thoughts to Heaven.
> For this did the most high One
> appear on earth as a poor child,
> desiring to carry on high with him
> all who would proclaim:
> Hallelujah!
> One he was with terrestrial creatures
> and at the same time with the heavens,
> the incircumscribable Word.
> The divine descent
> brought no change of place;
> the Son was born of the Virgin,

who, having taken God to her, heard it said thusly:
Hail, place of infinite God,
hail, door of the august mystery;
hail, unheeded warning to the unfaithful,
hail, fount of unfailing strength for the faithful,
hail, sacred vehicle of who watches over Cherubim;
hail, perfect dwelling of who watches over Seraphim;
hail, for virginity and maternity conjoined;
hail, for absolving all the sin of Adam;
hail, for having reopened the doors of Paradise;
hail, key to the realm of Christ;
hail, hope of eternal goodness
hail, spotless Bride!
All the bands of all the angels
were touched by the greatness of the work
of thine incarnation.
The inaccessible God
was seen by men in the midst of us,
and from each one came the cry:
Hallelujah!
Superb rhetoricians
stand like mute fish
before thee, O mother of God.
Incapable are they of explaining: "How
could you remain a virgin, and yet have given birth?"
While we, instead, are content to admire the mystery
and proclaim with faith:
Hail, dwelling of God's wisdom,
hail, treasure of Providence;
hail, revealer of the ignorance of the wise;
hail, revealer of mute tongues to the eloquent;
hail, that subtle reasoners went mad;
hail, for the myths of olden times that paled;
hail, for having shattered the sophistry of pagans;
hail, for filling the fishermen's nets with fish;
hail, for lifting ignorance up out of the abyss;
hail, for causing truth to shine so splendidly;
hail, bark of salvation for who wishes to be saved;
hail, harbor of this life;
hail, spotless Bride!
Wishing to save the world,

the Creator of every thing
came of his own will.
God, our shepherd,
appeared among us as a man.
Having thus called like unto like,
God proclaimed:
Hallelujah!
As a virgin art thou defended,
Virgin Mother,
and all who believe in thee.
The Creator of earth and heaven
made it so, immaculate,
that thy womb might teach
the world to sing:
Hail, column of virginity;
hail, door of salvation;
hail, initiator of rational fullness;
hail, fount of goodness;
hail, for giving new life to those born in error;
hail, for setting right the minds of those deprived of reason;
hail, for curing the minds of those who would pervert;
hail, for preserving chastity;
hail, for the pure bridal bed;
hail, bearer of good tidings for believers in the Lord;
hail, teacher of virgins;
hail, for adorning sacred souls for mystic marriages;
hail, spotless Bride!
Every song that attempts to match
the beauty of thy infinite mercy
is destined to fade.
If we should chant hymns to the number
that there are grains of sand on earth,
still would we not, O sacred King,
reflect the dignity thou hast showered
down on us; and we acclaim:
Hallelujah!

In the Nativity of the Lord

This is the *Inno in Nativitate Domini* by Sedulio.

From the rim of the Orient to the limits of the earth, let us sing of the
excellence of Christ, born of the Virgin Mary!

Beatified author of all things, whose wish it was to recloak the garments of a servile body, so that, by means of the flesh, flesh could be freed, and those to whom life had been given could be saved from perdition. Celestial grace visited the breast of the Virgin Mary. The womb carried mysteries unknown to her.

Of a sudden her body became the temple of the Lord. A virgin untouched by man gave birth to a Son.

The maid gave birth to Him whom Gabriel had announced, and of whom John had heard.

It was His lot to lie in a manger on a bed of straw. He who provides food even for the birds, had but little milk to drink. Celestial choirs and angels of God lifted their voices in song. To the shepherds a star announced the shepherd of every living thing.

At Compline

The following is attributed to Saint Ambrose.

We pray thee, O Creator of every thing, at this hour preceding night, that thou be clement and watch over us.

Let dreams and phantoms of the night be scattered. Keep us safe from our enemies and make us pure!

The Canticle of the Harlot

Accept me also, O Christ, you who once called another harlot "daughter": I beg you to lift me up out of the mud into which my actions have carried me.

That other harlot, weeping in your footsteps, and with a mortified soul, also cried out to you, to you who see all things:

O Christ, O my God, how can I look you in the eyes, I whose eyes have deceived everyone? How can I, who have brought down the wrath of God, ask comfort from you? Still, do me the favor of accepting this oil in expiation, and forgive me my impurities, that I might rise from the mud!

This woman who until yesterday had been a prostitute, when she caught the sweet aroma of your goodness that hangs over every thing, was horrified at her fallen condition and at the eternal suffering toward which she was hourly plunging: for the torments of Hell, for fornicators, are limitless and terrifying.

I am one of those who voluntarily **was** slipping steadily toward such torments.

That other harlot, once aware of these things, was no more a harlot. I, instead, though terrified, have remained in the slime of my actions.

To the Relic of the "Zone" of the Blessed Virgin

The author of this hymn is unknown. The relic seems to have been pre-served at Constantinople (as a matter of fact, some of the hymns in its praise are attributed to Saint Giuseppe Scevofilacio, custodian of relics in the patriarchal Basilica of Constantinople). The inhabitants believed that it protected the city. The relic was undoubtedly a belt or girdle, which is the meaning of the Greek word *zone*.

Thy venerated zone that belted the womb which God visited, O Divine One, is for thy invincible city a safeguard and a treasure.

Who, of all the countless mortals on this earth, hath tongue that can sing thy praises? Not even a celestial tongue could do it properly.

O Divine One, who birthed a vast ocean of celemency, let these lips attempt to sing thy praises; grant me the privilege of celebrating in song the virginal belt that circumscribed the universe; let me sing together with the angels of thy miracles, O My Lady, to thee who alone gave birth and preserved thy virginity.

Thy deed surpassed the imagination of man: unusual gestation, stu-pendous birth!

Thy zone, giver of life, with thy invisible power, struck down all other forces. And thou, O chaste one, along with thy garments, decided to enrich the city by bequeathing it thy treasures.

Thy zone and thy garments encircle us like a belt, causing salvation to shower down upon us. . . . O Mother ever Virgin!

Send us who praise thee waters of salvation and trophies from thy tomb.

Thou didst in olden times know beforehand of prodigies that would startle and frighten the enemies of God.

Therefore, we now ask thee to keep us encircled by thy belt, to give us strength and courage against our enemies, O Mother of the Virgin Birth.

To Saint Mary of Egypt

When thou didst issue forth from the shadows of sin and saw before thee the face of penitence, O glorious, out of love didst thou offer thy heart to Christ, His Mother interceding for thee.

In this manner didst thou obtain the pardon of thy sins and now dwellest with the angels. Thou, O wise Mary, by using the Cross, didst precipitate into the abyss the serpent of deceit which perpetrated the original sin. Thou didst choose chasteness, putting aside the carnal pleasures, and for this didst enter into the Saviour's bed, along with the Virgins, and there didst know honest delights.

Invoke Him, therefore, for my sake, that I might be pardoned of my sins and feel myself worthy of dwelling eternally with the angels.

O free me from these passions, from evil, thou who hast gained the divine state, mediator of men, of angels, of prophets and apostles and martyrs.

Let me lift my voice to sing of the day of thy mortal sleep, when those who, in veneration, saw thy body and laid it in the earth with great piety, as if life still dwelt in thee.

When still marked by the harlot's sins, thou were forced to hide thyself and flee from the Divine Presence.

But thou didst turn to the fount of all goodness, to the most piteous Mary, the spotless Lady, imploring her to free thee from horrors and errors; and she admitted thee to the presence of the Divine Wood on which the Word born of Her, arms outflung, gathered in the women. And since that time hast thou always dwelt in the company of the angels.

MOZARABIC LITURGY

Hymn of Praise

The Mozarabic liturgy consolidated itself in Spain after 711, the date of the Arab conquest. Up until the eleventh century all attempts to replace it by the Roman liturgy were unsuccessful. The name Mozarabians (in Spanish, *mozarabes,* in Arabic, *Musta 'ribah*) means "Arabianized," and was used to designate those Spanish Christians who embraced certain Arabic cultural forms during the period of the domination. Also, the liturgies were influenced by Mozarabian canticles, in which can be heard Oriental overtones.

> Thou Brightness of the Father's ray,
> True Light of light and Day of day:
> Light's fountain and eternal spring:
> Thou morn, the morn illumining!
>
> Glide in, thou very sun divine;
> With everlasting brightness shine:

And shed abroad on every sense
The Spirit's light and influence.

Thee, Father, let us seek aright—
The Father of perpetual light,
The Father of almighty grace—
Each wile of sin away to chase.

And Christ our daily food be nigh
And Faith our daily cup supply:
So may we quaff to calm and bless,
The Spirit's rapturous holiness.

All honor, laud, and glory be
O Jesu, Virgin-born, to thee:
All glory, as is ever meet,
To Father and to Paraclete. Amen.

Compline Hymn

In hymns of praise let us pass the first hours of the night. Now we ask thee, O Divinity, to listen to our hymn.

Grant forgiveness to all, lessen our fatigue, cleanse us of our sins and keep us far from shameful acts.

Let the true light illumine us, banishing all darkness from the soul, so that peace may abound and that each one believe, O Creator, in thee.

Compline Hymn

This hymn was used to mark the end of the Lenten period.

O gentle creator of light, thou who art also an immense light, a light in which the saintly and eternal Christ shines splendidly, and with him shines the Holy Spirit.

Banish the mists of this dark night. Keep the deceit of the serpent far from us, help us to arm ourselves with the Cross and fortify us in thy sacred name.

The malign one who, through the innumerable guises of his deceit, thrust creatures into a sinful state, and now enjoys the sight, and proclaims himself victorious, knows very well that he is conquered by the vast power of the Omnipotent.

Immortal father, shepherd of all creatures, strike down the dark adversary, and give us the light of thy sanctity, that we shan't know fear along the way.

O redeemer, king of all the earth, listen to the trembling cries of thy flock, strike down the insidious adversary, that we might participate in the beauties of the eternal life. . . . O Saviour.

Cause this night to pass peacefully for us, and keep the ugly enemy far; the sign of the Cross is ever victorious. O Christ, be with us!

All glory and honor, power and virtue to God, to His Son, Christ, to the Holy Spirit, the Word of which lights all the ages.

Hymn (Vespers)

O God the Father, holy one,
O Lamb of God, the Virgin's Son,
Engendered not of mortal wight,
Wellspring of life and prince of light.

Be thou our Saviour, Lord benign,
The only Son of God divine,
Christ Jesu, pilot of our barque,
And to our cry for succor hark.

Thou cam'st to earth to help thy folk,
To ease the captive of his yoke,
The fettered tongue-string to unbind,
To eyesight to restore the blind.

Ah! leave us not as orphans here,
Kind maker of the world give ear,
Spare us, good Lord, at any cost,
Who will'st that ne'er a soul be lost.

Artificer of moon and sun,
O Saviour, sole-begotten one,
Protect us from a death of woe,
Redeem us from our bitter foe.

May Christ our Master vigil keep,
And we in faith grow rooted deep,
Let Satan's armies melt as snow,
Unable to surprise his foe.

Through Jesus Christ may this be done,
Who reigneth with the Father One,

And deigned to teach mankind in brief
The holy Catholic belief.

Sing we in chorus "Glory be
To God the blessed Trinity,
To Father, Son, and Spirit, one
Or ever time and tide begun." Amen.

Hymn (Matins)

Maker of all, eternal King,
Who day and night about dost bring;
Who weary mortals to relieve
Dost in their time the seasons give.

Now chanticleer proclaims the day,
And calls the sun's awakening ray—
The wandering pilgrim's guiding light,
That marks the watches night by night.

Roused at the note, the morning star
Heaven's dusky veil uplifts afar;
Night's vagrant bands no longer roam,
But from their dark ways hie them home.

The encouraged sailor's fears are o'er,
The foaming billows rage no more;
Lo! e'en the very Church's Rock
Melts at the crowing of the cock.

Oh, let us then like men arise;
The cock rebukes our slumbering eyes,
Bestirs who still in sleep would lie,
And shames who would their Lord deny.

New hope his clarion-note awakes,
Sickness, the feeble frame forsakes,
The robber sheathes his lawless sword,
Faith to the fallen is restored.

Look on us, Jesu, when we fall,
And with that look our souls recall;
If thou but look our sins are gone,
And with due tears our pardon won.

Shed through our hearts thy piercing ray,
Our soul's dull slumber drive away;
Thy name be first on every tongue,
To thee our earliest praises sung.

All honor, laud and glory be
O Jesu, Virgin-born, to thee;
All glory, as is ever meet,
To Father and to Paraclete. Amen.

Midnight Hymn

In the silence of this obscure night we stand before thee, O Lord, continuing reverently and with vigilance the traditions given down to us by our fathers. By this vigil, we serve thee, O Paraclete.

In splendor thou art the peer of the Father, in subtlety the peer of Christ; in many guises art thou recognized, O Spirit, as the mystic King.

Turn thine eyes upon him who in the flesh is weak, and gather in those whom the ancient deceiver tricked with his black arts. Let not this flock be tainted with sin, for this is the flock thou didst, O Christ, redeem with thy blood.

Gather in the wandering sheep, O most pious shepherd, and in thine arms carry them to the Father.

The prince of Demons, wounded and wasted, angry and hungry, lets the prey drop from his jaws while slinking away.

Exult Christ the Lord; let choirs of angels dance and sing; let organs play; and three times let Him be proclaimed the Lord.

A Hymn for Rain

Under the dust, in arid squalor, lie the withered fields, the earth yellowing, dry, the soil crumbling, every attraction of nature now dead beneath the sun, no graceful greens of flowers to be seen on the land. A thirsty earth seeks rain: the fountain is dry, the rivers run no more, and the baked surface cracks by the minute.

Heat withers the countryside, fires the land, the odor of smoke clings even to the birds, nor do trees have leaves to cast a cooling shadow, while the mouth of the pilgrim is dry with dusty spittle.

Animals close their mouths to the wind, thinking to relieve their thirst, but in vain. Men close their mouths to the parched wind and hold their breaths; even the birds open not their beaks.

The fawn, driven mad by thirst, refuses her young ones; sorrowfully the mother abandons her loved ones, for she finds no grass to feed on.

Youths come to the well to draw water in vases, but since not a drop is there, they return home sadly, drinking their tears.

The ox lumbers out of the stall and goes about the fields seeking a tuft of grass. And in this manner herds die for want of pasture. The curved peasant goes bitterly to the woods, hoping to gather roots to feed upon; but the earth yields him no tender shoots of any kind.

Perhaps our sins brought on this famine, but, Dear Christ, forgive us our sins in a manner as grand as they originally were grand.

We implore thee, open up the sky and cause the rain to fall. Grant us the rain as in olden times it was granted.

O eternal Father, may thou be ever powerful and glorious; glory to thee, to Christ thy Son and the Holy Spirit.

Tonsure Ceremony

When one comes forth to have his beard blessed, after Mass has been said according to the ritual, and before the absolution is pronounced, the one to be blessed proceeds to the door where the priest waits. Taking some wax from the blessed wax, and putting a few particles on the right and the left and the center, the priest says:

In the name of the Father, the Son and the Holy Spirit.

The antiphon is recited: As the ointment descended from the head to the beard, from the head to the beard of Aaron, send this person, O Lord, blessings and life perpetual.

Verse: Here is what is good.

After reciting the Glory, the beginning of the antiphony is again recited. Then this oration follows:

As the ointment descended from the head to the beard, to the beard of Aaron, we ask thee, O Lord, to cause to descend down upon this thy servant the blessing of thy Majesty, so that he may come hither to bear witness to thy mercy and thy glory, so that he, O Lord, blessed with the Sacred Spirit, may feel himself armed in the faith of celestial grace. So be it.

O cleanser of souls, O God, who so loves equity and to whom sincerity is always welcome, amplify this servant's heart with purity and sanctity.

May he remain illumined by thy light and bedewed by thy ointment, absolved from every fault, that he may be found worthy of dwelling in the glorious light of thy Majesty, and may his heart be governed and possessed by the Holy Spirit throughout all the ages.

Benediction: O Christ our Lord, leader of all men who believe in thee, cause the ointment to descend from the head to the beard of thy servant with grace and blessings. So be it.

May he become a perfect man, under thy guidance, and be renewed in work and spirit. So be it.

May he unite with thee in his faith, that his life be made saintly. So be it.

ARMENIAN LITURGY

Preparatory Canticle for Sacrifice of the Mass

O profound and incomprehensible mystery that was without beginning! Above us you have dressed the realms in inaccessible light, and choirs of angels shine in transcendent glory.

With marvelous power you created Adam in the image of your sovereignty and surrounded him with the magnificence of your glory in Eden, place of delight.

Through your sacred and only Son did you renew and make immortal the beauty of Man, dressing Him in garments that can never be taken away from him.

O sacred spirit of God, who in raiments of fire did descend down upon the apostles, descend down upon us also with your wisdom as we cloak ourselves with this garment. In your house it is meet that one be saintly, and, since you alone are dressed in a splendid cloak and surrounded by the glory of sanctity, draw us along into your saintliness.

You who have extended your creator's arm to the stars, fill also our arm with strength, so that, by elevating our arms to you we may touch your realm.

May the diadem around our forehead protect our souls. May the star on our breast care for our senses, this star so similar to that of Aronne, beautiful, brilliant, a shining ornament of the sanctuary. O God, true monarch of all society, who on the earth is garmented in the cope, symbol of love, in order to have ministers worthy of your spirit, O celestial King, keep your Church unchanged and shower peace down on the advocates of your name.

A Prayer of Gregory of Naregh

With all our soul and with tearful sighs we pray to you and supplicate your glorious creative essence, O most merciful, O incorruptible, O eternal spirit so filled with tenderness, you who intercede for us with the Father of unmatched goodness, you who preserve the saints and keep sinners so pure as to render them living temples of the most high Father's spirit. O let our cries go not unanswered!

Free us of every impurity that displeases you, above all when we are in your presence, that our infirm minds may not be wholly unworthy of receiving the illuminating rays of your grace. Already we have come to know that you do not unite yourself with us except through the means of prayer and the sweet perfume of innocent habits. And, since it is true that one person of the Trinity came to be sacrificed and another caused this sacrifice to be the means of reconciliation with you, accept, we pray, our supplications, beatify us, make of us a precious habitation, pleasing, prepare us perfectly in all ways, that we, filled with joy, may partake of the banquet of the heavenly lamb and, without risking damnation, receive the gift of redemption, this gift which assures immortality.

May all traces of our poor human frailty be consumed and canceled out by this fire, in the same guise as happened to Isaiah the prophet, by means of that ardent fire placed in his hand by the angel. In every manner, in this same instant, be clement with us, and may your goodness be manifested as it was manifested through your divine Son, that goodness of the Father who gave his only Son that the celestial realm might become the dwelling of those who had been impure.

And I am also one of these miserable creatures who wishes to be received. Also I reaped the profits of Christ's blood, and stand in need of mercy. Save me by your mercy. Do it, that in all the universe the glory of the Father is known, that honor be His, that He be forever exalted.

For it is true that you are the power, charity, clemency, virtue and glory in the centuries of centuries. Amen.

Hymn for the Offering of Incense

In this temple of the Lord, open to offerings and vows, we now reunite humbly and in prayer to carry through the mystery of the august sacrifice about to be offered up; together, filled with joy, we turn about the sacred temple, bearing the most precious incense.

With goodness, O Lord, accept our prayers, as you accept this sweet aroma of cinnamon and myrrh, and keep us who make the offering in your name, so that we may forever and saintly serve you. For the intercession of your Mother and Virgin, accept the prayers of our ministers. O Christ our Lord, who, through your own blood, rendered the sacred Church more radiant and splendid in the eyes of Heaven, and who established the Church, the apostles, the prophets and saints along celestial models, all of us in this moment, priests, deacons and choristers, offer up the incense in your presence, as did Zacharias in times of old.

May our prayers, by means of this perfume, be pleasing to you, and rise on the air as did the sacrifices of Abel, Noah, and Abraham. In the name of the angels, preserve the Armenian See.

May you rise on transcendent joy and be limitlessly glorified, O Zion, daughter of light, O sacred universal mother, with your children. Adorned one, ornate one, O forechosen bride, brilliant, tabernacle of light resembling Heaven, for God daily shines on you. To reconcile us with the Father, and for our expiation, give us his most sacred flesh and blood, and, by virtue of this sacrifice, be merciful with all who have edified this temple.

The sacred Church recognizes and confesses its faith in the purity of the Virgin Mary, Mother of God, by means of whom to us have been given the bread of immortality and the wine of consolation. Pay homage to her with a spiritual hymn.

Canticle for Communion

O Church, mother of the faith, dwelling of the sacred marriage, adored bed! Dwelling of the immortal One who graced you with eternal beauties!

You are another gleaming sky that lifts itself from glory to greater glory, you are the one who regenerated all men, making them shine as splendid lights!

Now let us distribute this purifying bread,
And drink of this terrible blood
Which elevated us to the highest realms,
To the point of moving in the company of spiritual intelligence.
Therefore, come, O new sons of Zion,
Draw near to the presence of the Lord.
Look upon and enjoy our sweet and powerful Saviour.
You symbolize the ancient tabernacle,
But now you are the celestial tabernacle.

The first did shatter the diamond-studded doors,
But you have ripped the doors of Inferno from their fundaments.
The first triumph was over Jordan,
But you have triumphed over universal malice.
Joshua was the guide of the first,
But now the guide is Christ, the only Son.
This bread is the body of Christ,
In this chalice is the blood of the new alliance.
The greatest of mysteries reveals itself to you,
Here God is manifest.

Here among us is that same Jesus Christ, the Divine Word that did sit at the right of the Father, and who, sacrificed in the midst of all of us, took on himself the burden of the world's sins.

May He be eternally blessed, along with the Father and the Holy Spirit, today and throughout all centuries to come.

GELASIAN LITURGY

A Woman's Plea Against Sterility

O God who didst make fertile the barren Sarah through the seed of Abraham in such a manner as to cause her to know motherhood against even her fondest expectations, do likewise unto this servant of thine and cause her prayer to be answered.

Concede also to her fecundity as it was granted to those others, and bless the children she may have.

ETHIOPIC LITURGY

Introit of the Mass

Hallelujah!
I enter into thy house through the abundance of thy mercy.
I stand in adoration before thy sacred temple.
I confess to thee, O my Lord, for thou hast listened to words from my
    mouth.
I shall, singing, dance before thee, in the sight of angels.

I shall stand in adoration before thy sacred temple.

Thy priests are garbed in raiments of justice and thy saints proclaim with joy.

Sprinkle me, O Lord, with thine hyssop, and pure shall I be.

If me thou cleansest, more pure than snow shall I be.

Cleanse me of mine iniquities and my sins.

Defend thy servant from foreigners.

Thou hast given us bread from above.

Man hath eaten the bread of angels.

Mine hands shall be washed in the midst of innocents and I shall embrace thine altar, O my Lord.

Upon thine altar have I offered the victims of expiation.

Thou hast prepared for me the means to use against those who would plunge me into tribulations.

Thou hast showered my head with oil. How splendid is this cup!

I shall receive the chalice of salvation and invoke the name of the Lord.

Blessed is he who comes in the name of the Lord!

Great are blessings that come from the house of the Lord!

Hail, our Mother, Sacred Church, defended by strong walls, gleaming with topaz. O our Mother, O our Church, Hail!

Thou art that vase of purest gold in which was hidden the manna, the tabernacle of the bread that descended from Heaven, who gives life eternal to all.

Baptismal Formula

Lord, O Lord, good Father, our God, King of all things celestial and terrestrial, guardian, keeper of cherubim, look upon us, thou whose dwelling is in Heaven. Look upon thy creature.

Grant her the gift of Jordan's waters, O powerful and celestial One, and shower her with the blessings of the Holy Spirit. So be it.

A saintly water. So be it.

A water that cleanses sin. So be it.

A water that cleanses and regenerates. So be it.

Grant it, so that if there be some malign spirit hovering around her, it cannot touch her, who is baptized. So be it.

No spirit of the day can touch her. So be it.

No spirit of the night can touch her. So be it.

No spirit of deepest night can touch her. So be it.

No spirit of the air can touch her. So be it.

No spirit of pride from underground can touch her. So be it.

For all malign spirits are kept at a distance by thy power and are dispersed before the sign of the Cross of thy son. So be it.

In thy sacred name which we invoke, a name filled with glory and terrible in the presence of obstacles and adversity, whosoever is baptized expels from himself the old man, who is befouled with voluptuousness and error, and becomes a new man resembling his Creator, moving in the light of justice and the Holy Spirit. So be it.

And therein find again the eternal life. So be it.

Confirm their hopes. So be it.

May they remain before the throne of Christ. So be it.

May their sins be forgiven. So be it.

May they wear the celestial crown. So be it.

May this blessed water and oil so filled with glory be ever sacred, in the name of the Father, the Son, and the Holy Spirit, for the grace of thy people and all who brought to thee their children as servants to thy glory and the honor of thy Holy Son.

Gather them in thy celestial breast, shower them with the sweet odor of celestial greatness, in the name of prayers of angels and archangels.

O Lord, free thy people and bless their offspring, keep them and exult in them throughout all time. So be it.

Keep them strong in the true faith, throughout all their lives, and make them know the charity that transcends all, in answer to the prayers of all the saints and for the intercession of the Virgin Mary filled with grace, Mother of God, who is in all places saintly, and for Saint John the Baptist and martyr, precursor and companion of the life, and for all the saints since the beginning, as well as for thine only Son, glorious with thee and the Holy Spirit. So be it throughout centuries of centuries.

GOTHIC-GALLICAN LITURGY

The Collect of the Easter Mass

This formula dates from the sixth century.

O high and omnipotent God, who out of the mystery of the Cross brought about our salvation and elevated us to a level with thy servant David, in the threefold mystery of that Cross which manifests the unity of the Trinity, bringing the spirit of the Saviour to man, and filling the priest with Holy Grace, and, finally, endowing the King with flesh, O God, to thy Majesty we offer up our supplications, that to those whom in thy name thou didst consecrate through the washing away of sins, may thou also grant the grace to serve thee in sanctity and justice, that they maintain the unity of the faith through infusion of the Holy Spirit, and that they enter freely into the reign of Heaven along the peaceful path.

O God, who, having torn from its roots the plant of superstition, planted in thy Church the deep-rooted plant of faith, do look down from Heaven on this vineyard and grant that, with the irrigation of thy Grace, it fructify in abundance and yield many seeds.

ANCIENT GALLICAN LITURGY

Benediction of the People

This is taken from a *Missale Francorum* of the sixth century.

Bless, O Lord, this family that thou didst mold of clay and breathe life into by means of baptism: grant to all those who lost eternal life through the lips of Eve and were redeemed by the death on the Cross the right to glorify thy great merits.

Grant also that the perfidious adversary in them find nothing to work his evil on, that the divine piety in them find nothing to rebel against, that the vindictive flame find no motive to be cruel against them.

Instead, when that terrible day of judgment arrives, may they be summoned by the sound of the angels' trumpets, may their merits gain for them the eternal reward, and may they receive the triumphal palm.

LITURGY OF THE FRANKS

Prayer for Bringing Tears

Omnipotent and gentle God who for thy thirsting people caused a fountain of living water to rise out of the rock, now draw from our hard hearts the tears of compassion, that we may weep freely for our sins, and therefore, through thy mercy, be worthy of forgiveness.

We pray thee, O God, to gaze fondly down upon this oblation that we offer thee for our sins, and to cause rivers to flow from our eyes, that the fires of sinful flames might be wetted to extinction.

To Christ's Wounds

1 a) O knife that circumcised the sacred flesh of Christ, cut off our evil deeds,

1 b) O cheek of Christ, struck so harshly, teach us humility.

2 a) O sacred cords that bound the limbs destined to free us all,

2 b) O column to which Jesus was tied for flagellation, wash away our sins.

3 a) O lash that struck and wounded the tender body, placate those who offend us,

3 b) O sacred crown of Christ, grant us the gift of life and the rewards of Heaven.

4 a) O sacred Cross, beatified Cross, graced by the limbs of Christ, dispel all evil.

4 b) O you three nails that nailed Christ to the wood, pluck error from our minds.

5 a) The punctured veins permit us to support the suffering of the world.

5 b) And may the hammer that drove the nails heal all wounds, striking down perfidious sins.

6 a) Put an end to every wicked word, O mouth laved with a sponge of vinegar.

6 b) Body of Christ, pierced by the lance, thy love renders harshness sweet.

7 a) And thou, O body of Christ, set us free to partake of future glory.

7 b) Most splendorous Jesus, Saviour of sinners, cleanse us of crimes,

8 mercy for the bitter passion,
the flowing blood,
the sacred wounds.

Song of the Swan

1 O my children, I shall
sing the sad lament

2a) of the winged swan that crossed the sea.

2b) Weeping sadly, it cried to the sky:

3a) Of how it abandoned the land and soared high above the ocean.

3b) Poor winged thing, whither goest thou alone, alas, so sad!

4a) The splendid sky with humid wings thou canst never hope to reach.

4b) Swept by the waters, caught by the swirls of the tempest, I am an exile.

5a) No, I shall die in hungry troughs. Trembling, I sink. Seeing death, no longer can I lift myself.

5b) All around do fish abound in the waters. And yet I cannot in the wild tempest gain my nourishment.

6a) Show thyselves to me O dawns and sunsets of celestial reaches, O splendid astrals!

6b) Bring forth, clear Orion, dispel the clouds of sunset.

7a) While my heart is trembling so, gleaming shines the splendid dawn.

7b) Aided by the wind in flight I gain the rapid power of true wings.

8a) Joyously toward the notes came rolling celestial clouds.

8b) Exultant, toward the waters of the ocean, descended.

9a) With sweet songs it flies until it touches finally the land:

9b) All sing on high of the birds, of the aerial legions:

10 Glory
to the great King!

For the Sisters of the Madonna

Antiphony:
Mary the first-born, who became the Mother of Christ.
Mary, mother of James the minor, was born of Cleoph, a just man.
The illustrious descendant of Salome was Mary Salome.

Responsory:
Mary Magdalene and the two sisters gathered the spirits and mystic perfumes, desiring to soothe the bruised body.
And among themselves they asked: Who will move the rock away from the door?
Wondrous offspring: from a single vine came forth three shoots. From the shoots were born six men and the Creator.
For from Anne came three daughters, all named stars of the sea.
Above the throne of Solomon there is a seat. Under it are carved two hands with arms entwined. The symbol is explained in the Passion of Christ.
The Virgin Mother of piety leans against her two sisters, embracing them.

Antiphony:

Mary the first-born, espoused to Joseph, conceived without the seed of man.

Mary the mother of James the minor was espoused to Alphaeus, while Mary Salome was given unto Zebedee.

From her were born James the major and the other most beloved disciple of Christ.

Responsory:

O Jesus, instrument of divine light, sweet nutriment of the olive branch that two aunts, coming out in the mists of morning, wish to soothe with their ointments.

They shine like two lamps; in the shadow of the Cross they bear witness to the living flesh.

With the light of day the women are consoled by the splendid and terrible vision of the angel, who, rolling the rock away from the tomb, says unto them:

He is not here, the one ye seek, but he shall appear in all his glory, as ye shall see.

Today let us rejoice and lift our praises high to the two sisters of the glorious Queen, the daughters of Anne, who are crowned in Heaven.

Happy, happy aunts and sisters, who have blessed us with the gift of their virtue.

Anglo-Saxon Formula for Blessing Incense

This formula was adopted for the benediction of incense in the Salisbury Church. The term *thimiamata* strictly speaking, it does not correspond to incense, but rather means a mixture of incense and other odorous elements destined to be used in liturgical services.

O most sacred Lord and omnipotent Father, we invoke thy eternal and just mercy, that thou wilt cast thy blessings down upon the ingredients of this incense, making it an acceptable offering to thee. May it be blessed, this incense, through the invocation of thy sacred name, so that, wherever it touch and fall, it shall drive out every manner of demon and evil spirit, as did the incense of the Archangel Gabriel which he drew from the fish's liver and dedicated to Tobias. May thy blessing descend upon the ingredients of this incense, as those sweet aromas of thy prophet David descended when he sang:

May my song rise like incense in thy presence. And for us may it be perfume of consolation, of goodness and grace, so that these fumes will drive out every phantom from the mind and body, leaving us, as the Apostle Paul phrased it, smelling sweetly of God. May all the attacks of demons fly from this incense, like dust before the wind, like smoke before the dancing flames.

Grant, O merciful Father, that this incense of sweet odor remain always at the service of thy Church, for the use of the cult, that the value of its mystic symbol show us the way to the goodness of spiritual virtue. We ask thee, therefore, O omnipotent God of immense majesty, to cast thy blessing down upon this creation resulting from a mixture of various perfumes, that it might, wherever thy name is heard, put in flight all demons, malign spirits, and evil powers, thus keeping us pure in thy sight and permitting us to stand before thee, O Lord, in the fragrance of divine sweetness.

Entreaty and Proclamation of the Judgment of Cold Water

If in some manner he who has caused this man to be tried is at fault, either by works or deeds or science or other motives, give this one the power to swim above thee and harm him not for some blind reason that is unknown to him. I entreat thee in the name of Christ and command thee to obey in the name of Him who watches after every creature, Him to whom seraphim and cherubim sing praises of glory, saying: Sacred, sacred, sacred is the Saviour of the armies, who reigns and rules throughout the centuries. So be it.

After the entreaty and the benediction, the persons are divested of their garments and each caused to kiss the Cross. Then they are sprinkled with the Holy Water and the following is uttered:

I entreat thee, through the invocation of Our Lord Jesus Christ and through the judgment of the cold water, entreat thee in the name of the Father, the Son, and the Holy Spirit, in the name of the inseparable Trinity, the name of Jesus Christ and all the angels and archangels, in the name of the twelve Apostles, all the saints of God, in the name of that terrible Day of Judgment, the name of the fourteen ancients who each day laud God, the four evangelists, the twelve Prophets, the martyrs, confessors, virgins, princes, potentates, in the name of virtue, the cherubim and seraphim and all the celestial secrets.

I entreat thee in the name of the three children who praise God each day, Shadrach, Meshach, and Abednego, in the name of the countless thousands who suffered for Christ, in the name of Mary Mother of Jesus, in the name of all the people of God, in the name of the waters sprinkled on thee, in the name of all these, if thou knowest anything at all of this theft, hast seen or heard anything at all, hast carried off anything at all, hast hidden anything at all in thy house, hast a dirtied and guilty heart, may that heart vanish and the waters not sustain thee, against which trial no evil spirit can prevail. Accomplish this, O Lord Jesus Christ— thy name be praised—in order that all recognize thee as the blessed Lord who reigns for centuries and centuries.

Prayer for the Judgment of the Cheese

This is the formula used for the celebrated *judicium panis et casei.*

Thou shalt be the judge, O omnipotent Father, eternal God, who created earth and Heaven, formed the sea and built the sky itself and commanded that the sun, the moon, and the light shine splendidly over the just and the unjust.

Give us, O Lord, such proof of thy powers that the whole universe of earth and sky will doubt not that thou art God, that thou alone canst work wondrous things, O Lord Jesus, Son of God.

Cause them who are aware and responsible for the underlisted mis-deeds to have such tight mouths, throats, and jowls so as to be unable to swallow this cheese.

A Plea for the Judgment of the Burning Plowshares

O omnipotent God who created Heaven and earth and the seas and all things in them, who made man of thy own image, who sent us thy only Son, Christ Jesus, begotten of the Holy Spirit and the Virgin, in the name of that Holy Son our Lord Jesus Christ and the sacred Mother Mary, we invoke and pray thy Majesty to dispel by means of this judg-ment all slyful deceit and diabolic cunning, to dispel the enchantments of men and women and the occult powers of herbs, so that to all present thou wilt truly seem a lover of justice that no power of any kind can resist.

Therefore, O Lord of earth and Heaven, creator of the waters, king of all creation, in thy sacred name and as testimony to thy might, we now bless these burning plowshares in order to determine if this man is innocent of the crime of which he is accused. If he be innocent, let him walk thereon with bare feet. O omnipotent God, as thou didst free the children from the fiery furnace, and Susanna from false accusations, and Daniel from the lions' den, do now likewise through thy potent virtue keep the innocent feet of this man unharmed.

But if this man be guilty of the accusations as formulated, and dare to run the trial of proof by walking on the burning substance, cause his feet to manifest burns and boils, to thy honor, praise, and glory, that we, thy servants, may confide in thy name, and that the guilty repent of their sins and admit spontaneously what they have denied: for thou art the judge of the living and the dead and reign for centuries and centuries. So be it.

Medieval Casting-Out of the Demon

This text is singularly twisted, since it was originally taken from a traditional oral version handed down in a corrupt and barbarous form of Latin. Though we have done our best, the translation has presented great difficulties. The Latin, in places, is almost unreadable, and much of it reflects regional dialects of the time.

In the name of the Father, the Son and the Holy Ghost. I entreat thee and enjoin thee, O Devil, in the name of our Lord Jesus Christ, in the name of the virtue and the power of the Trinity, I entreat thee and enjoin thee, O Satan, and every diabolic power, to come forth from the body of this man, ———, and offend not his soul. Issue forth entirely!

Attempt not to hide or remain quiet or circulate or commit beastialities against the body and spirit of this man, against his raiment or his soul. Get thee away!

Leave not in the flesh, the bones, or in any other part of this man a trace or a sign of suffering.

Come out, O vile spirits, be ye one or many, whoever ye be, whatever be your names.

Issue forth quickly!

Issue forth from the head and hair of this man, from the topmost parts, from the forehead, the eyebrows, the eyes, the temples, the ears, the nostrils, the canals, the mutilations, the jaws, the tongue, the mouth's cavities, the teeth, the mouth, the throat, the craw, the after-craw, the shoulder, the shoulder blade, the palate, the windpipe, the respiratory canal, the chest, the brain, the lips, the jowls, the gums, the throat, the armpits, the spinal column, the back, the marrow—issue forth! Come out beneath the power of the Sacred Trinity and God omnipotent.

Pour like liquid out of the stomach, entrails, out of the thighs, the knees, the pores, from the heels, from the feet, the limbs, the nails, the articulations, the inter-articulations, the fingertips, the veins, the marrows, all the bones, the arteries, the flesh, from all the blood, from every humor, all the five senses, the genital organs, the seed, the groin, the cartilages, the bladder, the pit of the stomach, the urine, the sweat, and the lower fundament.

May it be cast out in the name of the crucified Christ, who rose again.

Issue forth from the bile, from the liver, from all the ligaments, from the intestines, from the stomach, from the ventricle.

Issue forth wholly from the spleen, never returning there!

Issue forth from the fat, from the reticulum, from the kidneys, from the heart and the subcardiac region, from the lungs, from every part of the heart and lungs. Issue forth from every part of the kidneys, every part of the loins, the butt, the ribs, the ilium, the trunk, the vertebrae, the cheeks, the lower cheeks, the vital fibers, the breath, the umbilical, the teats, the great intestine, the skin, the hair, from all his body, from all his food, his bread, his drink, all his victuals. Dare not come close or procure for this man diseases such as malaria, but be cast out and leave him pure, be cast out by the virtue of the Sacred Cross and our Redeemer Jesus Christ, who is the weapon of Christianity and our Saviour.

Driven out and defeated from the body of this man, then wander in deserted regions and alone. In the name and virtue of God the omnipotent, now issue forth in this moment, O vile spirit, from the body of
———.

Flee, fly, disappear, and leave this man ever in the service of Jesus Christ; leave him sane and healthy in body and mind. Issue forth, cursed one, and try not to hide or remain in any of his limbs, or in his breath, or cower in any corner of his dwelling. Put up no sly arguments. Touch nothing that belongs to him nor try to possess thyself of it.

Dare not invade his garments, his men, his women, his beasts. But, enchained and cast out of the empire, may the power and the glory of Jesus Christ, creator of the world, keep thee in regions far from the creatures of God.

Honor God omnipotent who rules over all things, who is obeyed by every element in the universe.

His virtue expels thee and forces thee to issue forth. For He is the one who set in flight the seven devils of Mary Magdalene.

He destroyed the realm of the dead, thy realm, and cast its rulers from their thrones. He himself is the Lord of virtue, he is the king and the glory that issued from the mouth of the Father before the time of Lucifer. We supplicate thee, O God, and invoke thee, that every vile particle in this man be cast out and that he be purified in that piety. We ask this in the name of Jesus and the Holy Spirit, O Father, that thy virtue may enter into this sick man and fortify him for the eternal life.

We have read in thy book, O Lord, that through the power of Jesus Christ the malign spirits can be driven out and their bearers cured of their sufferings, as it was stated Jesus said through his prophet Isaiah: He Himself bore our sufferings and our sicknesses and cured us where we were weak.

Thou, O Lord, Saviour of the world, said to thy apostles and to all that believed in thee, that they would have the power to ward off the evil spirits and to cure those who languish in sickness, if only they believed in thy name.

Thou didst say: Whoever asks to be saved in the name of the Lord, shall be saved. And all that is asked of the Father in my name shall be granted. Thou, O Lord, didst say: If ye who are wicked give your goods to your children, so much the more will the Father respond to ye when ye cry his name!

Thou, O Lord, didst say: If ye have faith and wish to move this mountain: it shall move.

We, O Lord, believe that thou art omnipotent and that thou art truly capable of all things. And now we invoke thee, O Sacred Trinity. O hear us, Jesus, our Saviour!

In the name of the Father, the Son, and the Holy Ghost, we ask that every diabolic agression against thy servant, ———, be driven away, and that he be restored to health, that he might enter into thy spirit. Thou, O Lord, didst say: the true in spirit need no physician, only the ailing. And thou didst affirm: I come not to save the just, but the sinners.

Thou, O God, and thou alone, with the Father, the Holy Spirit, mediator between men and God, be a physician for our sins: O Jesus Christ, Son of the living God, omnipotent Son of an omnipotent Father, thou art the creator. Send all the angels and archangels. Send Michael the Archangel, and Gabriel, and Raphael, that they might be present to aid and defend this man, ———, whom thou didst create out of dust and to whom thou didst give a soul, and for whom thou didst shed thy blood.

May they protect him, illuminate him and awaken him, render him tranquil when he sleepeth, and safe from all diabolic perfidy, and permit no malign spirit to enter into his body or his spirit.

Nor permit any malign spirit to offend or wound his soul, his body, his spirit, or tempt it in any manner.

Medieval Formula of Excommunication

This is taken from the *Formulae Veteres exorcismorum et excommunicationum* and was pronounced by the bishop, as the text itself indicates.

In accordance with the precepts of the Lord and the Apostles, and of Jesus Christ the Son, by virtue of the authority vested in the Apostles and in their successors, together with all of you, we do here and now cast from out the confines of the sacred Mother Church the aforementioned and wicked man; we do cause him to be separated from all society and every communion with Christians, and order him kept perpetually separated, both in this world and the one to come.

No Christian shall greet him or dare to kiss him.

No priest shall say Mass for him or give him the bread and wine of the Saviour.

No person shall unite with him socially or in any other form.

And if anyone do associate with him or take part in any of his works, that person or persons shall likewise be termed anathema, with the sole exception of those who may have contact with him in an attempt to lead him from error and into public penitence.

The present excommunication shall be held valid until such time as he comes to his senses, finds inspiration in divine grace, asks to do penance, and has in all ways humbly satisfied the Church of God he has offended.

An Invocation for the King

We invoke thee, O sacred and omnipotent Father, that, before God and men, from day to day, thy servant, ——, be made more worthy, that he be touched with the gift of thy piety and filled with the grace of truth; grant this to thy servant whom thou hast kept to the present day, whom thou didst raise up out of dust and endow with thy divine gifts.

We pray that he, participating in the divine abundance of grace, be permitted to attain that highest government, that he be kept safe on all sides from his enemies, that he know thy mercy, and that he reign happily over the people entrusted to his care. Grant peace and victory.

Consecration of the King

The allusion to England is explained by the fact that the Frankish Dynasty of the time claimed sovereignty over that land.

Omnipotent and ever-eternal God, creator and governor of earth and sky, creator and commander of men and angels, king of kings, Lord of lords, who permitted Abraham, thy faithful servant, to triumph over his enemies, and to Moses and Joshua granted innumerable victories, who elevated the humble David to the highest realm, freed him from the jaws of the lion, from the grip of the beast and from Goliath, as from the sword of Saul and the enemies, who showered down on Solomon the beautiful gifts of wisdom and peace, now turn thine eyes upon our humble prayer.

Shower down upon thy servant whom in supplication and prayer we have elected King of England and the land of the Franks the gifts of thy benediction and let him lean on thy strong right arm. Do this, that he, fortified in the faith as strongly as Abraham, filled with the gentleness of Moses, shining with the strength of Joshua, exalted by the humility of David, and gleaming with the wisdom of Solomon, may render himself seemly in thine eyes and walk along the path of justice securely. May he nourish and teach, defend and instruct all the churches of England and all the peoples under him; may he guide them with thy regal virtue against all enemies visible and invisible, in such a manner as never to betray the regal scepter of the Franks. With thy help, guide him in harmonizing them in faith and peace, both these peoples, so glorified by worthy love, objects for many years now of thy mercy. Let them continue to know thy mercy.

Thus protected by thee, conjointly protected by an invincible shield and surrounded by celestial arms, may he triumph over all enemies, provoke terror in the hearts of infidels and bring peace to those who have fought in thy name.

With thy blessing of multiple honors, shower down on him the blessings of the previously named faithful, put him on high in the regiment of the state, and bless him with the oil of the Holy Spirit.

Here he is blessed with oil.

Antiphony: Sadoc the priest did bless Solomon. Nathan the prophet did bless King John, and drawing near him, they said: Long live the king! And thou didst bless the priests, king, prophets, and martyrs who gained their realms through faith, worked justice in their realms, and saw their promises fulfilled.

May the sacred oil flow over his head, descend along his body, and penetrate to the innermost reaches of his heart. May he be worthy of the promises that, out of thy grace, the most victorious kings saw fulfilled. May he reign happily in the present century and aspire to the celestial court through the Lord Jesus Christ, thy Son, who was blessed with the oil in company with his friends; may he cause malevolent powers to weaken through the presence of the Cross, destroy the Tartar, conquer the Devil, and ascend victoriously to Heaven.

For in his hand will then be every victory, every glory, and every power, in God's realm and the unity of the Spirit.

Prayer for Consigning the Crown

God crowns thee with the crown of glory, honor, justice, and defense of the fortress, so that, by means of our blessing, with correct faith and good works, thou mayest wear the crown in the perpetual realm, which will be given thee by him who reigns for centuries of centuries.

For the King

This memorandum, which set forth the essence of regal functions—functions that were eminently Christian and priestly—ended with the following ritual:

It is just and right that the king now elevated to the throne should provide these three things for the Christian people who are his subjects. First of all, that the Church of Christ and all Christian people keep the peace at all times. Secondly, forbid violence or injustice on the part of any person of any level. Thirdly, that he show himself just and merciful in all decisions, that he and all of us may know the mercy of God.

The Prayer for All

Piously we ask thee, O Lord, to free us from all our crimes.

Through the intercession of the beatified and ever-glorious Virgin Mary, the Mother, and all the saints, we ask thee to keep the Pope and our curate, the king and our leaders, keep us, thy servants, and, finally, keep this dwelling, with all who dwell therein.

And all those who are close to us and familiar, or in our memories, to purify and illumine with virtue.

Give us health, keep our enemies, visible and invisible, far from us, thrust out the desires of the flesh that are in us, surround us with clean air, inspire us with charity for our enemies, pardon those who have offered us alms, forgive them their sins, and to all the faithful, living and dead, grant life on earth and eternal rest.

Ancient Prose of Cluny

Gentle Mother of the Saviour, hope of the world, hail, O gracious one!
Gate of Heaven, temple of God, safe port to which faithful fishermen
     can fly,
worthy bride of the sovereign King, toward all men gentle and filled
     with tenderness,
thou keepest us strong with thy care.
Light for the blind, safe pathway for our faltering steps,
Martha and Mary of our needs, thy love is for us.
Among the thorns was the flower, the flower which opened out into
     a celestial flower, thanks to thy great love.
Through thy word thou conceived the Word, birthed the King of
     kings, O Virgin emancipated from the human yoke.
Faithful to the King born of thy womb, thou nursed him and fed him,
     as mothers do.
United with him for so long, thou became a queen through thy virtue.
O Queen! In the name of the guilty, use thy offices with the King:
     may he pardon them.
May he, in his great goodness, restore them to life,
purifying them in every way, thus permitting them to dwell with thee.
     So be it.

ROMAN LITURGY

The Exorcism of the Water

I exorcise thee, O creature of water, in the name of God the Father
Almighty; and in the name of Jesus Christ, His Son, our Lord; and in
the power of the Holy Ghost; that thou mayest become water exorcised
for the chasing away of all the power of the enemy; that thou mayest
have strength to uproot and cast out the enemy himself and his apostate
angels, by the power of the same our Lord Jesus Christ, who shall come
to judge the living and the dead, and the world by fire.

O God, who for the salvation of mankind hast founded one of Thy
greatest Sacraments in the element of water, graciously give ear when
we call upon Thee, and pour upon this element, prepared for divers
purifications, the power of Thy blessing; let Thy creature serving in

Thy Mysteries, by Divine grace be effectual for casting out devils and for driving away diseases, that on whatsoever in the houses or places of the faithful this water shall be sprinkled, it may be freed from all uncleanness, and delivered from hurt. Let not the blast of pestilence nor disease remain there; let every enemy that lieth in wait depart; and if there be aught which hath ill will to the safety and quietness of the inhabitants, let it flee away at the sprinkling of this water, that they, being healed by the invocation of Thy holy name, may be defended from all that rise up against them. Through our Lord Jesus Christ, Amen.

For Heretics and Schismatics

O Almighty and Everlasting God, who hast compassion on all, and wouldst not that any should perish: favorably look down upon all those who are seduced by the deceit of Satan; that, all heretical impiety being removed, the hearts of such as err may repent and return to the unity of Thy truth.

Corpus Christi, at Vespers

Now, my tongue, the mystery telling
Of the glorious Body sing,
And the Blood, all price excelling,
Which the Gentiles' Lord and King,
In a Virgin's womb once dwelling,
Shed for this world's ransoming.

Given for us, and condescending
To be born for us below,
He with men in converse blending
Dwelt, the seed of truth to sow,
Till He closed with wondrous ending
His most patient life of woe.

That last night at supper lying,
'Mid the twelve His chosen band,
Jesus, with the law complying,
Keeps the Feast its rites demand;
Then, more precious Food supplying,
Gives Himself with His Own hand.

Word-made-Flesh, true bread He maketh
By His Word His Flesh to be;

Wine, His Blood; which whoso taketh
Must from carnal thoughts be free;
Faith alone, though sight forsaketh,
Shows true hearts the Mystery.

Therefore we, before Him bending,
This great Sacrament revere;
Types and shadows have their ending,
For the newer Rite is here;
Faith, our outward sense befriending,
Makes our inward vision clear.

Glory let us give, and blessing,
To the Father and the Son,
Honor, laud, and praise addressing,
And eternal benison.
Holy Ghost, from both progressing,
Equal laud to Thee be done. Amen.

Whitsuntide Vespers—The Veni Creator

Come, Holy Ghost, Creator, come,
From thy bright heavenly throne!
Come, take possession of our souls,
And make them all Thine Own!

Thou who art called the Paraclete,
Best Gift of God above,
The Living Spring, the Living Fire,
Sweet Unction, and True Love!

Thou who art sevenfold in Thy grace,
Finger of God's right hand,
His Promise, teaching little ones
To speak and understand!

O guide our minds with Thy blest light,
With love our hearts inflame,
And with Thy strength, which ne'er decays,
Confirm our mortal frame.

Far from us drive our hellish foe,
True peace unto us bring,
And through all perils guide us safe
Beneath Thy sacred wing.

Through Thee may we the Father know,
Through Thee the Eternal Son,
And Thee the Spirit of them both—
Thrice-blessèd Three in One.

Now to the Father, and the Son
Who rose from death, be glory given,
With Thee, O holy Comforter,
Henceforth by all in earth and heaven. Amen.

The Soul of Christ

Soul of Christ, sanctify me.
Body of Christ, save me.
Blood of Christ, inebriate me.
Water from the side of Christ, wash me.
Passion of Christ, strengthen me.
O good Jesus, hear me.
Within thy wounds, hide me.
Permit me not to be separated from thee.
From the malicious enemy defend me.
In the hour of my death call me,
And bid me come to thee,
That, with thy saints, I may praise thee,
For ever and ever, Amen.

The Blessing of the New Fire

O God through your Son, the cornerstone of our faith, you bestowed the light of your glory upon the faithful. Sanctify this new fire which was struck from flint and is destined for our use. Grant that we may be so inflamed with heavenly desires through this paschal feast that we may come to the feast of eternal light with pure minds. Through the same Christ, our Lord. Amen.

The Blessing of Palms

Hosanna to the Son of David! Blessed is he who comes in the name of the Lord! O King of Israel, hosanna in the highest.

O Lord, bless these branches of palm. Grant that the sincere devotion of your people may make them victorious over their enemy and zealous in works of mercy, and thus spiritually complete the ceremony which they outwardly perform this day in your honor, Through the same Christ, our Lord. Amen.

Prayer for Rain

O God, in whom we live, move and have our being, grant us the rain we need so that your answer to our present earthly needs may give us greater confidence to ask for eternal benefits. Through the same Christ, our Lord. Amen.

AMBROSIAN LITURGY

Easter Friday

Collect:

O God, eternal and omnipotent, who guided thy people across Jordan to the Promised Land; now that the ancient symbol has been unveiled through the grace of baptism, let thy adopted children dwell also in the celestial realm.

After the Communion:

Grant us this, O omnipotent God: after having put aside our resemblance to Adam, the first earthly father, after then having been reborn through the Easter rites, let us dwell in the image of our celestial Father.

The Fourth Sunday After Easter

Collect:

O God who, in order to reconduct an erring humanity to the proper path, gave them the light of truth to follow, now accord to all who profess the Christian faith the strength to renounce such practices and professions as are not in harmony with the precepts of that faith.

After spreading the corporal:

Thy inspiration, O Lord, precedes our every act, just as thy aid goes always with us. Therefore, grant that all our actions begin and end with thee.

During Advent

Prayer:

Arise, O Lord, in all thy majesty, and come; for only under thy protection can we hope to escape from the impending peril provoked by our own sins; only through thy grace can we make our way safely.

After spreading the corporal:

We pray thee, O omnipotent God, that the forthcoming solemnities dedicated to thy Son will enrich us with gifts for the present life and in the life to follow.

At the Third Mass of Christmas

Prayer:

Thou who art the creator and ruler of the world, do in these sacred days keep us piously on the side of grace and the Incarnation of thy Word through the Virgin Mary; for just as we were redeemed by thy piety, so shall we dwell safely under thy protection.

After spreading the corporal:

Thou, O God, who didst lift human nature up out of thy hypostasis, now let us consort with the divine Jesus Christ, for He deigned to consort with frail humankind.

Oblation:

May it please thee, O God, this oblation to the birth of Our Lord Jesus Christ; and thanks to this union, may we please Him, for he rules over our own nature.

On the Eve of Epiphany

O God, who on this day sent a star to reveal thy only Son to the Gentiles, we pray to thee that, as we have known thee in the light of the faith, we may one day be permitted to gaze upon thee in all thy glory. O eternal and omnipotent God who through a shining star gave witness of thy Incarnate Word, a star which brought the Magi forth to contemplate it, adore it, and offer up gifts unto it, we pray that this star of thy justice will shine spendidly and continually in our minds, and that our spiritual treasure remain always the Christian profession of thy faith.

Holy Saturday

Collect.

O God, fortress and eternal light, look again upon the wondrous mystery of thy Church, which mystery serenely carries out the work of human salvation as thou established it. Look at its entire orb and see how it uplifts, how it makes those who were old now youthful, how all is achieved through Him from which it began, Our Lord Jesus Christ.

Collect.

O God, who lifts up the humble and gives strength to the weak, thou who through the work of thy servant Moses wished to instruct the people of Israel, so that thy Law might serve as an admonishment also to us, do now exert thy power over those masses of people who must yet be baptized, grant us thy grace, mitigate terror, for thy mercy cancels out all faults, that what has been uttered as a threat might be converted into a cry for salvation.

The Prose of the Ass for the Festival of the Weak-Minded

This so-called Prose of the Ass was the second liturgical piece sung in the Office of Circumcisions, in the part called *Conducts ad tabulam*. The recitation took place in certain churches between Christmas and the Epiphany, while in others it was held on the Day of Circumcision. This latter became a popular feast day. During this celebration, with ceremonies that varied according to each church, the liturgy made use of an ass. Triumphantly received by canons and populace at the door of the church (at least according to the rite used at Sens), this beast was in some cases taken inside and up to the main altar. There would seem to be some uncertainty as to whether or not the ass was actually taken up to the main altar and dressed in sacred robes, in order that he, wise and judicious beast who had saved Christ from the persecutions of Herod, might listen to the reading of the ceremony (*tabula*) and the epistle. Many experts on the period in question, however, hold this opinion.

Out of the Orient arrived the ass, wise and beautiful, made to carry a load. Get along, Sir Ass, get along! Over the hills of Sichen, over the Jordan, he ascended to Bethlehem. Get along, Sir Ass, get along! More sprightly and surefooted than deer and mountain goats, faster than dromedaries. Get along!

The virtue of the ass has brought Arabian gold to the Church, incense and myrrh from the land of Saba. Get along!

While he drags a heavily laden cart, his strong jaws grind away at fodder. Get along!

At threshing time he separates the grain from chaff, eats barley with his feet and withers. Get along!

Say "Amen," O Ass, now stuffed so full. Repeat "Amen" and put aside your ancient habits. Get along!

For Pregnant Women

O maidservant of God, Mary Mother of Christ, hear this poor sinner who implores thee to keep from harm the unborn children in mothers' wombs. They, in truth, unbaptized, are still marked by the original sin, are destined to descend into limbo, a part of inferno.

O Mary, do come to the aid of these poor little ones who, through Adam's fault, are destined to remain forever deprived of the vision of God.

What an immense abyss is the judgment of God! Keep these little ones from perishing without fault and without cause.

What suffering was occasioned by that bite which Eve gave to the forbidden apple, for which death became the lot of all descendants!

But what a happy dialogue, O Mary, between thee and the angel, out of which new life arose for all the world!

And thy childbed, free of all suffering, outshines all other things.

For this canceled out the curse of Eve and gave a new blessing to all women.

To whom, then, may the weeping women in their pregnancy run for consolation, if not to thee?

Listen to them, O spotless Virgin, and may thy Son not hold the faults of parents against them.

Hear the desperate cries of the children destined to remain in the perpetual inferno of suffering.

And after having seen to their rebirth through the sacred rites of baptism, lift them up and let them dwell in eternal glory.

Crusaders' Hymn for the Taking of Jerusalem

1a) From all sides the faithful lift their voices, sing to God,

1b) Whose works are ever magnificent, throughout the universe.

2a) and let us take part in the feasting, our hearts cleansed for the forthcoming year.

2b) For glorious Jerusalem, so long in the hands of the Saracen, is now free.

3a) Let us proclaim the great might of the Franks, by whom Jerusalem was freed and returned to God.

3b) There is gladness, then, for she has been returned to Christianity, and already commands like a sovereign.

4a) Before her all France and Italy kneel down.

4b) Now Greece presents her gifts, and Arabia.

5a) Mesopotamia, Egypt, Africa, and all other peoples pass under her sway.

5b) Damascus, Tyrus, and other great ones send offerings.

6 While we celebrate the feast of
of Jerusalem, may we be privileged
to enjoy the bounties
of celestial Jerusalem!

For the Resurrection of Our Saviour Jesus Christ

Sun, moon, sky, stars, mountains, valleys, heights, plains, fountains, pools, rivers, seas, whatever flies, crawls or swims, lift up your voices to the glory of Christ!

Today the world's Redeemer returns victorious from the inferno.

O author of all things, we pray thee during this Easter period, to defend thy people against all threats of death.

Glory be unto thee, O Lord, who rose from the dead, unto the Father and the Holy Spirit throughout the centuries.

Prose for the Holy Mother

O shining Crosier and diadem of the King, shining in thy cloister as if of armor, already didst thou put forth flowers when Adam produced the human race.

Hail! Hail! Out of thy womb came other life than that which Adam took from his offspring.

O flower, it is not the dew that brings thee forth, nor the rain, nor the soft breeze, but divine splendor.

O Crosier, from the first hour of creation God had foreseen thy noble flowering.

And so created by His Word a golden substance, O admirable crosier!

How great indeed in power is the side of Man, out of which God created Woman's first form, a form in which were reflected all the beauties of creation!

Celestial instruments sound forth once more, the whole earth stands in awe before the worthy Mary, for God did truly love thee.

How lamentable it is, how one must weep, that through the wondrous creature Woman, tempted by the serpent, did flow the sadness of sin!

For this same woman whom God had made mother of all things did lacerate her womb with the barbs of innocence and bring endless suffering to her sex.

But thanks to thee, O Dawn, a new goodness was brought forth to atone for all the sins of Eve; through thee did mankind reap blessings in greater quantities than all the sins of Eve.

Therefore, O Blessed One, who gave humankind a new guiding light, gather up the limbs of thy Son in celestial harmony.

The Eleven Thousand Virgins

This complicated legend of Saint Ursula and the Eleven Thousand Virgins is a tale in which one finds a mixture of antique Roman legends, and even some from the Breton cavalier cycle. Probably the legend originated from a mistaken letter on an epigraph dedicated to the XI M(artyrs) V(irgins).

O Church, similar are thine eyes to sapphires and thine ears to Mount Bethel. Thy nose is like a mountain of myrrh and incense. Like the sound of splashing water is thy mouth.

Burning with a vision of the true faith, Ursula loved the Son of God, for which love she did put aside her husband in this world, looked steadfastly toward the beautiful light and said:

I burn to come to thee, to take thee unto me in Heavenly wedlock, to give myself over to thee along the pathway of a new life, as a cloud moves through the purest air.

Hearing Ursula speak thusly, quickly word spread from lip to lip.

They whispered: The ingenuous girl knows not what she says.

And noisily did they set about to tease her, and continued until the poor thing was struck down.

Then it was plain that scorn for the things of this world is as strong as Bethel.

And all of them came to know the sweet aroma of myrrh and incense, for scorn for the glories of this world rises to heights over all.

It was then that the Devil invaded her body and set about to defile her.

And these things were heard in a great voice by all the elements and they said before the throne of God:

Alas! The blood of the innocent lamb has been spilled at the moment of marriage!

And the sky heard, and lifted its voice in praise to the lamb of God, for through such precious pearls, made in the image of the Word of God, is the ancient serpent suffocated.

To the Sacred Relics

1a) With deep devotion let us venerate the heavenly King and Queen.

1b) The tresses of the Mother and the Son fill us with virtue.

2a) The illustrious Virgin's milk, the swaddling clothes of the Child, the cloth that washed the feet.

2b) The lowly manger of the humble King, the unusual tunic, touch the hearts of those who truly love.

3a) The pole of flagellation, the binding chains, did cut the knot of sin.

3b) The lashes, the crown of thorns, soothing balm of sins.

4a) The scepter, the Cross, the nails, the sponge, the iron lance, the blood that flowed so freely.

4b) The sheet and the sepulcher hiding the beautiful body, look after us always.

5a) The true title of the Cross assure the mind in the faith of miracles and true blood.

5b) The power of the staff of Moses and the stone tablets this does affirm.

To the Cross

May the Cross smile on me,
May the Cross be my glory,
The Cross of paradise,
May the Cross lift me up,
May the Cross be the light of dawn,
The door of life,
The good Cross,
May the Cross be my balm,
May the Cross bring me vigor and youth!

The Crown of Thorns

Wondrously fructifying thing, CLEAR, RED AND BLACK is the noble crown of thorns pressed down upon the head of Christ.

For the CLEAR and spotless flesh defies the crime of Adam, RED is the flower of passion, and BLACK death brought the suffering.

O garland of thorns, comfort us in the blood of Christ, bind us, O belt of thorns, in a belt of virtue, that the sly serpent strike us not without showing himself.

And thou, O Jesus, do make of the crown our diadem, that we may be washed pure of all our sins.

Carthusian Praises of Mary

Hail, O earth worthy of praise that produces green herbs and fruitful plants. Bedewing us with the essence of the Sacred Spirit, thou dost render more saintly our thoughts and make our works more virtuous.

Hail, O sacred substance of the earth on which the spit of God, irrigating that which had been prepared, fell and formed Man of thee, thus reforming the fallen human material from dust.

Hail, O ascents, up and down which the contemplative may walk.

Thanks to thee the humanity of Christ manifests itself, and the divinity is seen as humanized.

Hail, O earth so pleasing to God, sprinkled from above by divine showers, lifted up like a sweet bud by the Saviour, a new flower on a new earth, all renewed.

Hail, O door and entrance to the East, the door through which He entered into the temple and illuminated it with grace and piety.

Hail, smiling city in which the waves of the Holy Spirit built a dwelling worthy of Christ.

Hail, O dwellings so beautifully constructed by the hand of wisdom, dwellings that God edified and reinforced with the seven pillars of grace.

Hail! As beautiful as the moon, unique among the astrals as the sun, the favored of all. Advancing like the dawn, thou offered to the eyes of beholders that splendor which appears after darkness.

From the Assumption of the Virgin

The Mother of the great King and creator of all things is today elevated to a position above all the angels. Therefore let our voices rise up in jubilant songs of glory.

It was on this day that Mary the Virgin did rise to Heaven, departing this unworthy earth. Now gloriously does she reign with Christ. Let us then be glad! Now the Son hurries forth to meet the Mother, seats her on a throne higher than the highest star, and surrounds her with flights of angels.

Compline Hymn

Now the day is drawing to a close, inclining toward the hour of vespers, turning about from whence it came on the last rays of sunset. Following its pattern, it has encircled the world with shadows.

We unworthy sinners pray that thou wilt grant us retribution, not according to our deeds, O Christ, but according to the spirit of this invocation to thee.

A Hymn for Rain

O God, creator of all things, hear our prayer, and bring us rain, bring us heavenly showers. Thou who rulest over the seas and separatest them from the land, call down upon this arid earth the blessing of rain.

Thou who for Moses brought water from the rocks and guided his people, grant us the blessing of water. Thou who irrigated the whole earth with rains from paradise, and sated the hunger of six thousand souls with five loaves, Thou who turned the water into wine, in a like manner do now shower down upon thy earth the blessing of water. Thou who from the rib distilled water and blood, be not tardy in sending us rain for the crops. Why, O God, hast thou denied us, the flocks of thy pastures, why hast thou risen up against us? May thy ire be turned to peace. O Lord, God of Abraham, now send us rain for the crops and for our health. Come to our aid with rainy weather. Open thy treasures, thy celestial cataracts, with thy hand give us rain, that thy people be not desolate. All glory to the Creator. May he send us the rains, that our faith remain strong in the Actor and Molder.

To Christ

O Lord, thy goodness created me, thy mercy cleansed me of the original sin, thy generosity hath unto this day tolerated and sustained me, even though after baptism I did fall back into error and sin.

O most merciful Lord, thou dost wait for my conversion, and my soul awaits the infusion of thy grace, that it may attain, through proper penitence, a higher and better life.

Come to my aid, O Lord, who created me and who even now tolerates and keeps me.

I thirst for thee, hunger for thee, desire to fling myself at thy feet.

In the manner of an orphan deprived of his father, one who cries and trembles at the thought and memory of the missing image, so do I cry, O Lord, at the thought and memory of thy passion, thy flagellation, thy lashes, the memory of the Cross and how cruelly thou didst die for me, the memory of the tomb from which thou didst rise. I believe in thee wholly, my Lord, and, recalling with bitterness my exile from thee, do long to put myself in thy care and look upon thy face again.

Before the Cross

O sacred Cross which renews in us the memory of that Cross whereon our Lord Jesus Christ did give his life to restore to us eternal life, which through our sins we had lost, I adore and venerate thee, and glorify that Cross of which thou art the image. I adore and glorify our Lord Jesus Christ who through that Cross did work his goodness for us.

O adorable Cross of our salvation, our life and resurrection! O precious wood of liberation and salvation! O venerable image through which God gave us an image of distinction! O glorious Cross which we need only glorify!

Thanks to thee the inferno has been stripped of its terrors; it is closed to them thou hast redeemed. Thanks to thee the demons are put down, thrust aside and conquered. For thee the world renews itself and re-cloaks itself in the splendid garments of shining truth. Through thee human nature, contaminated by sin, finds its justification, is saved from damnation, freed from slavery, fault, and punishment, saved from death. For thee the heavenly dwelling is restored and completed. Through thee the Son of God, Himself a God, brought the name of the Father to us, exalting that name to the end. Through thee He prepared the Throne and installed the Realm. O Cross, chosen and prepared for goodness, neither the intelligence nor the tongues of men or angels can glorify thee sufficiently to tell of the great works achieved in thy name.

In thee are my salvation and my life; in thee alone do I glory!

For One's Enemies

O omnipotent and merciful Lord, grant unto mine enemies that which thou makest me desire for them. And if at times, through ignorance or through weakness, I should ask something for them that is uncharitable, do not grant it, O Lord, nor punish me!

Thou who art the true light, cause them in their blindness to see.

Thou who art the highest truth, correct them in their errors. Thou who art the true life, give life to their souls.

Through thy favorite disciple thou didst say: "He who loveth not is already dead!" Therefore grant, O Lord, them charity in their hearts toward thee and their neighbors, that they sin no more in thy presence against their brother.

Christ's Death

O tearful death, for which all things weep,
O lamentable death, for which the faultless wail,
O wondrous death, to which life was restored,
O death worthy of love, inspiration of the valorous,
O sacred death, O noble death, which destroys crimes,
O pious death, O fertile death, which brings rewards,
Stay ever before us, that the memory dominate us continuously and lift
    up the spirit and touch our hearts constantly, that our souls be
    illumined and prepared for action, that we be kept free of fault
    and know the gift of life. Amen.

Prayer, Praise, and Thanksgiving
by St. Francis of Assissi

Almighty, most Holy, most High and Supreme God, Holy and Just. Father, Lord King of heaven and earth, for Thyself we give thanks to Thee because by Thy holy will, and by Thine only Son, Thou hast created all things spritual and corporal in the Holy Ghost and didst place us made to Thine image and likeness in paradise, whence we fell by our own fault. And we give Thee thanks because, as by Thy Son Thou didst create us, so by the true and holy love with which Thou hast loved us, Thou didst cause Him, true God and true Man, to be born of the glorious and ever-Virgin, most Blessed holy Mary, and didst will that He should redeem us captives by His Cross and Blood and Death. And we give thanks to Thee because Thy Son Himself is to come again in the glory of His Majesty to put the wicked who have not done penance for their sins, and have not known Thee, in eternal fire, and to say to all who have known Thee and adored Thee, and served Thee in penance: "Come, ye blessed of My Father, possess the kingdom prepared for you from the beginning of the world."

And since all we wretches and sinners are not worthy to name Thee, we humbly beseech Thee, that our Lord Jesus Christ, Thy beloved Son, in whom Thou art well pleased, together with the Holy Ghost, the Paraclete, may give thanks to Thee as it is pleasing to Thee and Them, for all; He suffices Thee always for all through whom Thou hast done so much for us. Alleluia. And we earnestly beg the glorious Mother, the most Blessed Mary ever-Virgin, Blessed Michael, Gabriel, Raphael, and all the choirs of the blessed spirits, seraphim, cherubim, and thrones, dominations, principalities and powers, virtues, angels and archangels, blessed John the Baptist, John the Evangelist, Peter, Paul, the blessed patriarchs and prophets, innocents, apostles, evangelists, disciples, martyrs, confessors, virgins, blessed Elias and Enoch, and all the Saints who have been and are, and shall be, for Thy love, that they may, as it is pleasing to Thee, give thanks for these things to the most high, true God, eternal and living, with Thy most dear Son, our Lord Jesus Christ, and the Holy Ghost, the Paraclete, for ever and ever. Amen, Alleluia.

And all we, brothers, minor, useless servants, humbly entreat and beseech all those within the holy Catholic and Apostolic Church wishing to serve God, and all ecclesiastical Orders, priests, deacons, subdeacons, acolytes, exorcists, lectors, door-keepers, and all clerics; all religious men and women, all boys and children, poor and needy, kings and princes, laborers, husbandmen, servants and masters, all virgins, continent, and married people, laics, men and women, all infants, youths, young men and old, healthy and sick, all small and great, and all peoples, clans, tribes, and tongues, all nations and all men in all the earth, who are and shall be, that we may persevere in the true faith and in doing penance, for otherwise no one can be saved. Let us all love with all our heart, with all our soul, with all our mind, with all our strength and fortitude, with all our understanding and with all our powers, with our whole might and whole affection, with our innermost parts, our whole desires, and wills, the Lord God, who has given, and gives to us all, the whole body, the whole soul, and our life; who has created and redeemed us, and by His mercy alone will save us; who has done and does all good to us, miserable and wretched, vile, unclean, ungrateful, and evil.

Let us therefore desire nothing else, wish for nothing else, and let nothing please and delight us except our Creator and Redeemer, and Saviour, the only true God, who is full of good, all good, entire good, the true and supreme good, who alone is good, merciful and kind, gentle and sweet, who alone is holy, just, true, and upright, who alone is benign, pure, and clean, from whom, and through whom, and in whom is all mercy, all grace, all glory of all penitents and of the just, and of all the blessed rejoicing in heaven. Let nothing therefore hinder us, let nothing separate us, let nothing come between us. Let us all, everywhere, in every place, at every hour, and at all times, daily and continually believe, truly and humbly, and let us hold in our hearts, and love, honor, adore, serve, praise and bless, glorify and exalt, magnify and give thanks to the most High and Supreme, Eternal God, in Trinity and Unity to the Father, and Son, and Holy Ghost, to the Creator of all, to the Saviour of all who believe and hope in Him, and love Him, who, without beginning or end, is immutable, invisible, unerring, ineffable, incomprehensible, unfathomable, blessed, praiseworthy, glorious, exalted, sublime, most high, sweet, amiable, lovable, and always wholly desirable above all forever and ever.

In the Name of the Lord, I beseech all the brothers that they learn the tenor and sense of those things that are written in this life for the salvation of our souls, and frequently recall them to mind. And I pray God that He who is Almighty, Three in One, may bless all who teach, learn, hold, remember, and fulfill those things as often as they repeat and do what is there written for our salvation. And I entreat all, kissing their feet, to love greatly, keep and treasure up these things. And on the part of Almighty God and of the Lord Pope, and by obedience, I, Brother Francis, strictly command and enjoin that no one subtract from those things that are written in this life, or add anything written to it over and above, and that the brothers have no other Rule.

Glory be to the Father, and to the Son, and to the Holy Ghost. As it was in the beginning, is now and ever shall be, world without end. Amen.

Second Rule of the Friars Minor

In the Name of the Lord begins the life of the Minor Brothers.

The Rule and life of the Minor Brothers is this: namely, to observe the holy Gospel of our Lord Jesus Christ, by living in obedience, without property and in chastity. Brother Francis promises obedience and reverence to the Lord Pope Honorius and to his successors canonically elected and to the Roman Church. And let the other brothers be bound to obey Brother Francis and his successors.

Prayer to Obtain Divine Love
by St. Francis of Assisi

I beseech Thee, O Lord, that the fiery and sweet strength of Thy love may absorb my soul from all things that are under heaven, that I may die for love of Thy love as Thou didst deign to die for love of my love.

Prayer
by St. Francis of Assissi

Almighty, eternal, just, and merciful God, give to us wretches to do for Thee what we know Thee to will and to will always that which is pleasing to Thee; so that inwardly purified, inwardly illumined and kindled by the flame of the Holy Ghost, we may be able to follow in the footsteps of Thy Son, our Lord Jesus Christ, and by Thy grace alone come to Thee the Most High, who in perfect Trinity and simple Unity livest and reignest and gloriest God Almighty forever and ever. Amen.

Prayer of the Crucifix of Saint Damian
by St. Francis of Assissi

O high and glorious God, light up my heart.
Give me unswerving faith, certainty of hope, perfect charity; profound
    humility; wisdom and knowledge; that I might serve thee.

For the Passion

O children of the Church, weep with me today: the rocks are split asunder, the doors of the sepulcher are burst. Weep with me today for the bitter passion of the Son of Mary.

Therefore, be sad. With heavy heart gaze upon the great afflictions and sufferings which on this night the faultless One patiently underwent at the hands of the iniquitous Jews.

O unimaginable pain, here is the blood which purchased salvation for the human race. He who was the hope of Man took himself the pain and suffering, made himself as patient as a lamb, offered himself for our sins. Here He who redeems and liberates Man was made a prisoner and bound with cords. Like a thief was He tied, flayed, wounded with staffs, by His own creatures. And He was faultless.

How the Virgin weeps, how the disciples suffer, seeing the Lord in this moment! O magnanimous Father, out of charity to thee, the Son offers himself up in sacrifice. Impure sinners defile the Creator of the world, spit in His face, strike His chest, crying: Here is the guilty one who proclaims himself our God!

Man, it was through thy fault that Christ was put to death. He to whom all glory is due, goes obediently. They spit in His face. He falls to earth. With spears and thorns is He struck. Thus struck down and bound, we watch Him die.

Now the strong and invincible God is conquered, sentenced to death, He who with the blood and water of His sacred heart cured all the wounds of this grieving world.

O Judas, expert in sin, aware of the horrid crime, thou didst betray abominably, nor shall be forgiven. Woe unto thee! And woe unto them who acted with thee! They shall be torn apart in Hell, while the Son of the Virgin shall reign on high.

Now the spear is driven through Him whose works keep the world on its poles.

With His own heart he washes away the marks of sin. With all our hearts we must grieve for him, in the presence of God, and gaze at the harsh nails.

And you, perfidious Jews, who killed the Son of God, killed Him who called you out of the land of Egypt, who nourished you with celestial bread, make no sign of pardon to Him as He hangs suspended from the Cross.

Alas, the innocent One dies, the guilty is declared to be the just, while the true just is mortified, for evil is saved. Against all justice does death fall upon the just One, and fortune smiles on the unjust in equal measure. Let us weep and console ourselves upon this night.

O brothers of Judas, you who killed Christ, weep! Let your hearts be heavy with sin, that the Lord in His glory pardon you and admit you to His realm.

O Christian peoples, keep your hearts clean; venerate the Christ who died and was consumed for us; destroy the black net of sin; lift up your voices in glory to God, who holds compassion for all sinners.

Let us praise and adore the Son of God, who sacrificed Himself to destroy death and sin, who, dying, rose again to free us and call us to another life!

To the Virgin

O garment of the sun, bride of light, born of the Father, filled with divine spirit, show us the splendor of justice, thou who changed the beauty of Eve.

Thou walkest with the moon, shinest brighter than any star, hearest the songs of angels, Mother of light, Heaven's gate, now and forever.

On thy head is a crown of twelve stars in wondrous order; O Virgin, give us the Son as the stars give us rays.

O rose of the thorny plant, thou makest the lily bloom.

As clear as the dawn, splendorous, advance sweetly to us, come to us from the race of Jesse, from Aaron's rod, covered with flowers and leaves, O fruit of the almond tree.

Gleaming star of the sea, port of refuge, not all the storms of death can hurl us into inferno. Give aid to the shipwrecked on the seas of the world; intercede for them if they confide in thee.

O intact Lebanon, cypress of Zion, the river of Paradise encircles thee. Shower us with virtue, keep strife away. Let us know thy gift, and give us peaceful stars.

O Mother of Christ, the key of David, whose words can open the doors of the King and free prisoners from their cells, O Mother of Forgiveness, save us from the darkness of our miseries.

O tower of strength, shield of aid, a thousand breastplates gleam around thee. With thy power strike down all heresy. Through thy compassion, keep us from falling into sin through the idleness of our ways and of our nature.

In all the vast arch of Heaven there is none more worthy of praise than she, nor any similar to her, the Virgin Mary, bride of God, most humble Mother.

To the Virgin

O queen, divine light, pray for me,
O one more lovely than the rose, come to my heart.
Keep and protect Him, worthy of every praise,
Thy Son.
Hail, O Virgin, and keep me
From the assaults of Satan.
Hail, O precious arch of Christ,
the most beautiful flower.
O divine vase, O piteous fount,
be generous with thy gifts.
O sweet one, clement with all,
show us thy Son,
O splendor brighter than dawn,
after the exile.
May the Son of God
grant us many things,

and all to His glory.
Hail, O Virgin,
most high Mother,
hail, God's bride,
consolation in affliction.
He despairs not
who clings to thee
with all his soul.
Hail, O sure pathway.
guide us safely.
Hail, O celestial step to Heaven,
and forgive us.
Guide of the soul,
light in darkness,
shine for the wretched.
O forechosen from the beginning,
sovereign of the world,
O beatified, pleasing to God,
Queen of Heaven.
Have mercy on me,
O Virgin Mother,
in my exile.

To Saint Wenceslaus

I salute thee, O Prince of the Bohemians, father to the destitute, O merciful one, O Wenceslaus, illustrious of the illustrious. Enrich me with divine inspiration, that I may, enamoring myself of thee, sing of thy virtues, pray for signs of thy sanctity and proclaim thy miracles. For, without thy aid, my tongue cannot utter the glory of thy deeds.

When Christ desired to shower down glory and light on the land of the Bohemians, He, the true light of justice, caused thee to be born.

What tongue can relate thy great deeds, what lips can speak the miracles that in thy life thou worked, miracles that after thy death did claim the vows and prayers of the faithful?

Hear, then, my prayer, O Wenceslaus, and beatify me, O pious master; with thy prayers cleanse me of every impurity of the world, of the body and of the soul.

Since Jezebel thy mother and Cain thy brother harbored envy and rancor for thy works, they pushed thee along other pathways, with all the power at their command.

And thou in many ways didst show thyself great in thy love for Christ: on many nights thou went out, gathered up firewood in the forest and carried it on thy shoulder to the huts of the miserable and destitute, to the wretched and the needy.

To me, who am also wretched and needy and turn to thee, bring me the wood of life. Into my wicked soul, shred of every virtue, bring the divine breeze.

Busily in the fields thou cast the grain and worked the soil in the silence of the night, then gathered it at harvest time, gleaned it, crushed the grain, and made it into flour, and with divine care prepared the bread of the offering. Alone thou gathered the grape from the vine, pressed it, and distributed it to all the churches.

It was then that Satan instigated thy brother, who invited thee to a banquet and marked himself forever as an assassin, killing thee with his own hand and sword. Thus he made thee a martyr and destined thee for Heaven.

When he killed thee so ferociously, aligning himself on the side of Cain, thy blood spilled against the walls of the dwelling, and, though they were thrice washed, would not rub out: a sign of thy sanctity and thy goodness for all who beheld the sight.

The blood of Abel, now cries thy blood. O deign to vindicate to the terror of thy assassins thy blood with the sacred blood of Christ.

In this life permit me to venerate thy blood and thy martyrdom with such piety that, in the life to come, all my people and I may see thee seated next to Christ, the Son of God.

After three years thy body was exhumed and translated to the Church of Vitus in the city of Prague, from where, with a mighty sword, thou governest Bohemia.

There thou knowest peace, and art daily praised by the clergy and the people.

Here, in the name of thy good works, come manifestations and miracles, here whatever is asked is granted, here every plea growing out of true necessity is answered.

O sacred Prince Wenceslaus, hear my prayer and be not tardy in liberating me from this wicked and impure world. Call me up to thee in the eternal realm, that I may participate throughout all time, far from evil, in the divine glory.

Confiding in God

Neither this song nor those following it were born out of poetic inspiration. Rather, they were authentic forms of popular prayer orally repeated and handed down from generation to generation. They reflect a spirit of popular piety very seldom found in our religious history. . . . [These compositions] have such a popular stamp upon them as to make them seem at first glance the general heritage, used and abused, of the entire population. Certainly there can be found in them no particular evidence of poetic inspiration, not even that of a crude poet.

> My faults I tell to thee, God,
> to Jesus Christ my Lord,
> of the evil I have done,
> of the evil I have worked.
> Forgiveness I ask of thee,
> crying and weeping openly,
> and with the mind pleading,
> for I am so fallen.
> If thou wishest to forgive me,
> certainly thou mayest,
> but if justice must be used,
> I stand here ready.
> Do with me what thou will,
> my true Lord Jesus,
> for I think thou wishest peace,
> ever-beautiful King.
> Justice halts
> before pity for our faults,
> just are thy words,
> thou endest argument.
> If justice please thee,
> then punish me,
> though the thought is saddening,
> so am I fallen.
> If mercy please thee more,
> my sadness is not so sore,
> do thy will
> O beatified Father.
> If justice thou must do,
> so shall I receive my due,
> but if mercy be decreed,

just is thy work indeed.
To thy works, O Lord,
I sing, and praise the Word,
as pleaseth thee, the Maker
of every mortal creature.
Amen.

From the Song Or Alditi Mata Pacia

I would like to save my soul
and keep my spirit whole,
for Christ is my goal,
though to suffer not my wish.
When I rejoice, I say:
to Lord Jesus let us pray.
Then suddenly I turn away
like Peter from the fish.
I'm a rake when not in war,
battles with me are quickly o'er,
for the enemy does surely gore
me with my own arms.
Of judgment day and Hell,
my fears are greater than tongue can tell,
and yet I do damn myself well
each day, for all my deep alarms.
Though saddened am I in this mire,
virtue I do not acquire,
nor correct what brings His ire,
yet Paradise I long to see.
I would have Heaven's misericord,
with God I'm always in discord,
if with Him I were in concord,
death would not frighten me.
But it's bad to say it this way,
and worse not to want to fly away,
for though death has me for his prey,
I live in rollickeria.
I'm here to prove that Christ was right,
and so I sin with all my might,
many have I seen die without delight
and no repentance at all particularly pia.

If I am drawn into sin,
repentance isn't worth a pin,
where I can no longer sin,
to God would I return.
I'm here but to depart,
with no true repentance in my heart,
so let the sentence cast this upstart
down where mortals burn.
Death is already hard upon me,
to the fiery regions I go swiftly,
devils are dancing around me freely
to escort me to the door.
A wicked madman am I, a clod,
highly uncomfortable 'neath the eye of God.
I flay myself with my own rod,
leaving my flesh torn sore.
Since I am wicked and mad,
I live madly and am sad
that God is lost to the bad
in the world, by their madness.
Greater my madness, greater my terror,
for knowing clearly my own error,
since to me no light is fairer
than that which I in dying would caress.
O powerful, O generous,
O infinite tenderness,
three and One in essence blessed,
cure me of this madness.
Amen.

Lament of Love

Blessed be the day
of love that lighted,
with thy sweet touch,
my heart and righted
it with love of such
sweetness that my blighted
soul spoke, saying: Ohimé, Jesu ohimé,
love teareth me apart, ohimé.

How can my lips tell
of the gift to see
and know the deep well
of my sin, and repent me?
Thou entered in my cell,
I long now for thee.
Jesu, Jesu, Jesu,
what must this soul do?
I long for thee,
knowing not what to do,
feeling thy gift to me,
that did imbue
the spirit in me
with a spirit new,
made only to love thee.
Jesu, Jesu, Jesu,
what must this soul do?
Thou wishest me to love thee,
only to shower me with thy gifts,
O what error still is in me,
to make me flee thy gifts!
for which I pray thee:
send me strength which uplifts.
Ohimé, Jesu Ohimé.
love teareth me apart, Ohimé.
I would like to follow thee
in thy pain,
in thy sanctity,
through all thy reign,
such is my love for thee,
such is my pain.
Jesu, Jesu, Jesu,
What must this soul do?
Garlands I would like to wear
for thee, the crowned King,
and lay my vileness bare
while to thee I sing
of the love and the care
thou to wanderers bring,
Ohimé, Jesu Ohimé,
love teareth me apart.

For I have wandered far
from the light of thy grace,
and pray thee not to bar
me from thy face.
May this forlorn star
come to thee apace.
Jesu, Jesu, Jesu,
what must this soul do?
Sweet fruit of Mary,
when will I dwell
melodiously
inside thy shell?
Then I would wish from thee
nothing more to tell.
Ohimé, Jesu Ohimé,
love teareth me apart, Ohimé.
Safe in thy breast
I would burn without consuming,
in eternal love and rest,
thy light illuming,
my soul caressed,
my endless blooming.
Jesu, Jesu, Jesu,
what must this soul do?
O quiet solitude,
let me in, if it please thee,
make me a bride imbued
with love as constant as the sea,
and let this heart so rude
follow forever after thee.
Jesu, Jesu, Jesu,
what must this soul do?

To the Virgin

Let us salute devotedly
the Blessed Virgin,
and saying Hail Mary,
may she be praised forever.
Let us salute her sweetly
and with great solemnity,

for we know truly
that through her humility
was the Divine Majesty
enamored of her.
The angel set out to tell
of the lovely virgin girl,
and passing through the cell
did swirl
and tell us the nouvelle.
The angel said Hail Mary,
thou art filled with every virtue:
"Dominus be with thee
from whom comes every blessing
and all grace,
O we salute thee.
Blessed above all others
be thee always,
since thou art virgin
and free from ugly thoughts.
God sends me as His messenger,
that no one be kept waiting for the news."
Clinging to the column
in fright at the news,
tears streamed down
the High Virgin's cheeks,
fearful that the angel
had deceived her.
The Virgin was bewildered, and frightened too,
when she heard the angel speak.
She was honest and ashamed
and began to tremble fearfully—ashamed
of being with him, for she was
unused to company.

The Blessed Cross

Blessed Cross
perfecter of life
true and worthy Cross
for us so sweet
and heart-rending
—of the redeeming Christ,
—for every sinner,
—gladdened by Christ
—O my soul be worthy
—in the face of sin

From all depraved things
Keep it and guard it,
That it never burn with pain
Nor know suffering again.

Truly the Cross   —with great devotion
all of us must honor   —that in communion
for that passion   —we are worthy.
And who has no tears   —think on the torn
is of harsh bitterness   —Christ for our love.

Good is thy blessing
More than ever,
That for thy reason
Cast that cry.

Such is the Way   —of the soul and heart
to give voluntarily   —to redeeming Christ
against the spear's thrust   —and the painful nails
so painful was it   —the wicked Jews
when the hands and feet   —bound tight with pain.

O our Saviour
Who redeemed us
With the precious blood
from the mark of sin.
Pious King of love—beatified
By that glorious Father
So desirous of having
Perfect peace.
Look upon us, Christ,
Our redeemer.

To the Virgin

Praise be unto the Virgin Mary,
all praise be unto the beatified Mary,
called by Gabriel,
hail, full of grace.
Thou received the news,
sweet lady,
and then were named handmaiden,
for thou art hand in hand with God,
and out of these truly came
Jesus Christ the omnipotent.

Jesus Christ the eternal Lord,
Gabriel announced that coming
so worthy of honor,
and thou didst give birth
in the manger purely.
When the Child was born,
the star was seen;
it lit up all with
a light so clean.
The three wise men came carrying,
gifts they came bearing.
Herod was told
of the blessed Child
who would become King
and Lord of all the earth.
Herod caused all infants
of a year to be banished.
And Mary and Joseph
fled into Egypt
With Christ their Son.
For already the angel
had whispered: Cause the
Baby to flee.

Song of Praise

With heartfelt tears
we pray to the Mother.
allayer of all fears,
to receive our Brother.
Receive him in Paradise gladly,
where joy abounds happily,
where he with smiling face
will worship the Father.

Sacred Madonna Mary

Mother of every sinner,
we pray thee in the name of Christ
to pardon him.
O God and Father pardon him
in his turn

of every wicked thought and sin,
let him return.
Our Father to thee we say
our own bodies we will flay,
to come to know the Word
of Jesus Christ our Lord.

Prayer of Christ

O Father of mine I pray
thee this pain allay,
this cruel hurt so deep,
this harsh death I reap,
this suffering so strong,
borne so long,
and yet I know it will
remedy every ill,
so must it be with me,
for I have faith in thee.

In Praise of Christ

This oration, of which we give only an excerpt, is attributed, like so many others of the time, to the Beatified Brigida. Siena, fourteenth century.

Honor and glory be unto thee, my Lord Jesus Christ, who was conceived in the womb of the Virgin through the presence of the Holy Spirit and humbly dwelt therein until the time of thy birth. Then, after thy wondrous nativity, thou deigned to let the Mother touch thee with her pure hands and wrap thee in swaddling clothes and lay thee in the manger.

Blessed art thou, my Lord Jesus Christ, who wanted thy immaculate flesh to be circumcised, and wished to be called Jesu and offered unto the temple by thy Mother.

Blessed art thou, my Lord Jesus Christ, who wished to be baptized in the River Jordan by thy servant John.

Blessed art thou, my Lord Jesus Christ, who with thy blessed mouth personally spoke the Word of life, and who didst work many miracles.

Blessed art thou, my Lord Jesus Christ, who, fulfilling the word of the prophets, manifested in thyself the true God.

Honor be unto thee, my Lord Jesus Christ, who, during the passion and the death, dripped bloody perspiration from thy innocent body, and brought about our redemption, which thou wished to do; and in so doing, demonstrated the charity thou had for humankind.

Glory unto thee, my Lord Jesus Christ, for the derision and scorn thou underwent when dressed in purple and crowned with sharp thorns. And patiently bore the cruel spit in thy glorious face, and patiently withstood the blows on the face and body from the hands of iniquitous men.

Praised be thee, my Lord Jesus Christ, who as meekly as a lamb let them bind thee to the column and flagellate thee cruelly; and, bleeding, let them drag thee before Pilate and the people.

Blessed art thou, my Lord Jesus Christ, who patiently in the presence of Pilate listened to the opprobriums and vituperations and the lies. And heard the voices of the mob cry out that the thief and malefactor be freed, and that thou, most innocent, be condemned; with thy sacred ears thou heard the words.

Eternal praise and thanks be unto thee, my Lord Jesus Christ, who so meekly died for us, suffering such cruel pains. When thy blessed body lost its strength, and thou hung dead on the Cross, thy gentle eyes misted over, thy bloodless face turned pale and white, thy tongue became parched and dry: and thy mouth was wet with the most bitter drink. And hair and beard were matted with blood that flowed from the crushed and sacred head. The bones of thy hands and feet and of all thy body were disjointed and dislocated, to thy immeasurable agony; cruelly did the veins and nerves of thy precious body split asunder. So inhumanly flagellated and covered with sore wounds were thou that thy innocent flesh was most vilely torn and lacerated; thou suffered much. And still, my sweet Lord, thou hung from the Cross, and patiently in the hour of death, waited.

In Praise of Christ's Bodily Parts

Attributed to Brigida, Siena, fourteenth century.

My Lord Jesus Christ, since thy blessed nose was not horrified at the stench of the dead and smelling body of Lazarus, nor smelled the horrible stench which came from Judas the traitor when he kissed thee, therefore let thy precious nose be blessed, let it be praised, and may it be eternally sweet. Amen.

My Lord Jesus Christ, since with thy spotless teeth thou didst eat meagerly to sustain thy beautiful body, therefore let them be blessed and honored by all thy creatures. Amen.

My Lord Jesus Christ, since thy tongue never moved uselessly, nor could be stilled when thou had divine and fore-ordered things to say about justice, therefore let thy tongue be blessed. Amen.

My Lord Jesus Christ, since in accordance with the times thou wore a full beard on thy handsome face, therefore let that beard be honored and venerated throughout all times to come. Amen.

My Lord Jesus Christ, blessed be thy throat, thy stomach, and thy sacred inner parts, that they may nourish thy precious body with all due order, and perfectly sustain thy corporal life, and restore thy soul to joyousness. Amen.

My Lord Jesus Christ, blessed throughout eternity be thy precious ribs, thy shoulders, and thy back; may all earthly and spiritual men bless them; and if these men toil and sweat under earthly burdens, let them remember that from thy birth until thy death thou toiled and sweated to redeem us all, and bore great burdens of pain on thy back. Amen.

My Lord Jesus Christ, purest of the pure, may thy most innocent loins be blessed and praised above all angelic purity, which resides in Heaven, and above all innocent purity; for they remained chaste and virgin in the world. Therefore, no chastity or virginity can equal or resemble thine in purity. Amen.

My Lord Jesus Christ, by all the creatures of Heaven and earth, let thy thighs and legs and knees be revered and honored above all others; for in kneeling before God the knees paid reverence and honor. Thou didst kneel down before every thing, O Lord, with humility; before thy Disciples, and above all before Judas. Amen.

My Lord Jesus Christ, good teacher, may thy beatified feet be blessed and perpetually praised for having followed a path of such suffering in order to teach others the path to follow, and thou went along it barefooted. Live and reign with God the Father in the unity of the Holy Spirit, per omnia saecula saeculorum. Amen.

In Praise of the Virgin's Bodily Parts

Attributed to Brigida.

My Madonna, my Life, Regina of Heaven, Sacred Mother, very certain though I am that thy glorious body is praised perpetually in Heaven by the whole host of the celestial Court, nonetheless should I, unworthy though I be, like to praise thee on earth and sing to thy precious form with all my heart. Therefore, O my Madonna, Virgin Mary, may thy head and thy hair be crowned with a crown of glory. Just as one cannot count the hairs on thy head, so too are thy virtues beyond enumeration.

O my Madonna Virgin Mary, may thy most honest face be blessed with such radiance as to cause the faithful, seeing it through the shadows of this dark world, to be infused with spiritual consolation.

Blessed art thou, my Madonna Virgin Mary, whose eyelashes are more beautiful than the rays of the sun.

Blessed are thy most chaste eyes, O my Madonna Virgin Mary, that gazed with desire upon no earthly thing in this world; therefore, on whatever or whomever thine eyes did shine, their aspect surpassed the beauty of the stars.

O my Madonna Virgin Mary, all praise to the beauty of thy cheeks that glow with greater beauty than the dawn, which rises in colors of red and white. So did thy cheeks shine in splendor before God and all the angels; and never did thou flaunt their beauty out of mundane pomp or vanity.

O my Madonna Virgin Mary, may thy beautiful ears be revered and honored above the strength of the sea itself; for thine ears were ever turned against all foulness, and listened always to the true and good.

O my Madonna Virgin Mary, may thy sweet nose be glorified; for it did not keep the virtue of the Holy Spirit to itself, but breathed it forth sweetly, proof of thy love for the Most High God. Even when asleep, thou did not draw away from God's will. Let, then, thy nose be praised and blessed above all sweet things, even above the herbs and grasses that send forth their fragrance in thy honor.

O my Madonna Virgin Mary, may thy gracious tongue be praised in the presence of God and all the angels, above even the trees with their fruits; for never did thy tongue utter a word that harmed any person, but spoke ever prudently and usefully; it was sweet indeed to hear, more sweet than fruit to taste.

O Regina and Mother and Madonna Virgin Mary, may thy mouth and lips be blessed above the sweetness and odor of the rose and all the other flowers, especially for those most humble words thy mouth did speak when replying to the Angel of God who came to tell of His will, as the Prophets had foreseen. Thy virtue diminished the power of the Demon of inferno.

O Virgin Mary, my Madonna and consolation, may thy beauteous neck and shoulders be blessed and praised above the beauties of lilies and all the flowers; for never did these parts incline themselves except in honor of God, nor lift themselves for any other reason. But since the lily inclines itself and bends to the breeze, so did thou incline and bend to the will of the Holy Spirit.

O my Madonna, virtuous and sweet, may thy arms and hands and fingers be eternally honored and praised above all the gems, however precious; which gems resemble in beauty thy virtuous works. And so, as thy virtuous works brought unto thee the Son of God, so did thy arms and hands sweetly embrace Him and draw Him to thee in eternal love.

O my Madonna and my illumination, may thy saintly breasts be blessed and praised above all other sweet founts; for just as sweet founts give consolation and relief to the parched throat, so did thy breasts, nursing the Son of God, give relief and balm to the suffering and the needy.

O my Madonna Virgin Mary, may thy precious bosom be blessed and praised above all precious ore, however pure; for when standing below the Cross on which thy Son was nailed, thy bosom felt the hammers fall and the nails rive, until thy bosom heaved beneath the torture. And though thou loved thy Son, thou would have him undergo that bitter pain; that He might die to save the soul, that the soul might rise again; that the soul might not die forever; and so, in thy virtue thou stood steadfast, thus conforming to the will of God in all adversity.

O my Madonna Virgin Mary, delight of my heart, may thy most reverent heart be honored and praised above all other things of Heaven and earth, thy heart which loved God above all things, thy heart whose flaming charity showed itself to God on high in Heaven; for which God sent the Heavenly Son by means of the Holy Spirit to thy glorious womb.

O my Madonna, most fertile and Virgin Mary, may thy womb be blessed and praised above all fruitful trees of the field: for just as the seed which falls on good soil brings forth hundreds of plants for its possessor, so did thy seed bring forth, not hundreds, but hundreds of thousands of plants for the Father. And for this abundance of fruit of the field, the Lord is glorified: for still do the birds and beasts feed of this fruit. And so for the blessed fruit of thy womb, God is honored in Heaven, the angels rejoice, and earthly creatures live and are sustained.

O my Madonna, most prudent Virgin, may thy sacred feet be eternally praised above all the roots that continually give forth fruit, for thy blessed feet carried the Son of God—the most glorious fruit—in thy uncorrupted body; and thy virginity yet did remain intact. O how honestly thy sacred feet went their way! Truly, each footprint brought consolation to the celestial King, and caused the choirs of Heaven to sing happily. O my Madonna Virgin Mary, mother of all, in the name of God, the Son and the Holy Spirit, may that haven which carried the Son so gently be eternally praised above all thy bodily parts; for all the angels in Heaven now honor Him, and all the Churches of earth do pay him homage.

O my Lord, my King, my God, to thee all honor perpetually, to thee all praise and glory perpetually, to thee infinite thanksgiving, for having created that most worthy and honest Virgin who became the Mother, thus bringing consolation both to Heaven and to earth. May there be consolation also for those in purgatory. For he lives and reigns in saecula saeculorum. Amen.

Oration of Saint Brandano

All saints and disciples of the Lord, all saints and successors, pray for me. All saints of Princes, Bishops, Priests, Deacons, Subdeacons, Readers, Exorcisers, Servers, Martyrs, Confessors, Virgins, Monks, Clergy, Laity, Women, Men, Servants, Rich, Poor, Doctors, Workers; these and the saints of the perfect Trinity, let them be the glory of my soul and body, and my companion. Let them guard and keep me in seeing, hearing, tasting, smelling, and touching; in my flesh and blood and all my bones; in my nerves and veins and marrow, in the joints of my bones, in life, in death. Defend me, Lord, from the uplifted hand, from the left, from the right, from above and below, on sea and on land, in water and in fire, while entering and exiting, sleeping and awake, by night and by day, and in the hour of death and for all the days of my life. Keep me, O Lord, Sacred Trinity, omnipotent One, from all the perils on earth, from the perils of the sea, from wild fantasies, from four-footed beasts, and from those that drag themselves across the ground, and from serpents.

O omnipotent God, keep me safe from fire, lightning, thunder, hail, floods, earthquakes, from poison things, from envy, from the evil eye, from wicked words, perils, darkness, from all that flies in darkness, from the tempting demon of the day. Defend me, O Lord, against all evil and anger which stands opposed to Good.

At the Hour of Death

I pray to Sacred Madonna Mary and to the twenty-four precious saints and to all the angels and archangels; to all the patriarchs and prophets; to all the apostles and martyrs, confessors, virgins, and to all the other saintly and elect, that in this hour in which my soul departs the flesh, they come to my aid.

I pray to thee and ask mercy of thee, Saint Michael, Archangel of God, protector of mortal souls, and ask thee to free my soul from the hands of the enemy, that I might pass by the gates of the inferno and along the darkened path, that the dragon not rise up to take me, nor the lion, whose habit it is to seize sinning souls and drag them into inferno.

I pray to Saint Peter, Prince of Apostles, who holds the keys to Paradise, that he may open the door to me. O Dominus God omnipotent, creator of earth and Heaven, hear my plea and the mercy which I, a sinner, ask of thee; be merciful: receive me; I pray for thy mercy, for the modulation of the corpse; hear my plea: grant me in this life more life and health, and grant me time enough to do penitence; and in future centuries grant me forgiveness, indulgence, remission of all my sins, that I might live forever with all the saints. Amen.

To the Virgin
BY CARDINAL DI BERULLE

This prayer and those which follow are characteristic of that devoted humanism and piety inaugurated by the French school of the seventeenth century, against which one finds accented the severe form of Jansenistic piety.

You are a paradise wherein the serpent may not enter. The custodian angel which guards the gate is more fiery than was the earthly angel, and keeps malign spirits far from you.

You are a "closed orchard" and a "well-guarded fount," a treasure that God hid in the secret of wisdom, His wisdom, as one day you will have that secret hidden inside you, in your virginal breast.

Malign spirits cannot enter into you, nor do they have any knowledge of a treasure hidden in that manner; for them your graces are invisible and your privileges unknown; even your virginal state is hidden from them by your marriage to Saint Joseph, the scope of which is to keep the secret of virgin birth closed to demons; as Saint Ignatius says: *Ut partus ejus celaretur diabolo.*

An Offer of Oneself to the Virgin
BY CARDINAL DI BERULLE

Out of consideration for such elevated, sublime, and sacred matters, I offer myself, subject myself, and consecrate myself to Jesus Christ my Lord and Saviour, who did serve the Most Holy Mother, Virgin Mary. In perpetual honor to the Mother and the Son, I declare myself in a state of servitude, out of respect for her who is the Mother of my Lord, that I might more humbly and saintly bow down before such an elevated and divine quality of spirit; in her name I abandon myself as a slave, in honor of the gift of the eternal Word she gave down through herself and the Incarnation of her Son, which word it was His wish to communicate through her. I, therefore, give up all power over my own actions. I cede this power to the Sacred Virgin, put it wholly in her hands, out of homage to the great renunciation which she made through her Son Jesus Christ our Lord.

To her I cede the power that God gave me over myself, with the result that I belong no longer to myself, but to her; and to her, not to me, belongs the dominion over myself; I do this out of homage to the humble submission of Jesus Christ, who put Himself under her direction and guidance, both in His infancy and during the time of his sojourn on this earth.

To the Virgin
BY CARDINAL DI BERULLE

O fount of life and grace, refuge of sinners, I turn to you, that I might live in the grace of my God and avoid sin, and be kept from eternal death.

Grant me your special protection, let me partake of your privileges, and by virtue of your greatness and your right of property over me, let me obtain what I in my smallness am unworthy of obtaining. In honor of that wondrous moment when God was made Incarnate and you were made the Mother, I put myself wholly in your hands during these last hours of my life, hours which will be decisive for me throughout eternity.

O Virgin and Mother! O sacred temple of Divinity! O wonder of earth and Heaven! O Mother of my Lord, I belong to you because of your greatness and generosity, but wish to belong to you because of my dedication, resolution, and choice. I consecrate myself to you and to your only Son Jesus Christ our Saviour, and wish no day to pass that I do not pay Him and you some homage particularly reflective of my dependence on you, and my servitude for you, a spirit in which I wish to live and die. So be it.

To the Virgin
BY B. CAMBI DA SALUTIO

Is it possible, it is possible, is it possible, O most saintly Queen, that one may not have help from you?

And are you not the one, my Madonna, who became Mother of the

Lord and Queen of Heaven, for the purpose of helping the poor in heart, the afflicted and those with tribulations?

Are you not the haven and refuge for sinners, most saintly Madonna?

Why, then, do you not wish to help me and free me from my sufferings and tribulations?

O most saintly Queen, take care that this voice does not cry out that you abandon instead of come to the aid of the poor in heart, the afflicted, and those with tribulations. Take care, great Queen, that this voice does not come out, that you do lose your reputation and honor. And take particular care that these things are never said: A poor wretch, sorely tried and afflicted, at the extremes of his force, prayed to you with tears and great affliction in his heart, and he died that way, and you would neither free him nor listen to him.

Affections and Resolutions
BY SAINT FRANCIS DE SALES

Be confounded at your misery. O my God! how dare I appear in thy presence? I am, alas! but the corruption of the world; a sink of ingratitude and iniquity. Is it possible that I should have been so ungrateful as not to have left any one of the senses of my body, or of the powers of my soul, which I have not corrupted, violated, and defiled, and that not so much as one day of my life has passed which has not produced its wicked effects? Is this the return I should have made for the benefits of my Creator, and the blood of my Redeemer?

The Election of Paradise
BY SAINT FRANCIS DE SALES

O hell! I detest thee now and forevermore; I detest thy torments and pains; I detest thy accursed and miserable eternity, and above all, I detest those eternal blasphemies and maledictions which thou vomitest out against my God. And, turning my heart and soul toward thee, O heavenly paradise, everlasting glory, and endless felicity! I choose my habitation forever within thy Holy and most lovely tabernacles. I bless thy mercy, O my God! and I accept of the offer which thou art pleased to make me. O Jesus, my sweet Saviour! I accept thy everlasting love, and the place which thou hast purchased for me in this blessed Jerusalem; not so much for any other motive as to love and bless thee forever and ever

The Election of the Life of Devotion
BY SAINT FRANCIS DE SALES

O world! O abominable troop! No, never shall you see me under your banners! I have forever abandoned your trifles and vanities. O king of pride! O accursed king! infernal spirit! I renounce thee with all thy vain pomp, I detest thee with all thy works.

And, turning myself to thee, my dear Jesus! King of eternal glory and happiness! I embrace thee with all the powers of my soul! I adore thee with my whole heart, and choose thee now and forever for my king; with this inviolable fidelity, I pay thee irrevocable homage, and submit myself to the obedience of thy holy laws and ordinances.

O sacred Virgin! beloved Mother! I choose thee for my guide, I put myself under thy protection; I offer thee a particular respect and special reverence.

O my good Angel! present me to this sacred assembly, and forsake me not till I am associated to this blessed company, with whom I say, and will say forever in testimony of my choice, live Jesus, live Jesus!

Amorous Exclamation and Wailing Lamentation
BY MOLINOS

O divine Lord! How few the souls in this world who serve you with perfection! How few in number those who wish to suffer, who follow the crucified Christ, who embrace the Cross, who deny themselves and scorn themselves! O what a scarcity of pious souls! How few souls live and die for God! How few are perfectly resigned! What a scarcity of souls shining with simple obedience, with humility and self-knowledge! How few abandon themselves totally and put themselves in the hands of God, in His divine will! How scarce are pure souls and simple hearts which, stripped of their knowing, desiring, and wishing, are panting for negation!

O how scarce the number of souls who wish to let the divine Creator work within them, who suffer in order not to suffer, and die in order not to die! How few are the souls that wish to deny themselves, to cleanse the heart of its longings, desires, satisfactions, of its self-love and judgment! How few who wish to follow the path of negation and the inner light! Who wish to obscure themselves, dying for their senses and for themselves! How few wish to vow, purify, and lay themselves bare, that God might dress them and fill them with perfection! And finally, O Lord, how small is the number of blind, mute, deaf, and contemplative souls!

A Bride's Lament
BY SAINT JOHN OF THE CROSS

> Ah, where art thou hidden, Beloved?
> Heard thou me not call to thee?
> like a deer thou hast fled,
> having wounded me;
> crying, I followed: thou had fled me!
> Shepherds, you who go
> from hut to hut on the plain,
> if by chance you know
> him who caused my heart this pain,
> tell him for me: I die of this pain.
> In search of my love so sweet
> I shall go to these mountains and rivers,
> nor gather the flowers at my feet,
> nor fear misgivers,
> passing over the borders and rivers.
> O thick trees and wilderness
> planted by the hand of my Beloved,
> O grass of tenderness,
> all with flowers covered,
> tell me if here his shadow hovered.

To the Sleeping Baby Jesus
BY SAINT ALFONSO M. DE' LIGUORI

This song and those that follow, up to "*Praise Mary,*" form a part of the famous collection of spiritual songs so many times republished, modified, and corrected, that the Neapolitan saint composed for little children. Their spirit is rare indeed for Italian religious poetry, usually so courtly and formalistic. These poems have a freshness that made them favorites throughout the nineteenth century.

> The harmony
> of the skies
> stood still when Mary
> whispered sighs
> to Jesus in lullabies.

In a divine tone
the beautiful one,
in bliss
said this:
My baby, my Baby,
rest thy sweet head;
thou sleepest, and I,
before such beauty, am wont to die.
Sleeping, my sweet,
thou seest me not above,
but thy breath is sweet
and filled with love.
O beautiful closed eyes
that wound me,
when you are open,
how will it be?
The rosy cheeks
steal away my heart,
O God! must this child
from me part!
I force a kiss
upon the sweet lip,
pardon me, Dear,
'twas a slip, a slip.
She quieted then,
and in deep bliss,
on the Divine Face
placed a kiss.
He awoke,
filled with love,
regarded the Mother
above.
Ah God! how those eyes
stilled the Mother's
lullabies,
and hurt her!

On the Passion

O proud whips that of my Lord
tore the flesh like a cruel sword,

    pain Him no more, I pray,
    pain not the Way,
    torment Him no more.
    Flay the sins He died for.
    O harsh thorns that of my Lord
    pierced the head like a cruel sword,
    pain Him no more, I pray,
    pain not the Way,
    torment Him no more.
    Flay the sins He died for.
    O hard nails that of my Lord
    rived the flesh like a cruel sword,
    pain Him no more, I pray,
    pain not the Way,
    torment Him no more.
    Flay the sins He died for.
    O tyrannous lance that of my Lord
    cut the flesh like a cruel sword,
    pain Him no more, I pray,
    pain not the Way,
    torment Him no more.
    Cut away the sins He died for.

To Jesus

O my Jesus, who tortured thee and bound thee with those cords?
    It was I; I am guilty.
    Ah God! I ask thy pity!
O my Jesus, who struck that beautiful face so harshly?
O my Jesus, who flung the mud and spittle against thee?
O my Jesus, who lashed that beautiful flesh so cruelly?
O my Jesus, who pressed those thorns down upon thee?
O my Jesus, who laid that Cross upon that back?
O my Jesus, who filled thy mouth with bitterness?
O my Jesus, who drove those nails into thy hands?
O my Jesus, who drove those nails into thy feet?
O my Mary, who robbed thee of thy Son and killed Him?
    It was I; I am guilty.
    Ah Mary! I ask thy pity!

Praise Mary

Praise, praise,
praise Mary.
Praise Mary,
O faithful tongues,
let your voices rise
in harmony to the skies!
Mary, thou art a lily
of purity,
who was enamored of the Word
thy Son.
A light divine,
a beauteous dawn,
let the moon incline,
let the sun fawn.
With a powerful foot
thou ground
the ancient serpent
forever down.
Thy pure bosom
did afford
food to Jesus,
our Lord.
Now reign, sweet Queen,
midst angels'
voices
pure and clean.
Heaven gives thee
beauteous things,
thy crown is formed
in starlit rings.
O Mother Mary,
mystic flower,
aid my spirit
in this hour.

Prayer of the Italian Resistance

O Lord who raised up thy Cross among men, whose spirit revolted
against perfidy, against the interests of the powerful and the inertness

of the masses, give now to us who are assailed by cruel forces within ourselves, the same forces that once crushed Thee to earth, the strength to revolt.

God of Liberty and Truth, make us free: breathe life into us, tighten our will, multiply our strength, dress us in Thy armor. We pray Thee, O Lord.

Thou who were cursed, refused, betrayed, persecuted, and crucified, sustain us in this dark hour: be food for us, save us from dangers, comfort us during the bitter moments. As the adversary becomes darker and more confused, let us become more clear in mind and spirit. When we are tortured, seal our lips. Break us, but let us not bend.

If we should die, cause our blood to mix with thine and with our other Dead, that justice and charity might rise again.

Thou who said, "I am the Resurrection and the Life," grant to Italy in its suffering a generous and austere life. Free us from temptations; watch over our families.

On the wind-swept mountains, from the catacombs of the city, from the prisons, we pray to Thee: Give us peace. God of peace and all armies, God of joy and of the sword, hear our prayer.

LUTHERANISM

The Festival of the Reformation

Collect:

O Lord God, Heavenly Father, pour out, we beseech Thee, Thy Holy Spirit upon Thy faithful people, keep them steadfast in Thy grace and truth, protect and comfort them in all temptation, defend them against all enemies of Thy Word, and bestow upon Christ's Church militant Thy saving peace; through the same Jesus Christ, Thy Son, our Lord, Who liveth and reigneth with Thee and the Holy Ghost, ever One God, world without end. Amen.

The Festival of Harvest

Collect:

Almighty God, Most Merciful Father, Who openest Thy hand, and satisfiest the desire of every living thing: We give Thee most humble and hearty thanks that Thou hast crowned the fields with Thy blessing, and hast permitted us once more to gather in the fruits of the earth;

and we beseech Thee to bless and protect the living seed of Thy Word sown in our hearts, that in the plenteous fruits of righteousness we may always present to Thee an acceptable thank-offering; through Jesus Christ, Thy Son, our Lord, Who liveth and reigneth with Thee and the Holy Ghost, ever One God, world without end. Amen.

The First Sunday in Advent

Collect:

Stir up, we beseech Thee, Thy power, O Lord, and come; that by Thy protection we may be rescued from the threatening perils of our sins, and saved by Thy mighty deliverance; Who livest and reignest with the Father and the Holy Ghost, ever One God, world without end. Amen.

The Second Sunday in Advent

Collect:

Stir up our hearts, O Lord, to make ready the way of Thine Only-begotten Son, so that by His coming we may be enabled to serve Thee with pure minds; through the same Jesus Christ, Thy Son, our Lord, Who liveth and reigneth with Thee and the Holy Ghost, ever One God, world without end. Amen.

The Third Sunday in Advent

Collect:

Lord, we beseech Thee, give ear to our prayers, and lighten the darkness of our hearts, by Thy gracious visitation; Who livest and reignest with the Father and the Holy Ghost, ever One God, world without end. Amen.

The Fourth Sunday in Advent

Collect:

Stir up, O Lord, we beseech Thee, Thy power, and come, and with great might succor us, that by the help of Thy grace whatsoever is hindered by our sins may be speedily accomplished, through Thy mercy and satisfaction; Who livest and reignest with the Father, and the Holy Ghost, ever One God, world without end. Amen.

Matins—The Collect for Grace

O Lord, our Heavenly Father, Almighty and Everlasting God, Who hast safely brought us to the beginning of this day: Defend us in the same with Thy mighty power; and grant that this day we fall into no sin, neither run into any kind of danger; but that all our doings, being ordered by Thy governance, may be righteous in Thy sight; through Jesus Christ, Thy Son, our Lord, Who liveth and reigneth with Thee and the Holy Ghost, ever One God, world without end.

May God Bestow on Us His Grace
BY MARTIN LUTHER

> May God bestow on us His grace,
>   With blessings rich provide us,
> And may the brightness of His face
>   To life eternal guide us
> That we His saving health may know,
>   His gracious will and pleasure.
> And also to the heathen show
>   Christ's riches without measure
> And unto God convert them.
>
> Thine over all shall be the praise
>   And thanks of every nation,
> And all the world with joy shall raise
>   The voice of exultation;
> For Thou shalt judge the earth, O Lord,
>   Nor suffer sin to flourish;
> Thy people's pasture is Thy Word
>   Their souls to feed and nourish,
> In righteous paths to keep them.
>
> Oh, let the people praise Thy worth,
>   In all good works increasing;
> The land shall plenteous fruit bring forth,
>   Thy Word is rich in blessing.
> May God the Father, God the Son,
>   And God the Spirit bless us!
> Let all the world praise Him alone,
>   Let solemn awe possess us.
> Now let our hearts say, Amen.

All Praise to Thee; Eternal God
BY MARTIN LUTHER

All praise to Thee, eternal God,
Who, clothed in garb of flesh and blood,
Dost take a manger for Thy throne,
While worlds on worlds are Thine alone.
Hallelujah!

Once did the skies before Thee bow;
A virgin's arms contain Thee now,
While angels, who in Thee rejoice,
Now listen for Thine infant voice.
Hallelujah!

A little Child, Thou art our Guest
That weary ones in Thee may rest;
Forlorn and lowly is Thy birth
That we may rise to heaven and earth.
Hallelujah!

Thou comest in the darksome night
To make us children of the light,
To make us in the realms divine,
Like Thine own angels, round Thee shine.
Hallelujah!

All this for us Thy love hath done;
By This to Thee our love is won;
For this our joyful songs we raise
And shout our thanks in ceaseless praise.
Hallelujah!

Isaiah, Mighty Seer, in Days of Old
BY MARTIN LUTHER

Isaiah, mighty seer, in days of old
The Lord of all in spirit did behold
High on a lofty throne, in splendor bright,
With flowing train that filled the Temple quite.
Above the throne were stately seraphim,
Six wings had they, these messengers of Him.

With twain they veiled their faces, as was meet,
With twain in reverent awe they hid their feet,
And with the other twain aloft they soared,
One to the other called and praised the Lord:
 "Holy is God, the Lord of Sabaoth!
 Holy is God, the Lord of Sabaoth!
 Holy is God, the Lord of Sabaoth!
 Behold, His glory filleth all the earth!"
The beams and lintels trembled at the cry,
And clouds of smoke enwrapped the throne on high.

Christ Is Arisen
BY MARTIN LUTHER

Christ is arisen
 From the grave's dark prison.
We now rejoice with gladness;
Christ will end all sadness.
 Lord, have mercy.

All our hopes were ended
 Had Jesus not ascended
From the grave triumphantly.
For this, Lord Christ, we worship Thee.
 Lord, have mercy.

Hallelujah!
Hallelujah!
Hallelujah!
We now rejoice with gladness.
Christ will end all sadness.
 Lord, have mercy.

A Mighty Fortress Is Our God
by Martin Luther

A mighty fortress is our God,
A bulwark never failing;
Our helper He, amid the flood
Of mortal ills prevailing.
For still our ancient foe
Doth seek to work us woe;

His craft and pow'r are great
And armed with cruel hate,
On earth is not his equal.

Did we in our own strength confide,
Our striving would be losing;
Were not the right man on our side,
The man of God's own choosing.
Dost ask who that may be?
Christ Jesus it is He;
Lord Sabaoth His name,
From age to age the same,
And He must win the battle.

And though this world with demons filled,
Should threaten to undo us,
We will not fear, for God hath willed
His truth to triumph thro' us.
The Prince of darkness grim,
We tremble not for him;
His wage we can endure,
For Lo his doom is sure,
One little word shall fell him.

That word above all earthly powers,
No thanks to them, abideth;
The Spirit and the gifts are ours
Thro' Him who with us sideth.
Let goods and kindred go,
This mortal life also;
The body they may kill;
God's truth abideth still,
His kingdom is forever.

WALDENSIAN EVANGELIC CHURCH

From the Second Sunday of the Month

Let us pray: O eternal God who promised to make thy presence felt
to certain of thy children in a special way, we unite in thy name and

come to thee in search of that peace which surpasses all thought, a peace which thou alone can give to our souls by putting them in harmony with thy will. We thank thee, O Lord, for our creation and redemption, for the means of grace given us and the hope of glory; we pray thee to instil us with such a sense of thy mercy that we will forever praise thee constantly, not only with our lips, but with all our hearts.

O heavenly Father, help us to carry through our duties, and keep us always from the many temptations to which we are exposed. Fill us with the Holy Spirit, and in all undertakings let us feel that we succeed in the name of Him who loved us.

We pray thee to protect thy Sacred Church, illuminate its leaders, and through thy virtue sustain the missionaries who work for the cause of the Realm. Fortify those who fight for thy cause, and hasten the day in which every knee will bend before thee and every tongue proclaim thy glory.

Thou who rulest over the destinies of all people, bless our country, the King, and all the authorities who govern us. Gaze upon our families: bless the old ones, keep those strong who bear fatigues, inspire purity in the young, be the guide of our children who are taking their first steps; keep those whom we love from the perils in this life, and through thy grace reward them eternal life.

And now, O God, give us to understand thy Word, not according to the letter that kills, but according to the spirit that revives, and cause us —seeing in thy Word the glory of Jesus—to be transformed into the image of Him who is our blessed Saviour. So be it.

From the Liturgy of Good Friday

Omnipotent God, Father of mercy! We are gathered here in thy name to commemorate the anguished death of our crucified Redeemer. And before the Cross, even though we are incapable of comprehending the greatness of thy love for us, and incapable of explaining the mystery, we bless thee, our Father, fountain of grace, and confess thee as the author of our salvation. O Christ, who lowered thyself into the abyss for us, in thee on this day our gaze recognizes the spirit of our faith. We brought the evil, and thou underwent the suffering; we committed the sin, and thou wast nailed to the Cross! O Saviour, unite us with thee in such a manner that thy works become ours and that, by participating in thy death, we may rise again to live with thee. Come rule over us, and from this moment forth let us obey thee faithfully throughout all the days of our life.

O God of love, we pray to thee for all the peoples of the earth who are yet strangers to thy Word. Hear the prayers with which the Church pleas for their conversion, and shed thy light of truth on the multitudes still dwelling in darkness. Have pity on thy Church, so cruelly divided, obscured by so many transgressions! Shine down thy light on it as it shined at the dawn of the best days, and grant us times of restoration and peace. Bless our country, our King, and the authorities who govern us. Watch after our families; uplift the weary and troubled; direct the eyes of the dying toward the Cross, that they may find salvation, consolation, and life eternal.

And now, O God, bless the speaking of thy Word, and cause us not to be unreceptive in our souls to its message. We ask this in the name and love of Jesus Christ thy Son, to whom, along with thee, O Father, and the Holy Spirit, may there come honor and glory throughout all the centuries. Amen.

For the Waldese Feast

Let us pray: O God of our fathers, on this day in which we commemorate the benedictions granted by thee to our Church, which now worships and serves thee in full liberty, we invoke thy presence.

Let us praise thee with a profoundly grateful heart for the liberation thou hast worked; inspire the prayers and meditations which we carry out in the name of Jesus Christ our Redeemer, blessed throughout eternity. Amen.

For the Festival of the Church and the Reform

This festival is held on the first Sunday of November.

Let us pray: God omnipotent who brought light out of darkness, whose Word lighted the dark night of error and sin, we praise thee and bless thee for having made us aware and given us possession of the truth. Thou founded thy Church on the word of the apostles and prophets, and on the eternal Rock: our Lord is the Saviour Jesus Christ. Thou hast stood by thy Church during her struggle, and on this day we render thanks for thy steadfast faith. We thank thee also, O heavenly Father, for having given so many of thy children the opportunity to look upon the Sacred Scriptures, thus satisfying their thirst for truth and justice. We thank thee for having paid the price of an erring human tradition, bringing thy children under the sweet and blessed yoke of the supreme Shepherd, Jesus Christ, ever present in the midst of his works for the world.

O Lord, bless always thy universal Church and free it from the evils that afflict it. Remove from it the human errors that darken thy sacred truth, the false knowledge that contrasts with thy doctrine and thy promises, the faithlessness and lack of charity that disturb so many souls, the mundane threats around us, the divisions that weaken thy cause! In every part of the world give life to thy Church by instilling the Spirit in it; give new life also to each of those who is a member of it; let us commune with thy saints, and know the pure joy thou promised to all who love thee; and cause us to be faithful to the end of our days, so that, after our death, our souls may join those of the faithful who have passed from this life to dwell in glory forever.

Admonition of the Minister for Christmas Supper

You have heard, my brothers, how our Lord Jesus Christ instituted the Holy Supper. The Saviour wished that his disciples throughout all time should know of His coming and partake of the beneficence of His presence. On this day, Christianity rejoices because, "He is born"; but what sense would Bethlehem have for us without Calvary? He was born to die, and He died to save us, helping us to free ourselves from sin and come to know a new and eternal life. It is therefore good that we celebrate this Supper with all the solemnity of Christmas. The Sacred Board says unto us: the Saviour comes! He comes to reconcile us with God, to nourish our souls, to satisfy the thirst in our hearts, to enrich us with eternal goods.

And coming to us and giving himself to us, the Saviour says: "Come unto me! Dwell in me!" He is spiritually present here; let us then go to Him with our weaknesses and He will make us strong; let us go to Him with our hunger and we shall be fed; He will uplift us; He will gladden us; He will console us.

ANGLICAN COMMUNION

The Declaration of Absolution, or Remission of Sins

Almighty God, the Father of our Lord Jesus Christ, who desireth not the death of a sinner, but rather that he may turn from his wickedness and live, hath given power, and commandment, to his Ministers, to declare and pronounce to his people, being penitent, the Absolution and

Remission of their sins. He pardoneth and absolveth all those who truly repent, and unfeignedly believe his holy Gospel.

Wherefore let us beseech him to grant us true repentance, and his Holy Spirit, that those things may please him which we do at this present; and that the rest of our life hereafter may be pure and holy; so that at the last we may come to his eternal joy; through Jesus Christ our Lord. Amen.

A Prayer for Congress

Most gracious God, we humbly beseech thee, as for the people of these United States in general, so especially for their Senate and Representatives in Congress assembled; that thou wouldest be pleased to direct and prosper all their consultations, to the advancement of thy glory, the good of thy Church, the safety, honor, and welfare of thy people; that all things may be so ordered and settled by their endeavors, upon the best and surest foundations, that peace and happiness, truth and justice, religion and piety, may be established among us for all generations. These and all other necessaries, for them, for us, and thy whole Church, we humbly beg in the Name and mediation of Jesus Christ, our most blessed Lord and Saviour. Amen.

Matrimony—Prayers

O Almighty God, Creator of mankind, who only art the wellspring of life; Bestow upon these thy servants, if it be thy will, the gift and heritage of children; and grant that they may see their children brought up in thy faith and fear, to the honor and glory of thy Name; through Jesus Christ our Lord. Amen.

O God, who hast so consecrated the state of Matrimony that in it is represented the spiritual marriage and unity betwixt Christ and his Church; Look mercifully upon these thy servants, that they may love, honor, and cherish each other, and so live together in faithfulness and patience, in wisdom and true godliness, that their home may be a haven of blessing and of peace; through the same Jesus Christ our Lord, who liveth and reigneth with thee and the Holy Spirit ever, one God, world without end. Amen.

For a Person, or Persons, Going to Sea

O Eternal God, who alone spreadest out the heavens and rulest the raging of the sea; We commend to thy almighty protection, thy servant, for whose preservation on the great deep our prayers are desired. Guard him, we beseech thee, from the dangers of the sea, from sickness, from the violence of enemies, and from every evil to which he may be exposed. Conduct him in safety to the haven where he would be, with a grateful sense of thy mercies; through Jesus Christ our Lord. Amen.

In Time of War and Tumults

O Almighty God, the supreme Governor of all things, whose power no creature is able to resist, to whom it belongeth justly to punish sinners and to be merciful to those who truly repent; Save and deliver us, we humbly beseech thee, from the hands of our enemies; that we, being armed with thy defense, may be preserved evermore from all perils, to glorify thee, who art the only giver of all victory; through the merits of thy Son, Jesus Christ our Lord. Amen.

The Ordering of Priests

Almighty God and heavenly Father, who, of thine infinite love and goodness toward us, hast given to us thy only and most dearly beloved Son Jesus Christ, to be our Redeemer, and the Author of everlasting life; who, after he had made perfect our redemption by his death, and was ascended into heaven, sent abroad into the world his Apostles, Prophets, Evangelists, Doctors, and Pastors; by whose labor and ministry he gathered together a great flock in all the parts of the world, to set forth the eternal praise of thy holy Name: For these so great benefits of thy eternal goodness, and for that thou hast vouchsafed to call these thy servants here present to the same Office and Ministry, appointed for the salvation of mankind, we render unto thee most hearty thanks, we praise and worship thee; and we humbly beseech thee, by the same thy blessed Son, to grant unto all, which either here or elsewhere call upon thy holy Name, that we may continue to show ourselves thankful unto thee for these and all thy other benefits; and that we may daily increase and go forward in the knowledge and faith of thee and thy Son, by the Holy Spirit. So that as well by these thy Ministers, as by them over whom they shall be appointed thy Ministers, thy holy Name may be forever glorified, and thy blessed kingdom enlarged; through the same thy Son Jesus Christ our Lord, who liveth and reigneth with thee in the unity of the same Holy Spirit, world without end. Amen.

Holy Baptism—Prayer

Almighty and immortal God, the aid of all who need, the helper of all who flee to thee for succor, the life of those who believe, and the resurrection of the dead; We call upon thee for this Child [this thy Servant], that he, coming to thy holy Baptism, may receive remission of sin, by spiritual regeneration. Receive him, O Lord, as thou hast promised by thy well-beloved Son, saying, Ask, and ye shall have; seek, and ye shall find; knock, and it shall be opened unto you. So give now unto us who ask; let us who seek, find; open the gate unto us who knock; that this Child [this thy Servant] may enjoy the everlasting benediction of thy heavenly washing, and may come to the eternal kingdom which thou hast promised by Christ our Lord. Amen.

A General Confession

Almighty and most merciful Father; we have erred and strayed from thy ways like lost sheep. We have followed too much the devices and desires of our own hearts. We have offended against thy holy laws. We have left undone those things which we ought to have done. And we have done those things which we ought not to have done, and there is no health in us. But thou, O Lord, have mercy upon us, miserable offenders. Spare thou those, O God, who confess their faults. Restore thou those who are penitent, according to thy promises declared unto mankind in Christ Jesus our Lord. And grant, O most merciful Father, for his sake, that we may hereafter live a godly, righteous, and sober life, to the glory of thy holy Name. Amen.

A General Thanksgiving

Almighty God, Father of all mercies, we, thine unworthy servants, do give thee most humble and hearty thanks for all thy goodness and loving kindness to us, and to all men. We bless thee for our creation, preservation, and all the blessings of this life; but above all for thine inestimable love in the redemption of the world by our Lord Jesus Christ; for the means of grace, and for the hope of glory. And we beseech thee, give us that due sense of all thy mercies, that our hearts may be unfeignedly thankful; and that we show forth thy praise, not only with our lips but in our lives, by giving up ourselves to thy service, and by walking before thee in holiness and righteousness all our days; through Jesus Christ our Lord, to whom with thee and the Holy Ghost, be all honor and glory, world without end. Amen.

A Burial Prayer

Almighty and ever-loving God, we yield unto thee most high praise and hearty thanks, for the wonderful grace and virtue declared in all thy saints, who have been the choice vessels of thy grace, and the lights of the world in their several generations; most humbly beseeching thee to give us grace so to follow the example of their steadfastness in thy faith, and obedience to thy holy commandments, that at the day of the general resurrection, we, with all those who are of the mystical body of thy Son, may be set on his right hand, and hear his most joyful voice: Come, ye blessed of my Father, inherit the kingdom prepared for you from the foundation of the world. Grant this, O Father, for the sake of the same, thy Son Jesus Christ, our only Mediator and Advocate. Amen.

From the Eucharistic Prayer

And here we offer and present unto thee, O Lord, our selves, our souls and bodies, to be a reasonable, holy, and living sacrifice unto thee; humbly beseeching thee, that we, and all others who shall be partakers of this Holy Communion, may worthily receive the most precious Body and Blood of thy Son Jesus Christ, be filled with thy grace and heavenly benediction, and made one body with him, that he may dwell in us, and we in him.

Absolution Given by the Priest After Confession

Our Lord Jesus Christ, who hath left power in his Church to absolve all sinners who truly repent and believe in Him, of his great mercy forgive thee thine offenses; and by his authority committed unto me, I absolve thee from all thy sins; in the name of the Father, and of the Son, and of the Holy Ghost. Amen.

Hark The Glad Sound

Hark the glad sound! the Saviour comes,
The Saviour promised long!
Let every heart prepare a throne,
And every voice a song.

He comes the prisoners to release
In Satan's bondage held;
The gates of brass before him burst,
The iron fetters yield.

He comes the broken heart to bind,
The bleeding soul to cure,
And with the treasures of his grace
To enrich the humble poor.

Our glad hosannas, Prince of peace,
Thy welcome shall proclaim,
Anr heaven's eternal arches ring
With thy beloved name.

O Little Town of Bethlehem

O little town of Bethlehem,
How still we see thee lie!
Above thy deep and dreamless sleep
The silent stars go by.
Yet in thy dark streets shineth
The everlasting light;
The hopes and fears of all the years
Are met in thee to-night.

O morning stars, together
Proclaim the holy birth
And praises sing to God the King,
And peace to men on earth;
For Christ is born of Mary;
And, gathered all above,

While mortals sleep, the angels keep
Their watch of wondering love.

How silently, how silently,
The wondrous gift is given!
So God imparts to human hearts
The blessings of his heaven.
No ear may hear his coming;
But in this world of sin,
Where meek souls will receive him still,
The dear Christ enters in.

Where children pure and happy
Pray to the blessed Child,
Where misery cries out to thee,
Son of the mother mild;
Where charity stands watching
And faith holds wide the door,
The dark night wakes, the glory breaks,
And Christmas comes once more.

Christians Awake

Christians, awake, salute the happy morn,
Whereon the Saviour of the world was born;
Rise to adore the mystery of love,
Which hosts of Angels chanted from above;
With them the joyful tidings first begun
Of God incarnate and the Virgin's Son:

Then to the watchful shepherds it was told,
Who heard the angelic herald's voice, 'Behold,
I bring good tidings of a Saviour's birth
To you and all the nations upon earth;
This day hath God fulfilled his promised word,
This day is born a Saviour, Christ the Lord.'

He spake; and straightway the celestial choir
In hymns of joy, unknown before, conspire.
The praises of redeeming love they sang,
And heaven's whole orb with Alleluyas rang:

God's highest glory was their anthem still,
Peace upon earth, and mutual goodwill.

To Bethlehem straight the enlightened shepherds ran,
To see the wonder God had wrought for man,
And found, with Joseph and the blessed Maid,
Her Son, the Saviour, in a manger laid;
Amazed the wondrous story they proclaim,
The first apostles of his infant fame,

Like Mary let us ponder in our mind
God's wondrous love in saving lost mankind;
Trace we the Babe, who hath retrieved our loss,
From his poor manger to his bitter cross;
Then may we hope, angelic thrones among,
To sing, redeemed, a glad triumphal song.

Lord When We Bend Before Thy Throne

Lord when we bend before thy throne,
And our confessions pour,
Teach us to feel the sins we own,
And hate what we deplore.

Our broken spirits pitying see,
And penitence impart;
Then let a kindling glance from thee
Beam hope upon the heart.

When we disclose our wants in prayer
May we our wills resign,
And not a thought our bosom share
That is not wholly thine.

Let faith each meek petition fill,
And waft it to the skies;
And teach our hearts tis goodness still
That grants it or denies.

The Winter's Sleep Was Long

The winter's sleep was long and deep,
But earth is awakened and gay;
For the life ne'er dies that from God doth rise,
And the green comes after the grey.

So God doth bring the world to spring;
And on this holy day
Doth the Church proclaim her Apostle's fame,
To welcome the first of May.

Two Saints of God went by the road
That leadeth on to light;
And they gave up all at their Master's call,
To work in their Master's sight.

Would Phillip's mind the Father find?
Lo, he hath found the Way;
For to know the Son is to know the One
Whom the earth and the heavens obey.

And, James, 'twas thine by grace divine
To preach the Christian life,
Where our faith is shown by our works alone,
And love overcometh strife.

Lord, grant that we may brethren be—
As Christians live in deed;
For it is but so we can learn to know
The truth that to thee doth lead.

God Save Our Gracious King

God save our gracious King,
Long live our noble King,
God save the King!
Send him victorious,
Happy and glorious,

Long to reign over us;
God save the King!

Thy choicest gifts in store
On him be pleased to pour,
Long may he reign;
May he defend our laws,
And ever give us cause
To say with heart and voice
God save the King!

God bless our native land,
May heaven's protecting hand
Still guard our shore;
May peace her power extend,
Foe be transformed to friend,
And Britain's rights depend
On war no more.

May just and righteous laws
Uphold the public cause,
And bless our isle.
Home of the brave and free,
The land of liberty
We pray that still on thee
Kind heaven may smile.

Love's Redeeming Work Is Done

Love's redeeming work is done;
Fought the fight, the battle won:
Lo, our Sun's eclipse is o'er!
Lo, he sets in blood no more!

Vain the stone, the watch, the seal,
Christ has burst the gates of hell;
Death in vain forbids his rise;
Christ has opened Paradise.

Lives again our glorious King;
Where, O Death, is now they sting?

Dying once, he all doth save;
Where thy victory, O grave?

Soar we now where Christ has led,
Following our exalted Head;
Made like him, like him we rise;
Ours the cross, the grave, the skies.

Hail the Lord of earth and heaven!
Praise to thee by both be given:
Thee we greet triumphant now;
Hail, the Resurrection thou!

PRESBYTERIAN

Lord's Day Morning Worship

Invocation: Lord God, our heavenly Father, holiness becometh thy house. Grant unto us who tread thy courts clean hearts and right spirits. Remove from us, we pray thee, unworthy thoughts and the things that depress, and clothe us in the garments of praise. Enable us with one heart and one mind to bless thee whose mercies endure forever. May our worship in the name of Thy Son and under the guidance of Thy Holy Spirit be acceptable unto thee and enriching to ourselves, through Jesus Christ Our Lord, Amen.

Lord's Day Evening Worship

Invocation: O God, thou who art the Father of lights, with whom is no variableness nor shadow of turning; we seek the light of thy face at the hour of evening sacrifice. With the darkening of the world without, may there be the brightness of Thy presence in the house of prayer. Graciously forgive us our sins, and grant us such a vision of the Light of the world that the darkness of evil may be driven from our hearts, and that we may worship thee in spirit and in truth. Through Jesus Christ our Lord. Amen.

The Administration of Infant Baptism

The ritual should neither be hurried nor unduly extended. While the parents are bringing their child to the altar, the minister may repeat one or more appropriate passages of Scripture.

a. Do you now take God as your God in covenant, and as the God of your children?
Answer: I do

b. Do you renew the profession you made when you were admitted to the church?
Answer: I do.

c. Do you solemnly promise, if God shall spare your life and that of your children, to train them up in the nurture and admonition of the Lord; to instruct them in regard to their lost condition by nature, and to lead them to the Saviour; to pray with them and for them, to worship God regularly in your family; to set before them an example of piety; and to use all the appointed means for their salvation?
Answer: I do.

Then the minister shall say: The Lord bless you and your child and give you grace faithfully to keep this covenant.

Let us pray

Most merciful and loving father, we thank thee for the revelation of thy most gracious purpose toward us and toward our children. We thank thee for the ordinance of baptism and beseech thee to bless this sacrament, that the child whom we present unto thee in faith may be sanctified by Thy Spirit and receive into the family of thy children through Jesus Christ Our Lord. Amen.

Then all present reverently standing, the minister shall say to the parents: What is the Christian name of this child? Then the minister in pronouncing the name of this child, shall pour or sprinkle the water of baptism saying: I baptize thee in the name of the Father and of the Son and of the Holy Spirit. Amen.

Then the minister shall say to the Congregation: The child is now given to God in baptism and so received by Christ's appointment into this Church, and commended to the prayers and Christian nurture of God's people.

Father in heaven, thou who hast covenanted to be our God and the God of our child, we beseech thee that thy fatherly love may always be upon this child, that Christ may be his Redeemer and King, that the Holy

Spirit may dwell with him as Teacher, Comforter, and Sanctifier. May his life be precious in thy sight and when he comes to years of understanding, may he confess thee the only true God and Jesus Christ, whom thou hast sent; guard and guide him through the unknown years and at last receive him into the joys of thine eternal kingdom, through Jesus Christ, our Lord. Bless, O Lord, these parents and give them grace to fulfill their vows, and consecrate them anew to thy service. Let their home be filled with the joy and peace of Christ's presence. Bind them to one another with cords of divine love. Bestow thy blessing upon all the homes and the children of the Church, O Lord, leading them into all truth and guiding them in the service of Jesus Christ our Lord.

A Litany of Thanksgiving

It is good to give thanks unto God.
And to sing praises unto thy Name, O Most High.
To show forth thy loving kindness in the morning.
And thy faithfulness every night.

For the wonder and beauty of the natural world; for the sun that lights the earth by day and kindles the stars by night; for refreshing showers and running streams; for wooded hills and fruitful trees; for the wealth of the mountains and the harvests of the field.

We come before thee with thanksgiving.

For well-ordered homes blessed with joy and peace and contentment; for loving children and godly parents; for unfailing friends and wise teachers; for strength to labor and grace to endure trial and discipline.

We give thanks to thee, O God.

For our country and liberty we enjoy in this land of the free; for all righteous men in lawful authority, ordained of God through the voice of the people; for peace in our day, and the will to a just and enduring peace among people.

We bless the Lord, and forget not all his benefits.

For the unfailing words of Holy Scripture and the living word of him who is the way, the truth and the life; for the Church, visible and invisible, for the fellowship of all believers who love and serve one God and Father of all; and for eternal life through Jesus Christ our Lord.

Bless the Lord, O my soul, and all that is within me bless his holy name.

May the Lord continue to show his loving kindness to all his people.

And his righteousness to the upright in heart.
The Lord bless us.
And keep us
The Lord make his face to shine upon us.

And be gracious unto us.

The Lord lift up his countenance upon us.

And give us peace. Amen.

THE SALVATION ARMY

The Founder's Song
by William Booth

This and those to follow represent a limited example of the singular richness of hymn production in the evangelistic movements. These movements, like those of Christianity during its early period, have no liturgical prayers. Still, in the manner of the early Christians, the community takes its prayers from the individual inspiration of its various members.

O Boundless salvation! deep ocean of love,
O fulness of mercy, Christ brought from above,
The whole world redeeming, so rich and so free,
Now flowing for all men, come, roll over me!

My sins they are many, their stains are so deep,
And bitter the tears of remorse that I weep;
But useless is weeping; thou great crimson sea,
Thy waters can cleanse me, come, roll over me!

My tempers are fitful, my passions are strong,
They bind my poor soul and they force me to wrong;
Beneath thy blest billows deliverance I see,
O come, mighty ocean, and roll over me!

Now tossed with temptation, then haunted with fears,
My life has been joyless and useless for years;
I feel something better most surely would be
If once thy pure waters would roll over me.

O ocean of mercy, oft longing I've stood
On the brink of thy wonderful, life-giving flood!
Once more I have reached this soul-cleansing sea,
I will not go back till it rolls over me.

The tide is now flowing, I'm touching the wave,
I hear the loud call of the Mighty to Save;
My faith's growing bolder, delivered I'll be;
I plunge 'neath the waters, they roll over me.

And now, Hallelujah! the rest of my days
Shall gladly be spent in promoting His praise
Who opened His bosom to pour out this sea
Of boundless salvation for you and for me.

Have You Been to Jesus for the Cleansing Power?

Have you been to Jesus for the cleansing power?
Are you washed in the Blood of the Lamb?
Are you fully trusting in His grace this hour?
Are you washed in the Blood of the Lamb?

Are you washed in the Blood,
In the soul-cleaning Blood of the Lamb?
Are your garments spotless? Are they white as snow?
Are you washed in the Blood of the Lamb?

Are you walking daily by the Saviour's side?
Are you washed in the Blood of the Lamb?
Do you rest each moment in the Crucified?
Are you washed in the Blood of the Lamb?

Lay aside the garments that are stained with sin,
And be washed in the Blood of the Lamb;
There's a fountain flowing for the soul unclean
O be washed in the Blood of the Lamb.

Onward Christian Soldiers

> Onward, Christian soldiers,
>   Marching as to war,
> With the Cross of Jesus
>   Going on before!
> Christ, the royal Master,
>   Leads against the foe;
> Forward into battle
>   See his banners go.
>
> Onward Christian soldiers,
>   Marching as to war,
> With the Cross of Jesus
>   Going on before!

SEVENTH-DAY ADVENTISTS

Raise the Standard High

> Raise the standard high,
> Sound the gathering cry,
> Let the evil kingdom fall;
> With a purpose true
> And a will to do
> Sons of freedom, come ye all.
>
> Raise the temperance standard high, standard high,
> Shout the mighty battle cry; battle cry;
> Let the evil kingdom fall,
> Sons of freedom, come ye all.

Lord of the Sabbath

> Lord of the Sabbath and its light,
> I hail Thy hallowed day of rest;
> It is my weary soul's delight,
> The solace of my care-worn breast,
> The solace of my care-worn breast,

O sacred day of peace and joy,
Thy hours are ever dear to me;
Never may a sinful thought destroy
The holy calm I find in thee,
The holy calm I find in thee.

How sweetly now they glide along!
How hallowed is the calm they yield!
Transporting is their rapturous song,
And heavenly visions seem revealed,
And heavenly visions seem revealed.

O Jesus, let me ever hail
Thy presence with the day of rest;
Then will Thy servant never fail
To deem Thy Sabbath doubly blest,
To deem Thy Sabbath doubly blest.

Another Six Days Work is Done

Another six days' work is done
Another Sabbath is begun
Return my soul enjoy thy rest
Improve the day that God has blessed.

JEHOVAH'S WITNESSES

Forward You Witnesses

Firm and determined in this time of the end,
Prepared are God's servants the good news to defend;
He taught them to war and to conquer!
He taught them to war and to conquer!
Fearless against Satan's world conspiracy
With faith in Jehovah they face the enemy
Undaunted by threats or by rancor!
Undaunted by threats or by rancor!

Then forward, you witnesses, ever strong of heart,
Rejoice to endure all the battle's heat and smart;

Be glad that in God's war you too may have a part,
Before Satan's host will have perished.
Keep preaching, you witnesses, boldly without fear,
Go tell the glad tidings to all who will hear,
That all the signs show that the New World is near,
That the kingdom of God is established!

The Taunt-Song Against Satan

This challenge Satan boldly hurled into the face of God
The earth I'll rule, yes, all the world shall lie beneath my rod!
Above the stars of God I'll sit, exalted in the sky;
To me the mighty shall submit; I'll be like the Most High!

Yet to the abyss God has decreed, soon Satan must be brought;
For his rebel lion and his greed, he'll surely come to naught.
In chains of death he will be bound, with all his demon horde;
Beneath Christ's heel he will be ground; destruction his reward!

'Gainst Satan let the taunt-song ring, that he may hear his fate;
With joy let all the righteous sing God's triumph we await!
Rebellion will no more arise to mar the heav'nly scene;
All earth will be a Paradise of joy and love serene!

Joyful Service

Let's go forth with gladness now to serve our King;
All our gifts and talents to his work we bring;
Tho' but small our service yet thereby we prove
Our heart's full devotion and show forth our love.

In Jehovah's service there is work for all;
Loyal hearts and faithful heed his gracious call;
Sacred the commission we've received from heav'n;
Yes to us rich blessings thru the work are giv'n.

While we share with gladness in his service sweet,
Giving forth the witness to all those we meet;
For this wondrous favor to us here below
Granting us such service, our high praises flow.

*

Islam

ISLAM

Azan, or Call to Prayer

The prayers included here are those of the Hanafi sect of the Sunna. The service must be said in Arabic, and it is essential that the body and vestments of the officiant be purified and the prayer, preceded by the ritual ablution. The Azan is the call to prayer chanted by the muezzin.

> God is great! God is great! God is great! God is great!
> I bear witness that there is no god but God!
> I bear witness that there is no god but God!
> I bear witness that Muhammad is the Apostle of God!
> Come to prayers! Come to prayers!
> Come to salvation! Come to salvation!
> There is no other god but God!
> Prayers are better than sleep!

The Tahiyah

This is a morning prayer which is recited in the characteristic position, seated on the left foot with hands on the knee.

The adorations of the tongue are for God, and also the adoration of the body, and alms-giving!

Peace be on thee, O Prophet, with the mercy of God and His blessing! Peace be upon us and upon God's righteous servants!

A Khutbah of the Sacrificial Feast

The Khutbah is a form of free prayer spoken by the officiant during the two main feasts, the Idu'l-fitr and the Idu'l-azha. The latter, or sacrificial, feast is held on the tenth day of *zu-l-hijjah*. Early in the morning the populace comes together for prayers in the *'idgah,* an enclosure especially constructed outside the city for the festival. After the prayer has been said, the Imam takes his place on the *mimbar* (pulpit) and delivers an oration, or Khutbah, on the subject of the festival. Afterward, an animal is sacrificed, usually a goat, a cow, or a camel.

In the name of God, the Compassionate, the merciful.

God is Great. There is no God but God. God is Great! God is Great and worthy of all praise. He is Holy. Day and night we should praise Him. He is without partner, without equal. All praise be to Him. Holy is He, Who makes the rich generous, Who provides the sacrifice for the wise. He is Great, without an equal. All praise be to Him. Listen! I testify that there is no God but God. He is alone, without partner. This testimony is as bright as the early dawn, as brilliant as the glorious feast day. Muhammad is His servant who delivered His message. On Muhammad, and on his family, and on his Companions may the peace of God rest. On you who are present, O congregation of Moslemin, may the mercy of God forever rest. O servants of God! our first duty is to fear God and to be kind. God has said, "I will be with those who fear Me and are kind."

Know, O servants of God! that to rejoice on the feast day is the sign and mark of the pure and good. Exalted will be the rank of such in Paradise, especially on the day of resurrection will they obtain dignity and honor. On this day act not in foolish ways. It is no time for amusements and negligence. This is the day on which to utter the praises of God. Read the Kalimah, the Takbir and the Tamhid.[1] This is a high festival season and the feast of sacrifice. Read now the Takbiru 't-Tashriq. God is great! God is great! There is no God but God! God is great! God is great! All praise be to him! From the morning of the 'Arafah,[2] after every farz rak'ah,[3] it is good for a person to repeat the Takbiru 't-Tashriq. The woman before whom is a man as Imam, and the traveler whose Imam is a permanent resident, should also repeat this Takbir. It should be said at each Namaz until the

Salatu 'l-Asr of the Feast Day [tenth]. Some, however, say that it should be recited every day till the afternoon of the thirteenth day, as these are the days of the Tashriq. If the Imam forgets to recite, let not the worshiper forget. Know, O believers, that every free man who is a Sahibu-n-Nisab[4] should offer sacrifice on this day, provided that this sum is exclusive of his horse, his clothes, his tools, and his household goods and slaves. It is wajib[5] for everyone to offer sacrifice for himself, but is not a wajib order that he should do it for his children. A goat, a ram, or a cow, should be offered in sacrifice for every seven persons. The victim must not be one-eyed, blind, lame, or very thin.

If you sacrifice a fat animal it will serve you well, and carry you across the Sirat.[6] O Believers, thus said the Prophet, on whom be the mercy and peace of God, "Sacrifice the victim with your own hands, this was the Sunna of Ibrahim, on whom be peace."

In the Kitabu Zadi 't-Taqwa it is said that, on the 'Idu 'l-Fitr and the 'Idu 'l-Azha, four nafl rak'ahs should be said after the farz Namaz of the 'Id. In the first rak'ah after the Suratu 'l-Fatihah recite the Suratu 'l-A'la [Surah lxxvii] in the second, the Suratu 'sh-Shams [Surah xci]; in the third, the Suratu 'z-Zuha [Surah xciii]; in the fourth, the Suratu 'l-Ikhlas [cxii].

O Believers, if ye do so, God will pardon the sins of fifty years which are past and of fifty years to come. The reading of these Surahs is equal, as an act of merit, to the reading of all the books God has sent by His prophets.

May God include us amongst those who are accepted by Him, who act according to the Law, whose desire will be granted at the Last Day. To all such there will be no fear in the Day of Resurrection; no sorrow in the examination at the Day of Judgment. The best of all books is the Qur'an. O believers! May God give to us and to you a blessing forever, by the grace of the Noble Qur'an. May its verses be our guide, and may its wise mention of God direct us aright. I desire that God may pardon all believers, male and female, the Moslemin and the Moslemah. O believers, also seek for pardon. Truly God is the Forgiver, the Merciful, the Eternal King, the Compassionate, the Clement. O believers, the Khutbah is over. Let all desire that on Muhammad Mustafa the mercy and peace of God may rest.

A Khutbah for the Festival of the Breaking of the Fast

This feast, during which the Khutbah is recited, begins as soon as the month of Ramadan ends. Above all it is a festival of alms-giving (sadaqatu 'l-Fitr, from which the name of the festival 'Idu 'l-Fitr). The populace gathers together outside the city and, guided by the Imam, recites the prayers.

In the name of God, the Compassionate, the Merciful.

Holy is God who has opened the door of mercy for those who fast, and in mercy and kindness has granted them the right of entrance into heaven. God is greater than all. There is no God save Him. God is great! God is great! and worthy of praise. It is of His grace and favor that He rewards those who keep the fast. He has said: "I will give in the future world houses and palaces, and many excellent blessings to those who fast. God is great! God is great! Holy is He who certainly sent the Qur'an to our Prophet in the month of Ramadan, and who sends angels to grant peace to all true believers. God is great! and worthy of all praise. We praise and thank Him for the 'Idu 'l-Fitr, that great blessing; and we testify that beside Him there is no God. He is alone. He has no partner. This witness which we give to His Unity will be a cause of our safety here, and finally gain us an entrance to Paradise. Muhammad (on whom be the mercy and peace of God) and all famous prophets are His slaves. He is the Lord of genii and of men. From Him comes mercy and peace upon Muhammad and his family, so long as the world shall last. God is greater than all. There is none beside Him. God is great! God is great! and worthy of all praise. O company of Believers, O congregation of Muslims, the mercy of the True One is on you. He says that this Feast Day is a blessing to you, and a curse to the unbelievers. Your fasting will not be rewarded, and your prayers will be stayed in their flight to heaven until you have given the sadaqah. O congregation of Believers, to give alms is to you a wajib duty. Give to the poor some measures of grain or its money equivalent. Your duty in Ramadan was to say the Tarawih prayers, to make supplication to God, to sit and meditate [i'tikaf] and to read the Qur'an. The religious duties of the first ten days of Ramadan gain the mercy of God, those of the second ten merit His pardon; whilst those of the last ten save those who do them from the punishment of hell. God has declared that Ramadan is a noble month, for is not one of its nights, the Lailatu 'l-Qadr,[7] better than a thousand months? On that night Gabriel and the angels descended from heaven: till the morning breaks, it is full of blessing. Its eloquent interpreter, and its clearest proof is the Qur'an, the Word of God, most Gracious. Holy is God who says in the Qur'an: "This is a guide for men, a distinguisher between right and wrong." O Believers, in such a month be present, obey the order of your God, and fast; but let the sick and the travelers substitute some other days on which to fast, so that no days be lost, and say, "God is great!" and praise Him. God has made the fast easy for you. O Believers, God will bless you and us by the grace of the Holy Qur'an. Every verse of it is a benefit to us and fills us with wisdom. God is the Bestower, the Holy King, the Munificent, the Kind, the Nourisher, the Merciful, the Clement.

A Salatu 'L-Istikharah

Salatu 'l-Istikharah, literally "a prayer to curry favor," is a type of hopeful prayer frequently used. According to the Mishkat, IV:10, this particular prayer was taught by Muhammad himself to his disciple Jabir.

O God, I seek Thy good help in Thy great wisdom. I pray for ability to act through Thy power. I ask this thing of thy goodness. Thou knowest, but I know not. Thou art powerful, but I am not. Thou art knower of secrets. O God, if Thou knowest that the matter which I am about to undertake is good for my religion, for my life, for my future, then make it easy, and prosper me in it. But if it is bad for my religion, my life, and my future, then put it away from me, and show me what is good.

Burial Prayer

This is the prayer called Du'a, a generic term used to indicate supplication and distinguish it from Salat, a liturgic form of prayer. It belongs to the Salatu 'l-Jinasah funeral service.

O God, forgive our living and our dead and those of us who are present, and those who are absent, and our children, and our full grown persons, our men and our women. O God, these whom Thou dost keep alive amongst us, keep alive in Islam, and those who Thou causest to die, let them die in Faith.

Formula of Ablution

The ablution *wazu* is described by Muhammad as "the half of faith and the key of prayer" (Mishkat, III:3c), and is founded on the authority of the Qur'an, Surah v. 8, "O Believers! when ye prepare yourselves for prayer, wash your faces and hands up to the elbows, and wipe your heads and your feet to the ankles."

Before commencing the *wazu:* "I am going to purify myself from all bodily uncleanness, preparatory to commencing prayer, that holy act of duty which will draw my soul near to the throne of the Most

High. In the name of God, the Great and Mighty. Praise be to God who has given us grace to be Muslims. Islam is a truth and infidelity, a falsehood."

When washing the nostrils: "O my God, if I am pleasing in Thy sight, perfume me with the odors of Paradise."

When washing the right hand: "O my God, on the day of judgment, place the book of my actions in my right hand, and examine my account with favor."

When washing the left hand: "O my God, place not at the resurrection the book of my actions in my left hand."

The Verse of the Throne

This verse (Ayatu 'l-Kursi) is v. 256 of the Suratu 'l-Baqarah, or Chapter II of the Qur'an. It is related (Mishkat, book IV, c. XIX, part III) that 'Ali heard Muhammad say in the pulpit, "that person who repeats the Ayatu 'l-Kursi after every prayer, nothing prevents him entering into Paradise but life; and whoever says it when he goes to his bed chamber, God will keep him in safety, together with his house and the house of his neighbor."

God! There is no God but He, the Living, the Abiding. Neither slumber seizeth Him, nor sleep. To Him belongeth whatsoever is in heaven and whatsoever is in earth. Who is he that can intercede with Him but by His own permission? He knoweth what hath been before them, and what shall be after them; yet naught of His knowledge do they comprehend, save that he willeth. His THRONE reacheth over the heavens and the earth, and the upholding of both burdeneth Him not; and He is the High, the Great.

Prayer for the 'Aqiqah

The ceremony of the 'Aqiqah was originated by Muhammad himself and is carried out on the seventh day following the birth of a baby. It consists of a sacrifice to God, in the child's name, of two he-goats for a boy and one he-goat for a girl. The prayer given is usually recited by friends of the father during the banquet.

O God! I offer to thee instead of my own offspring, life for life, blood for blood, head for head, bone for bone, hair for hair, skin for skin. In the name of the great God, I do sacrifice this goat!

Prayer Inscribed on an Amulet

This prayer inscribed on an amulet known as Nad-I-'Ali is to 'Ali, fourth Caliph, cousin of Muhammad.

Cry aloud to 'Ali, who is the possessor of wonders!
From him you will find help from trouble!
He takes away very quickly all grief and anxiety!
By the mission of Muhammad and his own sanctity!

Prayer of Supplication

The Qunutu 'l-Witr is a special supplication recited after the Witr prayers, or, according to some, after morning prayers. The following is the one usually recited.

O God! direct me amongst those to whom Thou hast shown the right road, and keep me in safety from the calamities of this world and the next, and love me amongst those Thou hast befriended. Increase Thy favors on me, and preserve me from ill; for verily Thou canst order at Thy will, and canst not be ordered. Verily none are ruined that Thou befriendest, nor are any made great with whom Thou art at enmity.

The Overthrowing

In countries of Islamic faith the principal prayer is represented by scriptural recitation.

When the sun is overthown,
And when the stars fall,
And when the hills are moved,
And when the camels big with young are abandoned,
And when the wild beasts are herded together,
And when the seas rise,
And when souls are reunited.
And when the girl-child that was buried alive is asked
For what sin she was slain,
And when the pages are laid open,
And when the sky is torn away,
And when hell is lighted.
And when the garden is brought nigh,
[Then] every soul will know what it hath made ready.
Oh, but I call to witness the planets,
The stars which rise and set,
And the close of night,
And the breath of morning
That this is in truth the word of an honored messenger,

Mighty, established in the presence of the Lord of the Throne,
[One] to be obeyed, and trustworthy;
And your comrade is not mad.
Surely he beheld him on the clear horizon.
And he is not avid of the Unseen.
Nor is this the utterance of a devil worthy to be stoned.
Whither then go ye?
This is naught else than a reminder unto creation,
Unto whomsoever of you willeth to walk straight.
And ye will not, unless [it be] that Allah willeth,
     the Lord of Creation.

Prayer of Faith

O ye who believe! Turn unto Allah in sincere repentance! It may be that your Lord will remit from you your evil deeds and bring you into Gardens underneath which rivers flow, on the day when Allah will not abase the Prophet and those who believe with him. Their light will run before them and on their right hands: they will say: Our Lord! Perfect our light for us, and forgive us! Lo! Thou art Able to do all things.

Glorification of God Against Infidels

Is not He [best] Who created the heavens and the earth, and sendeth down for you water from the sky wherewith We cause to spring forth joyous orchards, whose trees it never hath been yours to cause to grow. Is there any God beside Allah? Nay, but there are people who ascribe equals [unto Him]!

Is not He [best] Who made the earth a fixed abode, and placed rivers in the folds thereof, and placed firm hills therein, and hath set a barrier between the two seas? Is there any God beside Allah? Nay, but most of them know not!

Is not He [best] Who answereth the wronged one when he crieth unto Him and removeth the evil, and hath made you viceroys of the earth? Is there any God beside Allah? Little do they reflect!

Is not He [best] Who guideth you in the darkness of the land and of the sea, He Who sendeth the winds as heralds of His mercy? Is there any God beside Allah? High exalted be Allah from all that they ascribe as partner [unto Him]!

The Works of God

Lo! Allah [it is] who splitteth the grain of corn and the date-stone [for sprouting]. He bringeth forth the living from the dead, and is the bringer-forth of the dead from the living. Such is Allah. How then are ye perverted?

He is the Cleaver of the Daybreak, and He hath appointed the night for stillness, and the sun and the moon for reckoning. That is the measuring of the Mighty, the Wise.

And He it is Who hath set for you the stars that ye may guide your course by them amid the darkness of the land and the sea. We have detailed Our revelations for a people who have knowledge.

And He it is Who hath produced you from a single being, and [hath given you] a habitation and a repository. We have detailed Our revelations for a people who have understanding.

He it is Who sendeth down water from the sky, and therewith We bring forth buds of every kind; We bring forth the green blade from which we bring forth the thick-clustered grain; and from the date-palm, from the pollen thereof, spring pendant bunches; and [we bring forth] gardens of grapes, and the olive and the pomegranate, alike and unlike. Look upon the fruit thereof, when they bear fruit, and upon its ripening. Lo! herein verily are portents for a people who believe.

Hymn of Praise

In the name of Allah, the Beneficent, the Merciful.
Praise be to Allah, Lord of the Worlds,
The Beneficent, the Merciful.
Owner of the Day of Judgment,
Thee [alone] we worship; Thee [alone] we ask for help.
Show us the straight path,
The path of those whom Thou hast favored;
Not [the path] of those who earn Thine anger nor
    of those who go astray.

Notes

1. Terms that indicate certain prayers. Kalimah, "the Word," is the Moslem credo (There is no god but Allah, and Mohammed is the prophet!);

Takbir is the expression *"Allahu akbar!"* meaning "God is great!"; Tamhid is the expression "There is neither power nor strength except in God, the Most High, the great One!"

2. 'Arafah is the eve of the 'Idul.Azha (sacrificial feast), when pilgrims scale the heights of 'Arafat.

3. This is the Persian term used for *salat,* the Islamic liturgical prayer.

4. Sahibu'n-Nisab is a legal term which identifies a person possessing sufficient means to permit him to pay the *zakat* (alms). As a consequence, it also identifies a person sufficiently able to pay for a feast or a pilgrimage to Mecca.

5. *Wajib,* literally "that which is obligatory," is a term used in Moslem law to describe an injunction caused by failure to observe certain practices. For example, the Moslem who fails to offer a sacrifice during the great festival is guilty of sinful omission; but if he holds that the sacrifice is not an institution of divine origin, he is only held to be a sinner, not an infidel.

6. *Sirat,* literally "a road," is used to indicate the bridge which passes over the infernal fires on the way to Paradise. Evil people fall off the bridge into the fire and remain powerless to reach their goal.

7. Lailatu 'l-Qadr, "the night of power," is a mysterious night of the Ramadan, the precise date of which is known only by the Prophet and a few of his close friends. In the Koran it is written that, during this night, "angels descend, and the spirit, as permitted by God, of all things is in peace and will remain in peace until the dawn" (XVII). The belief is that in that solemn space of a few hours every part of creation—animal or vegetable—kneels down in humble adoration before the Omnipotent.

CATHOLIC THEOLOGICAL UNION
BL560.P721961   C001
THE PRAYERS OF MAN NEW YORK

3 0311 00007 2467

BL
560
.P74
1961

BL 560 .P74 1961

The Prayers of man

DEMCO